ROARING GIRLS

THE FORGOTTEN FEMINISTS
OF BRITISH HISTORY

ROARING GIRLS

HOLLY KYTE

ONE PLACE. MANY STORIES

AUTHOR'S NOTE:
Spellings, capitalisation and italicisation have been silently modernised
throughout for clarity and consistency.

HQ
An imprint of HarperCollins*Publishers* Ltd
1 London Bridge Street
London SE1 9GF

This edition 2019

1

First published in Great Britain by HQ,
an imprint of HarperCollins*Publishers* Ltd 2019

Text copyright © Holly Kyte 2019
Illustration copyright © Becky Glass 2019

Holly Kyte asserts the moral right to be
identified as the author of this work.
A catalogue record for this book is
available from the British Library.

ISBN: 9780008266080

MIX
Paper from
responsible sources
FSC **FSC™ C007454**
www.fsc.org

This book is produced from independently certified FSC™ paper
to ensure responsible forest management.

For more information visit: www.harpercollins.co.uk/green

Typeset in Adobe Caslon Pro 11.5/17 pt by
Palimpsest Book Production Limited, Falkirk, Stirlingshire

Printed and bound in Great Britain by
CPI Group (UK) Ltd, Croydon CR0 4YY

Cover images: Dorothy Jordan by John Hoppner, 1791 © National Portrait Gallery
Duke of Aumale by Franz Xaver Winterhalter, 1846 © Bridgeman Images
Lady Diana Cecil attrib. to William Larkin, c. 1614 © Bridgeman Images

For Mum and Dad, for everything.

roaring girl: (**n**) a noisy, bawdy or riotous woman or girl, especially one who takes on a masculine role

OXFORD ENGLISH DICTIONARY

Contents

INTRODUCTION

Girls, we're told, are not supposed to roar. We're supposed to shut up, be quiet, stop nagging. We're supposed to calm down, dear. If we don't, we're bossy, we're aggressive, we're nasty, we're bloody difficult. We're a bunch of loud-mouthed feminazis and hysterical drama queens. If our skirts are too short, we're asking for it, but if we don't make an effort, we should be ashamed. If we don't speak out, how can we expect recognition? But if we do speak out, we get trolled. And that's in the twenty-first century, after four waves of feminism, when equality has supposedly been won.

Imagine, just for a moment, that you're a woman in the seventeenth century. In your world, feminism doesn't exist. You've been born into a rights vacuum. Your life is one long list of obligations and prohibitions. Your sole destiny as a wife and mother has been preordained since day one and the feminine ideal expected of you is to be chaste, modest, obedient – and, whenever possible, silent.

But what if you don't want to be silent? What if you want to roar?

Mary Frith was just such a woman. A notorious cross-dressing thief in Jacobean London, she was smashing up every rule in the book when she swaggered onto the stage of the Fortune Theatre in the spring of 1611, dressed in a doublet and a pair of hose, sword in one hand, clay pipe in the other, to perform the closing number of the play she had inspired. It was called *The Roaring Girl.*

A Roaring Girl was loud when she should be quiet, disruptive when she should be submissive, sexual when she should be pure, 'masculine' when she should be 'feminine'. She was everything a woman was not supposed to be, and in a world before feminism, she was society's worst nightmare.[1]

A WOMAN'S LOT

The eight Roaring Girls who feature in this book lived in Britain in the 300 years before the first wave of feminists fought tooth and nail for women's suffrage in the late 1800s, and during those centuries, the political and cultural landscape of the country changed almost beyond recognition. Collectively, these women witnessed the final wave of the English Renaissance and the last days of the Tudors. They saw their country rent by Civil War, their monarch murdered and his son restored. They found Enlightenment with the Georgian kings and experienced Empire and industrialisation in the long reign of Victoria. Britain was transforming at an astonishing rate, yet throughout this period – though it was bookended by female rule – a woman's legal and cultural status remained virtually stagnant. She began and ended it almost as helpless as a child.

The sweeping systemic changes needed to revolutionise a woman's rights and opportunities may have failed to materialise by the late nineteenth century, but the first rumblings of discontent had long been audible in the background. By the dawn of the seventeenth century, a radical social shift had begun to creak into action that would falteringly gather pace over the next 300 years. For although

Mary Frith was the original Roaring Girl, she wasn't the only woman of the era to find herself living in a world that didn't suit her, and who couldn't resist the urge to stick two fingers up at society in response; the seeds of female insurrection were beginning to germinate across Britain, and the women in this book all played their part in the rebellion.

From the privileged vantage point of the twenty-first century, it's easy to forget just how heavily the odds were stacked against women in Britain in the centuries before the women's rights movement, and how necessary their rebellion was. From the day she was born, a girl was automatically considered of less value than her male peers, and throughout her life she would be infantilised and objectified accordingly. Her function in the world would forever be determined by her relationship to men – first her father, then her husband, or, in their absence, her nearest male relation. On them she was legally and financially dependent, and should she end up with no male protector at all, she would find it a desperate struggle to survive.

By the age of seven a girl could be betrothed; at 12 she could be legally married. Her only presumed trajectory was to pass from maid to wife to mother and, if she was lucky, grandmother and widow. Any woman who tried to deviate from this path would quickly find her progress blocked by the towering patriarchal infrastructures in her way. Denied a formal education and barred from the universities, she would find that almost every respectable career was closed to her. She couldn't vote, hold public office or join the armed forces. The common consensus was that her opinions were of no value and her understanding poor, and consequently she was excluded from all forms of public and intellectual life – from scholarship to Parliament to the press. While the men around her were free (if they could afford it) to stride out into the world and participate in all it had to offer, she was expected to know her place and to stay in it – suffocating in the home if she was genteel; toiling in fields, factories, homes and shops if she wasn't. Genius was a male quality, and leadership a male occupation. Even queens would have their qualifications questioned by men who assumed they knew better.

The only 'careers' open to a woman during this period were those of wife and mother, but even if her homelife turned out, by chance, to be happy, these roles still came with considerable downsides. Legal impotence was perhaps the most obvious. In the eyes of the law, the day they married, a husband and wife became one person – and that person was the husband. From that moment on, the wife's legal identity was subsumed by his.[2] Her spouse became her keeper, her lord and her master, while she, as an individual, ceased to exist. Any money she might earn, any object she might own – from her house right down to her handkerchiefs – instantly became his, while all his worldly goods he kept for himself.[3] A wife could no longer possess or bequeath property, sign a contract, sue or be sued in her own right. In principle, she was now her husband's goods and chattels, and he could treat his new possession however he liked. If she were still in any doubt about what to expect from married life before she entered it, the Book of Common Prayer made it alarmingly clear: 'Wives, submit yourselves unto your own husbands, as unto the Lord.'[4]

If the marriage proved miserable, even unbearable, the wife was expected to endure it. Her husband could beat her, rape her, drag her back to his home if she fled – the law would look the other way. And if he strayed from the path of righteousness into another woman's bed, well, that was her fault, too; it could only be because she had failed to please him.

With no effective method of controlling her own fertility,

successive pregnancies were often an inevitable feature of a married woman's life, and this brought with it not only the terrors of giving birth, which, quite aside from the pain, could so easily result in her death,[5] but also the horrifying prospect that most of her children would likely not long survive. A couple during the early modern period might expect to have six or seven children born alive, but to see only two of them reach adulthood.[6]

If the marriage should break down altogether, a wife might find herself excommunicated – not just from society, but from those children, too. Like everything else, they belonged to her husband, and he could strip her of all custody and access rights with only a word. If desperate, she might try for a divorce, though if she did, she'd soon learn that she had little or no chance of ever obtaining one. Unless she was rich enough to afford a private Act of Parliament, and could prove her husband guilty of adultery and numerous other misdemeanours, including bigamy, incest and cruelty, the likelihood was all but non-existent. A husband looking to dispose of an unwanted wife, however, might have more luck – he had only to prove adultery in the lady. If all else failed, he could have her committed to the nearest lunatic asylum easily enough,[7] or perhaps drag her to the local cattle market with a rope around her neck and sell her to the highest bidder.[8]

For all these dire pitfalls, the onus weighed heavily on women to marry and have children, yet at any one time during this period an average of two-thirds of women were not married,[9] and their prospects were often even worse. The single, widowed, abandoned and separated made up this soup of undesirables, and with the notable exception of widows who had been left well provided for (they could enjoy an unusual degree of financial independence and respect), they were particularly vulnerable to hardship, poverty and ostracisation. The stigma of having failed in some way marked most of these women. And then, as now, women were not allowed to fail.

Forever held to a higher ideal, women have always had to be better. They alone were the standard bearers of sexual morality; they alone were responsible for keeping themselves and their family spotless. And since society saw no way of reconciling the fantasy of female purity with the reality of sex, it simply divided women into virgins and whores – idolised and vilified, worshipped and feared, loved and loathed. There could be no middle ground; even in marriage a woman's sexuality had to be strictly controlled, because left unchecked it had the dizzying power to demolish social order. All it took was one indiscretion and man's greatest fears – cuckoldry, doubtful paternity and the corruption of dynastic lineage – could come true. To avoid this chaos, women were subject to a different set of rules that were deemed as sacred as scripture: a man could philander like a priapic satyr and receive nothing worse than a knowing wink; if a woman did the same, she was ruined. Her reputation was as brittle as a dried leaf, and a careless flirtation or a helpless passion could crush it to dust. So rabid was this mania for sexual purity that it could even apply in cases of rape – so rarely brought to court and even more rarely prosecuted, though women undoubtedly endured it, and the shame, blame and suspicion that went with it.

These pernicious double standards permeated every form of social interaction between the sexes – even the very language they spoke. The nation's vocabulary had developed in tandem with its misogyny, resulting in a litany of colourful pejorative terms designed to degrade and humiliate any woman who proved indocile. Too chatty, too complaining, too opinionated and she was a nag, a scold, a shrew, a fishwife, a harridan or a harpy. An unseemly interest in sex saw her branded a whore, wench, slut and harlot. And if she ever dared succumb to singledom or old age, she deserved the fearful monikers of old maid, crone and hag. Terms such as these were part of people's everyday lexicon, and they have no equivalents for men.

Such thorough disenfranchisement – intellectual, economic, political, social and sexual – was the surest way to keep women contained, but despite these desperate measures, it remained a common gripe that women didn't stick to their predetermined codes of conduct anywhere near enough. They were sexually incontinent, fickle, stupid and useless. They gossiped, carped, prattled, tattled, wittered and accused. They had even started to write books. If they would not shut up and play the game, they would have to be forced, and in these tricky cases, ostentatious methods were called for.

A nagging, henpecking or adulterous wife who had overleaped her place in the hierarchy, for example, might be ritualistically shamed in a village skimmington or charivari – in which her neighbours would parade her through the streets on horseback, serenading her with a cacophonous symphony beaten out on pots and pans, and perhaps burning her in effigy, too. Alternatively, she might be subjected to the cucking stool – an early incarnation of the more notorious ducking stool – which essentially served as a public toilet that the offending woman was forced to sit on. And there could hardly be a more sinister or more blatant symbol of the systemic gagging of women than the draconian scold's bridle – an iron mask fitted with a bit that pinned down her tongue, sometimes with a metal spike, to quite literally stop her mouth.[10] This unofficial punishment, which was particularly prevalent during the seventeenth century, was mostly reserved for garrulous, gobby women who had spoken out of turn (or just spoken out) and challenged the authority of men, but it might also be meted out to a woman suspected of witchcraft – if she wasn't one of the thousands who were ducked, hanged or burned for it, that is.[11]

These elaborate tortures pointed to one simple fact: that the potential power women had – be it sexual, intellectual, even supernatural – scared the living daylights out of the patriarchy. In response, it did everything it could to suppress that power and preserve its own supremacy: it kept them ignorant, incapacitated, voiceless and dependent.

By the dawn of the seventeenth century, this sorry template for gender relations had prevailed largely unchallenged for millennia. It's a model so deeply entrenched in Western culture that it can be traced right back to the Ancients, who set the gold standard for excluding and silencing women, not only in their social and political structures but in their art and culture, too.[12] Its justification was based on one disastrously wrong-headed assumption: that women were fundamentally inferior to men. And for that we can blame both bad science and perverse theological doctrine.

Even today, we cling to the myth that men and women's brains are somehow wired differently – an idea that modern science is rapidly disproving.[13] But in 1600, the belief that gender differences were every bit as biological as sex differences was absolute. Ever since the Ancient Greek philosopher Aristotle hypothesised that women were a reproductive mistake – physically defective versions of men – it had been persistently argued in Western debate that they were mentally, morally and emotionally defective, too. It didn't help that seventeenth-century medicine had also inherited from the Ancient Greeks the nonsense theory that the body was governed by the 'four humours' – blood, phlegm, yellow bile and black bile – which in turn were thought to be linked to the four elements: earth, fire, water and air.

The belief was that a woman was comprised of cold, wet elements, while a man was hot and dry – a crucial difference that supposedly rendered her brain softer than his and her body more unstable. The catastrophic conclusion was that women had only a limited capacity for rational thought. It was no use educating them; their feeble brains couldn't bear the strain of rigorous intellectual study. They could not be trusted to think and act for themselves, which was why they required domination. And their bodies and behaviour had to be constantly policed, because women were famously susceptible to both sexual voracity and madness – which frequently went hand in hand and were often indistinguishable.

These pernicious, ancient ideas were only reinforced by Christian doctrine. The creation myth made it abundantly clear that Eve, the first woman and mother, who had been fashioned from Adam's rib for his comfort and pleasure, was the cause of original sin and the source of man's woe, while early Christian writers spelled it out to the masses that it was a wife's religious duty to bow to her husband's authority, because 'the head of the woman is man'[14] and to submit to him was to submit to God. By the seventeenth century, the damage had set in like rot. The message had been parroted and propagated by nearly every father, husband, preacher, politician, philosopher and pamphleteer across the land for thousands of years, until almost everyone – even women – believed it.

THE OLD RADICALS

With so many barriers in her way, so many erasures to contend with, it's a wonder that any woman ever made it into the history books. To dismantle such deeply embedded foundations is a monumental task

– so much so that we're still working on it today. In Britain, we have at least made progress enough for this to seem an unbearable world to live in – the Gilead of our nightmares. So how did any woman cope with it? How did any woman even begin to challenge it?

The truth is, the majority didn't even try. Browbeaten by continual put-downs and a lack of opportunity, they grimaced and bore it, most of them too poor, too ill-educated, too legally and financially dependent on men to have a means of protesting. Power and influence were not within the average woman's grasp, and if she were anything other than white, she faced almost insurmountable odds – the lives of black and brown women in Britain are particularly absent from the historical records, though they were certainly not absent from the country.

Faced with this dead end, some women chose to take pride in their domestic roles and make the best of their lot; others were so inured to misogyny that they accepted it as normal, even became complicit in it, conned into believing that they could somehow profit from playing nicely in this twisted game.[15]

But there have always been women who refused to play by rules that had so obviously been written by men, for men. Women who couldn't just keep quiet and carry on. Who didn't fit the narrow criteria of what a woman ought to be, and felt instinctively that they were as valuable as any man. How did these women – the clever, the curious, the talented; those who preferred women to men, who preferred sword-fighting to child-rearing, who preferred breeches to petticoats, learning to laundry, discussion to silence, independence to marriage; who yearned for the open seas, not the scullery, and dreamed of fame, not obscurity – how did *these* women negotiate the hostile world around them and find the outlets they needed for all their complexities?

There was only one way: they would have to rile, unnerve, disobey and question. They would have to forfeit the title of 'good girl' and become a Roaring Girl instead.

This book explores how just a few of them managed it. Together, the eight Roaring Girls collected here span the full spectrum of the social hierarchy, from a duchess to a slave, and encompass a rainbow of personalities: in these pages you'll find poets and adventurers, scientists and philosophers, actors and activists, writers and entrepreneurs, thieves and soldiers, ladies and lowlifes, wives and spinsters, mothers and mistresses, flamboyant dressers, plain dressers and cross-dressers, of every sexual preference – in short, all kinds of womanhood. Their roaring ways took various forms. Some of them used words, others action; some broke the law, others changed the law; some used their femininity, others threw it off entirely and appropriated the ways, manners and dress of men instead. All of them were playing with fire, and inevitably they sometimes got burned. For every admirer who cheered them on during their lifetimes, there were plenty more who denounced them as monsters, lunatics, freaks, devils, whores and old maids, and quickly forgot them once they were dead.

Indeed, to their contemporaries, their achievements might not have seemed particularly worth remembering. After all, they didn't conspicuously change the world – not one of them ruled a nation, wrote a classic novel, made a pioneering discovery or led a revolution. Yet progress can come in small, surprising packages, too. That the historical records took note of these women at all suggests that they were the exceptions, not the rule, living extraordinary, not ordinary, lives, and in the pre-twentieth-century world that was quite enough to get society in a tizz. By living differently, truthfully, loudly and unashamedly, these Roaring Girls were challenging the system, and – whether they knew it or not – making a difference. The imprint they made on history may have been faint, but it's there to be seen if we take the trouble to look. These women helped change our culture, however incrementally, and together they give a tantalising glimpse of the breadth, boldness and sheer brilliance of the legions of women who have fallen through the cracks over the centuries and tumbled headlong into the 'Dustbin of History'.[16]

IS THIS WHAT A FEMINIST LOOKS LIKE?

The urge to label such extraordinary women from history as 'feminists' is almost irresistible. Naturally, we want to 'think back through our mothers', as Virginia Woolf phrased it,[17] and find inspiring heroines to admire; it's our way of trying to bridge the gap between us, so we can all be on the same team. But to foist modern values and paradigms onto women who lived hundreds of years ago is to set ourselves a trap. If we take the dictionary definition of a feminist as one who supports 'the advocacy of women's rights on the ground of the equality of the sexes',[18] the majority of the women in this book don't qualify. Most would never have spared a thought for whether women should be granted equal rights with men – that was too big a question too soon, given the scale of the obstacles; they were usually far too busy trying to negotiate their own lives to worry about anyone else's. The human rights that women enjoy today would have been met with stunned disbelief by these women, and the word 'feminist' with a blank stare.[19] The women's suffrage movement was only just beginning to coalesce in the 1850s, so any woman who spoke out in defence of her sex before then was not a spoke in the wheel of any political or civil movement, buoyed by support from like-minded allies; she was a lone voice in a din of misogyny.

When examining the lives of historical women, there's no ignoring that their world was not our world; they lived by a different set of standards, a lower bar of expectation, and to try to force our modern concept of feminism to fit retrospectively would be foolhardy. As such, our Roaring Girls don't always behave in the ways we might want them to or say the things we want to hear. Many of them are a mass of contradictions. With their natural instincts so out of kilter with the social conventions of their day, the result was often paradoxical characters who were both products of their time and ahead of their time. To avoid disappointment, they should always be viewed against their own historical backdrop, rather than ours.

Which is why it can only ever be anachronistic to label these women simply as feminists. And yet, the spirit of feminism was not born with the word. There was no Damascene moment when the movement burst into being, fully formed and fully armed, like Athena sprouting from the head of Zeus. It didn't arrive with the first Suffragists in the 1860s; it didn't even arrive with Mary Wollstonecraft in the 1790s. Its birth was slow, incremental, painful and faltering, forged over centuries and across the world, by actions great and incidental, by people famous and forgotten.

What binds these women together, then, is not that they were feminists as we would understand them today, but that they all in some way broke the heavily gendered rules of what a woman 'ought' to be and began the work of rewriting them, exposing ignorance, reclaiming their freedoms and overturning preconceptions as they went. They may not have realised it, but that in itself was a feminist act. If we can allow ourselves to relax the remit of the word, we might call these formidable women a fraction of the many early feminists, proto-feminists, accidental, unwitting, even reluctant feminists, who, despite every effort to suppress them, dared to be extraordinary – who, between them, struck the first sparks of what would later become a blaze.

This book is intended as a celebration of these unconventional women's lives, in all their messy, three-dimensional wonder, in the hope of affording them a little of the gratitude and recognition they so richly deserve, and reclaiming some of the complexity that has historically been denied them. It's time we viewed such women not as saints or martyrs, heroes or villains, virgins or whores, masculine or feminine, but as real, contradictory, compelling human beings who laughed, loved, cried and fought their way through life, making the best of it, making mistakes – and each in their own way making history. Above all, it's a collection of stories about courage – the courage of women who, in a world that constantly told them no, stood firm and roared back the word yes.

Mary Frith

THE ROARING GIRL

It is Sunday, 9 February 1612, and a crowd has gathered in the churchyard of old St Paul's Cathedral to see a woman punished. Her crime is against nature; she has disgraced all womankind with her monstrous acts, and now, before the public and before God, she must admit her shame and be cleansed of guilt.

Barefoot and bare-headed, the woman walks out into the wan morning light, swathed in a white sheet and clutching a long taper. For those who can read it, a placard proclaiming her sin hangs around her neck. As she makes her way unsteadily across the cold flagstones of the yard towards the pulpit and carefully climbs the steps to the platform, the jeers from the crowd rise up and follow her.

From the pulpit stage, she looks out over her audience and sees a swarm of eager faces. They are waiting for the show to start, so when the priest begins his sermon, the woman takes her cue. She drops her eyes, suppresses a smile and does her best to cry.

The woman was Mary Frith, and six weeks before, on Christmas Day 1611, she had been arrested (not for the first time) at St Paul's

'I please myself, and care not else who loves me.'

MARY FRITH, OR 'MOLL CUTPURSE'
(c.1585–1659),
THIEF, CROSS-DRESSER, PERFORMER AND FENCE

Cathedral for walking the streets of London at night dressed in men's clothes. The result was a charge of public immorality, and a punishment designed to humiliate, disgrace and correct her: she would do public penance in a white sheet, at the open-air pulpit of St Paul's Cross within the cathedral grounds,[1] where all could bear witness to her forced repentance and the purification of her soul.

This symbolic ritual was a tried and tested disciplinary measure, already centuries old by 1612, but in this instance, it was a waste of time. The ecclesiastical court, which dealt with all lapses in personal morality, was attempting to shame and reform a woman who would not be shamed or reformed, and in the end, the event was more farcical pantomime than solemn ceremony. The penitent herself, it was observed, regarded her punishment with such merry disdain that she was drunk throughout the proceedings; for her, it seems, this was just another opportunity to play to the crowds. Her priest's sermon, meanwhile – a lengthy lecture denouncing her sin and calling on her to repent – was so mind-numbingly tedious that most of the audience lost interest and wandered off partway through. Those who stayed, however, were rewarded for their patience with precisely what they had come for: a free performance by 'Moll Cutpurse' – one of the most famous, and infamous, women in London.

THE THREE FACES OF MARY

When Mary Frith completed her act of penance at St Paul's Cross in 1612, her name – or at least that of her alter ego, 'Moll Cutpurse' – had been on the lips of most Jacobean Londoners for several years, especially those who frequented the playhouses, taverns, brothels and bear pits of Bankside, the lawless entertainment district of Southwark that lay conveniently outside the City's jurisdiction. Whether they loved or loathed her, feared or admired her, Mary's notorious career as a cross-dressing thief (or 'cutpurse'[2]) and street entertainer had fascinated the public, and by the time she'd reached her mid twenties, she had achieved cult celebrity status – so much so that several playwrights had already appropriated, refashioned and immortalised her persona as a wholly unconventional folk heroine.

Fifty years later, Mary's legend as one of the most enjoyably outrageous and controversial women of the age was still going strong, confirmed by the arrival in 1662 of a sensationalised 'autobiography', *The Life and Death of Mrs Mary Frith*, which, if it were what it pretends to be – the candid deathbed diary of a repentant sinner – would constitute an invaluable primary source for Mary's life and an important early example of life writing by an Englishwoman. As it is, the diary is almost certainly a fake. There is no credible evidence that Mary wrote it herself; after all, she'd been dead for three years before it appeared, and although up to 50 per cent of women in London were literate by the late seventeenth century (a much higher proportion than in most parts of the country), it's unlikely that a woman of low birth such as Mary would have been one of them.[3]

The book's numerous factual errors and omissions point instead to another hand, and given its erratic style, maybe even several. Falling into three distinct and sometimes contradictory sections – an opening address, an introduction summarising Mary's upbringing and a 'diary' of her life as a cutpurse – it comprises a string of unapologetic, entertaining, though often disjointed, anecdotes of her misdeeds, and seems to have more in common with the fictionalised criminal biographies that were popular at the time than it does with a genuine diary,[4] veering in tone from comic to defiant to political and even preachy.

This 'diary', then, is an unreliable account of Mary's life, though that's not to say it's worthless. Plenty of the details within its pages chime with what we know to be true. It's plausible that the authors had their anecdotes either directly from Mary when she was alive – an old woman entertaining anyone in the alehouse who would listen with tales of her outrageous youth – or from those who knew her, or, more likely, that they adapted them from the tales of her exploits that had been passed from gossip to gossip for decades. Mary had already written herself into London's folklore with her riotous escapades, leaving the diary's anonymous authors the task of matching, if not surpassing, these outlandish oral tales.

But herein lies the problem with Mary Frith. With the historical records frustratingly reticent on her real life (her appearances in them are few, though always revealing), much of what we know – or think we know – of her comes from the various fictionalised versions that appeared over the years, making her as slippery a character in death as she was in life. The legend who features in the 'diary', the character who walked the stage and the flesh-and-blood woman who left an imprint on the records don't always agree, splitting her image into hazy triplicate. The diarists were aware of the issue. Their excuse for the 'abruptness and discontinuance' of their story is that 'it was impossible to make one piece of so various a subject'.[5] This isn't just an unwitting admission of their own fudged documentation of her life; evidently Mary's baffling complexity made her as intangible to her contemporaries as she is to us.

Lower-class, lawless, unconventional and disobedient, Mary Frith was disturbing – but also strangely alluring; she represented an unusual kind of woman in the seventeenth century, one to whom society had no answer. By definition, such women lived a precarious life and needed cunning strategies to survive, and in Mary's case that meant barricading herself in behind a protective wall of myth and mystique, cultivating multiple personalities and perfecting her performance of each one until the real woman became as elusive as wisps of smoke. With so many Marys before us, it's as if she's laid down a challenge: to find the real Mary Frith, and catch her if we can.

A VERY TOMRIG OR RUMPSCUTTLE

The mystery authors of *The Life and Death of Mrs Mary Frith* do their best to get to the bottom of this unfathomable woman, but she is 'so difficult a mixture' of male and female, of 'dishonesty and fair and civil deportment', that they seem torn from the start between admiration and alarm. Faced with a cross-dressing thief who on the one hand must surely be morally reprehensible, but on the other was famed for her good humour and entertaining shenanigans, they delight in her one minute, sneer at her the next – sometimes all at once. Their introduction showers Mary with mock-heroic epithets: she is 'a prodigy', an 'epicoene wonder', 'the oracle of felony', the gold-standard bearer of thievery – a profession that is now in 'sad decays' without her; but she is also a 'virago', a 'bono roba' (prostitute), a monstrous hybrid of masculine and feminine, so unattractive that she was 'not made for the pleasure or delight of man'. Such a woman made little sense to her peers; she was as much a side-show freak as she was a folkloric heroine, and needed to be explained to the uncomprehending but fascinated public.

In their attempt to do just that, the authors begin at the beginning, with Mary's childhood, which, if the bare bones of their introduction are to be believed, served as a dress rehearsal for the role she would play in later life. With an air of surprise, they report that this natural rebel was born to perfectly ordinary, law-abiding parents – an 'honest shoemaker' and his wife, who lived in the Barbican area of London – in the latter years of Elizabeth I's reign (the exact year is unclear). Tender, affectionate and indulgent, Mr and Mrs Frith offered their daughter a humble upbringing, though a happy and stable one.[6] By rights, she ought to have been just another honest, hard-working young woman who soon married and settled into her predetermined roles of wife and mother. But no.

Mary's 'boisterous and masculine spirit' manifested itself early and would not be tamed. To curb her unruly ways, we're told that her parents took particular care over her education (which by the standards of the day meant teaching her to read but not to write, as well as a few domestic accomplishments), but their efforts had little effect. Young Mary was a child of action, not academia. She was an archetypal tomboy – 'a very tomrig or rumpscuttle' – fizzing with energy, and resistant to every norm of female behaviour: she would 'fight with boys, and courageously beat them'; 'run, jump, leap or hop with any of them', and ravage her pretty girls' clothes in the scuffles. She didn't care – her dresses hung awkwardly on her ungainly frame and only annoyed her.

Drawn to the places where the rabble congregated, this scrappy urchin spent most of her time at the Bear Garden, the rowdy entertainment arena wedged in among the playhouses of Bankside, where bear-baiting, bull-baiting and dog fighting kept the blood-lusty crowds amused. Here, in the fug of the bustling, stinking, noisy Southwark streets, all the vices were out on display: drunks and tavern brawlers, punters and prostitutes, cutpurses and cheats jostled along together, while down the road, above the gateway of old London Bridge, the heads of traitors sat on spikes, like gruesome lollipops in a sweet-shop window. Young Mary saw it all, and she wasn't fazed in the least; in fact, she fitted right in.

However unladylike, this was the world where Mary Frith felt at home, for she was 'too great a libertine … to be enclosed in the limits of a private domestic life'. As womanhood approached, she showed no interest in the feminine pursuits she was expected to learn: 'she could not endure that sedentary life of sewing or stitching', preferring a sword and a dagger to a needle and thimble. The bakehouse and the laundry were alien to her, and the 'magpie chat of the wenches' an irritation. Mary preferred a more direct form of expression. Even when she was young she was 'not for mincing obscenity'; by adulthood, the habit had developed into 'downright swearing'. Such profane language from a woman was unfeminine and unacceptable and, along with the rest of her behaviour, it had to be policed (as Mary would later discover – her reputed potty mouth would be listed in the court records as one of her many arrestable offences). To complete this picture of the ultimate anti-woman, we're told that 'above all she had a natural abhorrence to the tending of children', and steered well clear of becoming a mother (another claim that is borne out by the records).

If this character portrait is accurate, Mary was a woman destined to offend and perplex seventeenth-century society in every way. Indeed, so far was she from the meek, mild, modest woman that custom demanded that it was doubted she was a woman at all. She had unsexed herself, become a 'hermaphrodite in manners as well as in habit'; she was 'the living description of a schism and separation', combining the 'female subtlety' of one sex and the 'manly resolution' of the other – and to a society that only dealt in strict gender binaries, such a combination was profoundly unnerving.

A lower-class girl with no money, little education and scant opportunities had very few options in life even if she conformed, but if, like Mary, she either would not or could not conform, the choice was almost made for her. Such girls often found themselves tripping over into the wrong side of the law in order to survive, usually through thievery or prostitution, but even in that world there was a hierarchy to climb. If Mary wanted to live differently to most women, she would have to behave differently to most women. And if she wanted a modicum of the power and freedom that men had, then she would have to settle for power and freedom in the criminal underworld.

MOLL CUTPURSE

Too proud to beg, too wild for domestic drudgery and quite possibly too repulsed by men to contemplate prostitution, Mary Frith decided to make her living as a cutpurse. It was the most dangerous choice of all these unappealing options, for to embark upon a career of thievery automatically meant risking her liberty and her life. England in the early seventeenth century was a visibly savage place: legal punishments were reliably disproportionate to the crime and barbaric public executions were a favoured form of entertainment. With property deemed as valuable as human life – and frequently even more so – theft and burglary were among the country's capital offences; if Mary's fingers weren't quite nimble enough, she could be facing a stint in Newgate Gaol, or worse, the drop at Tyburn.[7] But in a city where ostentatious wealth rubbed shoulders with grinding poverty, the temptation to pick the glittering pockets of affluent bankers, merchants, lawyers and lords was just too great. Undeterred, or perhaps just desperate, Mary joined the hordes of cutpurses who plagued Elizabethan London early – probably when she was still a child – and quickly demonstrated a knack for getting away with it.

Undoubtedly it played to her advantage that law and order was then a haphazard thing – the professional police force had yet to be established and certain areas, including Mary's stomping ground of Southwark, fell outside the City's jurisdiction, making them attractive dens for every kind of vice. These areas were more or less governed by underground criminal networks. Magistrates relied on local volunteer constables to keep the peace and apprehend criminals, who in turn relied on members of the public to raise a 'hue and cry' whenever they spotted a misdemeanour. Mary was presumably so adept at sleight of hand that she mostly managed to pilfer unnoticed, though she wasn't always so lucky.

The records show that on 26 August 1600, when she was still a teenager, she was first charged by the Justices of Middlesex with stealing an unknown man's purse, while working in cahoots with two other women. She wriggled out of it on this occasion but was indicted again on 18 March 1602 for stealing a purse from a man named Richard Ingles, and again on 8 September 1609, for burglary.[8] Every time, she managed to secure a verdict of not guilty and escape a trip to Newgate – or the noose – so that by her early twenties she had made quite a career for herself. And with it came a well-earned new nickname: 'Moll Cutpurse'.[9]

The details of Mary's subsequent life as a cutpurse are filled in by *The Life and Death of Mrs Mary Frith* with unashamed glee. After a short preamble, Mary's so-called 'diary' embarks on a chain of anecdotes about her many misadventures, tricks and petty revenges, even providing a kind of instruction manual in places on how she and her colleagues successfully plied their trade. Helpful details such as dates are absent, and psychological self-analysis doesn't trouble her – 'It is no matter to know how I grew up to this,' she states dismissively, 'since I have laid it as a maxim that it was my fate.' She is, however, allowed the odd moment of reflection when it's to marvel at what an extraordinary creature she is. 'I do more wonder at myself than others can do,' she declares in awe, with the same air of amusement with which she relates all of her history. For the purpose here, more than anything, is to entertain with her oddity. Accordingly, her crimes are softened to 'pranks' and, like her literary descendant Moll Flanders, she is portrayed as an honest thief and magnetic heroine, her maxim for life: 'To be excellent and happy in villainy', because that has always been 'reputed equal with a good fame'.

Judging by these anecdotes, Mary's good fame was justified. She tells of being tricked into boarding a ship for the plantations of Virginia and her subsequent escape by paying off the captain, and of how, being poor and friendless, she then joined a gang of pickpockets, who judged her to be 'very well qualified for a receiver and entertainer of their fortunate achievements' – or rather a receiver of stolen goods. This was a life she rather took to, for although the danger was evident, she was 'loath to relinquish the profit', and seems to have quickly established a unique and powerful position for herself as protectress and confidante of this coterie of thieves. It was a mutually beneficial arrangement. Being 'well known to all the gang, and by my good dealing with them not a little in their favour', Mary was offered protection and anonymity in return – a real case of honour among thieves. She would share out the profits fairly, act as 'umpire in their quarrels' and lend money to the most desperate, thereby preventing them from committing dangerous robberies and effectively saving them from 'the hangman's clutches'. By fashioning herself as the fair, magnanimous champion of lowlifes in this way, Mary earned the respect and devoted loyalty of her fellow cutpurses, 'so that among all the thieveries they did, my name was never heard of; for they made it the chiefest of their religion to conceal me and to conceal nothing of their designs from me'. In effect, she had negotiated her way to the top of her own organised crime ring – and secured her own immunity in the process.

It was a wily strategy, though not foolproof – as we know, Mary occasionally found herself in hot water, but when she did, the pick-pocket community was allegedly swift to come to her rescue. In one instance, cited in the diary, when Mary is taken up for stealing a watch, she employs one of her gang to commit the ultimate theft in front of a packed courtroom, purely to get her off the hook. Once she had pleaded not guilty, she says, 'it came to this issue, whether that watch for which I was indicted was the gentleman's watch or no'. The constable who had apprehended her was called forward to deliver the watch for the gentleman to identify, but just as the constable was making his way into court, Mary deployed her secret weapon: 'one of my small officers dived into his pocket and sought out the evidence against me, and departed invisible'.

This neat trick naturally incensed the Lord Mayor, who immedi-ately suspected her chicanery, but with no evidence to hand, there was nothing he could do. Once again, the jury were forced to acquit Mary, leaving her free to continue with her shady dealings, undis-couraged and irredeemable as ever. Before long, she tells us, she had the confidence of famous highwaymen, too, and begins to cut a figure rather like a seventeenth-century Fagin, sending off her gang of pickpockets and robbers to do their light-fingered work and bring back the spoils to their mistress.

It's not known exactly when Mary Frith began to combine her pick-pocketing with transvestism, but it seems likely to have coincided with the advent of her entertainment career – a male-dominated industry like all the others – when she was in her early twenties.

I do more
wonder at myself
than others
can do

Counterintuitive though this decision seems for a thief whose life depended on anonymity, in around 1608 Mary began to see the advantage in developing her persona as 'Moll Cutpurse' into a public attraction; by simply donning a doublet, hat and cloak, she could become a 'character', who simultaneously drew the crowds to her and distanced her from them. It soon become her signature. Dressed in men's clothes, she would walk the streets of Southwark, challenging 'diverse gallants' to sartorial competitions and entertaining the crowds with her 'mad pranks', while her gang of footpads weaved through the distracted audience, cutting purses as they went. Now a decoy as well as a fence and low-level criminal mastermind, Mary Frith had pulled off a protean magic trick: she had become Moll Cutpurse, the charming, eccentric rogue who could never be caught in the act.

Mary's transvestism was unusual, but it didn't occur in isolation. It was part of a Europe-wide underground trend for female cross-dressing that first sprang up in the 1570s, reached a peak in the 1620s, thrived throughout the eighteenth century and continued on into the early nineteenth, when it rapidly fizzled out. The UK was particularly prone to this phenomenon, having one of the highest incidence rates in Europe – there are at least 50 recorded cases during this period of women living as men, either to work, marry or serve their country as soldiers and sailors – and it's easy to see the appeal.[10] A woman's clothes were ornamental rather than practical, designed to hinder, not help her. Her rigid stays and voluminous skirts accentuated her primary functions of mother and sex object, and were as cumbersome and restrictive as the social rules that bound her. To throw them off in favour of a doublet and hose offered a long list of symbolic attractions. For some women, sidestepping the arbitrary trappings of gender was a survival strategy or simple expedient, a handy disguise when in trouble, in love or going off to war.

For others, it was an expression of their complex sexuality, which, in an era before sexual categorisation, had only a one-size-fits-all model. For many more, it meant safety – from harassment, seduction, rape and prostitution, from forced marriages and unwanted pregnancy. And for the ambitious or adventurous, who, as Mary Beard puts it, had 'no template for what a powerful woman looks like, except that she looks rather like a man',[11] it meant a sudden open door to agency and opportunity. For those who dabbled, it was pleasingly provocative. For those who went the whole hog, it was a liberation. For all of them, it was a direct challenge to the intractable social codes that governed everyone's lives – an early feminist act of defiance.[12]

To a country that had long employed sartorial sumptuary laws to scrupulously to preserve the distinctions of rank in its citizens, this trend for female transvestism indicated their alarming lack of control over the distinctions of gender. The Bible had decried cross-dressing as an 'abomination unto the Lord',[13] a subversion of the 'proper' hierarchy between woman, man and God, as the pamphleteer Phillip Stubbes was keen to remind everybody in his 1583 *Anatomy of Abuses*. All cross-dressers, he wrote, were 'accursed'. Men who did it were 'weak, tender and infirm', degrading themselves to the status of feeble, powerless females.[14] Women who did it were hermaphroditic 'monsters' and presumptuous whores, attempting to steal a man's power and usurp his sovereignty.

It was this perceived power exchange that was key to transvestism's ability to unsettle and enrage society. In women, not only did it smack of insubordination, but with its elements of disguise, evasion and masculine aggression, it carried an intrinsic connection to both criminality and sexual incontinency. In 1615, a fencing master named Joseph Swetnam was so incensed by this fad that Mary Frith was spearheading that he published *The Arraignment of Lewd, Idle, Froward, and Unconstant Women* – a misogynist's rant in which he bloviated against the 'heinous evils' of women. The book was so popular it went through ten editions by 1637, and the concerns it spoke of went right to the very top. King James I, another notorious misogynist, voiced his own anxieties in January 1620, when he commanded that the clergy 'inveigh vehemently and bitterly in their sermons, against the insolence of our women' for 'their wearing of broad brimmed hats' and 'pointed doublets', for having 'their hair cut short or shorne' and for carrying 'stilettoes or poinards [daggers]'.[15] His decree then sparked a pamphlet war the following month between the anonymous authors of *Hic Mulier, or, The Man-Woman* and *Haec Vir; or, The Womanish Man*, who publicly fought out the big question: where these 'masculine-feminines' a monstrous 'deformity never before dreamed of', or emancipated slaves fighting for freedom of choice and self-expression?[16] It could not have been clearer that, even after decades of furiously debating the controversy, this new breed of woman that Mary represented encapsulated men's fears that 'the world is very far out of order'.[17]

Consequently, and perhaps inevitably, the panicked authorities frantically cracked down on this destabilising wave of transvestism in an attempt to stamp it out. Several women are known to have been arrested and punished for it long before Mary took it up: in 1569, one Joanna Goodman was whipped and sent to the Bridewell house of correction for dressing as a male servant to accompany her husband to war; in July 1575, the Aldermen's Court sentenced Dorothy Clayton to stand on the pillory for two hours before sending her to Bridewell Prison and Hospital because 'contrary to all honesty and womanhood [she] commonly goes about the City apparelled in man's attire'; in 1599, Katherine Cuffe was sent to Bridewell for disguising herself in boy's clothes to meet her lover in secret, as was Margaret Wakeley in 1601, because she 'had a bastard child and went in men's apparel'.[18]

Most of these women had been accused of sexual misconduct in connection with their transvestism and were using it as a form of disguise. Mary's motives, however, appear to have been quite different, with her cross-dressing driven partly by a need to advance her career as a crooked street entertainer, and partly by sheer enjoyment.[19] If she was aware of the hazards before she began, she was not put off; indeed, she seems to have been intent on exploiting every one of its discomforting associations. Her outfit of choice was usually a doublet and petticoat, mixing male and female dress, which, rather than disguising her femaleness, deliberately drew attention to her man-womanness. This was not a woman attempting to blend in and disappear; it was a woman who wanted to be noticed – a natural extrovert, who couldn't resist the overriding urge to step outside the conventional bounds of female experience and thumb her nose in a small but symbolic way at society's assumption that she was not fit to participate in the world as fully as men. Her method would have its advantages and disadvantages, but certainly Mary Frith had achieved her end: 'Moll Cutpurse' had gone up in the underworld – soon there was hardly a soul in London who didn't know her name.

THE ROARING GIRL

It was around 1610, when Mary was in her mid-twenties and had spent a good couple of years building her dubious reputation as a curious local personality, that London's playwrights began to take notice of her. And like her biographers, they, too, would mould her image to suit their own ends.

The theatre had come of age during Elizabeth's reign and, despite occasional closures due to the plague (in 1603–4 and again in 1606–9), it was maturing under James I. Nestled between the inns, bear-pits and brothels of Southwark, playhouses were grubby, raucous places, where 'all around were card-sharps, dicers, con men and money lenders, roaring boys and roaring girls',[20] and all of life, from nobodies to nobles, pooled together for their penny's worth of entertainment. They were also places where women, though welcome in the pits and the galleries, were still categorically banned from the stage.

Mary might not have been allowed to perform herself, but now, at the height of her fame, her alias Moll Cutpurse began to make cameo appearances in several comedic works of the day, taking the lead role in at least two. *The Mad Pranks of Merry Moll of the Bankside, with her Walks in Man's Apparel, and to What Purpose* was entered in the Stationer's Register by playwright John Day in 1610, and though it hasn't survived, the title gives a flavour of the jolly, affectionate take on her street performances that it likely contained. What has survived are two plays that both date from 1611 and feature very different treatments of Moll. One, Nathaniel Field's *Amends for Ladies*, gives her the short shrift you might expect, allowing her only a brief walk-on part and branding her a 'rogue', a 'whore' and a 'bawd'; the other would put Moll centre stage and overturn every assumption society held about her.

In the spring of 1611, Ben Jonson's *The Alchemist* had lately been performed at the original Bankside Globe Theatre by Shakespeare's company, the King's Men; Shakespeare himself, now approaching semi-retirement, was preparing *The Winter's Tale* for performance there in May. Across the river, between Whitecross Street and Golden Lane to the west of Shoreditch, on what is now Fortune Street, sat the Fortune Theatre, the rectangular (rather than polygonal) playhouse owned by theatre manager, brothel keeper, property dealer and pawn-broker Philip Henslowe and his son-in-law, the retired lead actor Edward Alleyn. There, the prolific dramatists Thomas Middleton and Thomas Dekker were presenting *The Roaring Girl*, a 'city comedy' to be performed by Prince Henry's Men (formerly the Admiral's Men), the second most important acting troupe after Shakespeare's.

The play's prologue makes it clear that Jacobean audiences were in for something new. No doubt they had turned up to watch this long-awaited piece with their own ideas of what to expect from a roaring girl, muses the speaker: she 'roars at midnight in deep tavern bowls'; she 'beats the watch' and controls the constables; she 'swears, stabs' and 'gives braves', causing mayhem wherever she goes. As the female equivalent of a noisy, riotous roaring boy, who had been a stock character of English literature since the previous century, she could mean nothing but mischief. But this would be the tale of a roaring girl who 'flies / With wings more lofty' – a new kind of woman, never before seen, 'whose notes till now never were'. Who could this woman be? The audience knew her name already. It was 'Mad Moll', of course, the actor cried, whose 'life our acts proclaim!'[21]

The play makes full strategic use of its audience's preconceptions, however, for its plot relies on the assumption that a woman like Moll Cutpurse – famed for wearing men's clothes, carrying a sword, smoking a pipe and thieving – would be every father's nightmare daughter-in-law. So when young lovers Sebastian Wengrave and Mary Fitzallard find themselves thwarted by Sebastian's father, Sir Alexander, who prohibits the match because of Mary's puny dowry, Sebastian's cunning plan is to pretend that he's in love with Moll Cutpurse instead, 'a creature / So strange in quality, a whole city takes / Note of her name and person'.[22] She is assumed to be a woman so repugnant that his father will overcome his financial misgivings about Mary Fitzallard and see her, by comparison, as a dream alternative.

It all goes according to plan. When Sir Alexander hears that Sebastian is to marry Moll he voices his outright disgust at his son's choice, describing her as nothing short of an aberration. She is a 'scurvy woman', 'a creature ... nature hath brought forth / To mock the sex of woman'. She 'strays so from her kind, / Nature repents she made her'. His judgement is unequivocal: Moll is a 'monster'.[23]

Panicked at the prospect of the censure and embarrassment that will surely follow if his son ends up shackled to such a creature ('Why, wouldst thou fain marry to be pointed at?' he asks Sebastian in disbelief),[24] Sir Alexander resolves to stop the marriage and employs a spy and trickster – the aptly named Trapdoor – to wheedle his way into Moll's service to 'ensnare her very life' and remove her from the picture. The traps are duly laid: because she is a woman and therefore surely vain and stupid, the villains try to flatter, trick and con her; because she is a cross-dresser and therefore surely a whore, they then try to seduce her, and because she is a thief and therefore surely greedy, they plant a trail of jewels in her path to make her fingers twitch.

When Moll swaggers on stage, however, first in mannish riding habit and later in full doublet and breeches, sword at her side and pipe in her mouth (played, confusingly, by a man pretending to be a woman dressed as a man), all the villains' plans – and their assumptions – are dramatically upended. Far from being the victim of this play, Moll Cutpurse is its undoubted heroine, outwitting her enemies at every turn. This is no monstrous whore; Moll is a model of chastity, wit and integrity, the moral heart of the action and (no doubt thanks to her real-life template) the most vibrant, fully formed character in the play. In her, the audience was confronted with an all-new image of female virtue: a woman who challenges her would-be seducer

Laxton to a duel for impugning her honour (and wins); who protects her enemies from a gang of marauding cutpurses rather than robbing them, and who is clever enough to see through Trapdoor's subterfuge in an instant. To defy the feminine ideal entirely, she is also staunchly anti-marriage, preferring 'to lie o'both sides o'th'bed' and retain her independence than to take orders from a man. If Sir Alexander knew her at all, she says, he would understand that she and Sebastian could never possibly marry – not because *he* could never want such a monster, but because *she* 'would ne'er agree!'[25]

Sebastian, at least, has the sense to realise that Moll is in fact the only person who 'has the art to help them', and that if his plan is to work, he must confide in her rather than dupe her. And his trust in her pays dividends, for by the close of the play, she has bested her foes, brought the lovers together and restored order and justice. Sir Alexander is left begging her pardon for slandering and prejudging her, begrudgingly admitting that 'Thou art a mad girl, and yet I cannot now / Condemn thee.'[26]

If we were to judge Mary Frith solely by *The Roaring Girl*, she would be a much easier figure to grasp, for Middleton and Dekker's version of her is remarkably close to our idea of a modern-day feminist heroine. To give this flagrantly unconventional female character such moral goodness, to have her triumph and be the agent of peace and harmony, when to the pamphleteers, the authorities and even the King she was a harbinger of social chaos, was a radical move. She is like no other heroine in Elizabethan and Jacobean drama.[27] Even Shakespeare's most famous cross-dressing women – Viola, Portia and Rosalind – do so for the purposes of disguise, to win or save their lover, and once their task is complete, order is restored and the threat that their cross-dressing posed is removed. They all end their respective plays back where they 'belong': married and in their 'proper' clothes. Moll is very different. Like her real-life counterpart, she cross-dresses because she wants to, and at the end of *The Roaring Girl* she is celebrated for refusing to bow to conformity and remains entirely herself – unmarried, in breeches and in full control of the action.[28]

This was a revolutionary female character to see in the theatre. In a play littered with low comedy (smutty jokes on her hermaphroditic qualities are everywhere – she is 'a codpiece daughter', a 'cutpurse drab', 'a monster with two trinkets', a 'gaskin-bride'[29]), Moll is never degraded; she is untouched by the slander and is the most powerful character on stage at all times. She also has all the best lines. The longest and most rhetorically slick speech in the play is hers, and as an impassioned diatribe against men's objectification and predation of women and the sexual hypocrisy that so easily branded them harlots, it forms the moral nub of the play. Her words are directed at her would-be seducer Laxton, but to all men by extension:

> ... *Thou'rt one of those*
> *That thinks each woman thy fond flexible whore,*
> *If she but cast a liberal eye upon thee,*
> *Turn back her head, she's thine ...*

Why, she asks, is a woman like her presumed immoral and considered fair game, and then cursed with a 'blasted name', just because she's 'given to sport' and 'often merry'? Is a woman not allowed to enjoy herself without inviting sexual advances? Apparently not. Nor was she always in a position to protect herself. Society preferred to ignore the unseemly truth behind its sexual politics, but here was Moll stating it plainly: that most women who ended up falling from grace did so not because they were morally corrupt, but because their circumstances were desperate. Forever at the mercy of poverty, chance and exploitative men who preyed on the vulnerable, it was all too easy for 'distressed needlewomen' and 'trade-fallen wives' to be used for pleasure and discarded as whores. Women who found themselves in dire straits would of course take all that was offered: 'Such hungry things as these may soon be took / With a worm fastened on a golden hook.'

Fallen women rarely found a public defender, but here, in the character of Moll Cutpurse, they had a fearless one who was stepping up and placing the blame firmly where it belonged: not with women, but with the sexual assumptions that served women so ill. The notorious thief had become the woman's champion,[30] who, despite the censure levelled at her, would always answer back and turn the gender tables: 'I scorn to prostitute myself to a man,' she roars in conclusion, 'I that can prostitute a man to me!'[31] It's an extraordinary speech for two male writers to put into a woman's mouth in 1611 – one that spoke such enduring truths that it still resonates today.

Mary Frith's madcap life may have been ripe for adaptation, but Middleton and Dekker took some bold liberties in their interpretation of it. Their portrayal of Mary as Moll Cutpurse is unquestionably rose-tinted, transforming her from the monster that society saw into an idealised blend of the 'masculine' and the 'feminine'. In their version, she is not even a thief – a twist taken up and perpetuated by Mary's 'diary', in which she insists that 'I never actually or instrumentally cut any man's purse, though I have often restored it.' There is little doubt that the real Mary Frith *was* a thief, but for the play's message to carry, and to please the Master of the Revels, Moll's moral character had to be blameless – even if that meant playing down her crimes and restyling the woman herself into a more appealing package for the theatre-going public.

Not one to let truth get in the way of a good story, Thomas

Middleton was blasé about his play's inaccuracies – in an epistle to accompany the play, he simply pleads artistic licence:

Worse things, I must needs confess, the world has taxed her for than has been written of her [here]; but 'tis the excellency of a writer to leave things better than he finds 'em ...

The legend of Moll Cutpurse – however romanticised – had now been enshrined in literature, but despite the airbrushing, the play still has something to say about the character of the real woman. In Mary Frith the playwrights seem to have recognised a free spirit, a merry, eccentric rogue, who they believed was not only harmless, but in a strange way heroic. This unusual woman, who was so openly disputing the status quo, didn't give a damn what people thought of her, and when Moll proudly owns this fact – 'Perhaps for my mad going, some reprove me – / I please myself, and care not else who loves me'[32] – it sounds remarkably like genuine admiration on the part of the playwrights.

In fact, it makes perfect sense that the theatre world should have embraced a figure like Mary. No doubt Middleton and Dekker spotted the lucrative commercial potential of such a larger-than-life celebrity, but the playhouse also occupied a liminal space on the fringes of society where, within the limits of censorship, misfits were welcomed, boundaries were pushed and the established order challenged. And with young boys in dresses playing the roles denied to women, theatre was an artform that relied on transvestism. This simple act of transformation – deemed wholly immoral off-stage – was so integral to the workings of pre-Restoration theatre that it was self-consciously worked into many of its plots, becoming a legitimate stage convention by which female characters could wrest some power and agency for themselves. These gender games could be exposed and toyed with at will by the playwright to remind audiences just how easily the divisions between masculine and feminine could be questioned and the hierarchies that relied on them overturned.[33] In the safe space of the theatre, the normal rules didn't apply.

It was in the dramatists' interests, then, to present cross-dressing as something exciting and titillating, but essentially innocuous, though in the real world it remained a different story. At a time when women were being whipped or sent to prison for cross-dressed misdemeanours, publicly flaunting one's transvestism on stage was downright dangerous. Yet that's precisely what Mary Frith now proceeded to do. As Moll recites the Epilogue to *The Roaring Girl*, she tells the audience that if the play didn't pass muster:

The Roaring Girl herself, some few days hence,
Shall on this stage, give larger recompense.[34]

And so she did. One day in April 1611, at the close of the play's performance, Mary Frith herself appeared on the stage, in full male dress before perhaps two or three thousand people, to perform an afterpiece (usually a short musical extra or jig performed after the main show). She was, it turns out, entirely complicit in this production that had so publicly appropriated her persona, and now she was taking full advantage of it for a little self-promotion.[35]

Did this appearance make Mary Frith the first woman ever to perform in a public London theatre? Very likely, yes.[36] But she was pushing the boundaries to their limits with this *coup de théâtre*. Women were not allowed on the stage, let alone in men's clothes, and in striding onto that proscenium, she was usurping a man's place, making a show of herself and blurring the distinction between make-believe and reality. It was a daring, transgressive, illegal act that would land her in big trouble.

CRIME AND PUNISHMENT

The London authorities didn't look on Mary Frith's antics with as kind an eye as the theatre world did. To them, she represented everything their king hated: she was a cross-dresser, a smoker (James I wrote a treatise against this 'filthy custom' in 1604)[37] and an upstart, uncouth, unbiddable woman. It's not known whether Mary managed repeat performances at the Fortune Theatre, or whether it was a one-off, but soon after her scandalous appearance on stage in April 1611, she was arrested and charged with multiple offences to prevent it ever happening again. Unlicensed, she had 'sat there upon the stage in the public view of all the people there present in man's apparel & played upon her lute & sang a song'. Not only that, she had engaged in 'immodest & lascivious speeches' with her audience, throwing out a bawdy challenge to those in the audience who thought she was a man: that 'if any of them would come to her lodging they should find that she is a woman'.[38]

This was unacceptable, not least because such a display would draw an undesirable crowd. Wherever Mary Frith appeared, a gang of roaring boys and girls was sure to follow. When Middlesex magistrates decided the following year, in October 1612, to ban all 'jigs, rhymes and dances after their plays' across England, they seemed to have Mary's performance in mind. The reason cited was that when similar 'lewd' entertainments had appeared at the Fortune Theatre, they had attracted hordes of cutpurses and other 'ill-disposed persons' at the end of every play, who shattered the peace and caused 'tumults and outrages'.[39] It was this, as much as her transgression on stage, that had goaded them into arresting her – Mary's very presence on the stage was seen as a threat to public order.

Her punishment was to be committed to Bridewell Prison and Hospital – a house of correction on the banks of the Fleet River in the City where petty crooks, vagrants, persistent drunks and fallen women were briefly incarcerated and subject to hard labour (usually beating hemp) and floggings. Mary appears to have been one of those who resisted correction, however, because within a year, she had reoffended: on Christmas Day 1611, she was caught at St Paul's 'with her petticoat tucked up about her in the fashion of a man with a man's cloak on her to the great scandal of diverse persons ... & to the disgrace of all womanhood'.[40] She spent the festive season back in Bridewell before being hauled before the Bishop of London in the New Year, answering fresh charges for what Mary calls in the diary her 'unseasonable and suspicious walking'.[41] She made her excuses, she says, claiming that she had been out late to attend a woman in labour, and was discharged with a small fine. Her revenge on the constable who arrested her, she tells us proudly, was sweet: having employed one of her 'imps' to trick him into believing he had inherited a great fortune, she enjoyed his disappointment immensely when he then learned that he hadn't.

In reality, Mary confessed to the Bishop a litany of other 'unwomanly' acts: that she had 'long frequented all or most of the disorderly & licentious places in this city', usually dressed as a man, including alehouses, taverns, tobacco shops and playhouses. That she had 'this long time past usually blasphemed & dishonoured the name of God' and 'associated herself with ruffianly swaggering & lewd company' – namely cutpurses, drunks and dissolutes, 'with whom she hath to the great shame of her sex often times (as she said) drunk hard & distempered her head with drink'.[42] This transcript of Mary's confession brings us closer to her true character than anything else can: by her own account, she was a hard-drinking, pipe-smoking, foul-mouthed cross-dresser who could usually be found bantering with the ragged company of the city's most disreputable alehouses – and occasionally picking a pocket or two. This was who she was, and this was the realm in which she ruled. But she was also a wily actress, and so before her godly accusers she launched into a dramatic apology, protesting that she was 'heartily sorry for her foresaid licentious & dissolute life' and giving a solemn promise that from then on she would behave 'honestly, soberly & womanly'.[43] Perhaps in that moment, when her liberty was at stake, she even half meant it.

Before her grilling in the Bishop's court was over, Mary's accusers succumbed to the age-old assumption that her cross-dressing must go hand in hand with whoredom, and so there came the inevitable charge that she had also been 'dishonest of her body' as a prostitute and 'drawn other women to lewdness' as a bawd (or madam). If the diary is to be believed, Mary did indeed have a sideline as a bawd, though even then, she managed to defy convention – as well as procuring women for men, she apparently also found 'the sprucest fellows the town afforded' for the pleasure of 'great women', and in one anecdote even convinces these fellows to pay maintenance for their illegitimate children.[44] The real Mary Frith, however, 'absolutely denied that she was chargeable with either of these imputations', and aside from the diary anecdote, there's no evidence to suggest she was lying. Nonetheless, the Bishop of London 'thought fit to remand her to Bridewell ... until he might further examine the truth of the misdemeanours enforced against her without laying as yet any further censure upon her'.[45] The authorities didn't know what to do with Mary Frith, so for want of any other ideas, they bundled her off to prison for the third time.

In time, the Bishop's court hit upon what it thought would be the perfect punishment for Mary: she must do public penance in a white sheet at St Paul's Cross – a purification ritual that would act as a second baptism and openly humiliate her, too.[46] Public shaming was an integral part of retributive law enforcement before and beyond the seventeenth century – the stocks, the pillory, the drunkard's cloak, skimmingtons and carting were among the standard punishments for errant citizens[47] – and though such draconian tactics may have worked on some, they seem to have yet again abjectly failed to 'correct' Mary. The prolific letter-writer John Chamberlain witnessed the scene at St Paul's Cross that day in February 1612 when Mary performed her penance, and he wasn't fooled by her act of contrition. With little sympathy for this 'notorious baggage', he wrote to a friend the following week that 'she wept bitterly and seemed very penitent, but it is since doubted she was maudlin drunk, being discovered to have tippled three quarts of sack [wine] before she came to her penance.' Her bleary-eyed speech of mock-repentance went unrecorded, but Chamberlain noted with some amusement that 'she had the daintiest preacher or ghostly father that ever I saw', who delivered his sermon so 'extreme badly' that most of the audience didn't bother to hear the end of it. Those who did, he said, 'tarried rather to hear Mall Cut-purse than him'.[48]

The event was nothing short of comical. And in the diary's account of the episode, Mary's defiance in the face of it is everything you would hope for: 'They might as soon have shamed a black dog as me with any kind of such punishment,' she says bullishly. For half a penny, she crows, she would have travelled to all the market towns in England in her white sheet, wearing it as a badge of honour rather than a cloak of shame.

Unrepentant, undeterred, unchanged, the Mary of the diary relishes every ripple of disruption she causes, and ensures she has the last laugh on the crowd who come to watch her: 'without any regard to the sacredness of the place' and 'in revenge of this disgrace intended me', her gaggle of trusty fingersmiths 'spoiled a good many clothes by cutting off part of their cloaks and gowns and sending them home as naked behind as an ape's tail'. We can only hope it's true: that all those who came to gloat over Mary that day left St Paul's with their bare arses exposed, even more humiliated than her.

THE QUEEN REGENT OF MISRULE

Unrepentant she may have been, but Mary Frith was not stupid. This latest brush with the law – her most serious and unsettling yet – convinced her that if she were to continue her Fagin-like career as a thief and fence, she would have to do so with a little more care and stealth. Her dalliance with the entertainment world meant that to the playwrights, players and pickpockets of London she was now a rebel heroine and a fascinating curio, but in the eyes of the law, she was a menace who was drawing too much attention to herself. In order to navigate such dangerous waters, Mary would have to negotiate this contradiction and twist her unusual position to her advantage.

Far from being the symbol of anarchy she represented to the outside world, within the confines of her netherworld, Mary prided herself on creating order out of chaos. According to the diary, she ran a tight ship and whipped the criminals of London into shape with 'rules and orders' to create 'a perfect regulation of this thievish mystery'. It soon occurred to her that she could use these managerial skills to confer upon herself a degree of much-needed respectability, and so, by 1614, two years after her run-in with the Bishop of London, she was calling upon her contacts to set up her own house as a brokery – a kind of 'lost property office', or 'insurance office', where victims of theft might reclaim their stolen goods (for a price). It was a new career move that earned her another new nickname, this time 'Mary Thrift'.

Her strategy was simple: to stay organised and in control, and to keep her house clear of 'any unseemly or lewd action'. In doing so, she could keep a low profile and her hands ostensibly clean, so that to the casual observer she was 'free from all manner of suspicion'. With no effective law against receiving stolen goods, and no organised police force, constables would turn a blind eye to her business dealings if, in return, they could mine her network of connections in London's criminal underbelly. It was a mutually beneficial arrangement that allowed Mary to straddle the fine line between the legal and illegal, and to assume a highly unusual position in London society. By protecting thieves who made it worth her while, but also helping the victims of theft to recover their valuables, she made herself an invaluable asset to both sides of the law.

The modus operandi of Mary's new business is evident in her dealings with a gentleman called Henry Killigrew, who in 1621 was robbed by a prostitute while he was still buttoning up his breeches. His first port of call was Mary Frith's office, for he had 'heard how [by her] means many that had had their purses cut or goods stolen' had managed to recover them. From a description of where this woman lived, Mary identified the thief as Margaret Dell, who was promptly arrested by the local constable of the parish of St Bride's and taken to Mary to be cross-examined. The alleged pickpocket's husband, Richard Dell, soon followed, accusing Mary of being 'a notorious infamous person' who was 'well known & acquainted with all thieves & cutpurses'. He demanded that his wife be released from her clutches, but Mary had the perfect retort. She had a legitimate commission from the authorities to examine criminal suspects and advised Dell to either leave her office or receive a beating. After the Dells lodged an official complaint in the Court of Star Chamber in May of that year for wrongful imprisonment, Mary found herself in court yet again on 4 June, and, as ever, she was unyielding in her defence. She had apprehended the thief fair and square, and if the Dells gave her 'any ill words or language' again, she warned, she would give as good as she got – 'in some tart or angry manner'.[49] Clearly, Mary was a woman of unusual influence, and was not one to cross.

This influence extended even to matters of life and death. Mary was careful to cultivate close ties with various lords of the court, which granted her enough authority to either save criminals from the gallows or condemn them as she deemed fit. Consequently, according to the diary, the thieves of London held her in such thrall, subjected as they were by 'love and fear', that they metaphorically crowned her the 'Queen Regent of Misrule'. For a woman of low birth, little means and an eccentric demeanour, this was an impressive rise to power, though it seems Mary had long been a queen in the making. Her role as sovereign of the London underworld was acknowledged in *The Roaring Girl* several years before, in a speech that shows just how much sway she held over the ne'er-do-wells of the city even before she set up her brokery. 'You do not know the benefits I bring with me,' says Moll:

> *No cheat dares work upon you, with thumb or knife,*
> *While you've a roaring girl to your son's wife.*[50]

In the years that followed, operating as a licensed fence and an intermediary between the thieves, the victims and the authorities, Mary would become – and remain – the undisputed ring-mistress of London's shady demi-monde.

To complement her new reputation as a figure of some standing, albeit in the murky hinterlands, Mary continued to feed her legend as a delightful peculiarity. Several of the diary's claims glory in her nonconformity, often concurring with other versions of her, and sometimes even outdoing them in eccentricity. The diary makes the specious claim, for example, that she was the first woman in England ever to smoke tobacco, a habit she took to with gusto, she says, 'because of its affected singularity', unwittingly sparking a trend in the process. In fact, women were known to have taken up this expensive new fad by 1590, when Mary was still a child.[51] That she swore like a trooper and 'loved good liquor, especially good wine' we know to be true, and her prowess with a sword is entirely plausible. When she boasts that she could 'use a backsword as well as the best of them' and once challenged an expert swordsman to a fight 'whom I so soundly beat that he was forced to lay it down and confess me the conqueror', she appears to be the very same Moll Cutpurse who wields one to such effect in *The Roaring Girl*.

Elsewhere, the diary unashamedly plays up the 'mad spinster' image that would have been almost as familiar to seventeenth-century readers as it is to us. Apparently, Mary's house was a cacophonous zoo, overrun with parrots, bulldogs, baboons, apes, squirrels and parrots, while the walls were hung all over with looking glasses, 'so that I could see my sweet self all over in any part of my rooms'. (Given the frequent assertion that Mary was no looker, one can only presume this is a snide little joke on the part of the authors.) On the flip side, she is also portrayed as a good sport: self-mocking, unconcerned, even delighted at her lack of personal charms. Indeed, according to the diary, she lacked every feminine accomplishment on the list (her singing voice, too, 'was the untuneablest thing that ever was heard'), and she couldn't care tuppence.

Mary's oddball status was almost certainly exaggerated for comic effect, but her history of daring performances in drag is a matter of historical fact, which lends one of the more improbable capers in the diary an air of plausibility it might not otherwise have. The story goes that Mary accepted a bet from her 'fellow humorist Banks the Vintner',[52] who wagered her twenty pounds to 'ride from Charing Cross to Shoreditch astraddle on horseback in breeches and doublet, boots and spurs, all like a man' – a showy stunt that could easily land her back in Bridewell. Mary was undaunted – 'I was for all such sudden whims,' she says, and in typical fashion she upped the stakes rather than backing away. To make herself as conspicuous as possible, she decided to carry a banner and a trumpet, too, and set out on the appointed day as resplendent as a cavalry officer.

She made it to Bishopsgate without drawing suspicion, but then a 'plaguey orange wench' yelled out 'Moll Cutpurse on horseback!' and set the crowds 'hooting and hallowing as if they had been mad'. 'Come down, you shame of women, or we will pull you down,' they bawled, forcing Mary to take fright and seek refuge in a friend's victualling house. The mob only followed, chuckling one minute, cursing her the next, unsure as ever whether they were enjoying her crackpot capers or heartily disapproved. When a wedding party momentarily distracted them, however, Mary slipped away, made it to Shoreditch, won her wager and breathed a sigh of relief that she was safely 'out of danger'. It's no wonder she was nervous – it could have gone much worse – but her imagination was caught up in the pride and pomp of her whimsical adventure: 'In my own thoughts …', she says (in a literary allusion unlikely to have come from her), 'I was squiress to Dulcinea of Toboso, the most incomparably beloved lady of Don Quixote.'

FEME COVERT

The Life and Death of Mrs Mary Frith roams freely through Mary's career as a thief, broker and professional provocateur, but there is one significant event in her personal life that it entirely neglects to mention. On 23 March 1614, when she was still in her late twenties and just starting out as a fence, Mary Frith did something wholly unexpected: she went to St Saviour's Church in Southwark (now Southwark Cathedral) and married a man named Lewknor Markham.[53]

This staggering omission isn't the first or only clanger to muddy the integrity of Mary's 'diary' – *The Roaring Girl* is also not mentioned and there is a thorny discrepancy over her age[54] – yet in this instance, it's easy to see why it might have been left out. For a woman who defied convention and resisted authority at every turn, and who, according to legend, was resolutely single and had no interest in men, marriage seems a particularly odd choice. This inconvenient detail simply didn't fit with the image of Mary that was being cultivated in the public consciousness; it disproved all the theories that she was an unnatural man-woman whom no man would ever marry, or a scorned woman who spurned all men, as the diary variously portrays her.[55] It didn't fit, either, with the Moll of the play, who was 'too headstrong to obey' a husband and had 'no humour to marry'.[56] For here she was, conforming to all the social conventions and acting like a perfectly 'normal' woman.

The records shed only a glimmer of light on the real story behind Mary's marriage to Markham, but it's enough to reveal that this was almost certainly no sweeping love story and that, as we might expect, Mary was not being quite the conventional good woman here that she at first appears to be.

On the contrary, Mary went out of her way to confuse the world about her marital status. Her primary motive for marriage seems to have been to manipulate the gender discriminations of coverture under English Common Law to maximise her freedoms, so that she could run her own business as a single woman, while at the same time claiming the legal immunity of a married one. Coverture laws decreed that when a man and woman married, they quite literally became one. In legal terms, at that moment a woman became a *feme covert* and her legal existence as an individual was nullified: she could no longer hold her own property or money, nor could she sign contracts or be sued in her own right. If she remained single, however, she retained these scraps of legal rights and was referred to as *feme sole*. Rather than submit to the disempowerment that these laws entailed for women, Mary decided to play the law for a fool. She became an expert at exploiting its loopholes, by posing as two different women – Mary Frith, *feme sole*, and Mary Markham, *feme covert* – as and when it suited her.

As a newly established businesswoman, for example, it suited her to be single. That same year, 1614, was when Mary set up her lucrative and semi-respectable 'lost property office', and for that she needed her legal independence. In order to have her cake and eat it, Mary seems to have negotiated a marriage settlement of convenience with Lewknor Markham, which allowed her to run her own business and retain her own earnings, despite being married, as if she were Mary Frith, *feme sole*.[57]

As a woman who flirted with crime on a daily basis, however, being Mrs Markham, *feme covert* and legal non-entity, could be extremely helpful. It meant that in the various lawsuits she was frequently embroiled in, she was virtually invincible, because the law would always assume that a married woman was acting under her husband's direction. Ten years later, in 1624, for example, when a

They might
as soon have
shamed a black
dog as me

hatmaker named Richard Pooke sued Mary Frith, spinster and *feme sole*, for some expensive beaver hats she had bought eight years before and still not fully paid for, her chief defence was that she could not be sued as a *feme sole*, because she was Mary Markham, a married woman, who was not legally liable for her own misconduct and therefore could not be sued. Pooke had been warned that Mary had used this trick before to overturn several previous lawsuits, but he fell into the trap anyway and, sure enough, Mary triumphed. It came out in this same trial that she and Markham had not lived together for years, and possibly never had, supporting the theory that, far from being a great romance, this was a marriage of convenience – and clever opportunism – on Mary's part.[58]

BEDLAM

There follows a gap of some 20 years before the records mention Mary Frith again, and when they do, it's to reveal another dramatic development that the diary fails to mention. Although perhaps this omission isn't so surprising either, because by the summer of 1644, when she was approaching 60, Mary was an inmate of the madhouse. On 21 June that year, the governors of Bridewell Prison and Hospital decreed that she, along with several others, 'be delivered & discharged out of the Hospital of Bethlem', as they were now 'recovered of their former senses' and well enough to be looked after elsewhere.[59] Bethlem Hospital, or Bethlehem, commonly known as Bedlam, was the notorious asylum then situated in Bishopsgate, where London's pauper lunatics were sent to be 'cured' of their madness.

The record gives no further details of why Mary was committed, and although there were doubtless plenty of her contemporaries who thought her mad, there was more than one way to end up in Bedlam. London's teeming, poverty-stricken slums, for example, were considered dire enough to send the city's inhabitants mad if they weren't already; the scholar Robert Burton, who had himself suffered from depression, observed in 1621 that England was a country that 'must needs be discontent', for it 'hath a sick body'.[60] But Mary Frith had always *thrived* in this world before. She was a formidable businesswoman, a shrewd criminal, a hardy Banksider. Now, as old age encroached, had a lifetime of hard drinking, tough talking and wild living taken its toll on her mental health? Had the stress of keeping up multiple person- alities and swatting away run-ins with the law pushed her to the brink?

The very notion of the robust Mary Frith having any kind of breakdown seems so incongruous that some have argued she may not have been mad at all but shamming madness to escape the war.[61] After all, in 1644, when Mary was released, England was a country riven by political division. The Civil War had been rolling on for two years already: divine-rights monarchy was facing an existential threat; King Charles I was at war with his own parliament, and up and down the land people were taking sides and falling into factions: Royalists versus Republicans. English society was floundering – any sane person might wish to avoid the unrest – and, performer as she was, Mary might have found it easy to play mad when she had to. But we shouldn't be so quick to assume. Even the most extrovert characters can be laughing in the dark, and the truth was that in Mary's day and beyond, women could find themselves carted off to lunatic asylums with alarming ease, thanks to the dangerously common belief that they were physiologically predisposed to insanity.

Doctors' casebooks across the country testified to the scores of women in Britain who were apparently 'mad'. Somerset physician John Westover, for example, treated three times as many women for mental disorders than men. Perhaps it was indicative of their restrictive, stultifying, frustrating existence, but the majority of those women were diagnosed with 'melancholy'; the others 'hysteria' or 'distraction'.[62]

The fault in these diagnoses lay with the archaic ideas that seventeenth-century medicine had inherited from Hippocrates and Galen, who had spouted the toxic theory that a woman's body was fundamentally unstable, prone to debilitating diseases of the mind and at the mercy of overwrought emotions. The cold, wet elements that supposedly comprised her body were believed to soften and weaken her brain, while her 'wandering womb', which roved around her body causing all kinds of havoc, would drive her to hysteria the moment it reached her head. Nervousness, depression, anxiety, hormonal mood swings and sexual desire might all be interpreted as madness in women, with virgins, widows and spinsters thought to be particularly susceptible. (The best cure, unsurprisingly, was believed to be sex and pregnancy.)[63] As a childless woman famed for her love of drink and her volatile, masculine behaviour, Mary fitted the template all too well. Perhaps it was always inevitable that her 'mad pranks' would one day land her in Bedlam.

If Mary wasn't mad when she went in, however, she may well have been by the time she came out. Conditions at Bethlem Hospital at the time were notorious. Corruption, abuse and neglect were rife, and from its cold, dank cells harrowing reports emerged of 'cryings, screechings, roarings, brawlings, shaking of chains, swearings, frettings, chaffings'.[64] The complexities of mental illness were so little understood that physicians used 'madness' as a woolly, catch-all term to cover every kind of affliction. Consequently, the 'lunatics' languishing within Bethlem's walls might include those plagued by voices, delusions, melancholy, rage, poverty or drink, as well as those with learning difficulties, epilepsy, dementia and anxiety. Among them, too, were those who were merely eccentric. The 'treatments' they were subjected to were invariably punitive rather than therapeutic, with inmates chained, starved and beaten, and often left to wallow in filth and excrement.[65] To complete the degradation of the inmates, come Sunday mornings, members of the public could pay a few shillings to stroll in and gawp, taunt the poor souls and even ply them with drink. No doubt there were many who queued up to see the famous Moll Cutpurse chained up in her cell, though what state they found her in will have to remain a mystery.

Mary's 'madness' was yet another inconvenient detail that didn't fit the Moll Cutpurse brief, and as a result, her later years look very different in the pages of her diary. Far from depicting a woman who was fading away and losing her mind, her biographers suggest she was now at the top of her game, operating at the highest levels of the criminal world as boss to even the most eminent male criminals. According to their account, Mary masterminded the feats of the famous highwaymen James Hind and Richard Hannam in the 1640s and '50s, and like them, she is portrayed as a highly vocal Royalist, who hosts a street party in honour of Charles I and stages a public protest against his enemies in the form of an allegorical bull-baiting, in which the Parliamentarians are cast as the ravaging dogs.[66]

Most scholars suspect this political subplot to be grafted on – a bit of Royalist propaganda on the part of the writers to savage Oliver Cromwell and his puritan protectorate and endear Mary Frith to the Restoration audience for whom her story was published.[67] Indeed, it's hard to imagine an irreverent, insubordinate character such as Mary supporting the absolute authority of King Charles I. At the same time, however, a character *less* puritan than Mary – whose life revolved around thieving, carousing, performing and cross-dressing

– is even harder to imagine. Whatever her genuine political allegiance (if indeed she had one), the last ten years of her life coincided with the strange decade after the country had executed its king, when Britain was ruled by a puritan republican regime. How Mary coped with the prohibition of everything she loved most, from the theatres to drinking to swearing, we'll never know; nor can we know her true feelings about her lost king. Come the Restoration of his son in 1660, however, the politic decision was made by her biographers to ensure that, whether true or not, this renegade woman would be safely remembered as a loyal subject of the Crown.

THE SINNER'S PENANCE

After all the brazen merriment and gleeful mayhem that has gone before, the diary culminates in an oddly remorseful end for Mary Frith, with the 74-year-old lying on her deathbed, weak and enfeebled and repenting her life of sin. She has fallen prey to a 'dropsy' – an excess of fluid – and as her body swells, she begins to see her condition as some kind of divine retribution for her life of vice, as every afflicted limb seems to 'point out the wickedness every one of them had been instrumental in, so that I could not but acknowledge the justice of my punishment'. Her hands, however, remain unaffected – proof, she maintains smugly, that they were the 'most innocent' part of her body, because she never cut a single purse herself.

This tacked-on repentance scene may be incongruous, but it was vital to the acceptability of *The Life and Death of Mrs Mary Frith* as a work of public entertainment. The authors claim to have published Mary's story not just because of the 'strangeness and newness of the subject', but for 'the public good'. And if a celebration of criminality is to masquerade as morally instructive, rather than gratuitously sensational, then by the laws of storytelling it must culminate either in reform or condemnation.

In literature then, at least, Mary Frith recants at her death, claiming 'with a real penance and true grief to deplore my condition and former course of life I had so profanely and wickedly led'. It's a nice try, but coming from a woman who had so consistently revelled in her wrongdoing and smirked at disapproval, this dramatic moral conversion feels rather too neat to have occurred in real life.

More convincing is Mary's appeal for us not to judge her too harshly, for, 'If I had anything of the devil within me, I had of the merry one, not having through all my life done any harm to the life or limb of any person.' Besides, she jokes, her illness is punishment enough, as it has finally accomplished 'what all the ecclesiastical quirks with their canons and injunctions could not do': made her abandon her doublet. Too swollen and sore to wear anything constrictive, she is grudgingly forced to 'do penance again in a blanket' and revert to her 'proper' female habit. Thus, in a moment sodden with symbolism, Mary's 'redemption' is complete – she is a Roaring Girl no more.

In the diary's final words, our heroine receives an unceremonial send-off, with Mary giving characteristically blunt instructions to be 'lain in my grave on my belly, with my breech upwards' so that she may be as 'preposterous' in death as she was in life. In reality, Mary's burial was somewhat more dignified. Despite another dud claim in the diary that Mary made no will, on 6 June 1659, just a few weeks before she died on 26 July, she did just that – and it reveals that she was a prosperous woman. Under her married name of Mary Markham, she left £20 to a relative named Abraham Robinson – a substantial legacy given that a labourer might earn £10 in a year and a house could cost under £30[68] – and the remainder of her estate to her niece and sole executrix Frances Edmonds. Her bequests made provision for a decent funeral, and so on 10 August, as per her wish, she was given a Christian burial at St Bridget's Church in Fleet Street – an end reserved not for the preposterous, but for the respected and well-to-do.

Mary Frith had died just a year shy of the Restoration – a new age of freedom and exuberance that would have suited her down to the ground. The Roaring Girl had fallen silent, and the play she had inspired had fallen out of fashion, yet her spirit would linger in the decades to come.[69] Her faux diary, published two years into Charles II's reign, would reignite her legend, casting her as a fervent Royalist for a renewed Royalist era, but she was also present in more nebulous forms. She was there, for example, in the actresses who would walk the stage legally for the first time, and be applauded, not punished, for donning men's clothes. She was there at the birth of the novel, in Daniel Defoe's Moll Flanders, who early in the next century would be 'as impudent a thief, and as dexterous as ever Moll Cut-purse was'.[70] And she was there in the new craze for criminal biographies that would perpetuate her myth still further – by adding highwaywoman to her list of misdeeds.[71] By the mid-eighteenth century she had taken her place in the rogues' gallery of famous dare-devils – from Robin Hood to Jack Sheppard – whose lawless lives have always strangely enchanted us and whose crimes we can't help but romanticise.

But when all the tall tales, exaggerations and embellishments are stripped away, what is left? We'll never know exactly what measure of the legend of Moll Cutpurse was present in the real Mary Frith, but despite all the sanitisation, decriminalisation and simplification, the teasing snippets of the living, breathing Mary captured in court transcripts and eyewitness accounts bear a striking resemblance to the Mary of myth. What we find in every version of her is an audacious, idiosyncratic, irreverent woman who used her own brass and ingenuity to rise through the ranks, from common cutpurse to famed entertainer to entrepreneur to folkloric heroine, causing shock, anger and amusement along the way. In the misfits' paradise on the peripheries of society, she found acceptance, safety, power and influence. She angered the authorities, captivated the playwrights, confused the biographers and divided the public. Hers was a life of constant peril and nagging insecurity, lived permanently on the edge – of respectability, legality, even sanity – and her strategy for survival was to hide in plain sight, wriggling and shape-shifting to exploit the loopholes, outfox her accusers and, whenever possible, get away with it altogether. This was a woman who wanted to be talked about but didn't want to be caught, and by manipulating her fluid persona and feeding her own glorified myth, she made sure that the character who endured was not a hardened criminal but a lovable rogue. If this virtuoso of evasion slips through our fingers now, it's probably because that's exactly what she wants.

Margaret Cavendish

MAD MADGE

Samuel Pepys had been trying to catch a glimpse of the famous Duchess of Newcastle for weeks. It was spring 1667, the lady was in London on a rare visit from the Midlands and everyone was impatient for a sighting. The rumours had it that she would visit Charles II's court on 11 April, and in the private pages of his diary, Pepys was on tenterhooks: 'The whole story of this lady is a romance, and all she doth is romantic. Her footmen in velvet coats, and herself in an antique dress ... There is as much expectation of her coming to court ... as if it were the Queen of Sweden.'[1] So, along with the curious, of which there were many, to Whitehall Pepys went – only to leave disappointed, for the Duchess never appeared.

A fortnight later, on 26 April, he spied her distinctive black-and-silver coach and velvety footmen as he was travelling through London. He craned and peered and saw just enough to conclude that she was 'a very comely woman', dressed just as the gossips had described: velvet cap, mannish black *juste-au-corps* riding jacket, hair covering her ears, neck bared and a number of fashionable black patches scattered over her face.

This little snapshot wasn't nearly enough to satisfy Pepys, so come 1 May he hastened to Hyde Park where she would be riding out along with the rest of the court in the May Day parade. Unfortunately,

'Though I cannot be Henry the Fifth,
or Charles the Second, yet I endeavour
to be Margaret the First.'

MARGARET CAVENDISH, DUCHESS OF NEWCASTLE (1623–1673),
PHILOSOPHER, SCIENTIST, WRITER AND PROTO-FEMINIST

everyone else had the same idea, and the Duchess was so 'followed and crowded upon by coaches all the way she went, that nobody could come near her'.

On 10 May they had another brief encounter as the Duchess made her way home through town to Newcastle House, in Clerkenwell. Spotting her carriage ahead of him, Pepys drove furiously in the hope of overtaking her, only to be thwarted yet again by a horde of '100 boys and girls running looking upon her' who were also desperate for a peek. In the end, she arrived home before Pepys could catch up with her, but he wasn't discouraged. 'I will get a time to see her,' he pronounced confidently.

And eventually, on 30 May, he did. The Duchess had boldly requested, and been granted, an invitation to the newly formed Royal Society – a Restoration temple to scientific advancement – and Samuel Pepys happened to be a member. There had been 'much debate, pro and con' by the fellows about whether or not a woman should be admitted at all. It had never happened before, and many were against it, some arguing that the Duchess's reputation would expose the Society to ridicule, others that it surely set an undesirable precedent. But at length the motion was carried, the lady invited – and a fuss expected. 'We do believe the town will be full of ballads of it,' Pepys noted, and when the day came, he hurried to the Society's headquarters, where he found 'much company, indeed very much company, in expectation of the Duchess', just like him.

At long last, Pepys had his chance to critique the woman at close quarters, and afterwards, as was his habit, he shared his impressions with his diary. His verdict, after all that, was damning:

The Duchess hath been a good comely woman; but her dress so antique, and her deportment so unordinary, that I do not like her at all, nor did

I hear her say anything that was worth hearing, but that she was full of admiration, all admiration.

This lady, supposedly so learned in natural philosophy, had been shown the Society's most innovative new experiments – 'of colours, loadstones, microscopes, and of liquors' – yet she'd had no insights or observations to offer whatsoever. In fact, she'd been virtually speechless. It had all been a great disappointment.[2]

Not many women could inspire such fascination on the one hand, and such scorn on the other. John Evelyn was also present that day and his diary entry was more succinct but no less scathing: 'To London, to wait on the Duchess of Newcastle (who was a mighty pretender to learning, poetry, and philosophy, and had in both published divers books) to the Royal Society, whither she came in great pomp.'[3] And there was the truth of it: Margaret Cavendish, Duchess of Newcastle, had trespassed on male ground. She was a 'mighty pretender' to scientific and philosophical learning, who'd had the temerity to publish her writings, cultivate her own eccentric style and wilfully make a spectacle of herself. Every man in that room was thinking it: *How dare she?*

LADY BASHFUL

It's little wonder Pepys was unimpressed with Margaret Cavendish's behaviour that day at the Royal Society; it was precisely the kind of public social engagement that made her inwardly squirm. From childhood, Margaret Lucas (as she was born) had been debilitatingly shy, so uncomfortable and tongue-tied among strangers that they thought her 'a natural fool'. But Margaret was no fool; addicted 'to contemplation rather than conversation, to solitariness rather than society, to melancholy rather than mirth', she was a dreamer, an observer, a sensitive soul.[4]

The one place she felt at ease as a girl was with her family, and the Lucases were one of the wealthiest in Essex. Descended from generations of self-made men, her father, Thomas Lucas, was something of a cavalier figure – in 1597 he was banished by Elizabeth I for killing one of her favourite courtiers in a duel, leaving his lover Elizabeth Leighton to bear the shame of giving birth to their illegitimate son. It would be six years, on James I's accession, before Thomas was pardoned and the couple were able to marry. They settled at St John's Abbey near Colchester and would go on to have a happy, respectable marriage and seven more children.

Margaret was the youngest, and although she would always regard her father as honourable and courageous, she would never know him personally – he was dead by the time she was two. Elizabeth took over the management of the Lucas estate (as the legitimate heir was not yet of age) and, as it happened, found she had a talent for the job. With the estate thriving under Elizabeth's captaincy, Margaret had an impressive role model in her mother, whose 'heroic spirit' and 'majestic grandeur' she was always quick to praise. Her glowing account paints Elizabeth as a doting, lenient mother, who raised her children with all the proper virtues – modesty, civility and respectability – though not without some snobbery; they were never 'suffered to have any familiarities with the vulgar servants' and were always decked out to look 'rich and costly'.[5]

While all this made for an idyllic childhood in Margaret's eyes, it left her ill-prepared for the adult world in one crucial respect. As was standard among the rich gentry, the three Lucas boys were all formally educated and sent to Cambridge, while the five girls were given only a rudimentary education, by an unfortunate governess whom Margaret remembered only as 'an ancient decayed gentlewoman'.[6] Like all high-born girls, the Lucas daughters were taught a few conventional feminine 'virtues' – singing, dancing, music, reading, writing, needle-work – but even these were 'rather formality than benefit'.[7]

Most of these accomplishments were of little use to Margaret. She had no interest in domestic pursuits and would later write with some pride: 'I cannot work, I mean such works as ladies use to pass their time withal ... needle-works, spinning-works, preserving-works, as also baking, and cooking-works, as making cakes, pies, puddings, and the like, all which I am ignorant of.'[8] Her interest lay elsewhere. For hours on end she would wander, lost in contem-plation, and soon found that she preferred to 'write with the pen than to work with a needle'. The blank page was a safe place, where her thoughts and ideas could roam freely. Even before she'd reached her teens she'd begun to write prolifically, filling 16 'baby-books' with observations, poetry and stories – though she later dismissed them as childish ramblings, which perhaps explains why they haven't survived.

Dress was another creative outlet, for Margaret had a bold sense of style and favoured creative, sometimes odd, ensembles – 'especially such fashions as I did invent myself' – to ensure that she came across as a true one-off, 'for I always took delight in a singularity'.[9] As an introvert who found it difficult to express her personality verbally, Margaret allowed her idiosyncratic outfits (which often had a mascu-line edge) to do the talking for her, and this, too, would set her apart from most of her sex. It was all very well to indulge her whimsy and burgeoning imagination in the cossetted environment of St John's Abbey, but in the wider world of seventeenth-century England, which valued obedience and conformity over flamboyance and originality, it left her rather more wilful and eccentric than was deemed accept-able in a woman.

The Lucases were a close-knit family. Margaret – a self-confessed physical coward who would jump at the sound of a gun and abhorred violence of all kinds[10] – was always so anxious that 'an evil misfortune or accident' might befall one of them that she would wake her siblings in the night to check they were still alive. Her fears were strangely prescient, for in 1642, when the Civil War broke out, there would be no escaping the unrest for the Royalist Lucases who, by then, were deeply unpopular in the Puritan county of Essex, thanks to their close involvement with Charles I's regime.[11] When local anger erupted into the Stour Valley riots on 22 August, mobs descended on St John's Abbey, ransacking and looting the Lucas home. The women in the house were imprisoned for several days while Margaret's brother, John, now head of the family, was held at the Tower for a month for raising an army for the King.

Margaret was 19 at the time and blindsided by the violence, writing later that 'this unnatural war came like a whirlwind',[12] but her loyalty to Charles I was unshaken, not least because she had developed an intense fascination with his French queen. In Henrietta Maria, the Parliamentarians saw only a dangerous woman whose influence over the King encouraged popery and tyranny; Margaret, however, saw the heroic queen of her dreams. Nursing a desire to 'see the world abroad', she offered her services to her heroine as Maid of Honour, and although her siblings worried that their gauche little sister might make a fool of herself in the worldly, sophisticated court milieu, Margaret got her way. She arrived in Oxford, where the court had been transplanted for safety, in the summer of 1643.

It didn't take long for Margaret's new life to pall. The daily routine at court was tedious, involving little more than waiting around in the presence chamber for orders or standing to attention for hours on end. The freedom she'd had at home to write was gone and she now found herself constantly on show, which, as her siblings had predicted, left her so crippled by shyness that she was rendered almost mute. Maids were expected to charm court visitors with their dazzling wit and conversation, but Margaret, 'dull, fearful and bashful' as she was, felt it safer to play dumb and 'be accounted a fool' than to make a poor attempt at worldliness and 'be thought rude or wanton'.[13]

So excruciating was this experience that Margaret would later fictionalise it in her 1668 play *The Presence*, in which she cast herself as Lady Bashful, the novice Maid of Honour who similarly gives the impression at Princess Melancholy's court of being 'a clod of dull earth'. But just as Lady Bashful turns out to be more than appearances would suggest, so Margaret felt there was a goldmine of ideas beneath her own gawky exterior. No doubt she was voicing her own aspirations when her alter-ego proclaims: 'I had rather be a meteor singly alone, than a star in a crowd.'

There was little chance of being a meteor at court, and inevitably Margaret came to feel she'd made a mistake, but her mother refused all her appeals to come home, feeling 'it would be a disgrace for me to return out of the court so soon after I was placed'.[14] She had no choice but to stick it out. And with the war intensifying, this would have life-changing consequences for young Margaret Lucas.

EXILES IN LOVE

By 1644, the Parliamentarians were gaining strength and the Queen, now pregnant with her ninth child, was in particular danger. Parliament had put a price on her head for high treason, citing her Catholic influence on the King as the primary cause of the war, so in April that year it became imperative for her to leave not just Oxford, but the country. With Margaret and the rest of her entourage in tow, Henrietta Maria went on the run, enduring a difficult birth and grave illness along the way. The group fled to Falmouth and on 30 June boarded a boat to the Queen's native France, where they were confident of a warm reception.

But first they had to survive the voyage. Buffeted by storm winds, they lurched over the waves, the Parliamentarian ships in hot pursuit, pelting them with shots. Henrietta Maria was as impressive as ever during the onslaught, commanding that if it should come to it, the captain should blow up the ship's ammunition store rather than allow them to be captured. Thankfully it didn't come to that; they reached Brittany alive, only to be faced with the dangerous coastal cliffs that stood between them and safety. A treacherous scramble to the top followed, before they eventually found asylum at a small fishing village, a ragged and far from regal-looking bunch.

This daring great escape had shown Margaret rather more of the world than she had bargained for. At 21, she was suddenly an exile and a refugee, and the harrowing experience left an indelible mark on her psyche. Time and again in the stories she would later write, beautiful, virtuous young ingénues would endure perilous voyages and find themselves shipwrecked in strange lands.

Traumatised but safe, Margaret was living an isolated, miserable life with the Queen at King Louis XIV's court at the Louvre in Paris when, in April 1645, William Cavendish, Marquess of Newcastle, arrived – a fellow Royalist exile who, having fled England in despair after a humiliating defeat at the Battle of Marston Moor, was also looking for comfort. On the surface, William was everything Margaret wasn't: a courageous soldier and renowned horseman, confident, worldly, charming and, as the former tutor of Prince Charles, highly educated. He was also a ladies' man, a rich widower and, at the age of 52, a full 30 years older than Margaret. And yet the pair had much in common: both were deeply romantic in nature and harboured high ideals, literary aspirations and a veneration of poetry, philosophy and plays. It wasn't long before William was wooing Margaret with passionate verses on a daily basis.

Unused to male attention, Margaret was wary at first. Marriage was not on her mind – on the contrary, 'I did dread marriage', she would later admit.[15] To a free-spirited woman of the seventeenth century, it meant a caged life of household management, the dangers of childbirth and unquestioning submission to one's husband, even if he turned out to be a drunkard, philanderer or tyrant. In later life, Margaret would even argue forcefully against marriage in principle, reckoning that 'where one husband proves good … a thousand prove bad'.[16] Had circumstances been different, she might well have chosen the shame of spinsterhood over the shackles of marriage, but as it was, she fell in love and married William in a quiet ceremony at the end of 1645.

Young, timid Margaret Lucas was now Lady Cavendish, Marchioness of Newcastle. It sounded grand, but as a prominent Royalist, William's primary Midlands estates of Welbeck Abbey and Bolsover Castle had been sequestered by Parliament, so in truth he had little to offer his new bride but his title. Margaret, in turn, was unable to access her substantial dowry of £2,000, as her brother, John, had been branded a 'malignant' by Parliament and also had his property confiscated, so when the couple set up home in William's Parisian apartments, the only option was for William to flaunt his name, reputation and continued spending in the hope of reassuring creditors that he was a safe bet. The bluff allowed them to live well enough on borrowed money, but it was a precarious existence. More than once over the next few years the creditors' patience would wear thin and William's steward would bring the worrying news that 'he was not able to provide a dinner' for them that day.[17] On these occasions, pawning their belongings and borrowing money from William's brother, or the Queen or anyone who would help them was the only recourse left.

Still, the Cavendishes put on a good show. William and his brother Sir Charles were enthusiastic, well-connected intellectuals who played host to some of the leading scholars, writers, scientists and philosophers of the day, including Thomas Hobbes and René Descartes. For Margaret, these soirées were accompanied by feelings of gnawing inadequacy, but by listening and observing (something she had always been good at), she found she could pick up second-hand all the latest philosophical theories and technological advancements to emerge from the Scientific Revolution that was sweeping through Europe. Margaret absorbed it all, quietly nursing a passion for big ideas and a longing to grapple with the invisible workings of the world. A woman with no education to speak of was suddenly an avid pupil at the cutting-edge of new thinking, and she found it utterly thrilling.

Less enthralling were Margaret's new domestic challenges – not least her antipathy towards home-making and the fact that, as time went by, babies stubbornly refused to appear. Given that William had fathered numerous children by his first wife, the problem was assumed to be Margaret's, so when there was still no sign of pregnancy two years into their marriage, her physician began to prescribe spa waters and a witches' brew of herbs to be syringed into her womb every morning and night.[18]

It's quite possible Margaret was secretly relieved when these remedies didn't work, for her own attitude to motherhood was ambivalent – society said it was her wifely duty to provide children and she felt that pressure, but the burning desire for them herself simply wasn't there. She could barely even understand it in other women. Dynastic motives made no sense for a woman, she would later argue, since 'neither name nor estate goes to her family' when she marries; and then, of course, she 'hazards her life by bringing them into the world, and hath the greatest share of trouble in bringing them up'.[19] Maternal instinct or affection didn't even enter the equation. Margaret would soon find other ways of perpetuating herself and her name that appealed far more ...

The couple thrived regardless. Conscious of her good luck in finding a husband who didn't suppress her ideas or curb her ambitions, Margaret was respectful and adoring of William – the model of a loyal, deferential, dutiful wife. In this, at least, she was happy to play the conventional woman. In no other part of her life would she be so conformist.

TRAITORS TO THE STATE

Despite their happiness together, the Cavendishes would be dogged in the first three years of their marriage by horrors both personal and national. By the summer of 1647, Margaret's sister Mary had died of consumption, and her beloved mother soon after, and by the end of 1648, the numerous Royalist uprisings of that year had all been crushed. The King had been imprisoned at Hurst Castle in Hampshire and his supporters purged from Parliament, and Margaret's brother Sir Charles Lucas, leader of the Essex rebellion, had been summarily executed by firing squad, without trial.[20]

The young woman who had anxiously checked her sleeping siblings for signs of life had now lost three members of her family in less than two years – one of them 'inhumanly murdered'[21] – and the following year her eldest brother Thomas would die, too. This torrent of grief left Margaret plagued by fears of 'death's dungeon'. With no faith whatsoever in an after-life, she would later write of life's cruel brevity, likening it to 'a flash of lightning that continues not and for the most part leaves black oblivion behind it'.[22] To many, this was heretical talk; to Margaret it was a perfectly rational hypothesis that only magnified her already nagging desire for immortality.

Unsurprisingly, during these years Margaret was diagnosed with 'melancholy' – a condition believed to be caused by an excess of black bile but what in reality must have been the cumulative effect of intense grief, financial worries and the stress of the ongoing political turmoil. With her budding interest in science, Margaret habitually self-medicated, purging herself with 'vomits' (emetics) and bleeds to rid her body of the 'humours' that she – and her physician – believed were making her ill.[23]

All the while the Civil War was building to its nightmarish crescendo. While Prince Charles had retreated to The Hague, where his sister Mary, wife of William II of Orange, could offer him refuge, the Cavendishes had settled in the affordable town of Antwerp in September 1648, where William maintained his tactic of blinding his creditors with extravagance by leasing the grand Rubens House from the famous painter's widow. Here, he, Margaret and his brother Sir Charles would resume their favourite pastimes of engaging in philosophical discussion, tinkering with telescopes and conducting scientific experiments in the family laboratory. And here, they would learn the shocking news of their King's fate.

On 30 January 1649, Charles I was executed for High Treason on a specially built scaffold outside London's Whitehall Palace for waging war against his own Parliament. In that moment, England forcibly rid itself of a monarchy that had survived for nearly a thousand years by pedalling a symbolic (if not literal) image of safety, order and stability, presided over by an untouchable, divinely appointed sovereign. Now the King was dead, that image was irreparably scarred, the body politic had no head and only the unknown remained.

For the Royalists, this cataclysmic event meant quickly regrouping, focusing their attention on their theoretical new sovereign, Charles II, and, despite further defeated rebellions in 1650 and 1651, never quite giving up on plans to restore him. For the Cavendishes, it meant accepting a life of indefinite exile in Antwerp. William learned that he had been banished from England on pain of death, putting his assets further out of reach than ever, and in early 1651, starvation once again became a genuine threat. 'I know not how to put bread in my mouth,' he fretted to a friend,[24] his panic rising – largely because his brother, whose financial contributions had kept this small family of exiles just about afloat, had now had his estates sequestered, too. The only way Sir Charles could regain them was to return to England and petition for them, which carried the risk of imprisonment or being forced to take the oath of loyalty to the new Commonwealth, which had replaced the monarchy. Reluctantly, Charles was persuaded to go, and as William's own estates were due to be sold off by Parliament and his wife was legally entitled to petition for one-fifth of their worth, it was decided that Margaret should accompany him. They set sail in November 1651, and on 10 December, with her brother John's help, Margaret nervously put her case before the Committee for Compounding at Goldsmiths' Hall in London. She wasn't quite prepared, however, for the callousness of their response. They refused her appeal outright, said they would sell off the entirety of William's estates, giving her no share of their worth whatsoever. William, they argued, was of the King's inner circle and therefore 'the greatest traitor to the State', which excluded him – and his wife, who had knowingly married him after his political exile – from their clemency.

Appalled to the point of speechlessness, Margaret's timidity silenced her when she longed to speak: 'I whisperingly spoke to my brother to conduct me out of the ungentlemanly place, so without speaking to them one word good or bad, I returned to my lodgings.' Utterly disheartened and 'unpractised in public employments', she didn't attempt to petition the Committee again.[25] As a relatively non-offending Royalist, Sir Charles would eventually have more luck, but for now his petition dragged on interminably.

Margaret was miserable: she missed William, worried about him, and was in no mood, and no position, to enjoy herself. London was a changed place since the war – it had now entered an age of aggressively enforced austerity: seasonal festivities were banned, the theatres closed, the royal pageantry gone. High-profile Royalists were wise to keep their heads down, so Margaret did just that, retreating to her rooms, and finding solace – therapy, even – just as she had as a child: in writing. Only now it took on a new significance. She kept it secret even from her husband at this early stage, but Margaret Cavendish no longer wished to write just for her own amusement. Never again did she intend to be silenced by powerful men or her own timidity. She had decided to become a published author.

LET WRITING BOOKS ALONE

It's hard to overstate how daring it was for Margaret Cavendish to even contemplate publishing her writing in mid-seventeenth-century England. Gagged by their poor education and mandatory silence, very few women had ever done so before 1640, and the handful who had were conscious of having overstepped their bounds into dangerously wanton territory and so tended to stick to 'chaste' and therefore 'suitable' feminine subjects: religious meditations and divine visions, poetry on love, friendship or God, domestic advice, recipes or cures. In the five years between 1616 and 1620, just eight new titles were published by women – 0.5 per cent of the 2,240 total.

But with the destabilising force of the Civil War came an undermining of all forms of established authority, and after 1640, during the war and Interregnum in particular, a mini-revolution took hold as women seized the opportunity created by the upheaval to publish books in increasing numbers. Between 1646 and 1650, new titles by women shot up to 69. And during the 1650s, almost five times as many books by women were printed than in the 1630s.[26] Aided by a brief lapse in the censorship laws,[27] this productivity boom hit both male and female writers, but women were the biggest gainers.

The rules of the game were slowly changing, but for women publishing remained a risky business. Even those who stuck to 'feminine' topics could still be attacked for disseminating their ideas. When Eleanor Davies published her prophetical visions in 1625, her husband was so enraged that he burnt her manuscript. And Elizabeth Avery, whose *Scripture-prophecies Opened* appeared in 1647, was publicly attacked for it by her own brother, who wrote in 1650, 'your printing of a book, beyond the custom of your sex, doth rankly smell'.[28] Lady Mary Wroth, meanwhile, encountered such vitriolic accusations of betraying her sex on the publication of her romance *Urania* in 1621 (notably from Sir Edward Denny, who in an acrid satirical verse labelled her a 'Hermaphrodite in show, in deed a monster') that she was forced to deny she had ever intended to publish it at all and attempted to withdraw all copies.[29] These ancestral trolls, who abused or ridiculed any woman who dared to speak out, intimidated their quarry, certainly, but didn't always succeed in silencing them. Women writers set about exploiting every loophole they could think of: some pre-empted attack with apologetic prefaces, others specifically addressed women or continued to confine themselves to modest, virtuous, 'feminine' subjects, while many chose to write anonymously or under a pseudonym.

When Margaret Cavendish strode into this daunting arena in 1653, however, with her first book, *Poems and Fancies*, she would take very few of these mitigating measures. Not only would she publish, she would do so under her own name and cover subjects that were considered exclusively male. This was a book whose dainty title belied its extraordinary contents. In lieu of the formal education she couldn't have, Margaret had spent her married life absorbing like a sponge every topic under discussion in her scholarly household – philosophy, science, literature, politics – and it had all filtered into her work. Her poems were not about love or friendship or God: they described fairies that lived at the centre of the Earth; a microscopic world contained in an earring; the terror of hunted animals; the futility of war; the elements; the universe; light, sound, matter and motion; and, most extraordinary of all, the scientific theory of atomism – a school of thought, derived from the Ancient Greek philosophers Democritus, Epicurus and Lucretius, which argued that particles of different sizes, shapes and properties comprised and governed the world. Her fancies were no less surprising: she wrote allegorical dialogues between Wit and Beauty, Earth and Darkness, Melancholy and Mirth; moral discourses on pride, humility, wealth and poverty; and fantastical prose that imagined a Royalist parliament as a diseased human body in need of a cure. It was a wildly abundant compendium of every style and subject that critiqued human nature and expounded dangerously materialist and atheistic views. Coming from a woman, this was not normal.[30]

Such an ambitious work would inevitably provoke outrage and ridicule, so Margaret also included copious prefaces, epistles and addresses in her book, designed to defend her decision to publish – the only placatory tactic she would employ. In her poem 'The Poetresses Hasty Resolution', she describes how her initial qualms almost prevented her from publishing at all. Reason urged her to 'do the world a good turn, / And all you write cast in the fire and burn',[31] but ambition made her impulsive. With a gambler's recklessness she 'resolved to set it at all hazards', for she had little to lose and immortality to win: 'If fortune be my friend, then fame will be my gain, which may build me a pyramid, a praise to my memory.'[32]

She expected censure, particularly from men, who would doubtless 'cast a smile of scorne upon my book, because they think thereby, women encroach too much upon their prerogatives; for they hold books as their crown ... by which they rule'.[33] The most obvious accusations, however – that she ought to be looking after her children and household instead of indulging her whims in writing – she could easily bat away, for she had no children and her husband's estate had been confiscated. As for any claims that she was just another aristocratic dilettante doodling away in her idle hours, Margaret would show just how seriously she took her work: she was as fond of her book, she wrote, 'as if it were my child', and, like a proud mother, was 'striving to show her to the world, in hopes some may like her'. The analogy was clever; it implied not only that her mind had achieved a lasting act of creation that her body could not, but that, far from being 'wanton' or 'rude', it was in fact 'harmless, modest and honest' for a woman to publish her work – as natural and virtuous as being a mother.[34]

Margaret faced one challenge even greater than public disapproval, though. She was a factory of complex, unusual ideas, yet her rudimentary home-tuition had left her without the tools to perfectly express them. In this she was nothing unusual; the state of women's education in the seventeenth century was even poorer than it had been in the last, especially for upper-class women.[35] King James I had disapproved of intellectual women and encouraged a culture of ridiculing them at court, and the attitude had stuck. Those upstart women who did acquire learning were viewed with suspicion, as the scholar Bathsua Makin knew well: 'A learned woman is thought to be a comet,' she wrote in *An Essay to Revive the Antient Education of Gentlewomen* (1673), 'that bodes mischief, whenever it appears.' The scholar Dr George Hickes noted the trend in 1684: 'It is shameful, but ordinary,' he said, 'to see gentlewomen, who have both wit and politeness, not able yet to pronounce well what they read … They are still more grossly deficient in orthography, or in spelling right, and in the manner of forming or connecting letters.'[36] Margaret was a prime example. Her handwriting was near-illegible, her spelling wayward, her rhymes and metre flawed, her grammar idiosyncratic and her punctuation conspicuous by its absence. She was acutely aware of it – her 'brain being quicker in creating than the hand in writing'[37] – but was often too caught up in a frenzy of creativity to be much of an editor. Her secretaries and typesetters had to pick up this slack, resulting in skewed interpretations of her meaning and rounds of later corrections.

Bowing to common opinion, Margaret concluded that it was simply 'against nature for a woman to spell right',[38] arguing that originality and wit were more valuable than the technicalities of form. Yes, her writing could be indulgent and baggy, her arguments incomplete and foggy, but to her a free and artless style was best: 'Give me a style that nature frames, not art, / For art doth seem to take the pedant's part.'[39] It's a convenient argument when the art is largely missing, but it ignores the real problem: her lack of education. It's been suggested that she might even have been dyslexic.[40] But having internalised the

'Tis true,
the world may
wonder at my
confidence

prevailing assumption that women were undeserving of education, blaming her own natural incompetence was the only defence she had.

For those looking for a straightforward feminist heroine in Margaret Cavendish, this is a problem. Keen to present herself as a wonder of the age, as something 'other' than the average woman, she voices the troubling suggestion that women are not naturally suited for intellectual pursuits more than once in *Poems and Fancies*: 'True it is,' she writes in one epistle, 'spinning with the fingers is more proper to our sex, than studying or writing poetry.'[41] And in her address 'To all writing ladies', despite urging them to push beyond their domestic sphere into the world of politics, religion, philosophy and poetry, she adds that 'though we be inferior to men, let us shew our selves a degree above beasts'.[42]

At this early stage in her career, when her ideas are in their infancy, Margaret is infuriatingly inconsistent on women's intellectual worth. With her own busy, capacious, ambitious mind fighting the remnants of patriarchal indoctrination, she flip-flops from apologist to agitator and back again. Elsewhere in the same book, she delivers a defiant 'up yours' to the snide world outside that's just itching to condemn her:

> *Tis true, the world may wonder at my confidence, how I dare put out a book, especially in these censorious times; but why should I be ashamed, or afraid, where no evil is, and not please my self in the satisfaction of innocent desires? For a smile of neglect cannot dishearten me, no more can a frown of dislike affright me ... my mind's too big, and I had rather venture an indiscretion, than lose the hopes of a fame.*[43]

This is the Margaret Cavendish that feminists adore, emerging from her chrysalis: singular, ambitious, confident of her intelligence and proudly dismissive of what others think. Over time, her ideas on women, like her ideas on natural philosophy, would develop into a much more coherent, formidable statement, but for now, she was primarily on the defensive, knowing damn well that her actions, though harmless, would be seen as provocative. With Sir Edward Denny's famous hectoring verse to Lady Mary Wroth still ringing in Margaret's ears three decades after it was written, she imagined men telling her, too, to go back to her sewing:

> *Work Lady, work, let writing books alone,*
> *For surely wiser women nere wrote one.*[44]

But Margaret would do no such thing, 'For all I desire, is Fame.' And fame she would get. Throughout her writing career, she would produce a staggering 23 books – accounting for over half of the total number of books (just 42) published by women between 1600 and 1640.[45] With her unabashed ambitions, and with few to rival her intrepid subject matter or prolific output,[46] Margaret would stand almost entirely alone in the century as a woman writer who could not be ignored.

MANY SOBERER PEOPLE IN BEDLAM

After nearly 18 months in England, Margaret grew impatient to return to William in Antwerp. She had sent her first book to the printers and even dashed off another (*Philosophical Fancies*),[47] and Sir Charles's estates had finally been released from sequestration, enabling him to buy back the family seats of Welbeck and Bolsover (though at a greatly inflated price) and stabilise the family's finances. So on 16 February 1653, just two months before *Poems and Fancies* was due to publish, Margaret set off back to Antwerp, reluctantly leaving her brother-in-law behind as he had succumbed to a fever.

With the lovers rapturously reunited, and the publication of her first two books imminent, Margaret's secret was out, and to her relief and gratitude she found in William a rare husband who entirely supported his wife's new career. He understood her literary ambitions because he had them himself, though he had the grace to recognise that she was the better writer. He would encourage her, write prefaces and the odd line or verse for her, praise her (blindly, some said), and together they sent out her books to their illustrious friends and waited nervously for the responses.

Anticipation was high when *Poems and Fancies* was due to appear in April – though not necessarily for the right reasons. Dorothy Osborne wrote excitedly to her betrothed, Sir William Temple, '… first let me ask you if you have seen a book of poems newly come out, made by my Lady Newcastle?' There was a concealed barb in her enquiry, however, as she clearly intended to despise it: 'For God's sake if you meet with it send it to me; they say tis ten times more extravagant than her dress. Sure, the poor woman is a little distracted, she could never be so ridiculous else as to venture at writing books, and in verse too.'[48] Margaret's reputation as an eccentric had preceded her, and for many her decision to write only confirmed their prejudices.

Once they had actually opened the book, reader responses were mixed. The 2nd Earl of Westmorland, Mildmay Fane, was an avid fan, scrawling a poem in praise of Margaret's talent inside his copy, while friends of the Cavendishes predictably gave it a glowing review. The highly cultured polymath and Dutch diplomat Constantijn Huygens wrote to a friend that it was 'a wonderful book, whose extravagant atoms kept me from sleeping a great part of last night'. Others were less impressed. Once she'd got her hands on it, Dorothy Osborne felt entirely vindicated in her assumptions that Margaret must surely be mad, sniping to Sir William: 'You need not send me my Lady Newcastle's book at all, for I have seen it, and am satisfied that there are many soberer people in Bedlam. I'll swear her friends are much to blame to let her go abroad.'[49] Margaret was not only compromising her womanly virtue by publishing a book; she was also guilty of an 'extravagant' kind of literature. Her 'free and noble style' that 'runs wild about, it cares not where'[50] was scatterbrained, unrefined and hard to follow – it was all far too unconventional for Dorothy Osborne.

Another worrying response came from friend and courtier Sir Edward Hyde, who offered the ultimate back-handed compliment that a woman could surely not have written so clever, so learned, so *masculine* a book, with 'so many terms of art, and such expressions proper to all sciences'.[51] The humble apologia, used so commonly by male writers and taken as intended – a rhetorical show of modesty aimed at endearing the writer to his audience – were in Margaret's case being taken as an admission that she was so inept she must be passing off someone else's work as her own. It was yet another accusation to add to the list of defences she was compiling for her next work, which was already underway.

On arriving back in Antwerp, Margaret had eagerly returned to a collection of essays she had started before her trip to England, but when she sifted through her papers, she was disheartened by what she found. It was obvious, even to her, that they were littered with errors and sagging under the weight of stunted arguments, half-baked ideas and distracting digressions. To revise them seemed too Herculean a task, so, true to form, in late 1654, she lazily published them anyway, as *The World's Olio* – a concoction of observations on all manner of subjects, literary, political, social and philosophical, that made up the rich stew or 'olio' of the title – and, without correcting the proofs, sent it out into the world to be assessed, warts and all.

Hampered, still, by the misconception that she was not up to the task at hand, Margaret again used prefaces to excuse her faults and lay the blame on her gender: 'It cannot be expected I should write so wisely or wittily as men,' she insisted, 'being of the effeminate sex, whose brains nature hath mix'd with the coldest and softest elements'.[52] She rejected the 'great complaints' from women, which were evidently becoming louder, that men had 'usurped a supremacy' over them since Creation. In fact, she argued the opposite, that 'Men have great reason not to let us in to their governments, for there is great difference betwixt the masculine brain and the feminine'. While men had the strength of an oak, women, she wrote, were like willows, 'a yielding vegetable, not fit nor proper to build houses and ships'.[53] They might exceed men in beauty, affections, piety and charity, but women didn't have the judgement, understanding and rhetorical skills of men.

There could hardly be a more depressing demonstration of the damage that systemic misogyny can do to a woman's self-esteem. For all her bravado, every word of this sprang from her insecurities at her failings and mistakes, and she had a long way to go before she truly understood the root cause of her disadvantage. In anticipation of more accusations of intellectual theft, she added numerous epistles to her book to protest that her work was her own, that 'my head was the forge, my thoughts the anvil to beat them out'. William was her tutor, and she his scholar, she admitted, but she had never received professional teaching from any 'proper' philosophers. The need to defend herself and her work would seemingly never end.

The year 1654 had been a bad one from the start: in February, the Cavendishes had received the news from England that Sir Charles had died, weakened by the fever he had caught the year before, and the effect was crushing. William had lost his brother, and Margaret a close friend, but both had lost the man they viewed as their saviour – Sir Charles had consistently lent them money and support, rescued the family estates from the Parliamentarians, even kept them from starvation. Margaret would later refer to him as 'the preserver of my life'.[54] They owed him everything, and his loss plunged the couple into melancholy and illness.

Work was Margaret's medicine this time, and despite the setbacks, her intellectual life was burgeoning. Friendships with scholarly types such as Constantijn Huygens allowed her to discuss her ever-expanding reading and the experiments she conducted in her laboratory, and to test her theories against other minds besides her husband's, while every spare minute was spent writing it all down.

Her next book, *Philosophical and Physical Opinions*, published in 1655, expanded on earlier ideas, offering an exhaustive theory of the natural world and all its phenomena, and her prefaces and addresses reflected this growing seriousness. She dedicated the work to Oxford and Cambridge, the universities she aspired to attend but was categorically excluded from.

The publication of *The World's Olio* the previous year had provoked yet more tiresome accusations that the work could not possibly be all hers, prompting Margaret to include in her prefaces increasingly irritable repudiations of the charges levelled at her by this 'ill-natured and unbelieving age'. She was repeating herself to no effect – a woman's word was worthless; the accusations only ceased when William weighed in on the debate in an epistle he contributed to *Philosophical and Physical Opinions*. It was plain to him that base prejudice was behind it all – 'Here's the crime,' he stated, 'a lady writes them, and to entrench so much upon the male prerogative is not to be forgiven' – and at long last, Margaret was beginning to understand this too.[55] As she grew weary of the battles to gain respect and recognition for her work, her own belief in what women could achieve, and what society said they could achieve, were becoming increasingly polarised.

In her dedication to the 'Two Universities', she forcefully argued her new stance, asking them to accept her work 'without a scorn, for the good encouragement of our sex, lest in time we should grow irrational as idiots'. She spoke from bitter experience when she wrote that men thought it impossible for women to acquire learning, 'and we out of a custom of dejectedness think so too, which makes us quit all industry towards profitable knowledge'. But as her confidence in her own abilities had grown, so too had her conviction that women had 'rational souls as well as men', and that it was their exclusion from intellectual, civic and political life that was the source of the problem; it left women to become 'like worms, that only live in the dull earth of ignorance … for we are kept like birds in cages, to hop up and down in our houses, not suffered to fly abroad'. Without the experience and knowledge that men had access to, it was no wonder women lacked their 'invention'. How could they thrive when 'we are never employed either in civil or martial affairs, our counsels are despised, and laughed at' and 'the best of our actions are trodden down with scorn'? And all because of 'the over-weaning conceit men have of themselves' and their 'despisement of us'.[56] Well, she'd realised her mistake and found her outrage. There was no natural inferiority in women; only prejudice against them. Margaret Cavendish the proto-feminist had been born.

VIRGIN VIRAGOS

Never one to pause for breath, Margaret plunged into her next book with a newfound confidence in both herself and in women. *Nature's Pictures Drawn by Fancies Pencil to the Life*, published in the summer of 1656, was another overwhelmingly diverse treasure chest of poems, fireside tales, animal fables, social satires and dialogues that attempted to pack in all of everyday life experience. It was her most ambitious, accomplished and visionary work yet, and the stand-out prose pieces all, in their way, offered revolutionary depictions of women.

In 'The Matrimonial Agreement', a woman's powerlessness in marriage is redressed when a sceptical bride strikes a bargain with her husband: if she suspects him of adultery, she has the right to leave him and take a share of his estate with her. In 'Ambition Preferr'd Before Love' the lady chooses not to marry at all, because 'Husbands will never suffer their wives to climb [Fame's Tower], but keep them fast lock'd in their arms, or tie them to household employments.' And in 'The Contract', a morality tale in the 'romancical' mould, scholarly women are unashamedly celebrated in the spurned heroine who wins back her betrothed by becoming a paragon of learning and a 'meteor of the time'.

'Assaulted and Pursued Chastity' is *Nature's Pictures'* most interesting fictional offering, though – an allegorical, romance-inflected romp that illustrates the sexual hazards to which women are perpetually exposed. Featuring a gun-toting, cross-dressing, self-educated, gender-fluid heroine who finds herself shipwrecked in fantastical lands and winds up fending off a predatory Prince, outwitting some dangerous canni-bals, leading an army into battle in defence of a Queen, making said Queen fall in love with her and ruling her own kingdom, it's pretty startling stuff for its time.[57] Too timid to fire a pistol herself,

We are kept
like birds in cages,
to hop up and down
in our houses.

Margaret was living out all her heroic fantasies by putting one in the unwavering hand of her heroine – and as the Prince advances on her with a smile, thinking it 'a shame to be out-dared by a woman', she shoots him without compunction. Later, when the Queen discovers her crush is a woman, Margaret even dabbles with the possibility of same-sex love – the Queen is 'angry that she was deceived, yet still did love'. Pushing the boundaries further still, she toys with the fantasy of same-sex marriage, as the Queen concludes that 'since I cannot marry her, and so make her my husband, I will keep her if I can, and so make her my friend'. The heroine's revelation to her troops, meanwhile, is met with undiluted approbation and a rousing cry for equality: 'Heaven bless you, of what sex soever you be'.

The last word, however, sadly goes to convention as the ending plucks our heroine from her boys' clothes and puts her in a wedding dress, as the wife of her would be rapist. It's disconcerting to say the least, but as a woman who flirted with the tropes of masculinity herself, Margaret knew not to push the transgressive image of the warrior woman too far. Amazonian 'virgin viragos' had traditionally signalled social disorder and disruption – dangerous, unnatural women who rejected their femininity and threatened to throw the established order of marriage and childbearing into chaos – but Margaret had flipped the idea on its head by using her weaponised virgin not to wreak havoc, but to bring about peace and social order.[58] Behind the smokescreen of the traditional marriage plot, she could argue the subtly radical notion that breaking with prescribed gender conventions might suggest impeccable virtue in women rather than immodesty, and that masculine get-up could be a kind of armour that afforded them empowerment, freedom and safety.

These tales are significant in portraying some of the earliest fictional heroines written by a woman in English, and it's heartening that in their intelligence, resourcefulness and courage they flouted all the tired rules of femininity and achieved a level of agency that their female audience could only dream of. And Margaret undoubtedly *did* dream of this stuff. She didn't fantasise about heroes who would come along to rescue her; she fantasised about being a heroic woman who could rescue herself. With so many autobiographical details filtering into these tales – perilous voyages from home, exile in a foreign land, men whose first wives are conveniently dispatched and whose libertinism is reformed by the love of a virtuous young woman – it's clear that Margaret was rewriting her own life as a romance adventure, and casting herself in the highly unconventional lead role.

If Margaret's reinvention of herself as a fictional heroine was ambitious, the inclusion in *Nature's Pictures* of her real-life autobiography was positively groundbreaking. Nothing quite like it had ever been published in English by a woman before. Their life writing had previously been either for private consumption or with a religious focus; ordinary, secular female existence was deemed unworthy of public attention. But Margaret begged to differ. At the age of just 33, in 'A True Relation of my Birth, Breeding, and Life', she set down her life story for posterity.

Aware that she was yet again straying from the well-trodden path, she had her defence ready. Vanity would be the first accusation, but others had done it without censure, so why shouldn't she? Some readers would consider it presumptuous, and wonder why she had written it all, 'since none cares to know whose daughter she was, or whose wife she is, or how she was bred, or what fortunes she had, or how she lived, or what humour or disposition she was of'. Her answer to this was simple and unashamed: granted, it might be of no interest or purpose to the reader, 'but it is to the authoress, because

I write it for my own sake, not theirs'. Here was a woman who freely admitted that her ambition (which 'inclines to vain-glory') was so great that she always had one eye on her legacy, aiming 'to tell the truth, lest after-ages should mistake, in not knowing'.[59]

This was a fine claim, but like all autobiographies Margaret's account was highly partial, glorifying her family as courageous, innocent victims of the Parliamentarians, and herself as a shy, melancholic writer who, despite her singularity and ambition, was a dutiful wife and loyal subject. For all her own spin-doctoring, however, here was also a prime opportunity to combat other people's; to publicly answer some of the gossip and exaggerations that had a habit of springing up around her. She slapped down the rumours that she had stood 'as a beggar at the Parliament door' and 'haunt[ed] the committees' during her trip to England, and scoffed that 'report did dress me in a hundred several fashions'. In producing this pioneering account of herself and attempting to set the record straight, Margaret was presciently asserting that women as well as men had a right to self-representation, to tell their own story as they wished, rather than languish at the mercy of other people's interpretations.

THE RETURN OF THE KING

By 1656, Margaret had been writing continuously for four years, but then suddenly the stream of publications stopped. 'My wit is drawn dry,' she admitted later,[60] though a lack of funds may also have been to blame. Just as her writing juddered to a halt, however, the political situation began to shift. Charles II had been living in Germany, but when an offer of support came in from the Spanish government, he moved his court to Brussels and tried to rustle up some rebellions in England. None of them amounted to much; in the end, the Royalists' plans had little impact compared with the death of Oliver Cromwell in September 1658 and the abdication of his son Richard as Lord Protector of the Commonwealth in May the following year. The Royalists had the power vacuum they needed, and in the chaos that ensued, the old stability of the monarchy began to look appealing once more. Negotiations with Charles began, and on 25 April 1660, Parliament voted unanimously for the return of the King. On hearing of the May Day celebrations, Samuel Pepys – once 'a great roundhead' in his youth[61] – reported dryly that there was 'great joy all yesterday at London, and at night more bonfires than ever, and ringing of bells, and drinking the King's health upon their knees in the streets, which methinks is a little too much'.[62]

The country's raptures continued when Charles arrived back in England on 26 May. William was so desperate to join his king that he followed in a rickety old boat that was barely seaworthy, and was overcome with emotion on his return home: 'Surely … I have been sixteen years asleep, and am not thoroughly awake yet,' he gushed.[63] For the time being Margaret had to remain in Antwerp as surety for William's debts, and in her absence England banished Puritanism and roared back to life. William hastily joined the queue of Lords who in August were presenting private bills for the reparation of their losses, and once he'd received royal assent, was finally able to borrow the money to release his wife and start paying off his debts.

When Margaret did finally return home, she wasn't quite as delighted with what she found as William had been. Despite her relief that her exile was over, her husband was still living in reduced circumstances in London, unrewarded by the King for his loyalty, while others had been showered with honours. It fell to his children to step in with financial help this time until he managed to claw back the rest of his scattered estates in September. That same month, however, his devotion to the King was at last rewarded with a decent position at court, as Gentleman of the Bedchamber, and the important salaried role of Lord Lieutenant of Nottingham.

Finances back on track, William announced that he and his wife would be settling in his Midlands estates of Welbeck, 20 miles from Nottingham, and Bolsover Castle, in Derbyshire. Margaret, who had never felt much at ease in garrulous urban society, was happy to retire to a quiet life in the country, though she and her husband would both be in for a shock when they arrived that autumn. William's parks had been uprooted, his livestock killed, his houses looted, and Bolsover Castle – occupied, garrisoned and part-demolished – was a ruin. Margaret later worked out her husband's financial losses to be a whopping £941,303.

It would take more loans and a grand restoration project, but within two years Welbeck, at least, had risen from the ashes and William was finally in a position to secure Margaret's jointure.[64] In the event of his death, he now granted his wife numerous properties, a yearly income of £1,025 and a life interest in Bolsover Castle, and over the next few years he would add even more to this inheritance – much to the consternation of his children.

In her new life in the country, Margaret tried to apply herself to housewifery, but despite an aptitude for elements of estate management (just like her mother), the lure of returning to writing became too great, and in 1662 she embarked on another publishing binge. First came a collection of plays that had been waiting patiently in her desk drawer since her days in Antwerp. Written when the English theatres were closed, and ignoring all the rules of standard drama, these plays were unlikely ever to be performed. Often long and oddly structured, chopping and changing between several plot strands, they have more in common with modern-day TV series, unifying through theme rather than time, place and action. They are particularly remarkable, though, in giving almost all roles and lines to women and exploring the far reaches of what they might desire. Their stories include warrior women who lead an army out to war in *Bell in Campo*, a group of 'academical ladies' who have rejected patriarchal society to live in a utopian all-female enclave in *The Female Academy*, and in her 1668 play *The Convent of Pleasure*, Margaret imagines another free and independent female space, established by the wealthy heiress Lady Happy, where the women declaim on why 'marriage is a curse' and enact a series of skits dramatising the hardships of childbirth and living with violent, drunken, profligate or philandering husbands to illustrate their point. Into this atmosphere has come a foreign Princess, of androgynous allure, 'a princely brave woman truly, of a masculine presence', with whom Lady Happy falls in love. 'Why may not I love a woman with the same affection I could a man?' she reasons – and this time Margaret allows her same-sex couple a fervent kiss before the dream is shattered.

It might seem odd that such gynocentric fantasies and anti-marriage sentiments should come from a woman so happily married, but Margaret's own good luck didn't prevent her from recognising the injustice inflicted on women by the institution, or from feeling the force of the oppression, loathing and derision that men routinely directed at them.[65] As in her fictions, Margaret's renegade feminist plays are mostly brought back down to earth with a bump with awkwardly conventional 'happy' endings – the Princess in the Convent of Pleasure turns out to be a Prince; the Female Academy proves vulnerable to the outside world and the Amazons must return to their 'proper' domestic sphere when the war is over. All the same,

Margaret was provoking much-needed debate about gender expectations here, and revelling in writing female characters who would surely have filled the patriarchy with dread.

She followed these plays with a book of topical orations, fulfilling her ambition of becoming a female Cicero (though she never took to the podium; for a shy, tongue-tied woman with much to say, the page was far more welcoming), but her next few projects would be retrospective in nature. Looking back on her earlier philosophical works with fresh eyes and a great deal more study under her belt, she found them seriously wanting, littered with rushed sentences, garbled ideas and misused or unexplained terminology. So in 1664 she produced revised editions of *Philosophical and Physical Opinions* and *Poems and Fancies*, swiftly followed by *Sociable Letters*, a collection of 221 epistles musing on 'the humours of mankind', which included vivid descriptions of everyday Antwerp life, social satire, analysis of her own ambitions, fears and shortcomings and the first extended critical appraisal of Shakespeare.[66]

Sticking with the epistolary form (the lack of rigid generic rules suited Margaret's wandering style), *Philosophical Letters* also appeared that year, which attacked the theories of the most revered male philosophers of the day – René Descartes, Jean Baptiste van Helmont, Thomas Hobbes, Walter Charleton, Galileo and Henry More – and invited challenges to her own opinions in return. This was a phenomenally brave and revealing move. Margaret was now so confident in her own philosophical opinions that she was engaging in public intellectual debate like any male scholar might.

Amid this flurry of publishing came another twist in the Cavendishes' fortunes. Money was still tight thanks to the expensive restoration of Welbeck, so William attempted to call in an old debt from the King, which amounted to nearly £10,000. It didn't quite work; the King refused to pay up, but in the summer of 1664, he offered William compensation in the form of a dukedom – a fair trade to William's mind. The decree was passed and on 16 March 1665 William and Margaret became two of the noblest (though certainly not the richest) people in the land: the Duke and Duchess of Newcastle.

THE BLAZING WORLD

Now in her early forties, Margaret was a name to be reckoned with. The Duchess of Newcastle's next book, *Observations upon Experimental Philosophy*, published in 1666, again skewered the works of well-known figures such as Robert Boyle and Henry Power, but particularly Robert Hooke's *Micrographia* – a book that recorded in intricate illustrations his findings under the microscope. As a founder member of the Royal Society, Hooke was delivering a powerful defence of its empirical modus operandi, but Margaret took issue with this approach. She and William owned a fine collection of microscopes and telescopes and, knowing how temperamental these early instruments were, she argued that they produced 'fallacies, rather than discoveries of truth', distorting more than they revealed and explaining only the exterior workings. Her rejection of experimentalism in favour of pure old-fashioned reasoning hasn't aged so well, but she was in good company at the time: philosophers Thomas Hobbes and John Locke and physician Thomas Sydenham all shared her scepticism and later produced their own attacks on the Society and its methods.

What has stood the test of time is the appendix Margaret wrote as a 'work of fancy' to amuse herself and her readers after all this heavy theorising. Conceived in the midst of the Scientific Revolution and in the wake of the Age of Exploration, *The Description of a New*

World, called the Blazing World was the most imaginative, exotic, genre-busting work of Margaret's career. A romance novella, fantasy adventure, philosophical utopia and theological debate all in one, this indefinable tale takes us to an alternate universe and makes a strong case for being one of the first examples of science fiction in English literature and – 150 years before Mary Shelley's *Frankenstein* – the first ever to be written by a woman.

Interplanetary flights of fancy had been imagined before in other languages, but Margaret was quick to assert her originality; hers was a world 'not such as Lucian's, or the French-man's world in the moon; but a world of my own creating'. And this was key to her romantic ambitions. As an 'Authoress', she could attain all the power in her imaginary world that, as a woman, she was denied in her own, for 'though I cannot be Henry the Fifth, or Charles the Second, yet I endeavour to be Margaret the First; and although I have neither power, time nor occasion to conquer the world as Alexander and Caesar did ... I have made a world of my own.'[67] If her readers liked this other world, they could elect to be her subjects, and if not, this was no tyranny: 'they may create worlds of their own, and govern themselves as they please'.[68]

In the first part of *The Blazing World*, which Margaret calls 'romancical', she upcycles many of the plot devices and philosophical ideas that appear in her earlier writings. A young woman is carried off against her will by a predatory man but is rescued by a shipwreck that carries her into another world, joined to her own at the North Pole. It's called 'the Blazing World' because its stars are so bright they light up the night as if it were day. In this fantastical paradise, the land is 'rich, and fruitful', the cities are made of marble, amber, coral and gold, and there is no use for guns because the inhabitants 'had no other enemies but the winds'. Here, human and animal merge.

There are men 'like foxes, only walking in an upright shape' or with 'heads, beaks, and feathers, like wild-geese'; 'some were bear-men, some worm-men … some bird-men, some fly-men, some ant-men', their skin a rainbow of colours – 'some of a deep purple, some of a grass-green, some of a scarlet', and so it goes on.

Quick as a flash, the young woman is married to the Emperor and, as Empress, is granted absolute power to govern this land as she pleases. Her first priority is to embark on a course of philosophical study – much like Margaret's own – to enable her to govern as wisely as possible. So begins the 'philosophical' part of the narrative, in which the Empress calls together the great thinkers of this world, its priests and statesmen as well as 'immaterial spirits', to question them on their system of government (a monarchy, of course) and consult them on scientific and philosophical matters, from astronomy and weather phenomena to natural history, mathematics, logic, atoms, theology and 'the beginning of forms'. Then she begins to make changes: she dissolves the societies she doesn't approve of and forms new ones, and even establishes her own female-centric religion, though she ensures that this world, unlike the real one, is conspicuously free from religious persecution, with the Empress keeping her subjects 'in a constant belief, without enforcement or blood-shed'.

In the final 'fantastical' section, Margaret pulls off a supreme act of vanity by making a surprise cameo as the scribe whose soul is summoned to help the Empress set down her founding constitution. In yet another same-sex tease, the two women form a deep, lover-like bond, travelling together to Margaret's world to observe William; their two souls inhabit his body for a time, before Margaret is appointed the Empress's chief advisor when invasion threatens her native country.

It's an audacious, inventive, wonderfully weird piece of fiction – the culmination of all Margaret's long-held ambitions to cast herself as a romance heroine, where the real and unreal, fantasy and auto-biography meet.[69] Here, Margaret the First, ruler of her own imaginary empire, uses her power to create a proto-feminist utopia, free from war and religious division, where there is 'no difference of sexes' and women can fully participate in civic life. Only in the wildest alternate reality did such things seem possible, so Margaret created in make-believe what she couldn't find in life: power, peace and gender equality.

As if to provide an antidote to her own oddity, Margaret's next book was far less radical and, probably for that very reason, her most respected work during her lifetime. *The Life of William Cavendish, Duke of Newcastle*, published in 1667, was a straightforward biography of her husband, whose reputation needed a little rehabilitation; his flight from the Battle of Marston Moor hadn't been forgotten and many of his rivals now thought him too old and unfit for political involvement. Unlike many of Margaret's previous works, it was taken seriously by most. The historian John Rushworth used it as a source for his work on the Civil War, and two women were inspired to write similar biographies defending their husband's war records: Lucy Hutchinson from the Parliamentarian side and Anne Fanshawe on the Royalist. Clearly, celebrating the achievements of her husband was considered a far more admirable use of Margaret's time than scribbling on natural philosophy, outlandish other worlds or indeed her own life. And it *was* a celebration: as well as detailing William's daily habits and activities, his upbringing and character, the book was a highly partial account of his political and military career, glorifying his successes, glancing over the stickier moments and hitting back at his detractors. This was William as Royalist martyr, a man who had stoically endured exile and financial castration for his loyalty to the

King. The result was still remarkable in its way – it was the first biography of a husband by his wife, and was produced by a female publisher[70] – but inevitably it was a romanticised portrait seen through an adoring lover's eyes.

As such, it still drew criticism. Samuel Pepys, always quick to belittle Margaret since she had disappointed him at the Royal Society earlier that year, began reading it the following spring but soon declared it a 'ridiculous history' that showed her to be 'a mad, conceited, ridiculous woman, and [William] an ass to suffer [her] to write what she writes to him and of him'.[71] William's crime in encouraging, rather than forbidding, his wife's writing is ranked almost equal with Margaret's insanity in writing it in the first place. The work was so overtly panegyric, likening the Duke's deeds to those of Caesar, and at the same time so banal (who cared what he ate for dinner, how long he took to dress or how much money he had lost?) that, for Pepys, it was rendered an undignified and vulgar exercise that made both of them look absurd and Margaret – as usual – mad.

ALL THE TOWN-TALK

During the Cavendishes' visit to London in the spring of 1667 – when Pepys chased Margaret all around town; when scores of children trailed in her wake; when she requested, and was granted, that historic visit to the Royal Society – one thing became quite clear: mad or not, the Duchess of Newcastle was now a celebrity. Restoration London was full of wonders, both thrilling and terrible. The backlash against Puritanism had ushered in a new era of licence, entertainment, flamboyance and festivity. The theatres had re-opened and women were walking their stages for the first time. Houses, shops, public buildings, churches and gaols had been reduced to charred skeletons, consumed by the most biblical conflagration the country had ever witnessed. And the Merry Monarch, Charles II, had presided over all, attended by his harem of mistresses. Yet still, this maimed, dazed and dazzled city was left open-mouthed with astonishment at the sight of Margaret Cavendish: the eccentrically dressed duchess who wrote fantastical books on mannish subjects and made 'legs and bows' instead of curtseys as if she were the heroine of one of her own romances.[72] The woman was a spectacle, and with that came the fame she had so long desired. But fame, she was learning, has its drawbacks.

The invitation to the Royal Society had caused controversy not just because Margaret was a woman, but because Margaret was Margaret. The fledgling Society's endeavours had arrogant, atheistic, revolutionary overtones, and consequently it had enemies. Margaret had even been one of them. She agreed with many of the Society's ideas and values, but she had criticised two of its leading members, Robert Boyle and Robert Hooke, in print not long before, as well as its whole programme of experimental research. Protective of the Society's reputation, many of its members had been against the admittance of a woman who attracted ridicule and criticism, and when she finally arrived, looking like 'a cavalier, but that she had no beard', and the ingenious remarks that this sea of men were waiting for failed to materialise, they congratulated themselves on being proved right.[73]

Pepys's fascination with Margaret curdled instantly, but John Evelyn, who had already started paying court to the Duke and Duchess at their house in Clerkenwell, was intrigued. After his first visit, he decided her oddities were a novel kind of amusement, proclaiming himself 'much pleased with the extraordinary fanciful habit, garb and discourse of the Duchess'.[74] His wife, on the other hand, gave a damning verdict. Mary Evelyn conceded to a friend that Margaret had 'a good shape, which she may truly boast of', but had little else positive to say. Her dress was 'fantastical', her 'curls and patches' overdone, her mannerisms affected, excessive and insufferable – just like her work: 'her gracious bows, seasonable nods, courteous stretching out of her hands, twinkling of her eyes, and various gestures of approbation, show what may be expected from her discourse, which is airy, empty, whimsical, and rambling as her books, aiming at science, difficulties, high notions, terminating commonly in nonsense, oaths, and obscenity'. Her ambition was nothing more than vanity, and what galled Mary most was that even wise, discerning men were taken in: 'I found Doctor Charleton with her, complimenting her wit and learning in a high manner; which she took to be so much her due, that she swore if the schools did not banish Aristotle, and read Margaret, Duchess of Newcastle, they did her wrong … Never did I see a woman so full of herself, so amazingly vain and ambitious.'[75]

What Mary Evelyn had missed was that much of this behaviour was Margaret's attempt at masking her own social awkwardness. Even in middle age, as a well-known author, she was gripped by shyness at society gatherings, causing her to overcompensate with overt displays of conviviality. Nerves would make her talkative, and in the wake of those accusations that her works were not her own, she chattered about her books 'more … than otherwise I should have done'[76] and learned passages by heart to prove her authorship.

The effect was quite the opposite of the one she was aiming for. A confident, ambitious woman translated as vulgar and arrogant, antagonising more conventional women like Mary Evelyn, who, like Dorothy Osborne, thought it improper and unchaste for a woman to write books at all, let alone books like Margaret's. Though not uncultured herself, Mary toed the patriarchal line when it came to the 'proper' purpose of a woman's life: they were 'not born to read authors and censure the learned', but to be of service to the sick, the poor, their husbands and children.[77] She couldn't help drawing comparisons between Margaret and the 'matchless' Katherine Philips, whose respectable poems on Platonic love and friendship had been published without her consent, and who therefore fitted the modest mould of femininity to perfection: 'What contrary miracles does this age produce,' Mary exclaimed in her letters. 'This lady and Mrs Philips! The one transported with the shadow of reason, the other possessed of the substance and insensible of her treasure.'

So alarmed was Mary by this new breed of woman that she would quickly remove herself from Margaret's presence for 'fear of infection', and hoped that 'as she is an original, she may never have a copy'.[78] Perhaps she had heard about Margaret's recent trip to the theatre at Lincoln's Inn Fields, where William's play *The Humorous Lovers* (thought by Pepys to be 'the silly play of my Lady Newcastle's') was being performed,[79] for on that occasion she wore a special dress of her own design that exposed her breasts, 'all laid out to view', revealing 'scarlet trimmed nipples'. Such an heroic, classical, barely-there costume might have been acceptable for a court masque or a portrait, but for a trip to the theatre this was a whimsy too far.[80] It was these kinds of theatrical displays that prompted Pepys to note in his diary that 'All the town-talk is nowadays of her extravagancies'[81] and left Mary Evelyn almost dumbstruck. Like Pepys and Dorothy Osborne, she could only conclude that Margaret Cavendish belonged in the madhouse: 'I was surprised to find so much extravagancy and vanity in any person not confined within four walls.'

It's not altogether surprising that some of Margaret's fiercest critics were women. This other-worldly being, who was 'not of mortal race, and, therefore, cannot be defined', who could only be compared with queens and romance heroines, was flouting all the rules that other women felt obliged to live by. When Margaret was around, women like Mary Evelyn were pushed to the sidelines, expected 'not to speak, but admire'[82] – and having always been taught to view other women as rivals rather than sisters, inevitably they sometimes resorted to jealousy, judgement, spite and even fear.

However, regardless of whether they approved of her or not, the public had made a mythical creature out of the Duchess; they talked about her, wrote about her and were desperate to catch sight of her. Margaret had courted the attention, and enjoyed being a visual spectacle, but as a social misfit striving hard to impress a sceptical crowd, she was bound to disappoint occasionally. As she struggled through the hobnobbing and learned what a fickle friend celebrity could be, perhaps the lustre wore off a little, for come July 1667, the Cavendishes returned to the peace and solitude of Welbeck, where Margaret was always happiest.

MARGARET THE FIRST

Margaret got straight back to work on her return to Welbeck, and over the next few years she concentrated on revising more works to prove just how much she had matured as a philosopher and writer. Her new editions reflected her broadened reading and contained tightened, simplified and in some cases reversed versions of her earlier arguments, with clearer explanations, defined terminology and the fancies expunged. Significantly, she also removed her most apologetic prefaces, no longer feeling the need to make excuses for her lack of education or to convince the world that what she had to say was worth hearing. After years of self-doubt, public censure and lonely trailblazing, Margaret had finally found genuine confidence as a woman writer, secure in the knowledge that her words and opinions were as valuable as anyone else's.

It was in the nick of time, as it turned out, because for all that anyone might have expected William – some 30 years older – to go first, it was Margaret who died suddenly on 15 December 1673. She'd been indefatigable to the last, but weakened by compulsive work, a sedentary lifestyle and years of self-inflicted bleeds and purges, she 'soon too active for her body grew'.[83] She was 50 years old.

As befitted a duchess and a celebrity, Margaret was given a grand burial at Westminster Abbey, and although William, elderly and grief-stricken, was too ill to attend, he arranged all the pageantry for his beloved, and collected for publication all the poems and letters from scholars, friends, philosophers and poets that had been written in celebration of her, in life and after her death. He joined her three years later, aged 84, and the two have lain side by side in stone effigy ever since, where Margaret, resplendent in state robes, holds an open book, pen case and inkhorn perpetually at the ready.

From her own day to this, Margaret Cavendish has been a divisive character. With each century extracting the caricature version of her that has best suited its own cultural values, from indulged aristocrat and raving madwoman to pioneering genius and visionary proto-feminist, responses to her have rarely been measured. For all those among her contemporaries who saw an 'illustrious whore' and 'atheistical philosophraster',[84] or agreed with Pepys, Osborne and Evelyn that she was mad, there were plenty who praised her achievements: Cambridge University addressed her as *Margareta I, Philosophorum Princeps* – 'Margaret the First, Prince of Philosophers'; the writers John Dryden, Richard Flecknoe and Thomas Shadwell dedicated works to both her and William, grateful for their patronage, while

Dr Walter Charleton believed she had 'convinced the world, by her own heroic example, that no studies are too hard for her softer sex'. Women writers, meanwhile, were inspired by her example. The astrologer Sarah Jinner published her first almanac in 1658, praising Margaret as an exemplar of the learned woman. And scholar, tutor and writer Bathsua Makin included Margaret in her catalogue of great women, alongside Elizabeth I, Christina of Sweden and Zenobia, Queen of Palmyra, in her 1673 *Essay to Revive the Antient Education of Gentlewomen*. By the end of Margaret's life, the 'Queen of Sciences'[85] had earned her place in English literature and, to a precious few, demonstrated that intelligence was genderless.

Eighteenth-century commentators were as torn as their predecessors, however. The general feeling was kindly, but perhaps only because Margaret's more challenging writings on natural philosophy and women's advancement had by then faded into the background; she was now known as a writer of dramatic fanciful tales and poetry, and as a 'perfect pattern of conjugal love and duty', whose crowning glory was her biography of her husband.[86] The writer, art historian and Whig politician Horace Walpole, however, was not generous. In 1758, he sneered at her 'unbounded passion for scribbling' and remarked that 'though she had written philosophy, it seems she had read none'. Walpole was at least egalitarian in his slights; he found both Margaret and William equally ridiculous, 'a picture of foolish nobility', tucked away together in state, 'intoxicating one another with circumstantial flattery on what was of consequence to no mortal but themselves!'[87]

Walpole's critique was harsh, but this was the image of the Cavendishes that carried over into subsequent centuries. Most nineteenth-century editors kept in line with public taste by selecting only Margaret's more frivolous works for publication (they particularly liked her poems on fairies), omitting anything they viewed as coarse or controversial. Yet despite this bowdlerisation, it was around this time that Margaret was first dubbed 'Mad Madge', a title that reduced her to some kind of lovable twit and entirely dismissed her intelligence, diversity and originality.[88]

Saddled with this dubious new moniker, her reputation was at its lowest at the onset of the twentieth century. Virginia Woolf shared Walpole's vision of Margaret as a 'lonely aristocrat shut up in her country house among her folios and her flatterers', scribbling away 'without audience or criticism', and her opinion was influential. Infuriated by her upper-class impunity to criticism and her informal, undisciplined, unscholarly approach to writing, she saw in Margaret a woman with all 'the irresponsibility of a child and the arrogance of a duchess',[89] whose imagination was allowed to run rampant, 'as if some giant cucumber had spread itself over all the roses and carnations in the garden and choked them to death'.[90] In the end, half admiring, half despairing, she summed up Margaret as 'noble and quixotic and high-spirited, as well as crack-brained and bird-witted' – only perpetuating the 'crazy duchess' theory.[91]

But this is the twenty-first century; as the Cheshire Cat would say, we're all mad here. The very traits that appalled our ancestors are what appeal to us today – Margaret's raw energy; her bold, riotous mind and unbridled curiosity; her daring, originality, versatility, ambition and eccentricity; take any of them away and it would dull her brilliance. At last she can be wholeheartedly applauded for confounding every traditional notion of what a woman should, or could, be: scientist, thinker, philosopher and one of the most flamboyant and prolific writers (male or female) of her era.

True, she was no ready-made feminist icon, but if anything, her faltering journey towards enlightenment only adds to her fascination. Throughout her imperfect career, we see almost in real time the development of a woman shaking off the barnacles of patriarchal thinking, building her confidence and learning to trust her own talent until she genuinely believes in what women can do. It's the culmination of this process, her extraordinary, genre-defying *Blazing World* – not her biography of her husband – that is now regarded as her greatest work; beloved by feminist scholars, it's one of the few still available in print.

Inevitably, Margaret's privileged social position allowed her the relative freedom to kick down barriers that other women couldn't, enabling her to achieve a number of historic firsts. But she was acutely aware of the perils of what she was doing. A woman of wit in seventeenth-century England 'loses her reputation', she wrote, for wit is sometimes 'satirical and sometimes amorous and sometimes wanton'; it strays into 'unfeminine' subjects and employs coarse language, all of which 'women should shun'. Judged by such standards, she may not have fitted anyone's definition of either a woman or a wit except her own, but it paid off in the long run – and it was the long run that mattered to Margaret. Fame and immortality were her heart's immodest desire, and while she found them during her lifetime, it's perhaps only now that she is gaining the reputation she both wanted and deserves. 'I would be known to the world by my wit, not by my folly,' she wrote. And, 'Who knows but after my honourable burial, I may have a glorious resurrection in following ages, since time brings strange and unusual things to pass.'[92] She was right. It would take nearly four centuries, but the day would come when the world was ready for Margaret the First, Duchess of Newcastle.

Mary Astell

OLD MAID

When Mary Astell's first biographer, George Ballard, began to research her life just five years after her death, in 1736, hardly a soul remembered her. Even his most knowledgeable antiquarian friends could come up with nothing. This was odd, because 30 years before, her name had been held in the highest esteem among the literati. Mary had been an unusually learned woman, a poet, a philosopher, a champion of gender equality and women's education, and a religious and political pamphleteer who had taken on Britain's most distinguished male scholars in public debate.

Yet even Ballard had only recently heard of her, through a chance meeting with a woman who went by the name of Frances Smith. Her real name was Elizabeth Elstob, and, like Mary, she had once been greatly admired. Twenty years before, Elstob had been a celebrated scholar of Anglo-Saxon – the first woman to achieve such a thing in Britain – but she had since fallen on hard times and been forced to flee London to escape her creditors. Ballard had found her working as an impoverished teacher, living under an assumed name, reliant on the charity of others – and full of stories about her great friend and mentor Mary Astell, who had similarly struggled to survive.

'If all men are born free, how is it
that all women are born slaves?'

MARY ASTELL (1666–1731),
POET, PHILOSOPHER, POLEMICIST AND THE 'FIRST ENGLISH
FEMINIST'

Ballard was shocked and baffled. How did women so learned, so respected, end up on the scrap heap, dogged by destitution and slighted by history? Mary Astell had known the answer. She had understood better than most the canker of gender inequality, and had foreseen her own impending obscurity. In 1705 she had tartly observed that 'since the men being the historians, they seldom condescend to record the great and good actions of women; and when they take notice of them, 'tis with this wise remark, that such women *acted above their sex* ... that they were not women who did those great actions, but ... men in petticoats!'[1]

Well, Ballard (though a dressmaker by trade) was an amateur historian himself, and meeting Elstob had inspired him to write a new kind of history: one that celebrated rather than neglected women's achievements. It would feature numerous biographical portraits of the great learned women of England and take him 15 years to complete, but Mary Astell was first on his list. Somehow, he had to unearth the details of her life and speak to all who had once known her, before this remarkable woman was forgotten forever.

O HAPPY SOLITUDE

Mary Astell was not an obvious candidate for poverty. At the time of her birth on 12 November 1666, her father, Peter, was a successful merchant in Newcastle's booming coal trade, while her mother, Mary Errington, came from a family of wealthy Catholic gentry in Northumberland, which had its own connections in coal. Indeed, the black stuff was everywhere in Newcastle, tainting the air and making its inhabitants rich. Mary's grandfather, father and uncle were all members of the Hostmen guild of Newcastle, a powerful group of businessmen who acted as coal brokers, monopolising export from the city. It was a heritage Mary would take pride in – proof of her class status, which she would cling to when life brought her low.

The family was prosperous enough to afford a spacious home on one of Newcastle's grandest streets, allowing young Miss Astell to grow up smartly dressed, well fed and waited on by servants. Her brother Peter was born two years after her, and another boy, William, when Mary was six, though he was dead within a week.

While Peter was sent off to school and later apprenticed to become a lawyer, Mary remained at home; there were no schools for girls in Newcastle at the time, so a formal education was not an option. Instead, Mary was taught only the rudimentary skills of reading, writing, knitting, spinning, sewing and other household tasks. Most girls would have been grateful even for this meagre training – in the North of England in the 1660s and '70s, 83 per cent of women could not even sign their names[2] – but Mary was ravenous for learning, and frustration set in early. While still a young child, she took matters into her own hands, learning the Bible and Book of Common Prayer almost by heart and taking herself off to the church library to expand her reading. Such precocity didn't go unnoticed; Mary was fortunate in having a bachelor uncle, Ralph Astell, curate of St Nicholas's Church in Newcastle, who was willing to tutor his young niece and pass on the benefits of his Cambridge education. She may have been as young as eight when they began an intense course of study that involved a weighty curriculum of theological doctrine, philosophy and poetry – and Miss Astell demonstrated a prodigious aptitude for every subject.

George Ballard would later note how naturally scholarship came to Mary: 'having a piercing wit, a solid judgement, and tenacious memory she made herself a complete mistress of every thing she attempted

Men seldom
condescend to record
the great and good
actions of women

to learn with the greatest ease imaginable'.[3] And this aptitude, coupled with the formative impact of an inspiring teacher, was a potent combination. Uncle Ralph was a published poet whose own understanding of the power of language was quickly absorbed by his eager and brilliant pupil. Just as influential were his religious and philosophical views, particularly those he'd picked up at university from a group of thinkers known as the Cambridge Platonists. They argued, after the ancient philosophers Plato and Plotinus, that the nature of the universe was spiritual rather than material, and that moral virtues and reason were God-given. The mortal life was meaningless, the appetites and senses a distraction; the important truths, and access to God, could only be attained through abstract thinking and intellectual reasoning. These teachings rooted themselves in Mary's core, and would inform the fundamental tenets of her spiritual and everyday life.

While still a teenager, she was inspired to try poetry for herself, and in these personal early works, her religious fervour and Platonist take on devotion were already fully formed. Abstemious and academic by nature, she began writing surprisingly jaunty verses on renouncing earthly pleasures in favour of nourishing her soul:

> *I dare not all the morning spend*
> *To dress my body, & not lend*
> *A minute to my soul ...*
> *O happy Solitude, may I*
> *My time with thee, & some good books employ!*[4]

Company and 'idle visits' were just an irritating interruption when the mind was occupied with study and contemplation.

Her poems might read like the work of an intense, anti-social teenager, but Mary maintained these principles throughout her life, developing a 'severe strictness of holy discipline' and observing every fast and vigil the Church of England had. With a nun-like fervour she tried to shake off the material wants and needs of the 'animal spirits' to concentrate on God: 'In abstinence few or none ever surpassed her,' Ballard wrote, 'for she would live like a hermit, for a considerable time together, upon a crust of bread and water with a little small beer ... She would say, abstinence was her best physic.' It was a lifestyle completely at odds with the new flamboyance of Restoration England, but her rationalist philosophy placed reason and divine contemplation above transient desires.

Based on such evidence, Mary might be taken for a tortured, humourless bore, but those who met her got quite the opposite impression: they found a sunny, serene soul, 'highly entertaining, and innocently facetious' in her conversation, whose strict asceticism was never accompanied 'with sourness or moroseness of temper'.[5] It just so happened that she believed in living spotlessly, with humility and charity, in imitation of Christ.

These were lessons she likely learned for herself, because Uncle Ralph, though an admirable teacher, turned out not to be the most exemplary of clergymen – frustrated ambitions led to a penchant for drink and his suspension from the Church in 1677 when he was found half-cut in the pulpit. Still, he had done a great thing in recognising and nurturing Mary's potential – not many men of the age would have deemed it worth their while. Like all good teachers, he had fanned the spark, kindling in her an intellectual discipline to complement her love of learning and a passionate belief in a woman's right to a life of the mind – a belief that would permeate everything she wrote and the way she lived for the rest of her life.

With any luck Mary's intense religiosity fortified her for the trials that life now threw at her, the first in 1678, when her father died. Despite his success as a businessman, the £500 that Peter Astell was worth upon his death couldn't stretch to support a family of five non-earners – his widow, his two young children, his elder spinster sister, who lived with the family, and disgraced Uncle Ralph. It fell to the Hostmen guild to supplement Mrs Astell's finances with monetary gifts and a loan of £21 to cover the funeral (which she was never able to pay back herself), and to take up the annuity paid to the aunt (another Mary, known as 'old Mrs Astell'). Any spare shillings from relatives were invested in the apprenticeship for ten-year-old Peter – the only Astell left capable of earning a wage. Mary, now 12, was left with no dowry and a prickly awareness of the burden that she and the two other Mary Astells in the family represented: a drain on resources who could bring in no income.

Three years later came an end to her education and the loss of another father figure when Uncle Ralph died, followed swiftly by old Mrs Astell in 1684. By 18, Mary had lost half her family, and her poetry began to reflect her darkening mood, with death, loneliness and frustrated ambition her favourite topics. 'What shall I do?' she despairs at the start of one poem – it was the burning question for any young woman as clever, independent and poor as Mary. She had no desire to be rich, admired or courted by men – 'These cannot my ambition please'. Her 'high born soul' was set on something loftier: to use her intellectual gifts, to improve the world in some way, to devote herself to God; only then could she be something 'truly great'.[6] But around her all she saw were closed doors: she couldn't go into business like her father; she couldn't go to university or be apprenticed in the law like her brother; she couldn't be ordained into the clergy like her uncle and in post-Reformation England, devout though she was, she couldn't even take her vows and enter a nunnery.[7] Caught in the trap of class propriety, genteel women were rendered helpless by the belief that earning a living was beneath them, making marriage the only viable career option.

With no dowry, though, Mary Astell would have been considered a poor catch by any prospective husband. This was by-the-by, as it happened, for marriage seems never to have tempted her. Though she didn't explicitly disclose her reasons – and why should she? – by the end of her teens, she already knew that wedding bells weren't for her. But that being the case, how did you solve a problem like Mary? A gentlewoman who couldn't work, wouldn't marry but wasn't independently wealthy? She would have to find another solution – one that few women had ever tried before.

BROUGHT TO MY LAST SHIFT

Unhappy and fidgety for change, Mary decided there was only one place to go if she was to revolutionise her prospects: London. The exact date of her departure isn't known; Ballard claims she was 'about twenty', and she may well have been prompted by local tensions that preceded the Glorious Revolution of 1688 – a treacherous act in Mary's eyes that saw the overthrow of the Catholic Stuart king, James II, in favour of his daughter Mary and her Protestant husband, William of Orange. Like most of Newcastle, the Astells had been unshakeably Royalist during the Civil War and, as a firm believer in hereditary privilege and established power, Mary's allegiance was unequivocally with the deposed Stuart king. From 1686, the still-polarised political factions in Mary's hometown spilled over into riots, and if she were already contemplating a new life in the South, the unrest may have been the nudge that encouraged her to jump. She had certainly been in London for some time by 1688.

It was a leap of faith. Mary had no family in London and no means of supporting herself beyond what little was left from her share of her father's will. The benevolence of family friends and their connections would be key to her subsistence. Or perhaps she dared to dream a little bigger ... Already an accomplished poet in private, she may have aspired to earn her living by writing from the start, though most would have dismissed this as foolhardy, as it had barely yet been established as a career option for women. Jaw-dropping figures such as Margaret Cavendish and Aphra Behn had gained fame and recognition from their plays, poetry and prose, and in the case of Behn, even scraped a living by it – the first woman in Britain known to have done so. But they had also been ridiculed and censured for their words – even a duchess like Cavendish had been labelled a madwoman for her ambitious philosophical fancies, while Behn – daring Restoration playwright, risqué poet and spy for Charles II – had always raised eyebrows and had died beset by debts in 1689, just as Mary was taking her first tentative steps towards independence. These weren't encouraging templates, and they certainly wouldn't do for a conservative, God-fearing young woman like Mary, who couldn't afford to have her reputation tarnished.[8]

So how did a woman earn a living as a writer, as Aphra Behn had done, but remain of the utmost respectability, as Aphra Behn and Margaret Cavendish had not done? Mary wasn't a roguish adventuress, nor was she an eccentric duchess. Nor had she any wish to churn out romance fiction and outré plays. A more suitable role model for her was the spotless Katherine Philips, lauded by all as the author of noble, elegant poems that elevated the bond of female friendship to something near divine. She was no business model, though – reluctant to publish her works, she had not earned a living by them. There were no precedents, no literary forebears, for what Mary had in mind. She would have to draw a new template: for an admired single woman who earned a good living by her pen. Success, however, would be a long time coming, and she would be sorely tested before it arrived.

Mary had settled in Chelsea, then a flourishing little town conveniently close to the city, where (then as now) life seemed charmed. A perfect mix of town and country, it was a patchwork of open fields and parks, with the Thames snaking past on one side, Charles II's private thoroughfare – the King's Road – bisecting it and a well-heeled, respectable crowd living in its 300 or so residences. Grand institutions were springing up along its streets, from boarding schools to the Royal Hospital (which was still a work in progress – it would be completed in 1692) and the Apothecary's Garden (now the Chelsea Physic Garden). So desirable a location was it that various noble-women had made it their home, including the King's wife Catherine of Braganza and the duchesses of Ormonde, Hamilton, Radnor and Mazarin. The tax record for 1694 shows that one in five of Chelsea's population were single women,[9] suggesting that its safe, genteel environs and comparatively low rents made it a particularly female-friendly spot.

The rents weren't quite low enough for Mary, though. By 1688 she had exhausted her funds and resources, and though she believed in the irrelevance of material pleasures, she had to admit there were some she couldn't survive without. At rock bottom, she appealed to the Archbishop of Canterbury, William Sancroft, for help. A man known for his 'good character' and frequent acts of charity, who had only recently been released from the Tower for refusing to swear allegiance to William of Orange, he exemplified everything Mary believed in. It's a shock to learn from her letter just how bad things were. She went to Sancroft as a 'humble petitioner' and revealed that she had been brought 'to very great necessity through some very unfortunate circumstances that I have lain under for some time'. The extent of this great necessity soon becomes apparent: 'I have pawned all my clothes,' she tells him, '& now am brought to my last shift'. In her frustration, she explains the cause of all her troubles – 'my Lord I am a gentlewoman & not able to get a livelihood' – spelling out the absurd trap she is caught in. Unable to work but 'ashamed' to beg, she asks instead for him to pity her 'unhappy state' and grant her an interview, so that she can give him a full account of her circumstances and prove herself worthy of his charity.

It's a stark, pitiful picture of a proud woman with no options left, but her supplication was rewarded. Her plight, and perhaps her eloquence, caught the Archbishop's attention and he granted her a meeting. What he found was a deeply devout, earnest young woman with a burning intelligence, quick wit and robust political opinions that chimed with his own – a girl who was surely destined for greater things than beggary. Convinced of her worth, Sancroft delivered Mary from destitution, both with cash handouts and useful contacts, and Mary made a gift of her gratitude, presenting him in 1689 with a hand-stitched volume of her poems. The frank, confiding dedication shows just how abandoned she felt by all who knew her and how adrift it had left her, as she thanks Sancroft for helping one 'who hath no place to fly unto and none that careth for her soul, when even my kinfolk had failed, and my familiar friends had forgotten me'.

This had been a perilously close brush with ruin; Mary had side-stepped catastrophe only through the charity of others, but charity couldn't be relied upon indefinitely. The need to find a sustainable way of supporting herself was now urgent. If she couldn't, she would forever be teetering on the edge of destitution, in danger of stumbling into the gutter.

LETTERS TO A CLERGYMAN

Success, when it came, happened almost by accident. Mary had been born into an age that believed in women's intellectual inferiority, but she had proven, to herself at least, that this belief was groundless. Now she yearned to prove it to a world of learned men, by participating in the buzzing intellectual life of the great city in which she had settled. Her inclination for abstract thought and intellectual reasoning meant that she favoured poetic, religious, philosophical and political works, and as she increasingly found herself picking holes in the latest writings by supposedly great men and nursing a growing impatience to have her say, she decided to do just that. Her first target was a clergyman, the theologian and well-known Platonist philosopher John Norris, whose *Christian Blessedness: Or, Discourses upon the Beatitudes* (1690) she had lately read and found fault with. And in an astonishingly confident letter, dated 21 September 1693 when she was 26, she frankly told him so. Her greeting must have knocked poor Norris sideways:

> *Sir, though some morose gentlemen wou'd perhaps remit me to the distaff or the kitchen, or at least to the glass and the needle, the proper employments as they fancy of a woman's life; yet expecting better things from the more equitable and ingenious Mr Norris, who is not so narrow-soul'd as to confine learning to his own sex, or to envy it in ours, I presume to beg his attention a little to the impertinencies of a woman's pen.*[10]

It's an ingenious opener, issuing an uncompromising demand to be treated as his intellectual equal. By insinuating that only the most stupid and 'narrow-soul'd' of men would chastise her for stepping outside of her domestic remit, and pointing with withering sarcasm to the 'impertinences' of clever women, she gave Norris no option but to take her seriously. He couldn't dare patronise her when she'd caught him in such a sophisticated rhetorical trap in her very first sentence.

This bold instigation of a correspondence with an author to express admiration and thrash out an argument was rare in women, but it did happen – aristocrats like Lady Conway and Lady Damaris Masham had conducted epistolary debates with philosophers – and Mary had the courage of her conviction that, although she wasn't an aristocrat and hadn't enjoyed the benefits of a higher education, thinking was 'a stock that no rational creature can want' – and she was particularly skilled at it.

Norris's *Discourses* had been written as a rebuttal to John Locke's empiricist theory that knowledge was derived from sensory experience. As an opponent of Locke and a follower instead of the rationalist French philosopher René Descartes, Mary had read Norris's theories that God was the cause of all things with interest, and she agreed with most of them, but she had found a flaw in the logic of one of his arguments and now corrected him on it with aplomb. God should be the sole object of people's love, yes, but not because He was the cause of all their pleasure, as Norris had stated. If 'God is the only efficient cause of all our sensations', she reasoned, then surely he was also the author of their pain and suffering, which, according to Norris's hypothesis, would exclude God from their love. Either Norris had got it wrong, or, as God did nothing in vain, pain must in some way do us good, thereby transforming it into a reason to love Him. It was one of the thorniest problems of Christian belief, but wrangling over the purpose of human suffering was one of Mary's favourite pastimes; after all, she – one of God's most devoted creatures – had experienced plenty of suffering and naturally sought a justification for it.

To his credit, Norris was impressed with Mary's doctrinal knowledge, clarity and persuasiveness – but most of all he was astonished 'to see such a letter from a woman'.[11] He conceded that she had hit upon the one weakness in his argument and managed to overcome his amazement long enough to invite further comments from her. So began a spirited correspondence between the obscure young woman and the renowned clergyman that explored complex questions on the metaphysical soul, the meaning of suffering and the nature of the love of God.

After ten months of lively debate, Norris was so pleased with their conversation that he thought it worthy of a larger audience. The entire correspondence should be published, he proposed, and though Mary recoiled at first, perhaps out of modesty or fear of criticism, she eventually consented. *Letters Concerning the Love of God* duly appeared in print, with Mary's name withheld. The principal wonder of this correspondence, Norris pointed out, was that it had been conducted 'between my self and a gentlewoman, and to add to thy wonder, a young gentlewoman'; this was novelty enough, but as Mary's letters were also of such 'surprising excellency', Norris assumed his readers would doubt that a woman had written them at all.[12] Like Margaret Cavendish's before her, Mary Astell's authorship would be questioned purely because her writing was deemed too good to have come from a woman. It would take a man's word to authenticate the work as hers – which Norris gladly provided – and the general response was that her letters were 'sublime'.[13]

The playing field was not yet level – Mary was still conspicuous mostly by her gender, and considered brilliant in spite of that – but where the uneducated Margaret Cavendish had been mostly dismissed as a crack-pot hobbyist a generation before, Mary was at least being recognised, thanks to her erudition, eloquence and pin-sharp reasoning, as a woman capable of taking on the most eminent scholars in the masculine arena of philosophical discourse. Her ambition was such, however, that good was never good enough. Her secondary motive in challenging Norris, beyond the theological question itself, had really been to challenge herself. Labyrinthine philosophical debates were meat and drink to her, and in Norris she saw a potential new tutor who could help hone her abilities, a sounding board to 'test my thoughts' against. As a 'raw disciple', she had brought her 'unwrought ore' to him to be 'refined' and was ready for criticism; in her ambition to be without fault, she asked him to point out her mistakes and help her find a system of philosophical principles that she could rely on in life. And Norris was nominally happy to oblige, though in practice he turned out to be more interested in discussing his own ideas than helping to develop hers.

The correspondence with Norris had at least allowed Mary to try her strength against a philosophy heavyweight; nonetheless, she was painfully aware that most men would have considered it a futile exercise, 'for knowledge is thought so unnecessary an accomplishment for a woman, that few will give themselves the trouble to assist them in the attainment of it'.[14] And why would they, when influential thinkers, such as the French Cartesian philosopher Nicolas Malebranche, to whose works Norris had introduced Mary, still argued that women's brains were too 'soft' to withstand the rigours of complex abstract thought?[15] The prevalent view was that if women were worth educating at all, it should only be in moral instruction, to make them better wives and mothers.[16]

Yet Mary was living proof that this was a nonsense argument. She and her unusually learned contemporaries such as Lady Damaris Masham and Bathsua Makin had now publicly demonstrated beyond all reasonable doubt that women were every bit as capable as men of intricate intellectual thought and that they, too, felt a need to expand their knowledge and improve their skills. But she was in a precious minority. Around her she saw scores of women whose identities were defined only by their roles as wives, mothers and housekeepers, and it begged the question: what of their minds? It disturbed her that women's intellects were maligned and neglected. If they were kept ignorant, how could they make informed life choices? How could they find the confidence and self-esteem to question subordination and stand up to oppression? And how would they ever be regarded as equals with men? These worries gnawed away at her until she reached the inevitable conclusion: someone had to help women improve their lot by asking these questions publicly, and that someone had to be her.

A SERIOUS PROPOSAL TO THE LADIES

During 1694, while wrestling with Norris over the question of God, Mary Astell had also been busy writing – and publishing – an explosive new work that tackled in magnificent style the desperate need for women's education. It was called *A Serious Proposal to the Ladies, for the Advancement of their True and Greatest Interest*, and again, no author name was given on the title page – perhaps because Mary was 'extremely fond of obscurity',[17] or perhaps to avoid the outrage she knew would follow from men who felt threatened by its contents. It was credited instead to 'a Lover of Her Sex', who directly addressed her sisters as serious, thinking creatures, and asked them in friendly but provocative terms, 'How can you be content to be in the world like tulips in a garden, to make a fine *show* and be good for nothing?' It was a challenge and a rallying cry, calling on the women of England to question their rights and mobilise to make a change. It was the kernel of a targeted, rational, intellectual argument that would one day be called feminism.

Her point was simple: men and women were intellectual equals, therefore women had as much right to an education as men. By now the question of whether or not women had the mental capacity for learning had been fiercely debated for nearly 300 years, with remarkably little progress to show for it. In Europe, the French–Italian writer Christine de Pizan was the first to pen a comprehensive defence of women as early as 1405. In *The Book of the City of Ladies* she offered a compelling catalogue of women's abilities and achievements in life and literature, from learning to inventing, creating and ruling, and deployed the allegorical figure of Lady Reason to argue that 'if it were the custom to send little girls to school ... they would grasp and learn the difficulties of all the arts and sciences just as easily as the boys do'.[18]

It hadn't been enough to create a sea change, though, at least not in England,[19] where throughout the sixteenth and seventeenth centuries numerous books and pamphlets bickered about the worth and capabilities of women – most of them written by men and expounding wildly misogynistic views. John Knox's *The First Blast of the Trumpet against the Monstrous Regiment of Women*, written in 1558 – the year Elizabeth I came to the throne – objected to women ruling the kingdom, while Joseph Swetnam's *The Arraignment of Lewd, Idle, Froward, and Inconstant Women* in 1615 objected to women in general.[20] By Mary Astell's day learned ladies were 'so unfashionable' as to have become a rarity, even among wealthy or

noble gentlewomen,[21] with women's illiteracy standing at an estimated 82 per cent between 1660 and 1700, compared to around 30
per cent for men.[22] Women were still primarily regarded as ornamental dynastic vessels for money, children and property that legally
they could not call their own. There was no need to educate them
for that – it was considered pointless.

When Mary entered the fray, she would not waste her time arguing
about whether women had the brain power to learn or not; she knew
they did and launched her polemic from a powerful position of taking
that fact for granted. Men, she said, 'must excuse me if I be as partial
to my own sex as they are to theirs and think women as capable of
learning as men are and that it becomes them as well'. Women had
a need and a right to an intellectual life, and in being denied that,
they were relegated to a life of triviality, in which they were taught
to value themselves only by their looks and their ability to attract a
husband – and in a grim irony they were held in contempt by men
as vain, frivolous, vapid creatures as a result. If women were only
given the opportunity, she argued, they could reach the same dazzling
heights as any man.

Her first task was to convince the ladies of this. They had been
told all their lives that their minds were good for nothing; it was a
difficult lesson to unlearn. Margaret Cavendish's assertion that it was
'against nature for a woman to spell right'[23] shows how even the most
ambitious of women had internalised the message, and Mary understood exactly where this seventeenth-century version of 'imposter
syndrome' came from. 'She who has nothing else to value herself
upon', she explained, 'will be proud of her beauty, or money and what
that can purchase.' Was it any wonder, she asked, 'when she hears
say that 'tis wisdom enough for her to know how to dress herself'
that a woman will dedicate herself to perfecting this skill?

Men must excuse
me if I be as
partial to my own
sex as they are
to theirs.

Drawing on her philosophical and religious convictions, which valued learning as godly and material pleasures as meaningless and regarded the 'immaterial intellect' as genderless, dished out equally by God, she urged women to take themselves seriously and aim higher. 'Since you cannot be so unkind to yourselves as to refuse your *real* interest', she implored them not to settle for a life of mediocrity, fixated on 'external accomplishments' such as beauty and fine clothes. Such ephemera were 'but sandy foundations to build esteem upon', and once they decayed and faded, a woman with nothing more in her armoury might easily panic and, being 'quite terrified with the dreadful name of *Old Maid*' make a terrible mistake in marriage. It's a message we still have trouble believing today: that inner substance beats outer beauty.

For women to occupy themselves solely with attracting men was to waste their energies on pleasing those who looked down on them for doing so. 'We value *them* too much, and ourselves too little', Mary wrote, 'if we place any part of our desert in their opinion.' This double standard, which led men to reproach and ridicule women for lacking the skills they were barred from learning ('So partial are men as to expect brick where they afford no straw'), made her seethe. Following this model, women were bred 'to be useless at the best, and in a little time a burden and nuisance to all about them', becoming an object of contempt even within their own family. Mary knew only too well just how damaging to the self-esteem that could be.

So why should women be 'content to be ciphers in the world' when they were perfectly capable of engaging in it alongside men? To Mary, the answer was obvious: they shouldn't. And her solution was education. To shore up her foundations and bolster her self-worth, a woman should be taught to think critically and logically. Only then would she be fully equipped to negotiate the world and make wise life choices – how to spend her time and money; who to trust with her life, property and money if she *did* decide to marry, and whether she wished to marry at all. She would understand the tenets of her faith, rather than blindly following doctrine. She would learn to question the ideas, rules and rulers around her. With ignorance safely banished, she might then enjoy a more purposeful, fulfilled and happy life.

Mary wasn't arguing all this to no purpose; she had a practical remedy. The 'serious proposal' of her title was to 'erect a *monastery*' or 'retreat' where women could escape the vanities of the world and find 'more substantial and satisfying entertainments'. An institution that would 'fit us to do the greatest good' in the world. A kind of secular convent where women could go to study and improve their minds. In short, a women's college.

The practicalities had been roughly worked out: the college would be funded by subscription, at a cost of five or six hundred pounds per subscriber, which would be pooled to create a modestly furnished institution. This had economic as well as social benefits: £500 was far less than the average gentlewoman's marriage dowry or the maintenance costs of a single daughter living at home, though it meant the college would only be open to heiresses and the daughters of 'persons of quality who are over-stocked with children'. The finer details were hazy, but, 'As to lodging, habit, and diet,' Mary wrote, 'they may be quickly resolved on by the ladies who shall subscribe,' for this would be a place of female autonomy, where women ruled. There would be a religious aspect to the programme, but she was clear that it was no nunnery; 'since inclination cannot be forced', no religious vows were to be taken. This was a necessary stipulation given that England's break with Rome 150 years earlier had resulted in the dissolution of all its monasteries, but the monastic model was the only template Mary had for such an institution. Before the Reformation, there had been around 140 convents in the country, and with the Church being the sole provider of girls' education, their schools and libraries had been invaluable. Now they were gone, Mary was proposing an academic replacement, a new solution for the scores of gentlewomen who, like Mary, either wanted or needed a safe, independent, meaningful life beyond their family or marriage.

The persistent 'woman question' had led others before Mary Astell to suggest such an institution (though not always for the right reasons). Most early suggestions for women's colleges limited their purpose to instructing women on their proper conduct as a maid, wife and mother, while others imagined more of an oubliette in which to lock away unsightly unmarrieds. (In 1621, for example, Robert Burton quipped in his *Anatomy of Melancholy* that grateful, unencumbered bachelors should build a monastic college 'for old, decayed, deformed or discontented maids to live together in'.) A true academic retreat for women was dreamed up by precious few. Margaret Cavendish had fantasised about it in her plays *The Female Academy* (1662) and *The Convent of Pleasure* (1668). And in 1673, scholar and royal tutor Bathsua Makin had opened a school for girls and talked of the importance of women's education in her *Essay to Revive the Ancient Education of Gentlewomen in Religion, Manners, Arts, and Tongues*, yet the suggestion still hung in the air that its value was mostly in offering them moral improvement and helping them 'to be useful in their places'. Mary, in contrast, was demanding something real and rigorous, aimed above all at personal fulfilment; her vision was ambitious and idealistic in a way that no one else's had been.[24] She imagined an all-female utopia, a 'happy retreat', where a community of women could live together in 'amicable society', unencumbered by the trappings of the outside world, employing their time in study, contemplation and self-governance. There would be no envy there, no censure, scoffing or raillery. Rich heiresses would be safe from fortune-hunters; single women would have provision and a purpose; and everyone would have a refuge where they could cultivate their minds. It was a place where women could find an alternative to marriage, in the 'purest and noblest friendship' with other women – which to Mary represented a different (and far superior) kind of sacred union: 'a holy combination to watch over each other for good, to advise, encourage, and direct'.

Such a place would have radical implications; it would 'amend the present and improve the future age', sparking, she hoped, a chain reaction whereby the 'pious and prudent ladies' who emerged from her college would go out into the world and inspire others to follow their example, triggering a movement that would revolutionise society's perceptions and expectations of women. Women could surely have no reason to disapprove of her suggestion, but men, she suspected, would resent it. She was right, they would, but she had the immunity of righteousness on her side. She argued, as feminists still must, of the mutual benefits of gender equality; that if men 'rightly understand their own interest, [they] have no reason to oppose the ingenious education of the women since 'twould go a great way towards reclaiming the men'. As mothers, women would have a profoundly beneficial influence over their sons, and as wives they would be respected partners rather than downtrodden minions. The only obstacle was men's fear of being outshone by their clever wives – and at this she could only tease: for 'if she be, 'tis his own fault, since he wants no opportunities of improvement unless he be a natural *blockhead*, and then such a one will need a wise woman to govern him'.

Mary modestly referred to her pamphlet as a 'rough draft and rude essay'. If fear prevailed and her proposal came to nothing, it would be 'but a few hours thrown away'. In truth, *A Serious Proposal* was a stunningly accomplished treatise – confident, clear-eyed, witty and conversational, powered by persuasive rhetoric, a relish for argument and the occasional acidic tang – and Mary couldn't suppress her excitement at what might be set in motion by it. At the thought of her college happily established, she was in raptures at the luminescent new breed of woman who would emerge from it – 'methinks I have already a vision of that lustre and glory our ladies cast round about them!'

THE MOST INGENIOUS MRS ASTELL

Despite the absence of her name on the title page, word got out that *A Serious Proposal* was Mrs Astell's work,[25] and given that it was an instant success (it went through four editions by 1701), she didn't mind at all. At just 28, she had established a bold, articulate, compelling public voice and loudly asserted her right to use it in protest.

Naturally, the pamphlet had the most profound impact on women – particularly a certain set of high-ranking, intellectually minded and predominantly single ladies who felt that this Mrs Astell was speaking directly to them and almost clairvoyantly addressing all their long-held frustrations. Women of means such as Lady Catherine Jones, Lady Elizabeth Hastings and Lady Anne Coventry, who would all become great friends and patrons of Mary Astell, were inspired to study and take philanthropic action, while scholarly women such as Judith Drake, Lady Damaris Masham, Elizabeth Thomas, Elizabeth Elstob, Lady Mary Chudleigh and Lady Mary Wortley Montagu were so fired up by her words that they snatched up their quills to write their own feminist works, including several poems in praise of 'Almystrea' – an anagram of Mary Astell.

It wasn't just women who admired her work, however. George Ballard reels off a list of scholarly men who were also deeply impressed. 'Dr John Walker very respectfully calls her, *the most ingenious* Mrs Astell', he writes, and 'the eminently learned Mr Henry Dodwell styles her *the admirable gentlewoman* Mrs Astell'.[26] The antiquarian

Ralph Thoresby referred to her as 'the celebrated Mrs Astell' in his diary, while John Evelyn described her writing as nothing less than 'sublime'.[27] Daniel Defoe, meanwhile, leapt upon the idea of an academy for women in his 1697 *Essay Upon Projects* – though, despite acknowledging his 'very great esteem' for Astell's work and 'great opinion of her wit', he claimed to have thought of it first.

Yet for all this praise, Mary's proposal faced numerous obstacles, with many resisting conversion to her ideas. The dramatist Richard Gwinnett wrote to his fiancée Elizabeth Thomas, 'I am pleased with her project, but do not think it likely to succeed.' The scholar Dr George Hickes, despite his general support of women's education, chided Mary for 'comparing of women with men' and belittled her writings as 'childish reflections'.[28] And as if to bat her down, the misogynist works kept coming, chief among them the wedding sermon preached by nonconformist minister John Sprint, published in 1699 as *The Bride-Woman's Counsellor*, on the weakness of women and their consequent need to be dominated by men, which might have given any bride cause to run a mile.[29]

The divided opinions on the proposal meant that it could only come tantalisingly close to becoming a reality. But come close it did, thanks to the benefaction of a 'certain great lady'. Elizabeth Elstob, who was well acquainted with Mary from the early 1700s, reported to Ballard that, although Mary never mentioned the woman's name, this lady was prepared to donate the vast sum of £10,000 to establish the proposed college. Some believe it was Lady Elizabeth Hastings – well known for her generous philanthropy and particular interest in women's education; others that it was Princess Anne of Denmark herself (the future Queen Anne). Whoever she was, her good intentions were thwarted. One Bishop Gilbert Burnet – a man who now sits slumped on the wrong side of history – 'powerfully remonstrated against it, telling her it would look like preparing the way for Popish Orders' and managed to dissuade this great lady from what would have been a historically significant act.[30] Absurd though it was, Mary Astell would not now be England's first founder of a women's college simply because, in a rare misstep, she had used the word 'monastery' to describe her academy. At a time when anti-Catholic feeling was still strong in England, with 'papists' excluded from power and public office and unable to vote, the terminology had damned her.

Fed up that her grand plan had not been realised, three years after *A Serious Proposal*'s publication Mary felt compelled to write an addendum to her essay. *A Serious Proposal to the Ladies, Part II* was produced in 1697 and served as a kind of DIY manual for women who, like Mary, were tired of waiting for academies that now looked like they would never come. Since no one else would help them, she encouraged women to educate and equip themselves with the knowledge they needed to determine their moral and intellectual purpose. Adopting the 'plain and significant language' she thought best for philosophical writing, she set about summarising the key philosophical principles expounded by her favourite thinkers, such as René Descartes and Antoine Arnauld, providing a toolkit for clear reasoning and distilling the debate on the source of human knowledge for her female readers. But again, her idealist ambitions would be frustrated. This heavy philosophical handbook proved less attractive to the book-buying public than her lively polemic, and the sales reflected it.

They may not have resulted in the revolutionary action that Mary Astell hoped for, but both parts of *A Serious Proposal* had made a significant dent in the patriarchal armour. Her athletic mind and exhaustive studying had ensured that her rhetoric was elegant, well reasoned and persuasive – a masterclass in this masculine art and a match for any learned gentleman. But as a single woman with no money and no rank, she had also struck a chord with women as an unassailably authentic voice. She knew exactly what it was like to be an intelligent, ambitious woman with nothing to do, nowhere to go and no way to live, and it gave her argument a force and integrity that few others (particularly male writers) had. She knew, too, that she was no exception – she had 'not the least reason to imagine that her understanding is any better than the rest of her sex's'.[31] Every woman was capable of the same intellectual attainments if only she had the opportunity and applied herself. *This* was how you solved a problem like Mary. You gave her an education and allowed her to be independent. You gave her a support network and allowed her to contribute to society, instead of shutting her up in a drawing room with trinkets and baubles, as helpless and dependent as a baby.

At the close of the seventeenth century, Europe was now staring the Enlightenment in the face – the period when the modern world of scientific endeavour, rational thought, individualism and tolerance would gradually emerge from the old – and in England, Mary Astell's would be the foremost female voice to proclaim not only that women had an absolute right to take part in this new Age of Reason, but that it was society's duty to enable their participation by providing the educational institutions they had every right to demand. Society, however, was nowhere near ready for such radical change. Britain would not even begin to solve this particular problem for nearly two hundred years.[32]

SOME REFLECTIONS UPON MARRIAGE

Mary's grand scheme to educate the women of England may not have gone according to plan, but she soon had another powerful feminist message for them that she could only hope would have more traction. Her second pamphlet, *Some Reflections Upon Marriage*, written in 1700, was occasioned by one of her Chelsea neighbours, whose story had become notorious. French heiress Hortense Mancini had been married off at 15 to the Duke of Mazarin – a rich man, certainly, but also a jealous, tyrannical, profligate and unhinged religious fanatic who was more than twice her age. After enduring seven years of cruel and deranged behaviour, she could take no more. She ran away from the Duke (and her four children) in male disguise and enjoyed numerous adventures on the road, including scandalous affairs with both men and women, before alighting in London and becoming one of Charles II's many mistresses. 'All the world knows her story,' John Evelyn observed when she died, racked by debt, drink and illness, in 1699, aged 52. And when the Duke and Duchess's sensational lawsuit reports were published soon afterwards, starkly documenting their intolerable marital battleground, Mary felt compelled to put pen to paper.

As a woman of strict morals, Mary couldn't excuse Hortense's behaviour, but neither could she accept that a woman should have to submit to such a husband just because he had assumed authority over her. She pitied the Duchess the 'unhappy shipwreck' of her life – a 'treasure' had been wasted on an unworthy lunatic – but because Hortense was duty-bound as his wife to obey him, she was legally in the wrong to leave him. It was a cautionary tale for all women, thought Mary, of 'the dangers of an ill education and unequal marriage'.

What followed was a critique on marriage and an appeal to women to truly understand what they were letting themselves in for: the loss of their legal status as an individual and all they possessed, and the obligation to submit to their husband in all matters – financial, familial, sexual – whether his demands were reasonable or not. The deal was to love, honour and obey. And in all but the most exceptional circumstances, it was an irrevocable bargain. To Mary, this was unacceptable:

> To be yoked for life to a disagreeable person and temper, to have folly and ignorance tyrannise over wit and sense; to be contradicted in everything one does or says and bore down not by reason but authority ... is a misery none can have a just idea of, but those who have felt it.

She conceded that marriage was 'the only honorable way of continuing mankind', but her opinion of it as an institution was low. It wasn't just men's fault – 'That is not pretended, for ... neither sex is always in the right' – but as the ones with the power, it was they who had earned her distrust, particularly when it came to motive: 'What will she bring is the first inquiry. How many acres? Or how much ready coin?' Some married for beauty, but they found 'time enough to repent their rash folly', while others married 'without any thought at all' beyond that 'it is the custom of the world, what others have done before them, that the family must be kept up, the ancient race preserved'. If the lady said yes to these overwhelming overtures, all she had to look forward to was life as 'a housekeeper, an upper servant'. Except that her lot was even worse, for she 'cannot quit his service, let him treat her how he will'. Marriage, then, was nothing less than a kind of slavery to which women had to martyr themselves for the benefit of society, and Mary could see no rational excuse for the imbalance: 'If all men are born free,' she demanded to know, 'how is it that all women are born slaves?'

With only the flattery of courtship to go by beforehand, most women were woefully unprepared for the realities of marriage. Even a lover who had professed himself the lady's slave became her all-powerful lord and master the moment the wedding was over. Could a marriage ever be truly happy under such conditions? The scarcity of candid contemporary testimonies on the state of private married lives makes the reality hard to gauge,[33] but when she looked about her, Mary evidently found what she expected: that unhappy unions outnumbered the happy. 'It is not to be wondered that so few succeed,' she wrote, 'we should rather be surprised to find so many do.' But what particularly galled her was that, if this 'blessed state' did turn out to be a disappointment, it was the woman who suffered most. A husband had 'a hundred ways of relieving himself' if his homelife became unpleasant: business, travel, drinking, gambling, whoring. But for most women, her 'business and entertainment are at home'; her consolations and distractions scant; she 'must be content and make her best on't' – in other words, she must put up and shut up.

This was the dire state of marriage in 1700 as Mary saw it play out time and again, and it offered women a spectacularly bad deal.[34] Again, she implored her female readers to aspire to something more – though admittedly other options were scarce. Even the beautiful, clever, wealthy Hortense Mancini had been 'taught to think marriage her only preferment, the sum total of her endeavours, the completion of all her hopes'. But an alternative was possible. Husbandless and fatherless, Mary herself was as free from male jurisdiction as any woman could be in 1700, and though it wasn't an easy option without cash, it beat a life of slavery hands down. For Mary, it came back to education – if a woman was 'taught to know the world, especially the true sentiments that men have of her and the traps they lay for her under so many gilded compliments', if she took the time to weigh up 'the good and evil of a married state', she could make a wise, informed choice.

Her case was persuasive, but there was an inherent conflict in Mary's views on authority and obedience in marriage that she could never fully resolve. As a High Church Tory Royalist, she believed (as many no longer did in the wake of the Civil War and Glorious Revolution) in the absolute God-given supremacy of the monarch and a subject's unquestioning obedience to that monarch; it was established order that kept the peace. Yet at the same time, she was working hard to undermine the authority of the husband, the state ruler of his family. This clash of ideologies prevented Mary from directly challenging the outrage of a husband's sovereignty – if a woman married she *was* duty-bound to obey him – but it was also the very reason *why* she was arguing that women ought to be immensely careful about whom they chose as their sovereign: 'She who elects a monarch for life, who gives him an authority she cannot recall however he misapply it … had need be very sure that she does not make a fool her head nor a vicious man her guide and pattern.' As marriage was a *voluntary* subjection, her flawed solution, rather than to smash up the patriarchal hierarchy, was to advise women not to marry at all.

To Mary, this seemed an easy enough choice to make, because, as her writings make clear, she didn't have much time for men – at least not in a romantic sense. Her own sexual indifference to them meant she struggled to imagine a heterosexual relationship founded on attraction, friendship and love. Instead, she could only view men as mercenary or sexual predators and had no advice for women who found themselves facing temptation.[35] Nonetheless her fears, for the most part, were valid. Like Margaret Cavendish before her, she worried that sexuality was dangerous for women. As Mary saw it, to remain single and chaste was the only reliable means of protecting your body, your reputation and your autonomy. It had worked for Elizabeth I,[36] but this was the bawdy new eighteenth century – enforced chastity was now looking old-fashioned and prudish rather than empowering.

Indeed, although the inequity of the married state was widely acknowledged, the virulence of Mary's stance was still baffling to some. Ballard claimed it was due to her own disappointment in a 'marriage contract with an eminent clergyman',[37] because, surely, a woman could only be so anti-marriage if she had been spurned herself? But given Mary's complete disinterestedness in men, this seems unlikely. More probable is that this was Ballard's attempt to soften the public's response to her uncompromising views, for, as he acknowledges, 'Some people think she has carried her arguments with regard to the birthrights and privileges of her sex too far.'[38]

As it happens, the evidence suggests that Mary *was* disappointed in love, but not by a man. The only clue to her romantic feelings comes, surprisingly, from her correspondence with John Norris. In their debate on divine versus earthly love, it becomes increasingly clear that the earthly love Mary is referring to is between women. Norris had convinced her that God was 'the only proper object of my love' – a principle she found easy enough to agree with, but putting it into practice was somewhat trickier. She couldn't prevent 'an agreeable movement in my soul towards her I love' and with it 'a displeasure and pain when I meet with unkindness'.[39] For all her self-denial, she found it 'a very difficult thing ... to love at all without something of desire' and she appealed to Norris for 'a remedy for this disorder', not out of shame, but because her religion demanded it. It didn't matter who the object of her desire was; it took her love away from God. With no other option, she tried to repackage her 'frequent disappointments' as some kind of divine lesson, and found other outlets for her passion – by championing women and investing in intense 'romantic friendships', which, to her, represented the purest form of love.[40]

There was enough demand for *Some Reflections Upon Marriage* for it to go through five editions in Mary Astell's lifetime, but inevitably she was labelled a seditious rebel for her attack on one of the principal foundations of Western civilisation. She was later forced to defend herself against accusations of blowing 'the trumpet of rebellion', stating that she was wholly opposed to sedition ('none can abhor it more').[41] Yet in saying so, she was admitting to the unresolved conflict at the heart of her character. All Mary's deepest-held views – on politics, religion and women – were in direct opposition on this issue of marriage. She couldn't abide political or religious dissent, but in this instance, dissent was necessary, because reason, which was always her guide, told her that such a dysfunctional dynamic had to be challenged. So out she went on a limb, a radical lone voice deploring the power imbalance between husbands and wives and the injustice it dealt out to women. Mary, and Mary alone, dared to argue that marriage might not be the greatest achievement of a woman's life and that it might not – should not – be her only option.

THE PAMPHLET WARS

With a taste, now, for polemic and pamphleteering, Mary Astell returned to it in 1704, but this time, perhaps due to the inertia she had met with on women's issues, she focused on her other passions: philosophy, politics and religion. Exhilarated and emboldened by the accession of a legitimate Stuart monarch to the throne in 1702 (and best of all a woman with Tory sympathies) in Queen Anne, Mary churned out five works in five years, which drew her right into the pulsing heart of contemporary public debate.

In 1704 alone she wrote three pamphlets in quick succession on the controversial topic of how to deal with Protestant dissenters, all of them arguing with style and restraint the High Tory line against Nonconformists, and all of them offering impressive take-downs of essays or sermons by eminent men.[42] In 1705 she followed these with a hefty 400-page defence of her faith, *The Christian Religion, as Profess'd by a Daughter of the Church of England*, in which she refuted the materialist ideas of John Locke and delved into the philosophical and theological foundations of her beliefs. Then in 1709 came her final work, *Bart'lemy Fair: Or, an Inquiry after Wit*, which took on an essay by the 3rd Earl of Shaftesbury, on the thorny subject of how to deal with religious fanatics.[43]

To most modern readers, these later works, heavy with now-antiquated political, philosophical and theological doctrine, are hard-going and lack the vital relevance of her fiercely argued feminist polemics, which can still hold the reader in thrall. Yet they, too, were ground-breaking in their way. Mary was an ordinary gentlewoman, entering the political fray on equal terms with famous intellectual men, and she could not only hold her own but rhetorically trounce any of her male counterparts. Women had written politically charged poems and plays before, but none had argued a party position in detail and engaged in pamphlet wars like this.[44] Mary was chalking out a new role for women in political public life. And although her pamphlets drew indignant responses from the opposition, her talents were recognised with (not always gracious) astonishment by her male peers,[45] who saw in her an eloquent controversialist whose arrows always hit the mark.

Mary's fame had now peaked. Her publisher had been consistently bringing out new editions of her books, and her skill and flair for debate had earned her a prominent place in society as a rare female polemicist. But it wasn't to last. Her ideas on women may have been astoundingly progressive, but her political and religious views were starting to look painfully out of date as the Whig supremacy and a new wave of liber-alism, materialism, scepticism and religious toleration took hold of the century.[46] By clinging to the old feudal system of absolute monarchy and class hierarchy and rejecting the emerging culture as trivial, frivolous and dangerous, she became a foot soldier fighting a cavalry charge.

Before long, she was attracting the attention of the vanguard of satirists who were fast becoming the talk of London's coffee-houses, and tellingly it was her writings on women that they targeted. No sooner had *Bart'lemy Fair* appeared in 1709 than Mary was lampooned twice in three months in Joseph Addison and Richard Steele's new society magazine *The Tatler*, as 'Madonella' – a spinster who had proposed to 'erect a nunnery' and was perpetually distracted by her lofty thoughts. She had been mocked on stage, too, in Susanna Centlivre's 1705 play *The Bassett Table*, as the 'little She-Philosopher' Valeria who is teased for founding a women-only college. Elizabeth Elstob received similar treatment, and the point was clear: learned women were a joke, a common caricature, peculiar old maids remote from the real world. It was a stock image that would persist well into the nineteenth century.

The backlash had begun and by 1710 events were conspiring to bring an end to Mary Astell's public life. Her ideas were now being mocked, her last two works had not sold well and, thanks to a developing cataract, writing was becoming arduous. The time felt right to step down from the rostrum. And besides, she now had a new and exciting project to occupy her. One that would allow her to pursue her longest and most passionately held dream.

A SOCIETY OF WOMEN

The education of women had always been Mary's primary concern. It was the gateway to a new kind of freedom, so when the opportunity arose in 1709 to finally put her ideas into some form of action, she grabbed it. Putting her public writing life behind her, Mary – now in her forties – decided to open a charity school for the daughters of outpensioners of the Royal Hospital in Chelsea, and she threw herself wholeheartedly into establishing and running it.

The school was part of a wider initiative of social reform during the early eighteenth century to introduce charity schools across Great Britain. The Society for the Propagation of Christian Knowledge (SPCK), established in 1698, saw Christian education as a means to raise the parish poor out of a life of indigence, and set about founding privately funded charity schools to teach children basic literacy and the Christian values of duty, obedience, patience and modesty to prepare them for humble but decent employment.[47]

Mary's first tasks were to secure rooms to rent in the Royal Hospital itself, to raise the initial funds and attract annual subscribers from middle- or upper-class patrons with a mind for philanthropy. Next, she had to set the curriculum and buy the necessary supplies. Unlike her proposed college, the school would cater for the poor, teaching 30 of Chelsea's disadvantaged girls the modest accomplishments of reading, writing, knitting, basic needlework and the tenets of Christian doctrine. It wasn't quite the towering intellectual retreat Mary had envisaged, cultivating an army of fiercely learned and independent 'she-philosophers', but it was a start, and it fulfilled her long-held need to do something practical to advance women's education. Even this modest endeavour would change the lives and prospects not just of its female pupils, but of its female staff, who would benefit from the employment opportunity – a schoolmistress could make up to £25 a year (a schoolmaster, of course, could expect more like £30), and might be provided with a rent-free house to live in as well. For single women with a basic education but nothing to live on, it was a respectable solution for independent living.

Indeed, it was the predominance of women in this enterprise that made it so unique. As with her college, men would play no part in Mary's charity school – instead, she took the unprecedented step in her report to the SPCK of directing that the school should be 'govern'd by seven trustees chosen out of the ladies & other gentlewomen who are subscribers; & is always to be under the direction of women'. And she had some magnificent women at her disposal. Throughout her years at the forefront of Chelsea's literary public life, Mary had accrued a remarkable circle of friends – a community of wealthy, pious, scholarly women whose magnanimity made the charity school possible. It was 'founded by a Lady of great quality', she told the SPCK, referring to her friend Lady Elizabeth Hastings, whose inaugural subscription of 5 guineas had led other ladies to follow her example, helping Mary raise the initial sum of £50 and open the school on 6 June 1709. Together, this society of women planned, subsidised, managed and sustained the school, contributing money and organising fundraising events. A similar trend for female autonomy occurred throughout the charity-school movement and constituted a kind of quiet revolution. For the first time, gentlewomen were mobilised to work collectively to a common purpose, finding a practical use for their wealth, time and energy.

Lady Elizabeth Hastings was just one of several aristocratic women in Mary's impressive group of friends, which now included Lady Anne Coventry, Lady Catherine Jones and Lady Mary Wortley Montagu. These women mostly shared Mary's High Church, Tory, Jacobite leanings, but more importantly they believed in her idealistic vision for piety, philanthropy and women's education. They had read her writings as young girls and the effect had been profound. Empowered by her words and her example, they had chosen to live independently, remaining single or widowed and in control of their wealth, swapping flashy court life for one of study, devotion and charity. Mary's serious proposal for a women's college had answered a deep yearning for purpose in each of their hearts, and although that great institution had never materialised, collectively these women got as close as they could to Mary's utopian vision. They became active patrons, supporting numerous girls' schools as well as a network of friends, servants, widows and spinsters – including Mary herself. And in doing so, they wielded more power to change lives than most women of the age.

Here was a living example of a profound spiritual and emotional sisterhood, committed to supporting one another in a society that was hostile to their way of life. Class and wealth were no obstacles to their friendship; Mary's extraordinary talents had become a conduit for social mobility, elevating her into the highest strata of society – an almost impossible feat for a single woman. These grand ladies admired her eloquence, her erudition and her strong opinions, and that was enough – she was the 'good and great Mrs Astell', 'worthy Mrs Astell', the 'celebrated and ingenious Mrs Astell'.[48] Their importance in her life, and she in theirs, was incalculable: she gave them ideas, encouragement and aspirations; they gave her financial stability and the respectability that as a poor, single, brazen woman writer she so badly needed. With her entire family now dead, it's arguable whether Mary could have survived her later years without them.

With a little help from her friends, then, Mary's life in middle age was full and rewarding. By 1712 she was financially secure enough to move from rented rooms into her own small house on Paradise Row (now Royal Hospital Road), overlooking the Chelsea Physic Garden. It's possible she was hired as a schoolmistress at the Chelsea School and gifted the house with the job. If so, she might have been earning a salary of £25 a year, but this was supplemented by regular contributions from her wealthy friends – from Lady Elizabeth alone she received £20 or £30 a year.[49]

By her early fifties, despite bouts of fevers, aches and pains so bad she expected and even longed for death, Mary had set up in new lodgings in New Bond Street (now Cale Street)[50] and was enjoying a busy lifestyle; she kept abreast of current affairs and scientific discoveries, soaked up the latest books and pamphlets, attended teas, dinners and card parties, wrote letters and of course made plenty of time for her devotions, including her habit of walking in all weathers from Chelsea to St Martin-in-the-Fields every Sunday to hear her favourite preacher. In 1720, imagining what a little extra cash might do for herself and her school, she succumbed against her better judgement to the capitalist impulse for speculation that was sweeping the nation thanks to the South Sea Company stock market boom.[51] But like so many of Mary's dreams, it all came to nothing. The South Sea Company Bubble burst before the end of August that year and Mary lost her small investment.

In 1724 she moved again, this time to Manor Street, possibly because, as a woman with Jacobite sympathies in the reign of the Hanoverian George I, she was now being pestered as a suspected conspirator by First Lord of the Treasury Robert Walpole's government cronies. They wouldn't even allow her 'to go to the chapel quietly', she complained.[52] Mary shrugged off the annoyance and stayed out of trouble, but her friends were concerned.[53] Lady Catherine Jones had for some time been trying to convince her to move in with her at Jew's Row where she could enjoy the care, protection and companionship of a dear friend, and in 1726, at the age of 60, Mary accepted the offer. Relieved at long last of the financial burden of supporting herself, she could breathe easy in her declining years, though perhaps with some sadness. The High Church Tory era in which she had played such an active part was over. The Stuart dynasty was failing to wrest back its throne from the Hanoverians. And to top it all, her publisher's business was in trouble and her books were no longer selling. The old world Mary loved was disappearing, and there seemed to be no place for her in the new Georgian Britain that was replacing it.

THE RECLAIMING OF THE SHREW

Mary's newfound life of ease was not to last long. Her end was imminent, and when it came, it was wretched. She had spent much of her life contemplating death, had sometimes even been impatient for it, but she must have hoped for a kinder meeting with her God than the one she received.

It began one day, probably when she was in her early sixties, when she discovered a lump in her breast. Her instinct was for secrecy; even as the lump grew painful and ulcerated, she tried to manage it as best she could herself. Doctors were expensive and specialists so hard to come by that dubious home remedies, even for cancer, were the usual recourse.[54] But in time, her physical state became intolerable and the horror of what she saw when she removed her dressings made it clear that 'there was an absolute necessity for [the breast] being cut off'. She sought out the Reverend Mr Johnson, a renowned Scottish surgeon, and entreated him 'to take it off in the most private manner imaginable' – being so anxious on this point that she 'would hardly allow him to have persons whom necessity required to be at the operation'.[55] Fixated on the sublime in the hope that it might deliver her from her fleshly torment, Mary bore the horror of the mastectomy with near-superhuman courage: 'She seemed so regardless of the sufferings or pain she was to undergo, that she refused to have her hands held, and … went thro' the operation without the least struggling or resistance; or even so much as giving a groan or a sigh.'[56]

Neither she nor Dr Johnson could know that by now her cancer was so advanced as to make the operation futile. She survived the surgeon's knife and the threat of infection afterwards, only to die a short while later, supposedly because the ordeal had 'much impaired her constitution'.[57]

As it became obvious that she was finally about to meet Him (though if ever there was a believer who might pray that God were a woman, it was surely Mary Astell), her morbid streak was given free rein. She welcomed death by summoning its physical manifestations to her, ordering 'her coffin and shrowd to be made and brought to her bed-side; and there to remain in her view, as a constant memento to her of her approaching fate, and that her mind might not deviate or stray one moment from God'.[58] Strange behaviour, perhaps, even in one as devout as Mary, but given all she had endured, one can hardly blame her for wishing to hasten the end.

When her death finally came it had the aura of an apotheosis, a martyr being released from their worldly sufferings into the soothing arms of God. The 'great and good Mrs Astell' was, according to Lady Elizabeth, 'five days actually a-dying', and in those last few days she wanted only to be alone with Him; she 'earnestly desired that no company might be permitted to come to her ... purely because she would not be disturbed in the last moments of her divine contemplation'. Her spiritual life was reaching its climax, and even her closest friends could not share in it. Lady Catherine was the last to see her, two days before her death, and she reported to Lady Elizabeth that Mary 'then begged to see no more of her old acquaintance and friends, having done with the world, and made her peace with God; and what she had then to do was to bear her pains with patience, cheerfulness, and entire resignation to the Divine will.'[59] They expected nothing less from their extraordinary friend.

Not two months had passed since the operation when she died on 9 May 1731, at the age of 65. She was buried in Chelsea on 14 May, with just a handful of mourners at her graveside. A modest, ascetic farewell for a modest, ascetic woman, and one that gives no sign of the magnitude of her achievements.

By the time of her death Mary Astell had been out of the public eye for over 20 years, and the world was quick to forget her. Her words couldn't reach the illiterate masses, and the feminist spark she had ignited in a select few had fizzled out by 1710, even before her death, with no tangible progress made and no immediate successor to show for it.[60] Her own books went out of print after the last run in 1730 and the history books ignored her, as she knew they would.[61] By 1736, when Ballard began researching her for his book, her name was virtually unknown.

And yet, tucked away in quiet corners, her influence was there, fiercely upheld by the women she had known and inspired. They pressed her books into friends' hands and told stories of her to one another, carrying inside them the glowing gem of self-worth that she had helped them find. The value of her assertion of a woman's right to be an independent thinking being with a legitimate public voice can't be measured, but it's there in the feminist arguments and bold lives of Lady Mary Wortley Montagu and Sarah Chapone, in the poems of Lady Mary Chudleigh and the Countess of Winchilsea, in the scholarship and educational zeal of Elizabeth Elstob, and in the creation of the Blue Stockings Society by the next generation.[62] It's even been argued that she snuck into the novels of Daniel Defoe and Samuel Richardson (both known to have read and admired her works) as a model for our earliest independent-minded fictional heroines.[63]

These murmurs of admiration were never enough to fend off her obscurity, though, which persists to this day. Overshadowed by more bohemian, more radical, more romantic characters like Mary Wollstonecraft, whose *A Vindication of the Rights of Woman* would be published almost 100 years after *A Serious Proposal*, in 1792, her name rarely comes up in mainstream discussion of early feminists. In the twentieth century, feminist scholars gave her works and life the detailed analysis they deserve, but her place in the public consciousness remains stubbornly non-existent.

And perhaps it's easy to see why. Her intense religiosity, entrenched conservative views and heavy philosophical bent are out of step with the twenty-first century, even offputting. After decades of instability that had overturned all that seemed permanent, when many were questioning all forms of authority, most of Mary's political beliefs focused on maintaining the hierarchies and institutions of the past. On the face of it, she hardly seems a likely candidate to spearhead a pioneering liberal movement. Too often she's been remembered as a prototype Mary Bennett, a staid, lonely old maid boring everyone with her sermonising, while her lighter, wicked side has gone largely uncredited. We know, for instance, that she kept a pet parrot, and that an anecdote from Elstob about its impish behaviour had Ballard doubled up in stitches, but, fearing this too frothy a detail for his high-minded subject, he omitted it from his biography.[64] With no surviving portraits of Mary, we have no idea what she looked like, only that she was reputed to be 'ill-favored and forbidding',[65] though others remembered her as hugely entertaining company.

Such reductions ignore the complexity and charisma of the real woman. Mary was an inconvenient mass of contradictions. A reluctant rebel, a radical conservative, an old-fashioned progressive, a Divine Rights monarchist who questioned authority, a High Churchwoman governed by rationality, a fair intolerant, a conformist dissenter, a cheerful ascetic, a pious wit – she was both perfect for, and entirely unsuited to, the Age of Enlightenment, and few since have known what to make of such a puzzling woman.

Mary Astell broke the mould for women, not ostentatiously but subtly. She confidently assumed her equal place with men in the public arena and commandeered their scholarly rhetoric; she spoke out in powerful, game-changing tracts that would outright reject the orthodoxy of male supremacy and form the foundation of a centuries-long movement that would change women's lives; and she sketched out a new template for an independent woman who could live without the protection or jurisdiction of men, earn her own money and win the admiration of her peers.

She has been called the first English feminist by scholars, not because she was the first to write on gender inequality or a woman's right to an education – she wasn't – but because she was the first English writer to assume the rational capabilities of women, the first to recognise that they needed safe, supportive institutions where they could develop those capabilities and, in the true spirit of the Enlightenment, the first to distil all that had gone before her into a sustained, coherent argument, powered by reason and philosophical principles. Crucially, she strove to improve the lot of all women, urging them to take pride and joy in their own intelligence and to proclaim, in a common cause, their right to an independence of mind and body – safe in the knowledge that the title of 'Old Maid' was one that 'none but fools will reproach her with nor any wise woman be afraid of'.[66] She was a woman who didn't seek fame, and mostly hasn't found it, but as a pioneering thinker, exemplary polemicist and tireless champion of women, her name should be on every feminist's lips.

Charlotte Charke

EN CAVALIER

On a summer's morning in Twickenham, 1717, a four-year-old girl patters down the stairs of her father's country house in search of a new identity. First, she sneaks into the servants' hall, where she carefully pins up her dimity coat in imitation of a pair of breeches. Next, using a broom handle, she retrieves her brother's waistcoat from its hook and buttons it up around her. Last, she straps her father's sword around her middle and dons his periwig and hat. Then she takes a moment to admire her work. The elaborate powdered curls engulf her tiny frame, the silver sword scrapes noisily along the floor and the laced beaver hat weighs heavily on her head – but Miss Charlotte is delighted with what she has created. She is the perfect image of her papa.

With great pomp and some difficulty, Miss Charlotte embarks on a solemn procession outside to find her audience. Only once she's in the garden does she remember that she is still wearing her girls' shoes, and they are ruining the effect, so she scrambles into a nearby ditch to hide them. There, she marches proudly up and down, bowing to all who pass and soon drawing the crowd she craves. Taking their giggles for approval, she walks herself 'into a fever in the happy thought of being taken for a squire', but this show cannot go on. Her parents are called to witness the spectacle, and that is the end

'I have, through the whole course of my life, acted
in contradiction to all points of regularity.'

CHARLOTTE CHARKE (1713–1760),
ACTOR, THEATRE MANAGER, WRITER AND CROSS-DRESSER

of Miss Charlotte's performance. Red-faced and scowling, the little squire is borne off home on the footman's shoulders and 'forced' back into her petticoats.

～✻～

The memory of this childhood pantomime stayed with Charlotte Charke all her life, not just because it made her smile but because it marked several prescient firsts in her life that together would form the foundation stones of her character: her first foray into acting, her first impersonation of her father and her first dalliance with cross-dressing. All of which she would weave into her notorious and fantastical career.

In March 1755, when Charlotte was 42, a series of adverts appeared in the *Public Advertiser* for her autobiography, to be published in instalments, which promised to chronicle the many misadventures of that extraordinary career. *A Narrative of the Life of Mrs Charlotte Charke* – actress, cross-dresser, vagabond and daughter of the famous actor, dramatist and Poet Laureate Colley Cibber – promised all the ingredients of a picaresque novel: 'mad pranks', 'theatrical anecdotes', a disastrous marriage, 'adventures in men's clothes' and 'surprising vicissitudes of fortune', with turns as a gentleman's valet, a strolling player and a pastry cook. It would be both tragedy and comedy, and Charlotte would play every role: hero, heroine, fool and penitent.

It's clear from the first that in this narrative we're in the company of a woman who doesn't take herself too seriously. Her opening act is to dedicate the work not to some eminent patron, but to herself – 'a *nonpareil* of the age', who cannot 'be matched in oddity of fame'. Addressing herself with a smirk, in the most mock-reverent terms, she praises the 'thoughtless ease' with which she has passed through her madcap life, and admires the many 'magnificent airy castles' she has built in her mind's eye.[1] There will be no vanity, no papering over her faults 'to escape a laugh', she assures her readers; all will be exposed for their amusement. This self-confessed sinner has decided, for the sheer novelty of it, to try on reform for size.

The prevailing good mood was deliberate, for with this book Charlotte wanted, above all, to entertain and to make money. As with all life writing, inevitably there is partiality, as well as omissions and exaggerations for comic and dramatic effect, but for all that, Mrs Charke is an eager, chatty and surprisingly reliable guide. Fully aware of how incredible some of her anecdotes seem, she is 'ready to make oath of the truth of every circumstance', claiming that she could refer any doubters to 'hundreds now living' who have witnessed her antics first-hand. And sure enough, despite her blasé attitude to dates, modern scholars have found little cause to doubt her version of events.[2]

In publishing her autobiography, however, Charlotte knew she was taking a risk. In mid-eighteenth-century Britain, women writers remained a rarity, and when they did brave publication, they were often still ridiculed and abused for exposing themselves and trespassing on male ground. Women's autobiography – pioneered by Margaret Cavendish in the previous century (see Chapter 2) – was particularly untrodden terrain; the number written by women before Charlotte came along can be counted on one hand, and secular ones were especially rare. Charlotte's was the first ever written by a British actress, and as it was 'the product of a female pen', she feared for 'the terrible hazard it must run in venturing into the world'.

All the same, she must have been quietly confident of capturing the public's interest. Attitudes to female cross-dressing had liberalised since Mary Frith's day (see Chapter 1), following the admission of women to the stage at Charles II's Restoration. As a practice it still held dangers – women were pilloried and imprisoned for offences related to transvestism during Charlotte's lifetime – but England had always been more lenient towards cross-dressers than other European countries, and it was willing to celebrate them when they met the right criteria. By 1755, it was almost bordering on an entertainment craze. In 1750, the famous Hannah Snell had thrilled London audiences with her tale of dare-devil cross-dressing as a soldier and marine (see Chapter 5), and actresses who made a career out of wearing breeches on stage, as Charlotte did, were the toast and tittle-tattle of the town – admired, lusted after and disapproved of in equal measure. In the entertainment world, at least, the more flamboyant the character, the more acceptable it seemed to be.

But Charlotte would push this newfound acceptance to its absolute limits, and the real world wasn't always so forgiving. By the time she had decided to give an account of her 'unaccountable life', she had been on a downward spiral from riches to rags for years. Her famous father had long since disowned her, and she readily admitted that publishing her story was partly an attempt to win back his favour. To manage this, however, she would have to walk a literary tightrope, flaunting her sensational singularity to attract an audience and earn a crust (rendering it as comic and endearing as possible in the process), while at the same time reassuring everyone – particularly her father – that she was a reformed character. She could not afford to fail; Charlotte Charke was writing for her very survival.

AN IMPERTINENT INTRUDER

In her own words, Charlotte was 'not only an unexpected, but an unwelcome guest' in the Cibber household when she arrived on 13 January 1713. The last of a dozen children (seven of whom died in infancy), this 'impertinent intruder' turned up after a six-year hiatus in a marathon of childbearing for her 45-year-old, asthma-exhausted mother. Despite their shock at this latecomer, however, Charlotte's parents adored and indulged her.

She had been born into a family of celebrities. Her father, Colley Cibber, was a playwright, a joint manager of Covent Garden's Drury Lane Theatre and one of London's most renowned comic actors, whose name had become synonymous with mannered dandyish roles, particularly that of Lord Foppington in his own play *The Careless Husband*. Charlotte's mother, Katherine Shore, hailed from the theatre world, too, as an actress and singer; she had once been taught by Henry Purcell and was said to have had one of the finest voices of her day. Her stage career had begun soon after she married Colley in 1693, though it didn't last long – by 1699 motherhood was her sole occupation.

There were advantages and disadvantages to being a Cibber – a liberal, well-heeled upbringing flitting between the family's London home near Trafalgar Square and their country residence at Twickenham was countered by the fact that Colley was despised by many. In 1730 he was made Poet Laureate by King George II – a role he held for 27 years and that, perversely, didn't then require much prowess as a poet. This was fortunate, as Colley didn't possess any; his skills lay in acting and playwriting, leading many to regard his appointment as a political reward for his loyalty to the Whig party and its leader, Robert Walpole. Colley's foppish affectations and dud verses became the frequent butt of jokes by the country's most caustic satirists and poets, including Henry Fielding, Jonathan Swift, John Dennis and, most famously, Alexander Pope in his 1743 version of *The Dunciad*, where Colley made an unflattering appearance as the King of the Dunces. Colley was careful to cultivate a veneer of nonchalance, off which these slights seemed to glance, though inside he was a seething cauldron of resentment.

His unedifying private life lost him even more friends – he was arrested in 1697 for sexually assaulting an actress, and again in 1712 for fathering an illegitimate child. His habitual gambling, meanwhile, led his detractors to publicly accuse him of failing to provide for his family. Whether these accusations were justified or not, it all jarred distastefully with the morally virtuous characters of his plays, earning him a reputation as a hypocrite, too.[3] Swayed by his enemies, history has not remembered Colley Cibber fondly, and, despite her continual defence of him, Charlotte's story would only reinforce this negative image. There was no denying, however, that she, like her elder brother Theophilus (also an actor and a notoriously dissolute character), was a chip off the old block. As a woman, Charlotte could never get away with the kind of libertinism that her male relatives indulged in, but she had nonetheless inherited the same reckless impatience, spend-thrift ways and innate theatricality. It was in evidence early on in that 'small specimen of my former madness'– her proud performance as a country squire when she was four. Even then, she recalls happily, she had 'a passionate fondness for a periwig'.

A comic actress had been born, but just as importantly, a cross-dresser had been born. On that occasion the 'drollery' of her figure, as well as her parents' soft spot for her, had protected her from any serious repercussions, and perhaps she thought they would always find her antics so adorable, but as time went on and her escapades became more elaborate, their tolerance began to wane. The following year, while the Cibbers were summering near Hampton Court, Charlotte took it into her head to play the victorious general and roped a troop of young locals into commandeering a donkey foal for the purpose. Using a garter as a makeshift bridle, attended by her ragamuffin gang and heralded by the 'huzzas' of her retinue, the foal's braying mother and 'a lad who scraped upon a twelve-penny fiddle',

Charlotte rode 'triumphantly' into town on her wobbly 'infantical Rosinante', fancying herself every inch the chivalric hero. But another tragic downfall was imminent. When her father spied her out of his window, he unceremoniously deflated her heroics, exclaiming, 'Gad demme! An ass upon an ass!' The 'surprise, pleasure, pain, and shame' that Charlotte saw in Colley's face that day left a stark impression on her. Her mother's response was less nuanced. She tied her daughter to a table leg and beat her with the birch.

Charlotte assures us that there were many more such escapades in her childhood, enough to fill a folio several times over – with her father often away and her mother frequently laid low with illness, she enjoyed an almost free rein. By regaling us with just a handful of these tales, she adequately proves her point: that she was a natural-born actress. From her earliest years, at every opportunity, life was a stage, and in all her miniature dramas the role she instinctively cast herself in was that of the male hero – the squire or the general, never the princess or the damsel. The infant Charlotte had already assessed the characters around her and decided that she wanted the power and agency of men, not the caged subjection of women, so without exception it was her father, not her mother, whom she chose to imitate. Already she was transcending the behavioural expectations of her gender, and already she was being punished for it, but she had started as she meant to go on.

DOCTOR CHARLOTTE

Charlotte's education was a 'genteel' and a 'liberal' one, 'such indeed as might have been sufficient for a son instead of a daughter'. This was a rare privilege for a Georgian girl, and one Charlotte heartily embraced. Aged eight she was sent to a school in Park Street, Westminster, and was an enthusiastic student, learning Latin, Italian and geography. Indeed, she applied herself with such intensity, she says, that it left her 'almost distracted' – a riff on the common misconception that women, with their soft, feeble brains, could be driven mad by too much study. To Charlotte's delight, she was fast becoming everything society feared and abhorred: a girl well versed in subjects it wasn't 'altogether necessary for a female' to know, with a natural antipathy to all things domestic. Her smattering of traditional feminine accomplishments included singing, dancing and music, but she handled a needle 'with the same clumsy awkwardness a monkey does a kitten'. Though too impatient to become a great scholar, she'd had a taste of the diverse world that was open to men but closed to women, and felt instinctively that it was where she belonged. This 'different turn of mind' would play a decisive role in her future.

After just two years of schooling, in the spring of 1723, Charlotte left Park Street to be home-tutored until the following winter, when she went to join her mother at the Cibbers' leased country house in Hillingdon, near Uxbridge, where Katherine had retreated for the sake of her asthma. Colley remained in London to be close to both Drury Lane and the social life he adored, while the rest of the couple's surviving children, all in their twenties, were marrying and settling down. This left Charlotte, now 11, restless, bored and largely unsupervised. To amuse herself, she turned first to guns. Frosty winter mornings were spent out on the common, where she became so excellent a shot that she trudged home with her 'feathered spoil' day after day and saw herself 'like the person described in Farquhar's *The Recruiting Officer*: capable of destroying all the venison and wild fowl about the country'.[4] Her mother made no move to curb this interest, until, that is, one of their strait-laced old neighbours protested that

Charlotte's behaviour was 'inconsistent with the character of a young gentlewoman' – at which, to Charlotte's great annoyance, her gun was promptly taken away.

People were beginning to notice that Charlotte was not quite what a young lady ought to be: there was no modesty, no quiet docility in her; instead, she was growing into a determined nonconformist, with alarmingly mannish inclinations. Over time, she found herself increasingly restricted, reined in and disapproved of, and when she then fell ill of a fever, her mother thought she'd found an efficient solution to both problems. She sent her daughter off to a relation in Thorley, Hertfordshire – a doctor named Hales – partly to aid her recovery, but also, says Charlotte, 'with the hopes of my being made a good housewife'. Surrounded by the doctor's dutiful wife and daughters, Charlotte had 'the nicest examples of housewifery perfections daily before me', but these paradigms revolted rather than inspired her. Proud of her scholarship and convinced she was destined for greater things than 'ornamenting a well-disposed and elegant table', Charlotte felt only contempt for these useless, docile creatures and heartily 'pitied their misfortunes'. Already it was plain to her that theirs was a life she could never tolerate for herself.

Of all the templates around her, it was Doctor Hales who interested Charlotte and he she chose to emulate. Fascinated by his work and spying another role to add to her dramatis personae, Charlotte began to zealously study physic – so much so that the doctor was soon entrusting her with odd jobs. But Charlotte was already several steps ahead; 'fancying myself a physician', she spent two years making a careful study of Hales and soon 'affected the solemnity and gravity which I had observed in the good doctor'. When Mrs Hales died in 1726 and Charlotte was sent home, she was ready, armed with her character notes, to debut her next role: Doctor Charlotte.

This charade was pulled off with worrying ease. Doctor Charlotte's first task was to persuade her sickly mother, who likely had no resistance left, to allow her to set up a drug dispensary in a small closet of the house: this was easily done. The teenage Charlotte then began to receive all the old ladies of the parish whenever they felt indisposed. She swotted up on the jargon (learning enough Latin words to 'confound their senses'), adopted the 'significancy of countenance' she had learned from Doctor Hales, and soon both men and women had 'a high opinion of my skill in the medicinal science' and were seeking her advice. In Charlotte's defence, she made a concerted effort to treat them efficaciously, consulting trusted medical manuals such as William Salmon's *Practical Physick* (1692) and Nicholas Culpeper's *Complete Herbal* (1653) to identify their ailments, and did so for free. But when her father stopped her credit with the apothecary and her supply of drugs dried up, she resorted to boiling up snails from the garden and prescribing those, instead. Her patients were none the wiser – delighted with their free healthcare, they were convinced they had never felt better, and their innocent gullibility tickled Charlotte so much that she was brought almost to the point of corpsing. As it turned out, Doctor Charlotte's remedies were mercifully ineffectual: for 'though, perhaps, I did no actual good, I never had the least misfortune happen to any of the unthinking credulous souls who relied on me for the restoration of their healths'.

This fad for physic soon exhausted itself, however, and Charlotte, 'as changeable as Proteus', decided that her next role would be that of a gardener – a much safer line of work. Always a keen mimic, she began her study of the family's gardener and soon had his mannerisms mastered, swaggering around with a bacon sandwich in one hand, pruning knife in the other, throwing out comments on seeds and plants, and occasionally shrugging her shoulders, scratching her head and demanding a beer. When the real gardener was sacked for being drunk and abusive, his understudy was ready. Charlotte had the full run of the garden and stables, chased off other prospective candidates for the job and was so caught up in her new role that she 'was entirely lost in a forgetfulness of my real self', making this her most method performance yet. Still half in character, 'with a significant wink and a nod', she rested on her spade one day and cheekily asked her mother 'whether she imagined any of the rest of her children would have done as much at my age'. Charlotte knew she was a kind of prodigy, though perhaps not quite the kind her parents might have wished for.

With her mother now paranoid that their dismissed gardener might rob or murder them in revenge, Charlotte spied an unmissable opportunity to step up and play the squire once more.[5] Having gathered all the valuable plate in the house by her bedside and armed herself with a trusty carbine, a blunderbuss, a musketoon and two brace of pistols, she hunkered down and waited for the attack. It never materialised but, not to be deprived of glory, Charlotte fired out of the window at the sound of a barking dog instead, which was enough to convince her panic-stricken mother that she had successfully fended off an intruder. Miss Charlotte was pleased with her career thus far: she had graduated from scholar to physician to workman to valiant hero – her diverse training for the stage was complete.

THE PROVOKED WIFE AND THE CARELESS HUSBAND

By age 17, before she had ever stood upon a stage, Charlotte Cibber had amassed an impressive array of acting credits and earned rave reviews from her credulous audiences. Her preference for male roles had continued unabated, but her next one would be uncharacteristically conventional, as she capped this wildly industrious adolescence with an ill-advised teenage wedding. Richard Charke was a talented musician, singer and composer who had been poached from a rival company by Drury Lane in 1729 to appear in its summer season. Charming, handsome, loved by the press and fought over by theatre managers, it's no surprise that when Charlotte met him and received a marked degree of attention, her head was turned. Believing herself in love, for the first time in her life she prepared to play the role that society expected of her. She even embraced it, thinking it 'a fine thing to be married'.

Looking back with the wisdom of maturity, it was obvious to Charlotte that Richard was merely a flatterer, and she a fool to believe his declarations of love. In reality, she realised, he had viewed her as little more than a solution to his 'desperate' cash-flow problems, thinking it 'no bad scheme to endeavour at being Mr Cibber's son-in-law', and she chided herself that it was for this worthless wretch that she had risked losing her father's affection.

Not that Colley opposed the marriage directly. Richard was not an advantageous match, but 'out of pure pity' at Charlotte's lovelorn state, her father gave his consent, and within six months, on 4 February 1730, the young couple were married at St Martin-in-the-Fields. Why Colley acquiesced so readily to this inauspicious union is a puzzle. Perhaps he genuinely believed the marriage would work; perhaps he was relieved that his odd, wilful daughter was finally conforming to conventional femininity; or perhaps it was just indifferent parenting. Charlotte appears to have believed the latter, for though at 17 she considered her father's consent 'the greatest favour he ever conferred on me', at 42 she obliquely reproaches him for not exercising a little more judicious parental tyranny, given that the bride and groom were 'both so young and indiscreet we ought rather to have been sent to school than to church'.[6] In hindsight, she felt certain 'that absence, and an easy life, would soon have got the better of the violence of my fondness' – for she knew by then that separating the young lovers would have saved her a good deal of trouble.

Separation would come soon enough, but first came the moment that Charlotte had really been waiting for her whole life: her first appearance on the stage. Colley had no objections to her following in his and his wife's footsteps – Theophilus and another daughter, Anne, had already established their stage careers – but most fathers in eighteenth-century Britain wouldn't have been so blasé at the prospect. Acting was a lowly, unstable profession for men, but for women it was downright disreputable. Excluded from performing in the theatre altogether until the Restoration of Charles II in 1660, actresses in Charlotte's day still carried the stain of immorality. To expose themselves publicly for money and the gratification of others suggested brazenness, immodesty and sexual availability, and these associations ran deep. Covent Garden was home to both London's theatres and its brothels, and the connection was not lost on the public imagination. Many celebrated actresses became high-profile mistresses, from Nell Gwyn to Mary Robinson, and if they fell on hard times, prostitution was considered an obvious recourse. Reputations depended on being able to successfully walk the knife-edge between career-defining allure and career-destroying scandal – a high-wire act that exemplified the sexual double standard, which saw actresses leered at and adored by men, but denounced as whores by them too. Seventy years after being allowed on the stage, these women were still not respected enough to be paid the same as their male counterparts or judged by the same criteria.[7]

But trouble-making, attention-seeking Charlotte was not likely to be deterred by such attitudes (in fact, she would make a career of cannily toying with them). There could never be any doubt that she was destined for the stage, and the opportunity arose not long after her wedding. Knowing that Charlotte was due to make her stage debut the following season, the actress Sarah Thurmond requested that Mrs Charke appear as the French maid Mademoiselle in her benefit performance of *The Provok'd Wife*, Sir John Vanbrugh's long-standing hit comedy about a bad marriage, at Drury Lane on 8 April 1730.[8] It was a decent role for a debut, providing some of the funniest lines in the play, and Charlotte remembered it fondly, observing wryly that she was so puffed up with pride that she experienced no first-night nerves – something she later recognised as bravado rather than prodigious talent. The prospect of appearing on the playbill gave her particular pleasure, though she was miffed to find that she wouldn't actually be named. To drum up intrigue, she appeared only as 'a young gentlewoman, who had never appear'd on any stage before', but anonymity was not to Charlotte's taste; she told everyone who would listen that *she* was the young gentlewoman in question.

Charlotte still had much to learn of her craft, but that first performance was met with the laughter and applause she craved, and a few weeks later she was able to reprise the role in another benefit. This time Mrs Charke was fully credited. Charlotte was on her way, but so was an interruption: just two months after her wedding, she found that she was pregnant, which might have been an occasion for joy had not the cracks already started to appear in her marriage.

The initial attraction between Charlotte and Richard had quickly dissipated under the strains of everyday life. Money was a constant worry; Charlotte noted with annoyance that although her father was 'greatly inclined to be his friend', Richard proved hopeless at making the most of these opportunities. Imprudent with cash herself,

Charlotte probably didn't help the couple's financial situation, but there was no doubt who was in the wrong when she learned that Richard was also fonder of taverns, gambling dens and 'a plurality of common wretches that were to be had for half-a-crown' than he was of her. The teenage, pregnant Charlotte was forced into the real-life role of the provoked wife, trailing around the bordellos of Covent Garden in search of her errant, careless husband.

Following the arrival of their daughter Catherine (or Kitty as Charlotte called her), who was christened on 6 December 1730, Richard's dissolute life continued unabashed, and in response Charlotte's affection for him dwindled to nothing. Her husband's libertinism would trigger no sobbing or wailing, no pleading or begging. Only a feeling of indifference, which was soon 'strongly attended with contempt'.

Neither her personal trials, nor the birth of her daughter, would be allowed to disrupt her acting career for long, however – not when it had only just begun. A month after the christening, by 11 January 1731, she was back on stage playing Mademoiselle, possibly out of financial necessity as much as desire, for she now knew there was no point in relying on Richard for support. If Charlotte's analogy of Mr and Mrs Sullen from George Farquhar's *The Beaux' Stratagem* is anything to go by, they were now 'a perpetual offence to each other', riling each other up like 'a gnawing vulture at the heart'.[9] The relationship grew increasingly untenable, and it seems that by 1733, like their fictional counterparts, they had 'agreed to part'.[10] Too poor to obtain the Act of Parliament required to gain a divorce, they had to settle for an informal separation, which gave Charlotte no legal protection whatsoever. Richard showed little interest in Kitty, and visited (Charlotte notes acidly) only 'when cash ran low'. As his legal wife still, she was obliged to hand over what money she had when he asked, and with the help of many an 'auxiliary guinea' from her father, she 'constantly supplied his wants' – with enough, she was sure, to buy herself some cuckold's horns.

WEARING THE BREECHES

By the summer of 1731 Charlotte's acting career was gathering pace. At first she had to settle for small roles in the principal plays, or mainpieces, and slightly more significant roles in the afterpieces – often comic musical pantomimes. But soon she was being chosen for more important parts and earning herself a pay rise, too, from a meagre 20 shillings a week to a still-meagre 30 shillings a week.

Her success as Lucy in George Lillo's tragedy *The London Merchant* that summer led Charlotte to her dream job as an actor in November 1731: her first 'breeches part' – as Mrs Raison in William Mountfort's *Greenwich Park*. 'Breeches parts' were a common feature of eighteenth-century plays and referred to female characters who, for plot purposes, donned male clothing to disguise themselves. Pioneered by Restoration actresses such as Nell Gwyn, Anne Bracegirdle and Susanna Verbruggen, these sex-swapping roles represented an empowering moment for women; challenging characters such as Shakespeare's Portia, Viola and Rosalind – previously always played by boys – gave actresses the chance to flex their acting muscles and allowed them to play their own subversive gender games on stage. On the other hand, they also provided yet another opportunity for objectification, as audiences sat goggle-eyed at the sight of so many shapely female legs in tight breeches. To 18-year-old Charlotte, who had spent her childhood marching around in her father's periwig and impersonating cheeky gardeners and sober physicians, nothing could come more naturally. Finally, she was able to play the man without censure or restraint – instead, she got applause and a pay packet.

As her standing in the theatre company grew, Charlotte was increasingly called on to fill the shoes of some of Drury Lane's leading ladies, including the revered actresses Mary Porter and Anne Oldfield. These were weighty roles that required her to master the highly stylised form of tragic acting that was then the norm, and for the first time in her career Charlotte felt a tremor at taking on 'such daring attempts'. The Drury Lane theatre managers, however, who included her brother Theophilus, had complete faith in her. Numerous parts were added to her roster between 1732 and 1733 – many of them breeches parts, and her flair (and partiality) for these roles did not go unnoticed. Soon she was given her first 'travesty role', which took breeches parts one important step further. These involved a female actress not just cross-dressing temporarily, but taking on a male character for the entirety of the play.[11] Depending on the role, this might require her to seamlessly adopt a male persona, or, in comedies and pantomimes, to ham it up in comic parody,[12] and Charlotte excelled at both. Just a few days after her first appearance at London's famous Bartholomew Fair in August 1732,[13] she was playing Roderigo at Drury Lane, Iago's gullible pawn in Shakespeare's *Othello*. Such roles, which Charlotte had been in training for all her life, would soon become her speciality.[14]

MUTINEER

It was all going so well, but over the next few years Charlotte's career would take several kamikaze turns that would set her life on an unpredictable course. In May 1733, she and the majority of the Drury Lane actors, led by her brother Theophilus, walked out in a complex dispute with the theatre's patentees, fuelled by personal dislike, professional mistrust, anger over suppressed wages and their own father's mishandling of his share of the patent.[15] An ugly stand-off ensued, in which the mutineers were illegally locked out of the theatre by armed guards, prompting them to sue the patentees, but after a fractious year, many of the players – including Charlotte and Theophilus – settled back at Drury Lane under new management.[16]

Once the dust had settled, however, Charlotte was still not satisfied. She wanted to play daring, complex female roles like the cross-dressing Silvia in Farquhar's *The Recruiting Officer*, and the conniving, sexually assertive Dol Common in Ben Jonson's *The Alchemist*. But at Drury Lane she had to fight for them, so when the season drew to a close in May 1734, she made a big decision: the only way to control the parts she played was to be her own boss, so she would try her hand at theatre management. On 20 May, the 'Mad Company' made its debut at the Little Haymarket Theatre with such entertainments as *The Beggar's Opera* performed in Roman dress, in which Charlotte, of course, took on the role of the womanising highwayman Macheath. She presided over a hectic few months in which, tellingly, almost every part she chose to perform was male. (In making travesty roles her trademark, Charlotte was risking her reputation and her family's displeasure; theatre manager and historian Benjamin Victor would warn actresses in 1761 that to take cross-dressing too far was to 'overstep the modesty of nature', but Charlotte was evidently unfazed by such mouldy, old-fashioned attitudes.[17]) The venture wasn't a financial success, but she had at least achieved a historical milestone: the first woman of the British theatre to manage her own troupe – at just 21 years old.

I had, even then, a passionate fondness for a periwig

The new season at Drury Lane was dull by comparison, and Charlotte made no secret of her frustrations. In 'a dispute about parts', she fell out with the new manager Charles Fleetwood and then exacerbated the feud by penning and staging a satirical farce, entitled *The Art of Management*, wherein she 'took no small pains to set him in a most ridiculous light'. Indeed, she wasn't subtle; she depicted Fleetwood as an idiot called 'Brainless', inciting him to retaliate by threatening her with legal action and buying up every copy of the printed text to halt its dissemination. Unfortunately for Fleetwood, there was no stopping audiences from enjoying the stage show.

Having unwisely burnt her bridges with Fleetwood more than once, Charlotte walked out of Drury Lane for good in early 1736 and joined the troupe of an up-and-coming young playwright who had taken up residence at the Haymarket: one Henry Fielding.[18] This was a decision that would anger her father (who until this point had continued to put in a good word for her at Drury Lane, despite the rift that her unconventional career choices had been causing between them) beyond the point of forgiveness. Fielding had already made an enemy of Colley by writing numerous satirical jibes about his lack of literary talent. Now, he had hired Charlotte to appear as Lord Place in his new play *Pasquin* – and her casting was no accident. The part entailed a direct hit at Colley, mocking his poor verses and obsequious connection to Walpole's Whigs; it was a calculated move that Fielding should want Colley's own daughter to play it. As for Charlotte, she had been overshadowed by her famous father for too long; she was now earning four guineas a week – and a name for herself. Papa would surely see the funny side …

Or perhaps she knew he wouldn't, and this was her little revenge for a lifetime of only half-noticing her and his role in causing the actors' mutiny, because this public lampooning of her father was not an isolated incident. She had already expertly pastiched his most famous role of Lord Foppington in a one-night benefit of *The Careless Husband* the previous summer at Lincoln's Inn Fields. Having been impersonating him since the age of four, she was by now an uncanny mimic of his affected mannerisms and comedy drawl. Then in March 1737 came the final insult in Fielding's *Historical Register for the Year 1736*, a satirical overview of the year that mercilessly ridiculed Colley's odes, as well as his habit of 'improving' Shakespeare through rewrites, while Charlotte's character Mr Hen, a Covent Garden auctioneer, took aim at the Whig government's corruption, auctioning off such values and virtues as honesty, patriotism, wit, modesty, courage and sense to the lowest bidders. Colley is known to have attended a performance at the Little Haymarket on 21 March and to have clapped and laughed his way through it, but in truth he never took mockery well. In his autobiography, *An Apology of the Life of Mr Colley Cibber*, published in 1740, he would express his true feelings about Fielding (a 'broken wit', as he called him) and the 'bad actors' he employed – his own daughter among them.

Colley would now wash his hands of Charlotte altogether. In their last ever meeting, likely to have occurred around this time, she recalls being summoned before a 'triumvirate' of accusers, including her father and eldest sister Catherine. She avoids detailing the charges they levelled against her, but no doubt they attacked her scandalous lifestyle as a single mother, her unseemly preference for breeches and travesty roles and her incendiary work with Fielding. Charlotte admits to being 'baited like a bull at a stake' and growing so obstinate that she 'answered nothing to their purpose', and so the encounter ended with Colley storming out of his own house, 'with a declaration not to return to it, 'till I was gone'. A surviving letter from Colley that likely dates from around this time shows how cold and unyielding he now was to Charlotte's appeals: 'You have made your own bed and therein you must lie', he wrote. 'Why do you not dissociate yourself from that worthless scoundrel, and then your relatives might try and aid you. You will never be any good while you adhere to him, and you most certainly will not receive what otherwise you might from your father.'[19] Unwilling to accept that her father could so ruthlessly reject her, Charlotte lay the blame fully with Catherine, her embittered sibling, the Goneril to her Cordelia, whom she suspected of poisoning Colley against her.

By now Charlotte had few supporters left. Her mother had died from an asthma attack in the midst of the chaos of the actors' mutiny, on 17 January 1734, leaving only Theophilus and her sister Elizabeth on her side. Theo would find acting jobs for her whenever he could, while Elizabeth, who doted on Charlotte like 'a favourite cat or mischievous monkey', took in her and Kitty. Charlotte could at least console herself that, by throwing in her lot with the vanguard of British theatre, she had taken a brave professional gamble. But it was all about to come crashing down.

Fielding's scathing lampoons had far-reaching consequences beyond Charlotte's familial relationships. One of their main targets, Britain's first prime minister Robert Walpole, had witnessed the increase in politically dissident plays with alarm and it prompted him to push through the Stage Licensing Act in June 1737, which outlawed the performance of plays in all theatres save those with a royal patent or special licence from the Lord Chamberlain. Essentially this left just the Theatres Royal at Drury Lane and Covent Garden, and the King's Theatre in the Haymarket.[20] Fielding's troupe was shut down and, like scores of other actors, Charlotte found herself out of work. Her spat with the management at Drury Lane suddenly seemed like an epic mistake.

Her options were now scant and mostly unappealing. Low, shameful work, crime or the workhouse would have beckoned for many women. But fired as always by her roving imagination and indomitable courage, Charlotte would do things differently.

After a failed attempt at running an oil and grocery shop in Covent Garden, she hit upon a scheme that was both ingenious and historically significant. Like almost every theatre manager in the country, if she wanted to remain in the business she would have to think outside the box to find a loophole in the Stage Licensing Act – and this she did. The act applied only to people, not objects, so Charlotte's answer was to establish a puppet theatre, where beautifully made marionettes would take the place of the actors on stage. Having obtained a licence from the Lord Chamberlain to run Punch's Theatre at the Old Tennis Court in James Street,[21] in March 1738 she embarked upon a run of serious, traditional plays, including Shakespeare's historics – but with an added innovation. Using 'mezzotintos of several eminent persons', she had the faces of her puppets carved to look like contemporary well-known figures, enabling her to dabble in topical satire with relative impunity. It's been observed that in doing so she was essentially pre-empting TV's *Spitting Image* by about 250 years.[22]

Charlotte's puppet shows did well, but even they didn't last long. A period of serious illness (induced by the gruelling performance schedule she imposed upon herself) and an oversaturated market meant that by 1740 she had been forced to sell her prized marionettes for £20 – a fraction of the near £500 she had paid for them.

Bad luck seemed to be stalking her, but there now comes a strange hiccup in Charlotte's history that is entirely of her own making. In an unusually cryptic disclosure, she mentions an 'honourable though very secret alliance' with a 'worthy gentleman' whose identity, for some reason, she has promised to hide. On the face of it, this seems to be a reference to her second marriage. The records show that on 2 May 1746 she married a Mr John Sacheverell – though oddly this man's name isn't once mentioned in her *Narrative*.[23] It's also unlike Charlotte to be quite so lax on chronology – nearly seven years out in this case. Her coyness is curious, because by now she was a widow. In the summer of 1736 Richard Charke had followed an acting troupe to Jamaica and within 18 months he was dead.[24] Charlotte was far from heartbroken at the news, and her wastrel husband's death meant she was free to marry again if she chose, but her studious avoidance of the word marriage suggests that this relationship took a different form – a tit-for-tat arrangement, perhaps, of sex or companionship in return for financial support, motivated by 'fondness' on his side and 'gratitude' on hers. The gentleman in question may even have been married.

If so, to publish any of these shady details would be fatal to Charlotte's reputation. She had recently seen her sister-in-law Susannah's career near destroyed by the exposé of her scandalous adultery, instigated by the abhorrent actions of Theophilus.[25] Charlotte would not make the same mistake; she would be careful to pay 'all due regard to decency wherever I have introduced the passion of love'. Whatever the nature of their liaison, it's clear this mystery man was helping her to survive, for when he died soon after their relationship began, Charlotte was left 'deprived of every hope and means of support'.

Saddled now with crippling debts she had no way of paying, the inevitable soon happened: Charlotte was arrested, for £7, probably in around 1741–2, and carted off to the bailiff's house. She was bailed out by a motley crew of female friends – all proprietors of Covent Garden coffee houses and brothels – but the most illuminating detail of this episode is that she was captured 'by dint of a very handsome laced hat I had on (being then, for some substantial reasons, *en cavalier*)'. To be '*en cavalier*' meant to be dressed in men's clothes – revealing that by now Charlotte had taken the significant leap of cross-dressing not just on the stage, but off it as well.

CHARLES BROWN

For a woman always so enamoured with playing the man, full-blown transvestism was perhaps an inevitable progression, and what could be easier – or more exhilarating – for Charlotte than to stroll off stage one evening in breeches, coat, wig and hat, and slip out the stage door into the street, leaving her tight corset and heavy petticoats behind? The nerves must have pulsed through her that first time, as she held her breath waiting for someone to look at her strangely, stop her, question her. But no one ever did.

So on an indeterminate date sometime in her late twenties, Charlotte decided to adopt the pseudonym of Charles Brown and live entirely as a man – and she's consistently inconsistent about her 'substantial reasons' for doing so. In the face of those who openly criticised this move as 'a very great error' – presumably her family – her excuse is deliberately evasive, attributing it vaguely to 'a particular cause' that bound her to another person, whose secret she was determined 'everlastingly to conceal'. Was this an attempt to shift the blame onto someone else and assuage her father's anger? Or does it hint at a clandestine relationship that required her to appear incognito? Occasionally, her cross-dressing was used as straightforward disguise to help her elude her creditors and avoid debtors' prison, but perhaps the most convincing reason she gives to justify her actions, and the easiest one to rationalise, is this: that she simply had a lifelong 'passionate fondness' for wearing men's clothes.

This predilection may have been an extension of her complex sexual identity or her flamboyant, theatrical personality, but even if those factors played no part, the benefits of cross-dressing must have seemed overwhelmingly attractive. It was such an absurdly simple trick – swap a dress for a pair of breeches, lower the timbre of the voice and add a swagger to the gait and suddenly a woman like Charlotte could outwit society's prejudice and enjoy all the freedoms a man took for granted. She could walk the streets as unencumbered as any gent in London, free from fear and harassment, with no one questioning her morals or her ability to work. It was an ingenious strategy for survival – and maybe even a pathway to success.

Charlotte had always instinctively felt that if she were to experience the world in full she would have to do so in male dress, but now she put it to the test. In her new identity, she went in search of work, and sure enough, there were far more job opportunities open to Mr Charles Brown than there were to Mrs Charlotte Charke. She soon found a job as a waiter for a lady named Mrs Dorr, the proprietor of the King's Head tavern in Marylebone, and quickly learned just how good she was at travesty parts. Having introduced herself as 'a young gentleman of a decayed fortune', she fooled both Mr and Mrs Dorr completely. Taken with this young man's sensitivity and 'melancholy aspect', his good breeding and ability to speak French with her foreign customers, Mrs Dorr made Charles Brown something of a favourite, inviting him to dine with her often and behaving 'as if I had been rather her son than her servant'. Charlotte was a talented actress, but even so the success of her male persona suggests just how learned and performative our gender signalling is. With her tall, slender frame and her gift for masculine mannerisms, Charlotte made such a convincing and charming young man that it even led her into some sticky situations – one of them (perhaps deliberately) resembling a farcical romance plot, complete with mistaken identities, scheming maid and risqué gender confusion. The Dorrs' mischievous maid excitedly whispered in Charles Brown's ear one day that a young female relative of Mrs Dorr's wished to marry him – having also told the lady in question that Charles intended to woo her. The whole story was 'trumped up' by the maid for her own amusement, Charlotte was certain, but still Charles had to make his excuses to the lady – he was too attached to the memory of his dear departed wife, he told her, to be able to consider marriage to another woman. Unsurprisingly, 'a strangeness ensued' between them after this encounter, and to make matters worse, rumours then began to swirl that Charles was in fact a woman. Her cover blown, Charlotte thought it best to remove herself from this awkward situation and so she parted company with dear Mrs Dorr, who, even after Charlotte had dropped the act, 'remained incredulous in regard to my being a female'.

Shortly afterwards, Charlotte found herself attracting the attentions of another amorous young lady, though this one was rather more tempting. She had been invited by the entertainer Jockey Adams to join his travelling troupe – as Charles Brown – in a town just outside of London, and while striding the stage as a charming young rake, she became the 'unhappy object of love' for a young lady in the audience – an orphan heiress, worth £60,000, who would have relinquished the lot to Charlotte 'had it been possible for me to have been what she designed me, nothing less than her husband'. Certainly, the girl's vast fortune was enticing – all Charlotte's worldly troubles would be over – but Charlotte was not so desperate, or so callous, as to play such a cruel trick on an infatuated teenager. As the girl had invited Charles to tea, Charlotte resolved to wait upon her, and 'by honestly confessing who I was, kill or cure her hopes of me forever'.

It was an uncomfortable meeting, to say the least. Charles bowed to the company and tried to position himself near the door but was 'soon lugged out of my chair' and 'awkwardly seated by her'. Nervous silences, tremulous voices and broken sentences followed, for Charlotte – usually so self-assured – was as terrified as her admirer by the delicacy of the situation, and became all the more so when the heiress's friends contrived to leave the two of them alone. But, as the young girl fought back tears, Charlotte steeled herself and made her confession. Like Mrs Dorr, the girl was utterly incredulous, being more easily convinced that Charles simply disliked her. Charlotte could only assure the girl of the truth, apologise and withdraw, leaving her to conclude that the episode was 'a most horrible disappointment on both sides; the lady of the husband, and I of the money'. When she returned to her troupe she found her colleagues panting to hear every detail of this blushing encounter – some of the men even offering 'to supply my place in the dark to conceal the fraud'. Charlotte gave them short shrift. She may have been hard up, but she would not sink so low as to defraud a young heiress of her fortune.

It would be easy to assume that anecdotes such as these are instances of Charlotte's theatrical imagination running away with her, that she included them in her *Narrative* to pander to the eighteenth-century craze for cross-dressing and the appetite for a titillating but ultimately safe glimmer of sex between two women. In fact, they're not nearly as far-fetched as they might seem. There are several known cases of fraudulent marriages between women occurring around this time: one cross-dresser named Mary Hamilton went on trial in Somerset in 1746 for conning Mary Price (who testified against her) into marriage under the name of Doctor Charles Hamilton – Henry Fielding would publish a fictionalised account of this case entitled *The Female Husband*. 'Samuel Bundy', who spent seven years as a man (some of them as a sailor) and married Mary Parlour in October 1759, was similarly exposed as being a woman some time after the wedding, with Parlour claiming ignorance. Bundy was subsequently prosecuted and imprisoned, while Ann Marrow was sentenced to the pillory and a six-month jail term 'for going in men's clothes, and being married to three different women by a fictitious name, and for defrauding them of their money and clothes' in 1777.[26] In all these cases, it wasn't the marriage of two women or even cross-dressing per se that did for them. It was the charges of fraud or theft. Cross-dressing had been outlawed in the Bible and publicly prohibited, but it had never been formally set down as a criminal offence. As a result, depending on the activities it was combined with, the response to it could still vary wildly, from imprisonment and corporal punishment to celebrity and even royal patronage. The possibility of lesbian sex, meanwhile, was such an alien concept to this phallocentric society that it was usually ignored. The befuddled authorities were more or less making it up as they went along.

Fraud and the total usurpation of male privileges, however, were another matter. Had Charlotte done the indecent thing and deceived the young heiress all the way to the altar, she would have been risking severe punishment. Perhaps she was put off by the tales of 'female husbands' such as Hamilton, Bundy and Marrow. Perhaps she'd even heard about the fate of German cross-dresser Catharina Lincken, who had been executed for sodomy in 1721 after marrying another woman.[27] Such horror stories make Britain's attitudes towards cross-dressed and homosexual women seem enlightened by comparison, but Charlotte was not quite daring enough to put them to the test. Plenty of women clearly were, however, and it's an electrifying thought that many more covert marriages between women may have slipped past the authorities altogether, which weren't scams at all, but genuine love stories.

JACK OF ALL TRADES, MISTRESS OF NONE

Charlotte emerged from these romantic escapades as poor as ever and was forced to scratch around to make ends meet, pawning her clothes and playing the odd role, until her brother Theophilus came to the rescue. Richard Annesley, 6th Earl of Anglesey, was looking for a manservant, and via a friend of Theo's, Charlotte was recommended for the job. The Earl was quite the knave – a bigamist who was rumoured to have defrauded his own nephew of his title, lands and fortune – but if she knew, Charlotte was unperturbed. Annesley evidently had as liberal an attitude towards cross-dressers as he did towards marriage, for after 'an open declaration who I really was, with a piteous account of my misfortunes', he readily hired 'Charles', knowing full well he was a she. For five short weeks, Charlotte enjoyed a reprieve from poverty, but her luck never did last long. When some officious friends convinced Annesley that it was improper to keep a transvestite valet – more so, apparently, than keeping several wives and stealing inheritances – his liberality caved under the pressure and he let Charlotte go.

A lesser person might have despaired at this point, and Charlotte admits that she now began to entertain a 'desire to die', but, by necessity, she dredged up every scrap of resilience and determination she had left and resolved instead to make 'a bold push'. She borrowed money from a friend and reinvented herself yet again, this time, rather unexpectedly, as a sausage seller. Door to door she went, with Kitty in tow, hawking her wares to her friends and taking pride in the fact that she had got herself and her daughter out of another scrape. Not everyone was so impressed. The gossips whispered that Colley Cibber's daughter was reduced to traipsing around town as a common street vendor, and soon the rumour mill went into over-drive. One story reached Charlotte that she was selling fish in the street and that when she had run into her father, she had slapped him round the face with a flounder; another claimed that she had turned highwayman and attacked him in Epping Forest in revenge for his neglect, reducing him to a gibbering, weeping wreck. 'A likely story,' Charlotte snaps, making clear her outrage at the 'ridic-ulous picture' these tales drew of her father. Since she has happily just given them a public airing in her memoir, however, it seems likely this outrage was manufactured. Perhaps, after all, she took more than a little pleasure in the thought of Colley fuming in his armchair, the latest instalment of his daughter's provocative work in his lap.

Charlotte's sausage-seller days came to an end prematurely, too – another bout of illness and a peckish dog who stole the remainder of her meat saw to that – and she spent the next few years, between 1742 and 1746, living by her wits, mixing acting and entrepreneur-ialism as the opportunities arose. She took on stints in pantos and at the Bartholomew and Southwark Fairs of 1742, put on benefit shows and ran her own season at the New Theatre, James Street, featuring her own play *Tit for Tat, or, Comedy and Tragedy at War* – a 'whimsical, comical, farcical, operatical, allegorical, emblematical,

Pistolatical impromptu medley', if you can imagine that.[28] In 1743, aged 30, she borrowed money from her uncle to start up her own eating house in Drury Lane – Mrs Charke's Steak and Soup House – until that, too, fell victim to her imprudence and bad luck, as she excitedly overspent, recklessly gave credit to out-of-work actors and took in lodgers who churlishly stole from her.

The following year she returned to acting, but destitution was never far away, and on at least one occasion her situation became so desperate that she resorted to sending another begging letter to her estranged father. His reply this time was even chillier than his last:

> *Madam–*
>
> *The strange career which you have run for some years (a career not always unmarked by evil) debars my affording you that succour which otherwise would naturally have been extended to you as my daughter. I must refuse therefore – with this advice – try Theophilus.*
>
> *Yours in sorrow, Colley Cibber*[29]

There is little doubt that Charlotte's bohemian, masculine lifestyle appalled her father, and that her public mockery of him had fatally skewered his pride. He knew full well, too, that Theophilus was also deeply in debt and could be of little help. But Colley was not one for self-torture. He enjoyed himself at his favourite club in fashionable Bath, while his embarrassing daughter walked the streets as a vagabond. Undutiful, unbiddable, unconventional and, worst of all, unfeminine, she had demonstrated the very worst qualities in a daughter. He would have nothing more to do with her.

A STROLLING PLAYER

By the close of 1746, London had become too hot for 33-year-old Charlotte. Her brief second marriage to John Sacheverell that summer was over almost before it had begun and her reticence on the subject suggests it was something she would rather forget. Her debts were mounting, her creditors were closing in; it was time to leave the city for the insecure but anonymous life of a strolling player. This was quite the come-down for a proud, even snobbish actress such as Charlotte. Strolling had officially been outlawed by the Licensing Act, leaving travelling players at risk of arrest for vagrancy, but, knowing the law wasn't strongly enforced outside the cities, ragged acting troupes would tour towns and villages all over the country, performing in small and often makeshift theatres (barns and pigsties often had to suffice), in their threadbare costumes and with cobbled-together props, to mixed audiences that might include the local gentry but also the local drunks. It was a far cry from the grand London theatres Charlotte was used to, where she had worked with the most talked-about writers and celebrated players of the day; now she was surrounded by 'despicable actors' who 'mangled and butchered' the works of the great poets and rendered the speeches of Hamlet and Othello in voices that gave her 'the strong idea of a cat in labour'. She was better than this and struggled to take the work seriously. Exploiting the audiences' wandering attention became a running joke for her and her friends: one evening, they decided to recite every random speech they could remember, regardless of the play, on a 'wild-goose chase through all the dramatic authors we could recollect'. Those 'who were awake' absolutely loved it.

But for all the laughs, the strolling life was hard, with gruelling schedules, stingy salaries and the constant threat of arrest. She travelled with Kitty around the West Country with various troupes between 1746 and 1750, discarding the name of Charlotte Charke and living solely as Charles Brown, and during these years she became so despondent that she was plagued with bouts of illness and 'a lowness of spirits'. Her greatest comfort, it seems, was a friend she refers to only as Mrs Brown, who nursed her and travelled with her. It's not known how they met – Mrs Brown may have been another strolling player – but the pair soon began to style themselves as Mr and Mrs Brown, with Charlotte adopting the role of husband. From the vantage point of the twenty-first century, the natural assumption is that this was a sexual relationship. Charlotte never says so, of course, but it's revealing that she and Mrs Brown presented their relationship in marital terms and stayed together until Charlotte's death, making this the most devoted, steadfast relationship of her life.

Charlotte's other great comfort on the other hand, her daughter, was about to cut herself loose after years of being dragged along in her mother's churning wake. At 19, Kitty now wished to marry another strolling player, John Harman, against Charlotte's wishes. She had immediately taken against Harman, whom she accused of being improvident and insolent towards her, but Kitty was as head-strong as her mother. The couple joined another strolling troupe and went their own way, and in January 1750, went ahead with the wedding. Charlotte did not attend.

With few other avenues available, Charlotte persevered with strolling, frantically trying to avoid destitution, but the final straw came when her managers abandoned the company for London, leaving her to manage everything alone, swiftly followed by her arrest for vagrancy in Minchinhampton. The night she spent 'in hell itself', in a damp, stinking prison, surrounded by men awaiting execution or transportation, left her shaken, and although her case was dismissed the next day, Charlotte had come to feel that the strolling life was not worth the trouble. Without delay, she and Mrs Brown quit the company and took a house together in Chepstow.

But what now? They could hardly live on air, so Charlotte, as the man of the house, embarked on a parade of professions that from anyone else might strain credulity. Each was as unsuccessful as the last, but Charlotte was ever resourceful and never defeatist: 'As I found one business fall off, I resolved to set up another.' First came a stint as a pastry cook (her lack of skill in the kitchen seemed irrelevant – 'as long as I was a Londoner, to be sure, my pastry must be good!'), then another as a pig farmer (when she managed to buy an old barrow instead of a sow). With borrowed money the Browns set up a fruit farm, only to find their orchard destroyed by vandals. Their pastry shop in Pill, near Bristol, did well for a summer while the ships kept arriving from Ireland, but come the winter, the ships vanished, and with them the Browns' trade. In January 1753, when Charlotte turned 40, she briefly became a proofreader and writer for the *Bristol Weekly Intelligencer*, and with that, this dizzying run came to an end. It had been a valiant – if sometimes farcical – attempt at entrepreneurialism, characterised by extraordinary perseverance and resilience, but the same old combination of ill luck and bad decisions had scuppered Charlotte's plans every time. Even when Mrs Brown inherited a little money from her uncle, Charlotte's anarchic spending habits laid waste to it in no time, despite her partner's restraining influence.

Charlotte was well aware of her ineptitude as a businesswoman. Acting was her calling, the one thing she excelled at, and it didn't take long to lure her back. After a brief stint with her daughter's troupe, which became increasingly tense thanks to Harman's continued rudeness, Charlotte received a letter from Theo, offering her a job as a prompter at the Orchard Street Theatre, in Bath, in September – and being 'heartily tired of strolling', she says, 'I readily embraced the offer'. But there was a catch: she had to appear not as Charles Brown, but in her 'proper character' – a condition that must have made Charlotte think twice. To bind herself back into a corset and petticoats after so many years would surely be unbearable. But she was desperate. Forced to weigh up her own desire for freedom and unconventionality with her need to eat, the latter had to come first.

It must have been a galling sacrifice, because she hated the job – it was exhausting, the manager was inept and it meant correcting actors who she felt were her inferiors. She lasted six months but, curiously, made no return to cross-dressing afterwards. To hammer this point home, she makes a great show of indignation in her memoir at a 'malicious aspersion' that she 'designed to forsake my sex again, and that I positively was seen on the streets in breeches' – an 'impertinent falsehood', she claims, aimed at making her look ridiculous. This uncharacteristic denunciation of the lifestyle she had pursued so unapologetically for so long seems to have been triggered by the fact that this rumour was 'brought to London and spread itself, much to my disadvantage, in my own family' – just at the moment when reconciliation with her family might be her only salvation. If she were ever to persuade her father to look on her more kindly, she would have to convince him that she had long renounced her peculiar cross-dressing ways. In casting Charles Brown aside, she was laying the groundwork for her next big role: the prodigal daughter.

THE LAST ACT

After an absence of eight 'contemptible' years, Charlotte gleefully returned to London in December 1754. Having already dabbled in playwriting, her latest money-making scheme was to attempt a novel – *The History of Henry Dumont, Esq; and Miss Charlotte Evelyn* would be a tale of the parental love she had long missed. She found a publisher, but 'being universally known to be an odd product of nature' she was persuaded to postpone the novel and instead write the most gripping story she had at her disposal: her own life.

Her publisher, Samuel Whyte, left an account of their business meeting, and though he wasn't a man predisposed to theatrical types, the picture he draws gives an unintentionally poignant snapshot of the abject penury in which Charlotte was now living. He talks of approaching her 'wretched thatched hovel' in Clerkenwell, accompanied by a bookseller, and being greeted at the door by a 'meagre, ragged figure' whom they took for a servant. (In fact, this 'squalid handmaiden', as Whyte calls her, was most likely the long-suffering Mrs Brown.)[30] So far, what they'd seen had looked far from respectable, but the tableau they met with when they got inside was nothing short of bohemian. There was Charlotte, sitting in state on a 'maimed chair', in 'dingy' petticoats, and surrounded by a menagerie. On one hob sat a cat 'of melancholy aspect', on another a monkey; a skeletal dog was curled at her feet and a magpie perched on her chair. A broken pair of bellows lay in place of a writing desk, while a cracked teacup served as her inkstand.

Whyte's response to this dejected scene is not to sympathise but to pontificate on Charlotte's long fall from grace – the 'once-admired daughter of Colley Cibber', he blusters, born to 'affluence, and educated with care and tenderness', had thrown it all away and 'finished the career of her miserable existence on a dunghill'.[31] Such would be the prevailing opinion in years to come: that a brattish, ungrateful, reckless daughter had rejected her father's gifts and ruined her own life.

Whyte's personal distaste for Charlotte didn't prevent him from recognising her as a bestseller, however; a deal was brokered and the first instalment of *A Narrative of the Life of Mrs Charlotte Charke* appeared on 1 March 1755, to be followed by seven others. It was a hit, as predicted, though not with the one man who mattered. Even by the second instalment it was becoming clear that Charlotte's charm offensive wouldn't work on Colley. She included a letter she had written to her father, now in his eighties, on 8 March, in which she had explained that she was publishing her life story and apologised for her 'thoughtless wildness'. She had even offered to throw herself at his feet in penitence. But the letter, she tells us, was returned unopened, and poor Charlotte just couldn't understand why. Had anything she'd done been really that bad? She was sure that none of her crimes were completely 'unpardonable'. Despite everything, she still felt 'bound by all laws, both divine and human' to love and 'tenderly revere' her father. Why did he not feel the same? Charlotte was heartbroken, and as usual she placed the blame firmly with Colley's 'cruel monitor', her sister Catherine. The only veiled recrimination she ever aimed at her father was the more damning image of him that she allowed into her memoir thereafter.

The final instalment of Charlotte's autobiography was published on 19 April. It had proved so popular that it soon appeared in book form, too, which itself went to two editions and was abridged for the respected *Gentleman's Magazine*.

I have been in a hurry from the hour of my birth

Charlotte had hit upon a rare success with her writing (her novel followed in 1756 and, though sniffed at by the critics, it did well), but it wasn't enough to solve her problems, financial or familial. By September 1755 she was treading the boards again with her brother Theo, and poverty would continue to pursue her well into the late 1750s, when her life would be blighted by a succession of losses. The first came on 12 December 1757 when, at the age of 84, her father died. Colley had remained sprightly, carefree and wealthy till the end, and he made sure that his two most disreputable children, the ones most like him, didn't profit by his demise. Catherine, of course, inherited the bulk of his estate, and with just £50 for Theo and an insulting £5 for Charlotte, Colley had had his final say. No record exists of how Charlotte reacted to the news, but the blow must have been profound. The father whose attention she'd craved but whose authority she'd defied had gone without granting her request for forgiveness. His love and support had been conditional – and spitefully withdrawn right to the very end. Perhaps Charlotte channelled her grief and frustration into her writing, because over the next couple of years she penned three short stories, which dealt with 'discordancy in families' and the dangers of living beyond one's means – things she knew plenty about.[32]

The following year marked Charlotte's final parting from her daughter Kitty, too, as she and her disagreeable husband moved to the West Indies in 1758 with a travelling company and eventually settled in America, where Kitty forged a career as a respected actress. And on 27 October that same year Charlotte's brother Theophilus, unable to get a licence to perform in London, set sail for Dublin with his mistress, only for his ship to be lost at sea. Many might have thought good riddance to a man who was generally regarded as an unpleasant character, but Charlotte had lost a dear brother and a rare source of dependable support.

'I have been in a hurry from the hour of my birth,' Charlotte wrote prophetically midway through her autobiography; and indeed, her own death would come rushing to meet her far too soon. This trag-icomedy would have no happy ending.

Her final stage appearances came in late 1759. On 7 August she applied to the Lord Chamberlain, the Duke of Devonshire, for a licence to perform a ten-night run of the comic opera *Galligantus* at the Haymarket, and the Charlotte of this letter seems much changed. Worn out by poverty, weighed down with grief and in an 'ill state of health', she is meek and humble, though still invoking the name of her dead father to persuade the Duke to 'permit the daughter, who was bred on the stage, to take an honest chance for those few nights'.[33] The Duke agreed, and on the seventh night of the run, 28 September, Charlotte also staged a benefit performance of Susanna Centlivre's *The Busy Body*, in which, of course, she took the lead role of the male fop Marplot. Her advertisement for this fundraiser reveals that her circumstances were as bad as ever. Her motive for the benefit, she wrote, was 'to settle me in business, being at present entirely dependent on chance for subsistence'. As usual she was down but not quite out – all she needed was the public to help her to 'a happier situation of life than I now enjoy'.[34]

Whether or not this latest business plan would have succeeded we cannot know, because Charlotte's time had run out. In November 1759 she applied for another licence that seems not to have been granted, and that winter she succumbed to illness, finally spent by the constant scrabble to work and live. She died at her lodgings in the Haymarket, at the age of 47, on 16 April 1760, after what must have been a bleak last few months. The event didn't go unnoticed in the press, however; her obituary featured in numerous newspapers, reducing this whirlwind woman to a few succinct words: the 'celebrated Mrs Charlotte Charke, daughter of the late Colley Cibber, Esq … a gentlewoman remarkable for her adventures and misfortunes'.[35]

Charlotte Charke took Shakespeare literally when he wrote 'All the world's a stage'.[36] Her natural tendency was to dramatise every adventure and misfortune in her life, and to prove just how consummate an actress she was, she would play every part in this voluminous drama. Not just the female ones – the rebellious daughter; the wronged wife; the doting mother; the diva actress; the prodigal daughter – but the male ones, too: the squire; the doctor; the gardener; the theatre manager; the entrepreneur; the rake and the husband. This kaleidoscopic woman made little sense to anyone else, because she refused to be moulded into one predetermined shape. It was both her strength and her downfall.

The British public had generally looked on Charlotte's unusual proclivities with a friendly, amused eye; yes, she was imprudent, odd and scandalous, but she was also entertaining. This enthusiasm wasn't shared by everyone, though; there were those for whom, like her father and her publisher, her story only confirmed that she was a bad example of womanhood; it 'could never be read by persons of her own sex, not wholly abandoned'[37] – they might be tainted or, God forbid, inspired by such a woman. As moral criteria tightened in the nineteenth and early twentieth centuries, people came to view Charlotte as an archetypal reprobate and undutiful daughter, 'one of those disgraces to the community that ought not to be admitted into society'. She had a 'disposition so wild, so dissipated, and so unsuitable to her sex'; she was probably a 'psychopathic lesbian', too, they screeched.[38]

Despite these histrionic responses, Charlotte's importance in the history of British theatre and early female autobiography has long been begrudgingly recognised. It's only in recent decades, however, that her significance as one of history's most charismatic rebel women has come to be appreciated. Through the fog of fusty propriety, a woman of immense restless energy and creativity emerges – intelligent, witty and confident, as well as incorrigible, impetuous and self-deprecating – one who could never be satisfied with the restrictions her gender forced on her. Though she'd be penalised for doing so, she would use her skills to find a new kind of freedom, to be both the heroine and hero of her hectic life story and to earn her own living as a woman in a man's world.

She believed herself to be dogged by ill luck, but chance wasn't the only author of Charlotte's problems. Her greatest ill luck was to be born into a society not yet ready to embrace a woman who had 'through the whole course of [her] life, acted in contradiction to all points of regularity'. To survive in a world where censorship stifled her every career move and where, by simply being herself, she forfeited her father's love, she had to draw on all her reserves of courage, ingenuity, determination and resilience. For an easy, comfortable life, she could have conformed, suppressed her 'natural propensity to a hat and wig' and won her father's applause. But then she wouldn't have been Charlotte Charke.

Hannah Snell

THE AMAZON

The rules on board ship were perfectly clear: women were not welcome. In 1731 the navy regulations stated plainly that a captain was 'not to carry any women to sea … without orders from the Admiralty'. By the 1750s they were grumbling that 'no women be ever permitted to be on board but such as are really the wives of the men they come to' – and the ship should be 'not too much pestered even with them'. Women were physically and mentally weak; they were a distraction to the crew; and every seafarer knew that they brought bad luck crashing down on any ship. Even men noted for their pragmatism were susceptible to this kind of delusional thinking. When Nelson's friend and colleague Admiral Collingwood discovered a woman on board one of his ships in 1808, he packed her off home immediately, declaring, 'I never knew a woman brought to sea in a ship that some mischief did not befall the vessel.'[1]

This centuries-old superstition was so embedded in naval folklore that it had been written into the rule book and become as good as fact. With seafaring and colonialism traditionally described in gendered terms – of manning female ships to master the female waves and conquer the female lands[2] – the fear was that allowing women a share of that mastery would be to invite a chaotic reversal of the established order and threaten male supremacy over the earth

'Ye dogs, I have more wounds about
me than you have fingers.'

HANNAH SNELL (1723–1792),
SOLDIER, MARINE AND PERFORMER

and sea. So when the first Admiralty Regulations were printed in 1731 they made it official: aside from the occasional wife, nurse or prostitute (who were admitted only begrudgingly and for the most part unofficially), women had no place at sea.[3]

And yet, particularly during the eighteenth century, a surprising number of women ignored this ruling – women who weren't content with the four walls of home, who yearned instead to experience the vastness of the seas and the heart-thrum of action, who were bold enough to throw themselves, unperturbed, into this all-male fray. There was one catch, though: if they were to go to sea on equal terms with men, they would first have to pull off an elaborate feat of camouflage and convince the world that they were men, too.

In May 1750, a woman named Hannah Snell returned home from sea, having done precisely that. For nearly five years she had lived, fought and flirted disguised as a man, and now she had arrived back in London with an extraordinary tale to tell. Within a few short weeks, she had caused a sensation: the famous Hannah Snell had a stage show and a sell-out biography to her name – and no wonder. Throughout the course of history, few things have fascinated and discombobulated society more than when its nurturers become fighters. From Zenobia, Boadicea or Joan of Arc in the real world, to the Amazons, Hua Mulan or Spenser's Britomart in the fictional, the courage, strength, incongruity and sheer 'unwomanliness' of warrior women have tended to elicit both excitement and fear. And with these febrile emotions often comes something more troubling: an impulse to repackage them, make them a little more palatable and a little less threatening. Hannah Snell would be subject to – and even complicit in – this very kind of identity manipulation, leaving subsequent ages the task of finding the real image beneath the overpaint.

YOUNG AMAZON SNELL

The main source of information for Hannah Snell's life is *The Female Soldier*, the biographical account that was published in July 1750, soon after her return to England. But this account was not written by Hannah. Like most women born without privilege, she was only semi-literate; what she needed was a scribe to take down her story, and in publisher Robert Walker she found an enthusiastic one. Being every bit as keen as he was to make some ready cash, Hannah granted Walker the exclusive rights to her story, and the result is an assault course for historians trying to get at the truth. For every record that corroborates the claims made in *The Female Soldier*, there are several others that expose the sleights of hand, time shifts and fact-twists that Walker frequently employed to reel in his audience and manipulate his narrative to fit his purpose. His job was to sell Hannah's story as outlandish but true, and to sell Hannah herself as a sympathetic, courageous character who, despite her transgressive behaviour, would pass the strict eighteenth-century criteria of a good and virtuous woman. It was a marketing exercise as much as anything else, and as such there must always be a pinch of salt on hand when reading *The Female Soldier*.

Proceeding cautiously then, we find from the outset that, despite Walker's promise to treat his subject 'fully and impartially', Hannah is his undisputed heroine throughout. He is downright effusive in his encomiums: Cleopatra, Semiramis and the Arcadian shepherdesses were all pretty good, he argues, but none of them were a patch on Hannah Snell. She was a woman born to a life of heroism, he says, and her soldierly ways were in evidence from very early on.

She arrived on 23 April 1723, during the reign of George I, into a large family who lived on Friar Street in Worcester, most of whom demonstrated a distinct fancy for the military. The eighth of nine children, Hannah had three brothers who would all become either soldiers or sailors, while all but one of her five sisters would marry military men. This martial trend in the Snell siblings derived not from their father, who was a humble hosier and dyer, but from their grandfather, 'the illustrious Captain-Lieutenant Sam Snell', who had reportedly fought and died at the Battle of Malplaquet in the War of the Spanish Succession in 1709. Of all his grandchildren, however, it was Hannah who would give old Grandpa Sam a run for his money.

Hannah's parents – another Samuel and his second wife Mary – were by no means rich, but they could afford to 'bring up and educate a numerous family'. For the girls, of course, this meant acquiring only the most basic of skills; they were taught to read 'exceeding well' but not to write, and this was fine by Hannah, for she had no aspirations to be a woman of letters. By the age of ten her heart was set on adventure; 'the seeds of heroism' had already been 'implanted in her nature, and she used often to declare to her companions that she would be a soldier if she lived'. She got her practice in early, forming 'a company of young soldiers among her playfellows' (appointing herself as chief commander) and parading them through the city of Worcester on a regular basis. Hannah's battalion of child recruits became a well-known sight around the town as they performed their drills, and earned the affectionate nickname 'Young Amazon Snell's Company'.[4]

Walker skims briskly over the remainder of Hannah's childhood, alighting on Christmas Day 1740 when she was 17. By now, both her parents were dead, and with no other source of support, she moved to London to stay with her sister Susannah and her husband, James Gray, a carpenter, who lived in Ship Street, Wapping. Theirs was a modest household, where Hannah would have been expected to pay her own way. How she managed this remains a mystery – domestic service, street-hawking or bartending in a local tavern are all possibilities – but any work she might have come by would likely have been both unskilled and poorly paid. By 1743, however, after three years of eking out a living, she must have thought she'd found the solution to survival – maybe even happiness. Wapping was a riverside parish frequented by seafaring folk, and, attracted by their roistering ways and hair-raising tales, Hannah had taken a shine to one of them – a Dutch sailor named James Summs. Walker, always keen to stress his heroine's virtue, assures us that Hannah's friendship with Summs developed into a 'mutual though not a criminal passion', and that the fellow made his addresses following all the rules of propriety. When he asked for Hannah's hand, she consented, and the two were married on 6 January 1744 at Fleet Church, when she was 20 years old.

Marriage was supposed to be a woman's end goal, the safe option that would set her life on a straight, narrow and predetermined path, but for Hannah, it would trigger the strange series of events that was to make her life remarkable. Had the marriage been a successful one, she might have settled into the conventional life of wife and mother, sitting at home waiting for her husband to return from sea – the anxious (and, though Hannah may not have realised it, often impoverished) life of many a sailor's wife.[5] As it turned out, James Summs soon revealed a less gallant side to his character. He was 'the worst and most unnatural of husbands', who 'not only kept criminal company with other women of the basest characters, but also made away with [Hannah's] things in order to support his luxury and the daily expenses of his whores'. Already cruelly disillusioned, Hannah was about to meet with another complication when she learned that she was pregnant. The news did nothing to reform her husband. Summs was now deeply in debt and when Hannah was seven months gone, he deserted her and ran off to sea, leaving her to face 'all the shocks of poverty' alone. Wretched as her situation was, perhaps Hannah was glad to be rid of him, for Walker tells us that she 'patiently bore herself up' and returned to her sister and brother-in-law, whom she could always rely on for support.

Hannah's daughter, Susannah (named, presumably, after the dear sister who had taken her in), was born two months later, but the ray of light she brought would be fleeting, for at just seven months old, she quickly sickened and died. At this dreadful moment, Walker doesn't dwell on emotions – indeed, he rarely does; instead, he gives only the most perfunctory information: that Hannah made sure the baby was 'decently interred at her own expense at St George's parish, Middlesex'. Her state of mind is passed over without comment – perhaps it was too painful for her to recount – but it can be guessed at. At any rate, one thing seems certain: this was the moment that decided Hannah's future.

'THE REAL SOUL OF A MAN'

As Walker tells it, now that Hannah was childless, she made the radical decision to go in search of her perfidious husband, which would inevitably entail going to sea, and to maximise her chances of success, 'she boldly commenced a man'. It may seem an odd and risky course of action, but Hannah was by no means the first or only woman to choose such a dare-devil option.

Popular ballads that sang of young girls who ran off to sea in breeches had a long tradition dating back to the sixteenth century, but in the late 1600s, in keeping with the Europe-wide trend for female cross-dressing that was now in full swing, reports began to emerge of women trying it for real – reports that multiplied throughout the 1700s.[6] Their paths to freedom varied. On the very peripheries of society, female pirates such as Mary Read and Anne Bonny – who met on the high seas during the golden age of piracy and swashbuckled their way straight into court and very nearly the hangman's noose in 1720 – terrorised the oceans in a bare-faced rejection of the established rule of law. Others turned patriot instead and, like Christian Davies, served their country as soldiers. Davies joined the British Army in 1693 (also supposedly in pursuit of her husband), fought in the Nine Years' War and the War of the Spanish Succession, and was only found out when she was wounded at the Battle of Ramillies in 1706. Lauded for her courage, she became the first female Chelsea Pensioner in 1717 and was even granted a pension by Queen Anne. By the time an account of her life had been published in 1741, two years after her death, her story was legendary.[7]

Then there were those who, like Hannah, decided to enlist in naval crews and become a tar.[8] There are more than 20 reports of such women between the late seventeenth and early nineteenth centuries in Britain, accounting for almost half of the 50 known cases of cross-dressing women during this period, from Mary Lacy, who served in the Royal Navy for 12 years from 1759, first as William Chandler and then, once her secret was discovered, as the first known female shipwright, to the mysterious William Brown, a 21-year-old from Grenada who, according to the muster list of the *Queen Charlotte*, was dismissed from service on 23 May 1815 for 'being a female' – the first black lady tar in British naval history, whose real name and story we'll probably never know.[9]

Why any woman would actively choose such a life when conditions on board were so intolerable that most men had to be press-ganged into it and would desert at the first opportunity is a big question – one that has rarely been answered satisfactorily by the accounts and ballads that have come down to us. These tales usually adhere to the same formula: that dainty young ladies like Hannah and Christian Davies donned breeches and ran off to sea in search of their lost lovers. But this excuse – perceived as the only comprehensible motive for a woman wanting to run away to sea or battle – was trotted out so frequently that 'when an actual case of a woman seaman was reported, the theme was often tacked on' by newspaper reports and storytellers.[10] No other explanation could reassure the public that their heroine was still recognisably feminine and heterosexual, and the possibilities that she might choose this path to improve her social and financial lot, to escape the boredom or servitude of her life, to have an adventure or simply because she felt more at home living in breeches, were not even considered. In short, the 'lost lover' motif was so prevalent, and the chances of finding these errant lovers so remote, that it can almost certainly be dismissed as a genuine motive.

Mary Lacy, whose account of her life in the military is considered one of the most historically reliable, was unusually honest about why she chose the life she did: having started out as a domestic servant, she grew resentful of both her position and the beatings she received from her parents, and when she was left distraught by a thwarted flirtation with a young man, 'a thought came into my head to dress myself in men's apparel, and set off by myself'.[11] Her decision was impulsive, childish even, to run away and escape a life she detested, while her enlisting was entirely opportunistic and spur-of-the-moment – a gentleman asked her if she'd like to go to sea, and not knowing what else to do, she said yes.

The same could easily have applied to Hannah. Life as a woman had dealt her a bad hand – she had obeyed the rules and become a wife and mother, and all it had done was leave her jilted, destitute and grief-stricken. With the yearning for excitement that she had nurtured since childhood tugging at her petticoats, the temptation to be someone else when Hannah Snell's life was proving so utterly miserable must have been irresistible. To Walker, this could only mean that Hannah had 'the real soul of a man in her breast' – what other explanation could there possibly be for such an intrepid woman?

Going to sea would be hard – perhaps she didn't yet realise how hard – but surely it couldn't be any tougher than making her way as a poor single woman. It's an indicator of just how stifling a woman's existence was compared to a man's that to live as a sailor represented incarceration to him, but freedom and independence to her. The low, sporadic wages that were an insult to him were gratefully received by her, while the peripatetic lifestyle of the seafarer offered her a liminal space where she could learn new skills and experience a life beyond the confines of her gender – a luxury that he did not need. If it turned out badly, however, she had one major advantage over her male colleagues – she could escape the ship in one easy move by revealing her sex and being discharged.

Whatever her motivation, Hannah was done with petticoats and penury. She was done, for now, with being a woman. In a new community, with a new identity, she would try her luck as a man and see if it served her any better. Walker tells us that on 23 November 1745, less than two years after her marriage, she picked what must have been the first male name that came into her head – that of her brother-in-law, James Gray – donned a suit of his clothes, snuck out of the house in Ship Street 'unknown to any' and vanished into thin air. She was going on an adventure, and she wouldn't reappear for nearly five years.

SOLDIER, SOLDIER

Under her new name of James Gray, Hannah made her way from Wapping to Coventry, ostensibly in pursuit of her husband. Ignoring the fact that Bonnie Prince Charlie and his Jacobite troops were currently marching from Scotland in what would be their last attempt to invade England and restore the Stuart kings, Walker has Hannah, seemingly oblivious to their approach, alighting in Coventry on 26 November 1745, the very same day that the Jacobites reached Preston. Almost immediately, she found herself pressed into military service in Captain Miller's company, part of General Guise's regiment; as she stood watching the drums beating up for soldiers, she was spotted by a corporal who 'by force put a piece of money into her hand, and insisted she should drink with him'.

The lax attitude to official documentation meant that her little act of identity theft was surprisingly easy to pull off. Naval officers weren't overly concerned with checking who their new recruits actually were and they didn't bother to carry out a physical examination – at times of conflict, as almost the entire eighteenth century was, they were desperate for men: young or old, sick or well, vagrant or criminal, volunteered or press-ganged, butch or effeminate, they weren't fussy and didn't ask too many questions. Walker gives few details of Hannah's actual transformation, but Mary Lacy's and Christian Davies's accounts suggest that a severe haircut, a change of clothes, a little padding in the waistcoat, a heavier gait and a lower tone of voice were enough to fool the negligent or indifferent.[12] With fashion such a strong signifier of rank, gender, even occupation in the eighteenth century, these simple measures were enough for a woman to be taken for a smooth-faced, androgynous boy.[13]

After three weeks in Coventry, Hannah and 17 other new recruits were sent north, on foot, to join Guise's regiment in Carlisle, where the Duke of Cumberland was busy routing the Jacobite garrison left behind by Bonnie Prince Charlie, who, having turned back at Derby, had retreated back to Scotland on 20 December. The march to Carlisle took three weeks, so by the time Hannah arrived in January 1746 all remnants of the Jacobite occupation were gone, saving her for now from any military engagement. (The rebels would face their final defeat a few months later, at Culloden.) Instead, she was 'instructed in the military exercise, which she now performed with as much skill and dexterity as any sergeant or corporal in his Majesty's service'. Her time in Carlisle wasn't to last long, however. Disaster soon struck when a sergeant named Davis attempted to embroil her in the seduction of a young lady. What he didn't bargain on was Hannah's compassion for her fellow sister: 'her virtuous soul abhorred with a becoming detestation the criminal intention', so 'instead of acting the pimp, she went and disclosed the whole matter to the young woman, and warned her against the impending danger'. When Davis's seduction duly failed, he suspected Hannah, or rather James Gray, of sabotaging his plans in order to claim the lady for himself, and his revenge was brutal. He accused James Gray before the commanding officer of 'neglect of duty', for which Hannah was sentenced to 600 lashes, 'five hundred of which she received, having her hands tied to the castle gates, for a crime which Nature put it out of her power to perpetrate'. She was only spared the last 100, Walker tells us, because of the 'intercession of some of the officers'.

The situation worsened when a young man named George Beck joined the regiment, who had not only been born in Worcester but had lodged at the Grays' house in Wapping alongside Hannah; he would almost certainly recognise her. Cruelly punished for an offence she didn't commit and now in fear of discovery, she decided to desert, for 'no dread of punishment was equal to that of shame, which she must have unavoidably undergone had her sex been once discovered'. On the spur of the moment, she made a new plan. With a yen to go abroad, she decided the naval city of Portsmouth seemed a likely place to start, though now, as a deserter, trudging through the country-side in her army uniform seemed distinctly unwise. A new disguise was needed, and about a mile outside of Carlisle the answer presented itself. In the fields beyond the town she came across some pea pickers hard at work who had discarded their coats nearby ... It would not be theft, but a trade: she pulled off her regimental coat, swapped it for one of theirs and set out on her month-long journey to the south in the safety of another's clothes.

This is a thrilling start to Hannah's adventures. There's just one problem: Walker's account and the historical records don't quite add up, to the extent that this early part of Hannah's military career, from 1745 to 1747, seems likely to have been an invention.[14] The problems start with her baby daughter. The parish records state that Susannah Summs was buried at six months old on 31 January 1747, which means that in late 1745, when Walker has Hannah supposedly making her way in male dress to Coventry after the absconsion of her husband and the death of her child, she must in fact have been still with her husband, either just pregnant or about to be. If Walker's dates were correct, she would have been in the early stages of preg-nancy during the 500 lashes she is meant to have received in Carlisle. Six hundred lashes were considered the most a person could endure before death, so it seems unlikely that Hannah and her unborn baby could have withstood 500 and emerged unharmed. Then there is the question of the concealment of her sex during this punishment.

Walker was aware of this potential plot hole, which he blamed on the hurried production of the book, but since there were 'some particular incidents' in Hannah's tale that some attentive readers might wonder at, because they 'may carry with them an air of improbability', he thought he'd better add in a later explanation. His solution is that, 'At that time her breasts were but very small, and her arms being extended and fixed to the city gates, her breasts were towards the wall, so that then there was little or no danger of her comrades finding out the important secret which she took such uncommon pains to conceal.' Our credulity is at snapping point here and Walker knows it.[15]

With a sigh, then, we have to concede that this part of Hannah's story doesn't pass the stress test. Why it might have been added is another question – extra lurid material to boost their bestseller? To protect another deserter, or perhaps associate Hannah, however tenuously, with the English resistance to the Jacobites? Only she and Robert Walker can answer that.

FIGHTING LIKE A GIRL

After a shaky start, Hannah's story checks out far more convincingly from 1747, though still with the odd glitch. According to *The Female Soldier*, after an uneventful month in Portsmouth, the search for her errant husband largely forgotten, Hannah unashamedly sought adventure. 'Disdaining a life thus led at home in indolence and ease, [she] resolved still to go abroad' and enlisted – as James Gray, of course – as a marine in Captain Graham's company, of Colonel Fraser's regiment, in turn part of Admiral Boscawen's fleet of ten naval and East India Company ships, which were fighting it out with the French

East India Company for control of their Indian trading posts in the First Carnatic War of 1746–8. She boarded the *Swallow*, a British sloop-of-war, which was bound for the East Indies to seize the French-held island of Mauritius and the Indian east-coast town of Pondicherry, in retaliation for the French's recent capture of the English-held Madras. On 23 October 1747, the *Swallow*'s captain, John Rowzier, noted in his log that 'a lieutenant of marines and five private centinels' joined the crew, and sure enough, one of them was James Gray.

The ship weighed anchor and made for India on 1 November. Hannah's horizons were broadening, quite literally, but within the confines of the ship, her daily life was now decidedly unpleasant. Seamen lived crammed together in the stuffy, putrid lower deck, each with just a 14- to 16-inch space for their hammock and no privacy whatsoever. Food rations were meagre and unhealthy, consisting mainly of sea biscuits, hard cheese and salted meat, and the drinking water rank. Maintaining personal hygiene was not an option, so deadly diseases, particularly scurvy but also typhus, tuberculosis, dysentery and smallpox, were rife, and should the crew kick against their lot, the punishments were harsh – even the smallest misdemeanour could earn a seaman a flogging.

Conditions on board ship were so unbearable that most men were there against their will, kidnapped by press gangs that were sent out, particularly during wartime, to forcibly recruit any man who was not of the gentry class. And for their labour and the loss of their liberty they were not even well remunerated: a sailor's pay was low and could take years to materialise. It was a dire existence, and the well-to-do commissioned officers, who enjoyed far better conditions on the quarter deck, knew it. They were reluctant to grant shore leave for fear that large numbers of men would desert the moment they reached land, because, as Dr Samuel Johnson put it, 'No man will be a sailor who has contrivance enough to get himself into a jail; for being in a ship is being in a jail with a chance of being drowned.'[16]

During these months of confinement, the promise of the occasional visit from a prostitute was one of the few carrots (along with a good supply of beer and rum) that might just keep the sailors in line and (it was hoped) curb incidents of sodomy on board – the punishment for which was death. This temporary admittance of women was certainly not acceptable practice, but rather 'a necessary' and 'unavoidable evil'[17] to keep the hungry, angry, sex-starved crew from mutiny.[18]

Such was the life that Hannah had signed up for and, somehow, she adapted well. By the time they reached Lisbon, 'James Gray' had become 'a favourite amongst them all'; she helped to wash, cook and mend linen – all standard female occupations, as it happened – but was also stationed on the quarter deck in case of engagement, where 'her business was to fight and do what mischief she could with the small-arms which they had on board'. Young as she was, she had quickly become 'a little tar of note'.

There would be no gentle initiation into this new life of hers – the voyage to India was hazardous. At Lisbon, the ship was already in need of repairs from storm damage, and the rough seas were only set to continue. In constant danger of shipwreck, the *Swallow* creaked its way to Gibraltar in January 1748, and then on to Cape Town, arriving safe and remarkably unscathed on 6 May. There was little time to recuperate from the journey. On their arrival, Admiral Boscawen ordered the fleet to Mauritius, with an audacious plan to kidnap a French soldier and learn from him the might of the French force. Hannah readied herself along with her shipmates for her first taste of warfare, and, though a 'raw marine', she was eager to 'distinguish herself by her

intrepid behaviour'. All the same, she may have been relieved when
the mission was called off, as Boscawen chose instead to save his troops
for the main event: the invasion of Pondicherry.

The *Swallow* left Mauritius on 28 June and headed for the coast of
India where the French were stationed at Pondicherry, ready and
waiting. When the crew arrived a month later at Fort St David, an
English settlement 12 miles south of Pondicherry, they set up camp
two miles outside of it, and here the British forces (comprising the
marines, the East India ships and 3,000 Indian troops) were readied.
On the morning of 8 August they began their march towards
Pondicherry, camping out along the way, and for the next month lay
siege to the town, digging trenches all around it and setting up their
cannons. All in vain, as it turned out. Continual gun and mortar fire
plus the threat of monsoon rains made progress difficult, and as
conditions worsened, the siege began to crumble; for Hannah and
her fellow marines, it meant slogging away 'middle-deep in water'
for hours on end with very little to show for it.

According to Walker, it was in the final few days of this beleag-
uered siege that Hannah took a dangerous hit from the enemy fire.
Lauding her bravery, he describes how, guns blazing, she fired 37
rounds of shot, only to be brought down by a barrage of musket balls
in return. She was left seriously wounded, with six shots in her right
leg, five in her left and one in her groin, which spelled particular
danger, not just to her life but to her disguise.

Our heroine was in a fix – she was taken to the hospital at
Cuddalore, just south of Fort St David, and placed under the care
of Dr Belchier, but such was her determination not to be found out
that she omitted to tell the surgeons of the wound in her groin. For
her own safety, she could have dropped the act there and then, but

no, 'she resolved to run all risks, even at the hazard of her life, rather than her sex should be known'. Her only option was, somehow, to tend to this wound herself, so when the gnawing pain became unendurable, 'she intended to try an experiment' – she would extract the ball from the wound herself. With undisguised glee, Walker explains how she 'probed the wound with her finger till she came where the ball lay, and then upon feeling it thrust in both her finger and thumb and pulled it out'. With the help of an Indian nurse, Hannah then applied healing salves to her wounds and, allowing the surgeons to treat her leg injuries, she managed a full recovery in three months. To Walker, this episode was the ultimate expression of Hannah's 'invincible courage and resolution': she would rather 'have her flesh tore and mangled' than be exposed.

It's an extraordinary story, and if the accounts of lady tars tell us anything it's that the improbable isn't necessarily impossible. But Hannah's determination to persist with her stressful charade in such dangerous circumstances is perplexing, not least because the consequences for unmasked female sailors and soldiers were far from severe. They were discharged from service, yes, and humiliated, undoubtedly, but there was no punishment, not even a reprimand – if their sex was discovered when they were about to be flogged, as Charles Waddall's was when tied to the gangway to receive two dozen lashes for deserting the *Oxford* man-of-war in 1771, the punishment was immediately stopped. Waddall – another young lady who claimed to be chasing her errant lover, probably because she knew this was a safe excuse that would be well received – was not only spared; she was given half a guinea by the Admiral and sent on her merry way.[19] Likewise, 17-year-old Margaret Thompson, who joined the navy as George Thompson in 1781, avoided three dozen lashes by the revelation that she was a woman. The response was nothing worse than astonishment at the 'blooming youthful girl' suddenly in the sailors' midst.[20] By now, the threat posed by female cross-dressers had been largely overwhelmed by the force of their entertainment value; these shocking, amusing, arousing curiosities would go unpunished – if they stayed within the strict parameters of what was socially redeemable. Provided the lady's aim had been to search for her lost lover, preserve her virtue or serve her country in a fit of patriotism and not to commit sexual deviancies, fraud or theft, and as long as she eventually resumed her 'natural' feminine role and didn't expect to be considered a man's equal just because she donned his clothes and did his job as well as him, then her subversive act could be tolerated, celebrated in newspapers, ballads, plays and books, even rewarded with royal patronage, as Christian Davies's story had proved.

Which begs the question: would anyone prize the secret of their gender over their life, when the alternative was so lenient? Hannah, it seems, did – and she wasn't alone. In almost every account we have, women tars and soldiers never chose to disclose their sex, no matter what the provocation. Their new life of freedom and adventure was far too precious to give up willingly; they only ever did so when they were forced.

While Hannah was convalescing, Walker tells us that her shipmates transferred from the *Swallow* to the *Eltham* man-of-war and sailed off to Madras. So on her release from hospital, she was temporarily put on board the *Tartar*, before being transferred to the *Eltham* on its return, at which point she and her crewmates sailed for Bombay and arrived, their ship leaking and battered, a fortnight later. After a five-week hiatus, the *Eltham* made its way back to Fort St David, where Walker claims it was caught up in the great hurricane on 13

April 1749 that sank the *Namur*, though miraculously it emerged unscathed.

He also insists – just to prove his heroine's impeccable feminine sensibilities beyond any doubt – that during the crew's shore leave at Fort St David, Hannah had to frequently avert her gaze and close her ears at the debaucheries of her shipmates. Her acting abilities in these moments impressed him, for despite overhearing 'the most execrable oaths that could be invented' and being 'eyewitness of a thousand unseemly actions … which almost shocked her', she always remained mindful of the character she was playing. As a 'brother tar', she was 'not only forced to connive at, but seemingly to countenance and approve' of this rowdy behaviour, so while her colleagues were busy bedding the local ladies, Hannah adopted an imperious swagger to deflect attention from the fact that she was not. More than this, Walker refuses to tell, as he skips over the next few months until the *Eltham* weighed anchor and set sail for England on 19 November 1749.

Hannah's exploits in India would form the bedrock of her tale when she returned to London: it would be the basis of her petition for a naval pension and would prove critical to her popularity – it was an heroic tale of adventure and bravery, of survival against the odds, of resourcefulness in the face of exposure. But again, there's a snag: the official ships' musters don't quite agree with Walker. The dates and locations set down in the records suggest that James Gray was still fit and healthy and sailing with his crewmates in the *Eltham* to Bombay when he was supposed to be in hospital, and that the *Eltham* was not in Fort St David in April 1749 when it was supposed to have been hit by the hurricane that sank the *Namur*. On top of that, it turns out that, in the months that Walker skips over, James Gray was involved in a second siege that goes entirely unmentioned in *The Female Soldier* – at the Fort of Devicotta.[21] After this, Walker's account and the official records converge and diverge with dizzying rapidity, for a month and a half after the siege of Devicotta, on 2 August, James Gray was indeed hospitalised at Cuddalore and had to convalesce for two months under Doctor Belchier, which matches Walker's version closely, but he then set sail for England with his crew on 19 October 1749, exactly a month earlier than Walker claims. Like a blurry photograph, the details in the two sources almost, but don't quite, coalesce to form a comprehensive image.[22]

Verifying the truth of Hannah's injuries is even more difficult. There are no hospital records of James Gray's condition, and no evidence of Hannah undergoing a physical examination to verify her wounds. Was James Gray hospitalised with injuries to match Hannah's? Or did he succumb to scurvy or malaria, as many of his shipmates did? Twenty of the *Eltham*'s crew were sent to hospital during August and September that year, and a disease would certainly involve a much less intimate physical examination than leg and groin injuries.

If Walker's account is inaccurate on these points, it's worth asking why. Simple human error, honest mistakes creeping into what Walker admitted was a hurried publication, is one possibility. But it's been plausibly argued that Walker and Hannah may have cooked up a different version of events quite deliberately. For one, the siege of Pondicherry was a far more famous skirmish than that of Devicotta – it had been widely reported on at home and Hannah's death-defying involvement in it would doubtless excite readers more. And if she were to be granted a navy pension – a need, rather than a want, for most sailors – it would rely on her being injured in battle, rather than falling ill.[23] If this be the case, we might curse Walker and Hannah for their lax ways with the truth, even if we can't fault their cunning.

'THE DISAGREEABLE TITLE OF
MISS MOLLY GRAY'

The question of how women like Hannah managed to pull off their daring disguises is a fascinating one. Even if she had the demeanour, gait and voice of a bawdy sailor down to a tee, how could she not be discovered in the close confines of a sloop-of-war? The lack of hygiene on board helped – with few or no opportunities for bathing, and sailors living and sleeping in the same clothes, there would rarely be an occasion for getting undressed, apart from those notorious floggings. And another of those occurred in Bombay when Hannah was accused by the ship's first lieutenant of stealing a missing shirt – a petty, trumped-up charge to punish her for a minor act of insubordination (she had refused to sing for the officer, resenting 'with true fire and spirit such an imposition on her will'). She was given 12 lashes but evaded detection this time, Walker tells us, because 'she stood as upright as possible, and tied a large silk handkerchief round her neck, the ends whereof entirely covered her breasts'. This was another moment of reckoning for Hannah – or any woman trying to conceal her sex: just how much did she value her new life as a marine? Enough to endure a barbaric punishment that she could easily avoid by disclosing her true identity.

How Hannah negotiated the more personal trappings of being a woman is equally hard to establish – these are not the kinds of details that make it into polite eighteenth-century literature. Other cross-dressing women of the time can give us some clues, however. The German cross-dresser Catharina Lincken, who also served in the military in the early 1700s, was discovered to have used a primitive kind of she-wee – 'a leather-covered horn ... fastened against her nude body' – to enable her to urinate standing up, while Christian Davies is believed to have used something similar: a 'silver tube' that she acquired from another female soldier.[24] And though it was never dared mentioned in documents of the time, it has since been argued that nutrition on board ship was so poor that women's periods may well have stopped, solving one problem at least, or that blood-soaked rags could be passed off as some kind of venereal disease.[25] Whatever the tactics, a successful transformation took courage, ingenuity and more than a little luck.

Hannah evidently had all three, as well as a talent for mimicking masculine mannerisms, but even so, she drew suspicion. Her portrait, sold alongside her biography, depicts her as being of a strong, stocky build (a bonus when it came to wrestling with rigging in all weathers, handling a heavy musket and hiding her curves), but it was noticed during the *Eltham*'s journey back to England that 'James Gray' was of a strikingly youthful, smooth-skinned appearance. His crewmates teased him 'for want of having a rough beard', and took to giving him 'the disagreeable title of Miss Molly Gray', which naturally made Hannah nervous. With impressive sangfroid, she met these jests 'not only with a smile and an oath, but with a challenge ... to prove herself as good a man as any of them on board'.

To demonstrate her masculinity beyond doubt, she threw herself into the crew's high jinks at their next dock, Lisbon. When the sailors went gallivanting ashore, Hannah 'would be one of the most forward to promote the scheme, and would seem to take a peculiar delight in carousing'. She even went so far as to compete with a fellow sailor, Edward Jeffries, over a Portuguese woman who had taken a shine to her. Jealous of his rival, Jeffries suggested they draw lots for the woman, and it was only Hannah's luck at losing the draw that got her out of this sticky situation.

Walker takes great delight in reporting these close encounters between Hannah and her pseudo-lovers; with lesbianism not yet a concept in the British psyche, the tease of two women being almost but not quite *in flagrante* was all part of the inexpressible appeal of cross-dressed women in the eighteenth century, as long as any hint of sexual ambiguity was ultimately quashed. Whether Hannah ever indulged in anything more we can't know, but flirtation was certainly a safe, easy trick that women could employ to imitate the ways of men (Mary Lacy made no secret in her memoir of the fact that she flirted with as many women as she could to aid her disguise). Obeying convention, Walker reins in the titillation just in time, rescuing his heroine from any genuinely licentious activity and reassuring his readers that 'all her compliances were indeed forced, and all she did was the result of necessity, and not choice'.

Apparently it served her purpose, because by behaving in this overtly loutish way, Hannah 'prevented [her crewmates] from carrying the joke too far' and 'the name of Miss Molly was here perfectly buried in oblivion'. Skilled actress that she was, she had learned to curse and flirt and drink grog alongside her fellow men with absolute conviction, but Walker could only sell his heroine if she were also pure, virtuous and unequivocally heterosexual, so he has it both ways, stressing that 'by acting such parts as in secret gave her the utmost disgust' she both silenced the jokers and 'returned at last to her dear native home as pure as when she first set out'. With that, his readers could indulge their double standards without the slightest twinge of unease.

Hannah had survived a great deal on her adventures and managed to keep her disguise intact under extraordinary pressure, but the long journey home had a few more unpleasant surprises in store. Just a day after the *Eltham*'s departure from Fort St David, 'the only sincere friend she had on board', Lieutenant Richard Wagget, died from a long-standing illness that she had been nursing him through, and his loss 'shocked our heroine greatly'. Then came a staggering discovery about her long-lost husband. A chance meeting with a sailor who had heard of James Summs's fate revealed that he had met a gruesome end, having been executed for murder following a brawl in Genoa. With no evidence to support or contradict this story, it could be entirely true or entirely fabricated, but it's been noted that Summs's death does at least provide a convenient resolution to this particular loose end, freeing Hannah from her 'official quest' of searching for her lost lover and allowing her to return home.[26]

This she did on 25 May 1750, when the *Eltham* sailed into Portsmouth harbour seven months after leaving India (Walker has the ship arriving a week later, for reasons known only to him and Hannah). A weekend of revelry with her shipmates ensued, during which Hannah indulged in one last flirtation, with 'Miss Catherine', a young woman she had briefly met on her last visit to Portsmouth, who quickly became 'a kind of sweetheart' – or at least, a convenient and agreeable means by which to avoid another drinking binge with her shipmates. Her fellows approved of her choice, gave smutty toasts 'to the successful battering of Miss Catherine's Fort' and excused her, while she sauntered off to enjoy her lady friend's 'amorous caresses'. Poor Miss Catherine seems to have been the loser here, for Walker tells us she fell in love with James Gray and would've happily married him, leaving Hannah in the awkward position of having to gently explain to the lovelorn girl that 'common prudence obliged her to postpone the match for a short time till she could return to London, and not only get her pay but her discharge'. To which Miss Catherine tearfully acquiesced.

Having thus neatly extricated herself from another same-sex dalliance, on 27 May 1750, Hannah and a company of ten other tars set out from Portsmouth, with their five shillings 'conduct money'[27] in their pockets, and by way of Petersfield and Guildford made their way home to London. She had seen exotic wonders, experienced grim hardships and known extraordinary adventures, but now her life as a marine was officially over.

FAREWELL, JEMMY GRAY

Late one night at the close of May 1750, Hannah arrived on her old doorstep in Wapping, and when her sister Susannah opened the door, their reunion was joyous. Despite her sister's long absence and strange apparel, Susannah knew her 'almost at the first glance' and 'ventured, contrary to all seeming decency and good manners, to throw her arms about our young marine's neck'. In her excitement, Hannah ran upstairs and woke her brother-in-law, the real James Gray, whose identity she had borrowed so freely for the last few years, with a torrent of grateful hugs and kisses. It made her giggle that in his befuddled state, Gray was utterly perplexed and nonplussed to find 'such odd and uncommon civilities from a stranger in his regimentals', but once the penny finally dropped and Hannah had assured him of the 'innocence of her intentions', she was welcomed home with delight. Gray plied her with refreshments, then sat her down, eager to hear her fabulous tale.

Hannah had begun to shed the skin of her alias, but as she hadn't yet collected her army pay and feared discovery before she could do so, revealing her identity to the public would have to be carefully managed. She bided her time until 9 June, when she and her shipmates went to Downing Street to claim from their regiment's agent the several years' worth of pay they were owed. Hannah walked away with £15, as well as two suits of clothes, which she quickly sold for an extra 16 shillings, and only then, with her pay packet safely in her pocket, had her alias James Gray served his last official purpose. She now felt free to discard him.

It had to be done immediately, she knew, while she had so many witnesses. After all, her messmates were the only ones who could corroborate her incredible story. So when the crew decamped to a pub to celebrate their newfound wealth, Hannah seized the moment. As Walker tells it, she knew the truth would tickle rather than upset them, so she began by playing a little game. Addressing the crowd in a tone of great solemnity, she informed her shipmates that it was 'very probable ... that not one of you will ever see your friend and fellow-soldier, Jemmy Gray, any more'. Dismayed cries of 'God Forbid!' rang out, at which Hannah burst out laughing, and in the bawdy, bantering style that now came so easily, she joked with her bedfellow Master Moody that 'Had you have known ... who you had between a pair of sheets with you, you would have come to closer quarters. In a word, gentlemen, I am as much a woman as my mother ever was, and my real name is Hannah Snell.' A hushed astonishment fell upon the gathering, until one by one her friends piped up that they refused to believe it – this was 'one of Jemmy's merry conceits to amuse them', surely? It was only when her sister and brother-in-law confirmed her story that her friends accepted it, and erupted into raptures on her bravery, compassion and forbearance in response. Never once, in all the hardships she'd endured, had they ever heard her complain, they said – perhaps women weren't such weak, delicate little creatures, after all.

In a word, gentlemen,
I am as much
a woman as my
mother ever was

As for Master Moody, he was so enamoured of Hannah and her story that he proposed marriage on the spot, but she refused. Mindful of 'what miseries and misfortunes' she'd been subjected to through the 'hard-heartedness and inhumanity' of her last husband, she was now 'fully determined, if she knew her own mind, never to submit herself to the marriage yoke any more'. Rather than rely on a husband to support her, Hannah followed her friends' advice and decided to petition the Duke of Cumberland, the Captain-General of the British Army, for financial compensation for the injuries she sustained while on active service, and this scene she craftily orchestrated, too. For maximum impact, she dressed in her male attire, and on 16 June delivered her petition 'with her own hands' to the Duke as he sat in his carriage in St James's Park. As intended, this display got her noticed. The Duke read her petition there and then, and promptly ordered Colonel Napier, the Adjutant-General, to investigate the veracity of her claims.

Within a week the newspapers were reporting the story – and already skewing the facts, claiming that she had been 'seven years in a Marine Regiment' and that 'her sweetheart being pressed into the Marine Service, she put on men's clothes, and entered into the same regiment, went to the East Indies in the same ship with him, and was his messmate while he lived (he dying in the voyage)'. More important than the details, however, was that the press and the public were captivated by her story. 'She behaved with great intrepidity as a sailor and soldier, and her sex was never discovered, by either sweetheart, or any of her comrades, 'till she made the discovery herself by the above-mentioned petition,' thrilled the papers.[28] It was the start of a whole new career for Hannah – as a feted and fictionalised celebrity.

THE JOVIAL TAR

It's not known how Hannah and Robert Walker met, but Walker was an influential figure in the publishing industry, a canny businessman and an innovator in the serialisation of books. It's likely that he read of Hannah's escapades in the newspapers in mid-June and, with an eye for a sensational bestseller, hurriedly approached her with a book deal. Knowing that her navy pay would soon dry up and that she would be wise to capitalise on her novelty value, Hannah granted him exclusive rights to her story and together they presented an affidavit to this effect to the Lord Mayor, swearing to the truth of her tale, witnessed by her sister Susannah and signed by Hannah with a cross on 27 June. The first edition of *The Female Soldier* duly appeared with lightning speed on 3 July. It had been hurriedly thrown together due to the 'impatience of the town to have it published', Walker wrote in defence of any errors, and the release of a second, much longer edition in nine-part serialisation less than two weeks later is testament to its instant popularity.

Hannah's publicity machine was now in full flow, and a stage show was perhaps the inevitable culmination of such intense media interest.[29] Whoever came up with this bright idea (and Walker implies that it was down to Hannah's 'more than ordinary ambition'), the theatrical potential of her story was quickly seized upon, and though she wasn't a performer in any official sense, she had spent the last few years method acting as though her life depended on it – how hard could it be before a theatre audience? In the end, it wasn't hard at all. On 29 June 1750 – several days before her biography even appeared – Hannah took to the stage of the New Wells Theatre in Goodman's Fields for her first performance, and it proved so popular that she repeated it 60 times over the following 70 nights, in a run that lasted until 6 September and earned her a decent weekly salary.

One of many vaudeville-style acts that played out each night at this fringe theatre, Hannah's show began as just a couple of songs performed in her sailor's garb, though it quickly developed into a much more complex piece, including a demonstration of her manual exercises in full regimental uniform, complete with supporting cast. Each performance was met with 'universal applause' – not because of her vocal talents (she readily admitted to having no 'judgement in music'), but because it was titillating, patriotic fare and all done with 'great decency and good manners'.[30]

This enthusiasm was likely down to the sheer novelty of her act. A woman brandishing a sword on stage in military uniform audiences had seen before – Hannah was part of a popular eighteenth-century theatre tradition of women in breeches parts taking on the roles of female soldiers[31] – but this show was unique in one important particular: Hannah wasn't just an actress *pretending* to be a female soldier; she was a *real* female soldier. And that audiences had never seen before. The military exercises she performed on stage were elaborate and finnicky, comprising 74 individual movements, some with several 'motions' in each, while the musket she used weighed 12 pounds and had a 46-inch-long barrel, with a 17-inch bayonet on the end.[32] To wield such a thing with dexterity required skill, strength and practice – an untrained amateur could not have done it – and the veteran soldiers in the audience conceded that Hannah managed it with all the ease of a professional. This show was more than just a cash cow; it provided a vital piece of evidence – perhaps the most convincing of all – in support of her authenticity as a trained female soldier.

Hannah Snell was everywhere you turned in London: she was in print and on stage; several portraits of her, both in military uniform and in a gown, were sold on street corners, while a ballad celebrating her deeds circulated around town. And this warm reception was beginning to pay dividends beyond the entertainment world, too. Satisfied with her petition for compensation, Colonel Napier handed the Duke of Cumberland a certificate that supposedly verified her wounding at Pondicherry (though it's not clear how, as no physical examination of Hannah is known to have taken place),[33] and the Duke's response was that 'such an Amazonian lady as Mrs Snell deserved some encourage-ment, and that her heroic achievements should not be altogether buried in oblivion'. By 27 June, the press was claiming that the Duke had 'been pleased to order her to be put upon the King's List, by which she will obtain a pension of thirty pounds per annum, for her life'[34] – a benefaction that came with the proviso that she maintain her soldier's persona for the entertainment of the masses.

Hannah was perfectly happy to oblige, for she had already 'determined to continue so to do' and had 'lately purchased a new suit of decent man's apparel as an incontestable proof of her aversion to the present fashionable hoop' – the most telling evidence yet that she cross-dressed as much for pleasure as for practicality. This was a risky way to end the story of a cross-dressed woman. Such accounts usually concluded with the comforting confirmation that the lady was a reformed virago and retired adventurer who had reverted to the habits of conventional femi-ninity, either by stepping out of her breeches and back into her 'proper' attire or by marrying. Hannah would pointedly do neither within the confines of *The Female Soldier*. On the contrary, at this stage in her life, aged 27, she was determined to continue to cross-dress and to eschew marriage forever. Little wonder, then, that Walker felt the need to overcompensate with lashings of defensive praise.

This is no
false attack;
I will have
my man

To disarm any critics who might judge her harshly for continuing with her curious peccadillo, he points out how integral Hannah's transvestism now was to her continued success. She was highly conscious, he said, that 'had she made her appearance upon the stage in petticoats, she would have made but an awkward figure, and that all her performances would have been lifeless and insipid', and she wasn't so naïve as to imagine that her newfound fame would last. The public would soon get bored of this peculiar woman with her madcap story, so she was 'determined to make hay whilst the sun shines, and, like the laborious ant, to lay up a little stock to support her against a rainy day'. It was only sensible, he argued, for her to capitalise on her moment in the spotlight, and for this reason 'her resolution to decline the female garb for ever hereafter is not so blameworthy as some may perhaps be apt to imagine'.

To make it absolutely clear where our sympathies and our cash should go, Walker ends his account with an abundance of goodwill towards his heroine, ladling on the praise for her ambition, her bravery, her metamorphic skills and her ability to 'preserve her chastity amongst a whole crowd of military men' by avoiding rape and seduction.[35] He then goes on to explain Hannah's next move. With her future now dependent upon her continuing to adopt male dress, she had hit upon a plausible, long-term career that could successfully incorporate it: the 'jovial tar' would become the 'jovial publican'. Using her stage earnings and the promised pension from the Duke of Cumberland, she intended to open a public house, which she would aptly call The Woman in Masquerade, and the painted sign outside would leave punters in no doubt of its USP: the famous Hannah Snell, in breeches and jacket on one side and in regimentals on the other. Walker heartily approves of this new scheme, and hopes his 'readers will likewise'. His PR machine could not have worked harder to sell Hannah – unconventional and 'unfeminine' as she was – as the perfect man-woman, with all the heroism of a warrior and all the purity of a maid. So far it had done its job, but the Amazonian Mrs Snell's 15 minutes of fame would not last much longer.

DOWN AND OUT

The Female Soldier draws to a close in September 1750, when the last instalment of the serialisation was published and Hannah's future, at the age of 27, was still uncertain, so to understand her remaining 42 years we must scavenge what we can from other sources. From this point on, her life was not without incident, but her run of good luck appeared to be over.

Despite the press's optimism, there's no evidence that the hoped-for pension from the Duke of Cumberland ever materialised, but Hannah had a back-up plan: as Christian Davies had done before her, she would apply to the Royal Hospital Chelsea for a pension instead. This application was more successful: on 21 November 1750, 'Hannah Snell, alias James Gray' was admitted as an out-pensioner at the Royal Hospital and granted five pence a day for the rest of her life.[36] It was something, though by no means enough to live on.

By now, she could no longer rely on her stage career to fill her purse, for as she'd predicted, it was short-lived. Her season at Goodman's Fields had closed on 6 September that year, and notwith-standing an extra four-night run at the New Wells Spa in Clerkenwell from 11 September, this was the end for her London shows. Audiences in the capital had lost interest, but Hannah was not willing to give up on this source of income quite yet, so she decided to do what Charlotte Charke had done several years before: she would try the provinces and become a strolling player. Off she went, touring her act around the country, and it was when she was visiting her home town, of all places, that the next mishap of her life occurred. In November 1751, the *Derby Mercury* reported that 'They write from Worcester, that the famous heroine Hannah Snell, formerly a soldier, has been lately committed to Bridewell, by one of the magistrates of that city, for a misdemeanour.'[37] This tantalising snippet omits far more than it reveals, giving no information whatsoever on the precise nature of this 'misdemeanour', but bridewells were houses of correction that had sprung up around the country in imitation of the London original, and were reserved for petty offenders of the 'disorderly poor'. Inmates would be briefly incarcerated for crimes such as 'dishonesty', disorderly behaviour, prostitution, beggary or vagrancy, sometimes even madness, with both men and women subjected to the 'corrective' punishments of whippings and hard labour. Since the Stage Licensing Act of 1737 had outlawed strolling players as vagrants, it may well be that vagrancy was Hannah's only crime. Alternatively, she may have become so strapped for cash that she was forced to live by dubious means, or perhaps, unable to leave her military bravado behind her, she'd even been involved in a brawl.

Whatever her offence, her life took a more positive, if surprising, turn a few years later. Leaving the stage behind her (there is no record of her performing beyond 1751), she appears to have settled in Newbury, Berkshire, and despite Walker's insistence that she was 'resolutely bent to be lord and master of herself, and never more to entertain the least thoughts of having a husband to rule and govern her', she must have changed her mind, for she *did* marry again, not once but twice. Evidently by 1759 she did indeed know that James Summs was dead, for in November of that year, at the age of 36, she married Richard Eyles, a carpenter with whom she had two sons.

After Eyles died, she then married a Richard Habgood, at Welford on 16 November 1772, when she was 49.

It's a dramatic volte-face for a woman supposedly so against remarrying. Maybe she fell in love – twice. Or maybe, with her military past no longer novel enough to earn her a decent living, survival had just become too hard as a single woman.[38] Fortunately, her second and third choices seem to have been happier than her first, though there was sadness during these years, too, for in the mid-1760s, her sister Susannah and brother-in-law James Gray, who together had been so supportive of her in the past, both died of consumption, having been consigned by abject poverty to separate workhouses.

Despite Georgian Britain's growing commercial success and the rise of a new 'middling sort' of affluent professional, Hannah's family, like swathes of the country, were floundering, and with no official state support, they were penalised for it rather than helped. Hannah herself had only one asset – her remarkable history as James Gray – and even though public interest in her had waned, she continued to trade on it. And not everyone, it turned out, had forgotten about her. In January 1771, one newspaper was still keen to pounce on her late fame and trumpet her every action as full-blown heroism, reporting how a pugnacious Hannah had rescued a 'poor countryman' from a press gang that was terrorising the London neighbourhood of Newington Butts. If the anecdote is to be believed, Hannah, now in petticoats, 'collared and shook' the man's captors and challenged them to a fight 'with fists, stick, or quarter-staff'. 'Ye dogs,' she bellowed, 'I have more wounds about me than you have fingers. This is no false attack; I will have my man.' And so she did. She restored the captive fellow to his wife, looking for all the world like the fierce, heroic warrior readers knew of old.[39]

But you can't always believe what you read in the papers – an eyewitness account a few years later paints a much sadder picture. On 21 May 1778, a clergyman named James Woodforde visited the White Hart pub in Weston Longville, Norfolk, specifically to see the famous Hannah Snell. There, he found her back in breeches (having been granted 'the liberty of wearing men's clothes' by the Crown, 'and also a cockade in her hat, which she still wears') and talking 'very sensible and well' of her madcap youth. These days, he learned, she 'travel[led] the country with [a] basket at her back, selling buttons, garters, laces etc' – an ageing eccentric, forced to peddle knick-knacks and tales of past glories in exchange for scraps. The revelation of this sad come-down moved Woodforde to charity. He purchased a few buttons, gave her two shillings and six, then went about his business.[40]

Her next appearance in the records is the most peculiar yet, and one that further demonstrates just how slippery the business of identity could be in the eighteenth century. In December 1779, when Hannah was 56, two separate newspapers reported her untimely death: 'Hannah Snell, the female soldier (well known in many parts of this kingdom) was found dead on Mousehold Heath in the precinct of Woodbastwick,' proclaimed the *Ipswich Journal* on 18 December, and the *Newcastle Chronicle* a fortnight later. The first thought that springs to mind is murder. Had the famous Hannah Snell really been butchered on a lonely common when out walking one night? Thankfully, no, she hadn't. We know this, first, because the newspapers also reported that the inquest returned a verdict of 'natural death', and second, because the body on the common was not Hannah Snell's at all. It was a curious case of mistaken identity. With no forensics or official records available to aid identification, the shaky methods of chance documentation or personal recognition were relied upon instead, and on this occasion they got it wrong. That the body on the common was assumed to be Hannah's suggests that it belonged to another middle-aged woman with a fancy for men's clothes, who may even have been dressed as a soldier – another Roaring Girl whose story will never be known.

MILITARY HONOURS

The newspapers were as surprised as anybody when, some 12 years after her reported death, they discovered that 'The veteran heroine, Hannah Snell, who distinguished herself many years ago, by repeated acts of valour, and who served in the Navy in a man's habit, is still alive.'[41] She was not, however, in a good way. By 1785 her third husband had died and money was scarce again, for in June of that year she petitioned the Royal Hospital Chelsea for an increase to her pension. They agreed to raise it from five pence to a shilling a day 'in compassion to her infirm state of health', which both physically and mentally was now deteriorating.[42] A few years later, on 6 August 1791, when she was almost 70 years old, she was admitted to the dreaded Bethlem Hospital – the country's most notorious lunatic asylum, now sited at Moorfields – 'being at present a victim of the most deplorable infirmity that can afflict human nature'.[43]

There's no knowing exactly what this 'deplorable infirmity' entailed. Thirteen years before, James Woodforde had found Hannah's conversation eminently sensible, and those admitted to Bedlam could be suffering from any number of mental health issues – depression, anxiety, dementia or the fearful symptoms of syphilis – all bundled together under the vague umbrella term of 'madness'. Whatever Hannah's illness was, she survived only six months after admission, dying – for definite this time – on 8 February 1792, at the age of 69.

By the late 1700s reports of the conditions at Bedlam varied wildly, from accusations of negligence, corruption and physical abuse to claims of its unusual cleanliness and sympathetic treatment of its inmates. In 1814, however, the philanthropist Edward Wakefield told a parliamentary committee that 'Many women were locked up in their cells naked and chained, on straw, with only one blanket for a covering, and the windows being unglazed, the light in winter was shut out for the sake of warmth.'[44] It seems probable, therefore, that Hannah died – frail, confused and distressed – in a cold, dark cell, stripped of her clothes and her dignity and shackled like a criminal. Such living conditions can only have hastened her decline.

In death, Hannah was afforded much more dignity. As a Chelsea Pensioner, she became the second woman ever to be interred at the Royal Hospital Chelsea (after Christian Davies in 1739), though even this turn of events adds another twist to her tale. On 3 February 1792, just a few days before her official date of death, one James Gray was also buried at the Chelsea Hospital. The mismatching dates are problematic, but their proximity seems altogether too coincidental to be unrelated. Odd though it may seem for Hannah to have been buried under her assumed name, it remains plausible – her stint as James Gray had been the defining era of her life; it had made her famous, earned her an income and granted her a freedom she could never have found otherwise. Perhaps this was the dying woman's last request, to be buried not as Hannah Snell, who had suffered so much, but as the famous female soldier who had won the admiration and affection of a nation.

In recent years, Hannah Snell's story has been viewed with a scepticism that her contemporaries never entertained. So seduced were her eighteenth-century audience by the sensation and derring-do of her tale that the misinformation, distortions, embellishments and omissions passed unnoticed. In the intervening centuries, interest in her has come and gone and come back again, usually in tandem with the periodic waves of feminism, with books, articles, plays and even a rock opera drawing on her life, but cynicism has gradually replaced credulity. Some have labelled her a fraud, others even fictitious.[45] It's true, the tale that has come down to us is undoubtedly a spin piece that cleverly manages Hannah's image to fire up and then soothe the British middle-classes. Yet in the scraps of documentary evidence, in the testimonies of her contemporaries, in the accounts of other women who successfully went to war in disguise, the stamp of authenticity is discernible, even if some of the details have been embellished in places and worn away in others.

In his version of Hannah Snell, Walker plays to his audience by consciously balancing the masculine and the feminine, the sexual and the pure, so as to neatly offset the one with the other. Hannah is a mannish woman, a valiant warrior, a principled patriot, a flirtatious tar, a consummate actress and an independent heroine, but she's also a wronged wife, a bereaved mother, a chaste maiden and a preserver of virtuous young women. The reality was likely a messier, less contrived, more interesting jumble of all these qualities – a young woman who was sick of the constraints of traditional femininity, who enjoyed the boisterous, ribald life of being at sea, who craved adventure and was always on the lookout for the next opportunity. Such a woman is no longer seen as an enigma who must be explained, or a gender anomaly that needs to be excused.

For hundreds of years, the 'no women allowed' rule meant that their role in the armed forces had to be either unofficial or covert. Despite the long history of women supporting their country during wartime and picking up male roles both on the home front and in the field, it's only in the last 25 years that women in the forces have been allowed to step outside of their auxiliary roles and stand side by side with men.[46] Since 2001, they have served (and died) on the frontline as medics, bomb-disposal experts and fighter pilots, although the unease at women engaging in combat roles has persisted – the ban was only officially lifted in 2015. The breakthrough came following a Ministry of Defence review, which confirmed what many people already knew: that women were every bit as capable of fighting for their country as men. Hannah Snell and her sister soldiers had proved it centuries before.

Mary Prince

GOODS AND CHATTELS

The family arrives at the marketplace of Hamble Town, Bermuda, at four o'clock in the afternoon. They find the square dotted with eager pale faces, laughing and milling freely, and anxious dark faces like theirs huddled together in groups, still and alert like cornered prey. Stopping before a large house, the mother shuffles her three daughters into a line, backs to the wall, arms folded across their scratchy shifts. She weeps openly as she does this. Moments later the auction master approaches, eyeing the family with disdain. Which of the girls is the eldest? he asks, and the mother points wordlessly to Mary, who is watching him warily from the end of the line.

At 12 years old, Mary already knows not to resist when the master takes her hand and pulls her into the street. He turns her slowly, calling out to his customers: come, come, have a look! They do come, but they don't just look. Smartly dressed men press in around her, prodding, grabbing, probing – butchers assessing a lamb. They talk casually about her body as if she cannot understand them, and their words make her flinch. Panic rising, she clasps her hands flat across her chest and pushes down hard to try to slow her clattering heart.

The bidding starts at just a few pounds, but she is fiercely bartered for – £57 is a good price for so young a slave, remarks one voice in

*'I have felt what a slave feels, and I know
what a slave knows; and I would have all
the good people in England know it too.'*

MARY PRINCE (1788–C.1833),
SLAVE, ABOLITIONIST AND THE FIRST BLACK WOMAN TO PUBLISH
HER LIFE STORY IN BRITAIN

the crowd. No one is listening. Their attention is on the master, as he brings forward the next miserable soul whose life is for sale.

~.✕.~

Mary would be 40 years old before she would get her first taste of freedom, when she arrived in London from Antigua in 1828. That day, she passed through customs as goods and chattels, just another item in the luggage of her 'owners', Mr and Mrs Wood – she had no home, no nationality and no rights, but the moment she set foot on English soil, she became a free woman. In theory, at least.

English merchants had begun to trade in African lives in earnest during the 1640s, and by the mid-eighteenth century, Britain was one of the major players in the lucrative commodification of black lives, shipping 50,000 slaves across the Atlantic to its colonies in the Americas and the Caribbean every year – slaves who were shackled and crammed like livestock into the lower decks, trapped in the heat, stench and putrefaction of a human cesspit, to be worked in plantations that produced the cotton, tobacco, sugar, salt and coffee that the white people craved. As many as one in eight of them didn't survive the journey.[1]

By the time Mary Prince arrived in London, the argument for abolition had been building for decades, but it had not yet won the fight. Slavery in the British colonies was still entirely legal, though for years there had been some confusion about the status of slaves who had been brought over to Britain by their owners. There was no law in the statute books that clarified it, only the general belief, derived from a court ruling in 1569, that 'England has too pure an air for slaves to breathe in'. The influential case of the slave James Somerset, in 1772, presided over by Lord Mansfield – in which Somerset had escaped from his master on arrival in England, believing himself to be free, only to be recaptured by his master, who disagreed – had established in principle that no man or woman could be enslaved in Britain by ruling in Somerset's favour.[2] But this ruling applied only on British soil, becoming null and void as soon as the slave returned to the colonies. Even in 1828, this caveat still existed, because although the slave trade had been abolished throughout the British Empire in March 1807, slavery itself had not been; it remained common practice for upstanding British families to own slaves in far-away countries and to force them to work for no pay.

This was the legal trap in which Mary Prince found herself when she arrived in London: she was free while she remained in England, yet not free if she attempted to leave – a no-win choice between freedom in exile or slavery at home. Her owners, the Woods, who had mistreated her for the last 13 years, had no intention of granting her release – or manumission – from slavery so that she could return home to Antigua a free woman; in fact, they did everything in their power to prevent it. So when tensions between them rose to such a pitch that Mary decided to exercise her newfound human right and leave, she was stuck in limbo, one of the estimated 15,000 black people living in Britain,[3] most of whom occupied the lowest echelons of the social hierarchy.

Mary ventured into the city, but to live alone and friendless as a lower-class woman in the early nineteenth century was hard enough; to live alone as a black woman and former slave was almost impossible, and it quickly became apparent that she would need help. She found her way to the Anti-Slavery Society offices in Aldermanbury, East London, and there met the society's secretary, Thomas Pringle, a key player in her story and a man who would prove her most tireless champion. He took her on as his servant, and before long, emboldened by her new supporters, Mary made an extraordinary decision. If the only way she could ever return home as a free woman was if slavery was abolished, then she would have to shock the British people into understanding just how necessary abolition was. She would publish an account of her blighted life to help persuade them to grant every slave in the British Empire their freedom.

Mary Prince wasn't the first slave in Britain to protest in this way – Ukawsaw Gronniosaw, Ignatius Sancho and Olaudah Equiano had all published memoirs and letters before her – but she was the first female slave to do so, and it would be no easy task. To begin with, she was only semi-literate, so Pringle organised for Mary to dictate her life story to a writer friend of his named Susanna Strickland. After all, Mary's was precisely the kind of first-hand testimony the Anti-Slavery Society needed to give ballast to their message. To convince a public that was disinclined to accept the word of a slave, however, Pringle and Strickland would have to do everything they could to present Mary as a reliable, sympathetic witness. Pringle's contribution was to bolster Mary's account with a supportive preface, extensive supplement, notes and appendices. Slaves before Mary had met with incredulity and hostility when they had attempted to publish, so her story would need all the corroboration it could get.[4] Strickland, meanwhile, saw to it with a few strategic cuts and tweaks that Mary's words and moral character would appear pristine. Their close involvement with the text would serve to strengthen Mary's account in the short term, but in the longer term it would raise troubling questions over its authenticity.

The finished pamphlet, *The History of Mary Prince, A West Indian Slave*, appeared in 1831, when Mary was 43 years old, and it told in detail of her wretched life of hard labour and abuse in Bermuda and Antigua, and her struggles to gain her freedom in London. Her account would be shocking – like all slave narratives, it is a catalogue of human brutality – and difficult for her audience to read. But it was Mary's self-appointed duty to challenge their complicity and tell them what they didn't want to hear, and so she began to speak.

FAMILY FOR SALE

From the moment Mary Prince was conceived, she was the legal property of farm owner Captain Charles Myners, of Brackish Pond in the British-held island of Bermuda. Her mother was his household slave, and her father a sawyer belonging to one Mr Trimmingham, and when baby Mary arrived in 1788 she, too, passed, unsuspecting, from human being to chattel.

For the first few years of her life Mary remained blissfully unaware of this fact, too young to understand her bondage or even to register the first time she was sold. She was still an infant when Myners died and his slaves were divided up; she and her mother were handed over to 'old Captain Darrell', whose daughter and son-in-law, Captain Williams, became their new mistress and master. This couple had very different characters. The Captain was a 'harsh, selfish man'. His returns from sea were dreaded, even by his wife, who lived in fear of him and was frequently left distraught by his enjoyment of 'other female society'. Mrs Williams, on the other hand, was kind, so much so that, in Mary's eyes, they almost managed to transcend the condition of owner and slave: 'My obedience to her commands was cheerfully given: it sprung solely from the affection I felt for her, and not from fear of the power which the white people's law had given her over me.'[5] Mary even loved her, though she observed that Mrs Williams didn't dare treat her slaves so well whenever her husband came home.

The years spent with the Williamses were often surprisingly pleasant. Mary's mother gave birth to five other children – three girls and two boys – so Mary grew up in the comforting nook of her own family, rough-and-tumbling with her sisters and brothers, as well as the Williamses' daughter, Miss Betsey, who was of a similar age to Mary. 'The tasks given out to us children were light,' she says, 'and we used to play together with Miss Betsey, with as much freedom almost as if she had been our sister.'

Almost. But even in this 'kind' household, it was clear that Mary and her fellow slaves were a thing apart. The two little girls ran around happily together, and for her part, Mary loved her dear friend. There was no escaping, however, that she had been gifted to Miss Betsey and was 'made quite a pet of' by her in return. Mary's wording says it all. 'She used to lead me about by the hand, and call me her little nigger,' she says, revealing the disturbing imbalance immediately at play between them. It was only a child's game, but already the little white girl knew that the little black girl was her possession, more toy than genuine friend; she had assumed her supremacy from the start. Neither child was aware of the evils of their respective roles in this arbitrary hierarchy; they knew no different and didn't question it. On the contrary, Mary considered this 'the happiest period of my life, for I was too young to understand rightly my condition as a slave, and too thoughtless and full of spirits to look forward to the days of toil and sorrow.'

Those days came soon enough, and they would teach Mary just how little control she had over her own life. When Mary was 12, Mrs Williams found she could no longer afford her, so she hired her out to a Mrs Pruden, who lived about five miles away and needed a nurse for her small baby. It wasn't a terrible fate in the scheme of things – Mary was fond of the baby and Mrs Pruden struck her only the once, which was evidently considered a blessing – but she was dismayed at having to leave her family, Mrs Williams and Betsey. When she heard soon afterwards that Mrs Williams was dead, Mary and her mother genuinely grieved her loss. They didn't yet know it, but her death would have dire ramifications for them far beyond their immediate sorrow.

Just three months later, Captain Williams remarried, and in order to fund the wedding he decided to sell Mary and two of her sisters, Hannah and Dinah. This would mean the break-up of Mary's family and naturally she was distraught. Betsey Williams was outraged, too, though she mostly took umbrage at the prospect of having her property snatched away; 'You are *my* slaves, and he has no right to sell you,' was her bitter and petulant response.

But sell them he did. And when the day came, Mary's mother prepared 'her little chickens' for market, dressing her girls in new coarse linen shifts (osnaburgs), as if preparing them for death: 'See, I am *shrouding* my poor children,' she wailed, 'what a task for a mother!' She called for Miss Betsey to 'take your last look of them' and, to the sound of their mother's weeping, the children made their way to the market place at Hamble Town (now Hamilton, the capital of Bermuda). This would be the day when Mary first truly understood that white people saw her not as a thinking, feeling human being, but as an animal or a piece of meat. As the vendue master paraded her in the street, the dehumanisation of the moment was not lost on her: the buyers 'examined and handled me in the same manner that a butcher would a calf' and 'talked about my shape and size in like words – as if I could no more understand their meaning than the dumb beasts'.

The 12-year-old Mary endured the prods and jabs of strangers and the imminent loss of her family, and even from a distance of some 30 years, the memory of her fear was still powerful: 'My heart throbbed with grief and terror so violently, that I pressed my hands quite tightly across my breast, but I could not keep it still.' She was right to be scared, for her younger sisters were both sold to different owners, 'so that we had not the sad satisfaction of being partners in bondage'. Within minutes, their family had been physically rent apart. The three children now stood alone in the world with no rights and no protection, and their 'poor mammy went home with nothing'.

This systematic dismantling of black families – a swift way of destabilising community ties, weakening kinship bonds and, by extension, reducing the likelihood of a united resistance – was an all too common scene played out at every slave sale, and Mary gives a rare first-hand female perspective on its horrors. Olaudah Equiano described similar scenes of pain and horror at the Barbados slave market at which he was sold, where 'relations and friends [were] separated, most of them never to see each other again'. It was done 'without scruple' by the white folk, he wrote.[6] To corroborate this episode in Mary's story Pringle includes in a footnote an eyewitness account of a slave sale in the Cape of Good Hope, in which a family of slaves were 'exhibited on a table, that they might be seen by the company' and 'literally torn from each other' as they were sold off to separate masters. The eyewitness noted how 'the tears, the anxiety, the anguish of the mother' and the 'touching sorrow of the young ones, while they clung to their distracted parent' contrasted drastically with the 'marked insensibility and jocular countenances of the spectators and purchasers'. Likewise, Equiano noticed the 'eagerness' in his buyers' faces, while Mary, on the day of her sale, saw a strange indifference in the crowd, 'who were looking at us so carelessly', ignoring her family's anguish. 'They were not all bad, I dare say,' she adds quickly – perhaps in concession to her white interviewer – 'but slavery hardens white people's hearts towards the blacks; and many of them were not slow to make their remarks upon us aloud, without regard to our grief – though their light words fell like cayenne on the fresh wounds of our hearts.'[7] Pringle's eyewitness agreed; to him, this callousness in the face of such suffering spoke volumes about the 'miseries of slavery' and its 'debasing effects upon the hearts of its abettors'.

THE LICK OF THE COWSKIN

After the grief of losing her family, Mary now had to endure life under her new owners, and it quickly became clear that, so far, she had been lucky. The identity of her new master is protected in the narrative. Pringle chips in here to say that the full names of slave owners 'to whom conduct of peculiar atrocity is ascribed' were omitted to protect their living relatives, and also, presumably, to avoid libel suits, so Mary's master is referred to only as Captain I– of Spanish Point. It has since been deduced, however, that he was Captain John Ingham, a privateer and shop owner.[8] It was night-time when Mary arrived at Ingham's house and as she approached she met two slave women in the yard. On seeing this nervous young girl shuffling towards them, the ladies lamented her fate and told her she must 'keep a good heart' if she were to live there. Almost immediately, she discovered what they meant.

Heart-sore at parting from her family, Mary's first act on entering the house was to retreat to the shadows and weep, but Ingham's wife was pitiless. Snatching Mary's hat from her head, she greeted her with the words, 'You are not come here to stand up in corners and cry, you are come here to work.' She would be given milk and potatoes to eat; she would sleep under a blanket on the hallway floor and she would be put to work immediately on a full roster of household chores, which included looking after the Inghams' baby.

This was a daunting enough welcome, but then, just as Mary was going to sleep, she witnessed a dreadful scene. A French slave named

Hetty, whom Captain Ingham had captured on a privateering venture, was bustling around the house and seemed to Mary 'the most active woman I ever saw' – she tended to the farm animals, put the children to bed and cooked the dinner. Mary had noticed her particularly, because hers 'was the only friendly face I had as yet seen, and I felt glad she was there'. That first night, however, she heard Mrs Ingham call out to Hetty from her bedroom to ask if a certain chore had been done. The moment Hetty replied that it hadn't yet, Captain Ingham leapt from his bed and ran downstairs 'just as he was, in his shirt', carrying a 'long cow-skin' (a thong of twisted hide). 'I heard immediately after, the cracking of the thong, and the house rang to the shrieks of poor Hetty, who kept crying out, "Oh, Massa! Massa! Me dead. Massa! Have mercy upon me – don't kill me outright."' Mary huddled under her blanket, trembling 'like a frightened hound' as Hetty's screams filled the house, fearing 'that my turn would come next'. She had been sold straight into hell, and soon came to feel of her new home that 'The stones and the timber were the best things in it; they were not so hard as the hearts of the owners.'

At the Inghams', Mary was taught to wash, bake, pick cotton and wool, cook and tend to the animals, but more than that she was taught of man's disturbing capacity for cruelty. For that first night was only the prologue to a relentless series of violent episodes that Mary witnessed under their roof, where such repugnant treatment of all their slaves – adults and children – was commonplace. Two little boys called Cyrus and Jack received daily blows, as well as pinches to their cheeks and arms, 'often for no fault at all'. Believing themselves to have been granted a licence by both the law and the prevalence of violence among white slave owners, the Inghams had clearly disabled their conscience and absolved themselves of guilt, for 'Both my master and mistress seemed to think that they had a right to ill-use them at their pleasure.' And of course, as she'd feared, Mary's turn soon came next. 'To strip me naked – to hang me up by the wrists and lay my flesh open with the cow-skin, was an ordinary punishment for even a slight offence,' she says. A broken jar, a spilt pail of milk, even if it was the master's fault, could easily result in a hundred 'licks' of the cow-skin, or as many as it took 'till I was unable to stand, and till he himself was weary'. The whip wasn't their only instrument of torture, however – Mrs Ingham ('a fearful woman, and a savage mistress to her slaves') would deal out blows 'from her hard heavy fist', while Captain Ingham, in response to one of the cows getting loose, once took off 'his heavy boot' and 'struck me such a severe blow in the small of my back, that I shrieked with agony, and thought I was killed; and I feel a weakness in that part to this day'. He went on to whip her, too, she recalled, just for good measure.

The Inghams' methods of oppression included more calculated forms of psychological and physical torture, too. Mrs Ingham particularly liked to inflict sleep-deprivation on Mary, deliberately sitting up late, sometimes until morning, to make her work all night: 'often I have dropped down overcome by sleep and fatigue, till roused from a state of stupor by the whip, and forced to start up to my tasks'.

But it was Hetty, whom Mary had come to call 'aunt', who, even when pregnant, bore the worst of their cruelty. When she died at a young age, her fellow slaves were convinced that the Inghams had 'hastened' her miserable end 'by the dreadful chastisement she received from my master during her pregnancy'.[9] Mary's account of Hetty's demise – triggered, of all things, by a cow that had got loose – is harrowing:

> My master flew into a terrible passion, and ordered the poor creature to be stripped quite naked, notwithstanding her pregnancy, and to be tied up to

a tree in the yard. He then flogged her as hard as he could lick, both with the whip and the cow-skin, till she was all over streaming with blood. He rested, and then beat her again and again. Her shrieks were terrible. The consequence was that poor Hetty was brought to bed before her time, and was delivered after severe labour of a dead child. She appeared to recover after her confinement, so far that she was repeatedly flogged by both master and mistress afterwards; but her former strength never returned to her. Ere long her body and limbs swelled to a great size; and she lay on a mat in the kitchen, till the water burst out of her body and she died.[10]

The suffering Hetty endured was so great that the slaves all agreed that death was 'a good thing for poor Hetty', but Mary was left traumatised by her end: 'The manner of it filled me with horror. I could not bear to think about it; yet it was always present to my mind for many a day.'

Violence – the inevitable end point of all racism – had been normalised by the system of slavery; it was the standard method for keeping vast numbers of people subjugated. But the Inghams' extreme, unprovoked ferocity is hard to comprehend, fuelled by what comes across as unmitigated and unwarranted rage, as if forever meting out revenge for some non-existent crime. To conclude that they, and every other sadistic slaver, were just naturally vicious characters would be reductive and unsatisfactory – no answer at all. Pringle understood this, and having seen with his own eyes the effects of slavery on both black and white people during his six years living in a slave colony in South Africa, he had a theory to explain it. 'Slavery is a curse to the oppressor scarcely less than to the oppressed', he wrote in his supplement. 'Its natural tendency is to brutalise both.' The masters may have had the power, but they were in no way the victors in this battle. Pringle's experiences in South Africa had left him convinced of the need for

the abolition of slavery, not just for the physical and mental preserva-
tion of black people, but for the moral redemption of white people.
He was even 'inclined to doubt whether, as regards its *demoralizing*
influence, the master is not even a greater object of compassion than
his bondman'. He had seen decent people poisoned, degraded and
shamed by their role as slavers, becoming capable of cruelties (worse
even than those of Mary's owners) that British folk back home in their
drawing rooms would scarcely believe. To justify slavery, the public had
always been fed the line that black people were indolent savages, inferiors who deserved, even needed, to be dominated, but in narratives
like Mary's they could see for themselves that it was the whites who
were the savages, and it was slavery that made them so.

Following her atrocious death, Hetty's onerous duties fell to Mary, as
did her punishments. Even after a severe flogging, Mary was expected
to get up and continue her work. Any slight mistake, accident or
slip-up meant fierce retribution: 'There was no end to my toils – no
end to my blows. I lay down at night and rose up in the morning in
fear and sorrow; and often wished that like poor Hetty I could escape
from this cruel bondage and be at rest in the grave.'

If the Inghams were trying to break Mary's spirit, and with it any
possibility of insurrection, they almost succeeded. But not quite. Mary's
courageous heart beat fiercely even at this young age, and if death
would not come to release her, she resolved to try to release herself.
After one needless punishment too many, she ran away, fleeing to her
mother at the Williamses' – a daring act of rebellion that would ultimately be fruitless. Grieved to see her daughter so ill-treated, Mary's
mother tried her best to protect her, hiding her in a hollow in some
nearby rocks and bringing her food and drink at night. When Mary's
father discovered that she had run away, however, he knew he had no

choice but to take her back to the Inghams – she was their legal possession, after all. His appeals to them to treat her kindly were ignored, and even when Mary found the courage to speak up and tell them she could no longer bear the floggings, it did no good. 'I was obliged to submit … mothers could only weep and mourn over their children, they could not save them from cruel masters – from the whip, the rope, and the cow-skin.' Mary was the legal property of the Inghams and, for now, there was nothing that she or her parents could do about it. She would remain where she was, suffering the same horrific treatment almost daily, for five long years.

A VERY INDECENT MAN

In 1805, when she was about 17, Mary swapped one hell for another. She was joyful at first when Captain Ingham sold her off to a new master on Turk's Island,[11] but that joy soon drained away. So far, she had been a domestic slave, attending mostly to household chores, but she was about to experience life as a plantation slave. Now the property of a Mr D— of Grand Quay – since identified as Robert Darrell[12] – she was handed a half-barrel and a shovel on arrival and immediately put to work knee-deep in his salt-water ponds. The slaves worked from 4 a.m. until 9 a.m., at which point they were given a little maize boiled in water, before being sent back into the ponds to work through the heat of the day, 'the sun flaming upon our heads like fire'. Such conditions bred horrendous physical side-effects: the unrelenting heat caused 'salt blisters in those parts which were not completely covered', while 'our feet and legs, from standing in the salt water for so many hours, soon became full of dreadful boils, which eat down in some cases to the very bone.' They endured this all day, until dark, when they went to sleep 'in a long shed, divided into narrow slips, like the stalls used for cattle'.

As for Mr Darrell himself, Mary soon realised that she had merely gone 'from one butcher to another'. His torments varied in nature. To humiliate her, he made a spiteful joke of her name, calling her 'Mary, Princess of Wales' – it being a 'common practice with the colonists', Pringle tells us, 'to give ridiculous names of this description to their slaves' as a means 'of expressing the habitual contempt with which they regard the negro race'.[13] And of course the floggings continued, though by now, Mary says, 'there was nothing very remarkable in this' – it was the 'common usage' of slaves on that 'horrible island'. Just as Captain Ingham had done, Mr Darrell 'often stripped me naked, hung me up by the wrists, and beat me with the cow-skin, with his own hand, till my body was raw with gashes', although Mary noticed one chilling difference between the two men: 'my former master used to beat me while raging and foaming with passion; Mr D— was usually quite calm. He would stand by and give orders for a slave to be cruelly whipped, and assist in the punishment, without moving a muscle of his face; walking about and taking snuff with the greatest composure.

'Nothing could touch his hard heart,' Mary adds, 'neither sighs, nor tears, nor prayers, nor streaming blood.' If Darrell's slaves got sick, they were given hot salt water to make them sicker. If they couldn't keep up with the others, they were put in the stocks and flogged. Even the old and infirm were not spared. Mary tells of Darrell's barbaric torture of an old man named Daniel: he beat him with a 'rod of rough briar' and then flung salt water on the wounds 'till the man writhed on the ground like a worm'. Daniel's wounds never healed; they became 'full of maggots, which increased his torments to an intolerable degree'. The sickening sight of this old man's sufferings struck pity and fear into the hearts of the other slaves, for 'in his wretched case we saw, each of us, our own lot, if we should live to be as old'.

Darrell's son, Master Dickey, was quick to learn the ways of his father. Another slave, Ben, became so hungry one day that he resorted to stealing some rice from the store. He was caught for this little theft, and though he pointed out in his defence that he'd seen Master Dickey do the same many times, Darrell locked him up overnight, starved him, hung him up and flogged him. Dickey's own revenge, once he'd learned that the slave had informed on him, was brisk and terrible – he ran a bayonet through Ben's foot. Master Dickey was also happy to target the vulnerable. When an elderly slave named Sarah, whom Mary says was infirm and 'not quite right in her head', wasn't able to wheel her barrow fast enough, Dickey threw her among the prickly pear bushes. 'By this her naked flesh was so grievously wounded, that her body swelled and festered all over, and she died a few days after.'

As with the Inghams' treatment of Hetty, this was murder by degrees. Mary is just as anxious to tell these appalling stories of her fellow slaves' sufferings as she is her own, 'for when I think of my own griefs, I remember theirs'. It's all part of her mission – not just to tell the public her story, but to speak for all slaves, to make it clear, if there were any doubt (and it seems there was plenty), that her case was by no means isolated. She cleverly appeals to the Brits' pride in their own civility when she says, 'The people in England, I am sure, have never found out what is carried on [at Turk's Island]. Cruel, horrible place' – the implication being that if they had, their sensibilities would have been far too affronted to ever have condoned it. Her descriptions of what she has lived through are deliberately graphic, because, as she says, 'the truth ought to be told of it' – and it was only those like her, who had experienced it first-hand, who could do so. This is the real crux of her protest and her motivation for publishing her story:

... what my eyes have seen I think it is my duty to relate; for few people in England know what slavery is. I have been a slave – and I have felt what a slave feels, and I know what a slave knows; and I would have all the good people in England to know it too, that they may break our chains, and set us free.

The power to change things was in the hands of the British people, so Mary aimed her appeal squarely, unavoidably, at them. It was the white law-makers, and only them, who could free every slave in the British colonies, and laws were only changed when public opinion was swayed. It was vital that Mary persuaded her readers of the true 'horrors of slavery'.

Mary stayed on Turk's Island for about ten years – she is lax on dates, but we can hazard a guess that she was in her late twenties by the time she left, and the reason was Darrell's retirement. He returned to Bermuda and took Mary with him to wait on his daughters. She was glad of it, relieved to be free of the salt ponds of Turk's Island and to be going home, where she might be reunited with her family.[14]

She was not, however, free of Mr Darrell. She spent several more years working for him in Bermuda and seems to have entertained a misguided belief that, away from Turk's Island, his behaviour would improve. She was soon proved wrong; the violence showed no signs of abating; instead, she discovered the full extent of his depravity during this period. Stoked up by drink, he would beat his own daughter to the point where she 'almost killed her', forcing Mary to intervene on at least one occasion at the sound of the girl's screams – for which, of course, she was 'licked' by the whip in return.

Darrell was also given to subtler, though no less disturbing, forms of abuse. Mary (or more likely her editor) refuses to be explicit on this point, but what is said is revealing enough: 'He had an ugly fashion of stripping himself quite naked, and ordering me then to wash him in a tub of water. This was worse to me than all the licks. Sometimes when he called me to wash him I could not come, my eyes were so full of shame. He would then come to beat me.'

Undoubtedly, this was not the whole story. From this obfuscated detail we can infer that Darrell's persecution of Mary extended to sexual abuse, though the full extent of it has almost certainly been purged from the narrative in deference to the sensitivities of Mary's nineteenth-century audience. Though she is not allowed to speak freely, we must listen to what Mary is trying to tell us here, for there are hints at further atrocities elsewhere that also go half-spoken. In one instance, when Darrell caused Mary to drop some plates and knives, 'he struck me so severely for this, that at last I defended myself, for I thought it was high time to do so. I then told him I would not live longer with him, for he was a very indecent man – very spiteful, and too indecent; with no shame for his servants, no shame for his own flesh.' Her insistent repetition of the words 'indecent' and 'shame' are telling. Darrell's behaviour, whatever it was, disturbed Mary greatly – enough to make her stand up to him that night and escape to a neighbouring house. But again, her courage in leaving got her nowhere; she was forced to return the next day, 'not knowing what else to do'. Resistance was futile. Consent was not required when the man in question owned you; sexual abuse was just another commonplace element of the slave experience if you were unlucky enough to be a woman. The American abolitionist and former slave Harriet Jacobs knew this well. In her much more explicit 1861 account of her own experiences, it was resoundingly clear what she meant when she wrote: 'Slavery is terrible for men; but it is far more terrible for women.'[15]

What my eyes
have seen I think
it is my duty
to relate

THE PROMISE OF FREEDOM

Having spent over a decade with the deplorable Darrell, Mary was desperate to leave him, and when an opportunity finally arose she grabbed it with both hands. Another slave owner, Mr John Wood, was going to Antigua, and Mary eagerly requested to go with him. Wood was reluctant, but when his wife saw that Mary could work hard, they agreed to purchase her from Darrell for £100. Her motive for leaving was unequivocal: 'The truth is, I did not wish to be any longer the slave of my indecent master.' That word again …

This would be a fateful decision – and as Mary admits, one of her own making. In some ways, with the Woods, her lot had improved. She had escaped Robert Darrell, and her tasks were mainly domestic – attending to the bedchambers, nursing the Woods' child and washing their clothes in a nearby pond – but affliction was never far away. Years of physical hardship had led to rheumatism, which was now so bad she had to walk with a stick. She also developed an acute skin infection called St Anthony's fire in her left leg – a condition that, in severe cases, could prove gangrenous and fatal. For months she was relegated to a grubby outhouse full of insects and vermin, where the only care she received was from a kind lady who lived next door, who sent round an old slave woman to bring her soup and make her a hot bath to ease her pains.

In many other respects, Mary's lot was much the same as before. The Woods were not kind to her. On one occasion Mrs Wood sent her 'to be put in a cage [prison cell]' and had her 'flogged, by the magistrate's order, at her desire' the next morning; this was for a petty quarrel Mary had with another slave woman over a pig. Indeed, Mrs Wood 'was always abusing and fretting after me', as if she harboured some personal vendetta against her – perhaps because Mary was learning to defend herself against the barrage of harsh treatment and 'ill language' she faced: 'At last my heart was quite full, and I told her that she ought not to use me so; – that when I was ill I might have lain and died for what she cared; and no one would then come near me to nurse me, because they were afraid of my mistress.' She had made an enemy of her mistress by being so outspoken. Mrs Wood immediately reported Mary's insubordination to her husband, who raged at her and packed her off to find another owner. She would have done so, gladly – she approached a free black man named Adam White and asked him to buy her – but she quickly discovered that Wood was toying with her, for when White approached him he was told that Mary was not for sale. It was the Woods' perverse pleasure to express their annoyance at her every action but to continually refuse to sell her.

Now a self-possessed woman in her early thirties, Mary wanted more than anything to be free, and there was one other route by which she might achieve this: to purchase her freedom herself. So, with the spirit of an entrepreneur, when the Woods were away, she began to save up some money by taking in washing and selling coffee and yams to the captains of ships. It was a long shot; she would need to cobble together at least £100, and the Woods had already shown how determined they were to keep her shackled, but presumably it felt better than doing nothing. Perhaps she turned to those who she thought might have the power and influence to help her, for by now she was also in a long-term sexual relationship with a white man named Captain Abbot, which would last for seven years. Little is known about how they met or the nature of their affair – this scandalous liaison was one of the inconvenient facts of Mary's life that Susanna Strickland (rather than Mary) decided to excise from her narrative. Abbot is mentioned in the *History* only as a gentleman who once lent Mary some money in one of her failed bids to buy her freedom. His role as her lover would come out much later, under oath in a courtroom ... [16]

It was also around this time that Mary discovered religion. While she and the Woods were away in the country one Christmas, she was invited by another slave to go to a Methodist meeting and there she heard 'the first prayers I ever understood'. She had already been baptised almost ten years before, in 1817, but the prayers and hymns and the promise of forgiveness at this meeting had a profound impact on her that her previous experience of the church had not. Once home, she became an avid member of the local Moravian Church[17] – a fact that she kept from her mistress, in the knowledge that she would undoubtedly prevent her from going. 'But I felt I *must* go', and so, in a small act of rebellion, Mary would sneak away to hear the preachers after she had delivered the children their lunch at school, and there in the chapel she learned that religion gave as it took away; it taught her that she was a sinner – which she hadn't been much aware of before – but it also taught her to read, and offered her, for the first time in years, a welcoming community ready to enfold her in the warmth of kindness and the comfort of absolution.

Some time after she began to attend church, Mary met a former slave named Daniel James – a carpenter and cooper who had managed to purchase his freedom. The acquaintance turned to romance, and when Daniel proposed marriage Mary said yes, though such was the importance of her newfound faith that her acceptance came with the proviso that he attend the Moravian church with her. He must have agreed, for they were married there at Christmastime 1826, when Mary was about 38 years old.[18]

Predictably, the news of Mary's marriage did not go down well with her master and mistress. When Mr Wood heard of it he 'flew into a great rage', demanding of Daniel what right he had to marry one of his slaves, while Mrs Wood seemed particularly bothered by it – 'She could not forgive me for getting married,' says Mary, 'but stirred up Mr Wood to flog me dreadfully with the horsewhip.' As she had grown older, however, Mary had gained in courage, and developed a headstrong habit of answering back. 'I thought it very hard to be whipped at my time of life for getting a husband – I told her so. She said that she would not have nigger men about the yards ... or allow a nigger man's clothes to be washed in the same tub where hers were washed.' This was ugly, unashamed racism, which betrayed in Mrs Wood not only the white supremacist's desire for racial segregation, but also her more personal, vindictive urge to commandeer every minute of Mary's time and to segregate husband from wife.

Indeed, Mary's status as a slave meant that she 'had not much happiness in my marriage', for understandably it 'made my husband sad to see me so ill-treated'. With a little money now put by, Mary asked again if she could buy her freedom with the help of a Mr Burchell, who was willing to advance her the remaining money if she worked it off in his service, but again the Woods refused. The very suggestion was an affront to their rule. Mary was 'a black devil', ranted Mrs Wood. 'Who had put freedom into my head?' she demanded to know. Mary explained to the uncomprehending woman that 'To be free is very sweet', but there was no convincing her mistress that Mary deserved her liberty every bit as much as she did. Out of pure spite, it seems, she 'took good care to keep me a slave'.

The situation might never have changed, but for the fact that, in 1828, the Woods decided to return to England for a time to send their son to school and settle their daughters back at home, and they took Mary with them as nanny to their youngest child. It meant parting from her husband, but Mary was willing to make the journey – she believed, somewhat naively, that the British climate would cure her rheumatism. Even more tantalising was the rumour Daniel had heard that, once she alighted on English soil, where no man or woman could be enslaved, Wood intended to free her. Buoyed by her own optimism, Mary left for England in good spirits, with every expectation of returning to her husband before long as a healthy and free woman.

FREE IN ENGLAND

Mary's hopes for improved health in England were dashed immediately, for almost the moment she stepped foot in London in 1828, at the age of 40, she suffered an acute attack of rheumatism that made the mounds of washing she was constantly tasked with an agony to perform. The pain was so bad she couldn't even stand at the washtub – instead, she was forced to kneel or sit on the floor. The Woods barely seemed to notice. They worked her as hard as ever, and if she dared complain, she was accused of laziness. Once the family was settled in Leigh Street, Bloomsbury, Mary was presented with five bags of laundry from the sea voyage and expected to work her way through them. Hackles raised, Mary stood firm: she was not physically capable of doing the work, she argued, and if the Woods were not willing to show her any compassion in her illness, she was sorry now that she had come with them to England. A battle of wills ensued: the Woods would repeatedly pick fights with Mary and order her to leave, and when she then argued for her freedom, they would refuse it, threatening instead to send her back to Antigua or turn her out of doors. Mr Wood would never sell Mary her freedom; instead, he dared her to 'go and try what freedom would do for me, and be d—d'.

At first, Mary didn't quite dare. She was well aware of her rights – 'I knew I was free in England,' she says – but she also understood her impossible predicament as well as the Woods did. She could stay as their subject, to be worked into the ground for no pay, but be reunited with her home and husband, or she could walk out of their house and take her chances as a free woman with no home, no friends, little money – and no husband. There was danger in this latter option. In such a hostile environment, only the occasional few managed to escape the hand dealt them by the colour of their skin. A number of black Africans had been living in Tudor England before the country had fully engaged in the slave trade, arriving either as merchants, members of aristocratic retinues or by hitching a ride with English privateers – and they often played an active and specialist role in society.[19] Once England had begun to capitalise on the trade in human flesh in the 1640s, however, most black people in Britain were there as a direct or indirect result of slavery. For the majority, a life in domestic service was the best they could hope for – their occasional appearances on the margins of aristocratic portraits are a testament to their position on the sidelines of society, as expensive, exotic accessories whose main purpose was to help around the house – but there were exceptions. Ignatius Sancho, for example, had been born on a slave ship circa 1729, but on coming to England he had risen, thanks to his quick mind and self-education, to become first butler to the Duke and Duchess of Montagu and later a well-connected writer and composer. Then there was Dido Belle – even more of a rarity: born in 1761, she was the illegitimate mixed-race daughter of a slave woman and a British naval officer, who lived the life of a refined aristocrat in Britain, only because she'd had the good fortune to be entrusted by her father to the care of his uncle, Lord Mansfield – the very same Lord Chief Justice, who in 1783, had presided over the landmark slavery cases of James Somerset and that of the *Zong* massacre, both of which ruled in favour of the slaves over the slavers and helped build the case for abolition – influenced, some believed, by Mansfield's affection for Dido.[20]

But these were the exceptions, not the rule. Mary had neither access to learning nor upper-class connections: 'I did not know where to go, or how to get my living,' she says, and aware that she would struggle to survive alone in London, where she 'did not like to leave the house'. So for the moment, she stayed where she was, being worked as relentlessly as ever.

The day soon came, however, when Mary's implacable owners pushed her too far. She had been in England for nearly three months, and the Woods had just threatened to expel her for a fourth time, when she resolved that she 'would not be longer thus treated, but would go and trust to Providence'. She had been with the Woods for 13 years, had 'worked for them like a horse', but now she was ill and no matter what she did, no matter how hard she toiled, she couldn't please them. Her parting words to her owners had been characteristically forthright, and in answer they drove her out of the door, throwing abuse after her as she went.

It was done. Mary had made the biggest decision of her life, sacrificing her home in Antigua in order to throw off her shackles, but what now? She turned to the only people she could think of for help – the Moravian missionaries. With the help of the Woods' shoeblack, Mr Mash, she found their mission house in Hatton Garden, told them her story and was allowed to leave with them what few belongings she had. It was only when she returned to the Woods' house to retrieve her trunk that it dawned on them how badly their constant goading had backfired. Too proud to face her themselves, they sent a friend after her to sweet-talk her into coming back, but Mary's answer was categoric: 'I can stay no longer to be so used.' Now she had found her courage, she would not let it go.

Luckily, Mr and Mrs Mash were able to offer her refuge; Mr Mash was familiar with Mary's situation and he and his wife pitied her, so for the next few months they sheltered her, nursed her and brought in a doctor to treat her rheumatism. Then, in November 1828, at the recommendation of a woman she knew named Hill, Mary approached the recently formed Anti-Slavery Society.[21] There she met Thomas Pringle, a Scottish poet who, following his eye-opening six-year stint in South Africa, had been appointed the society's secretary. Profoundly moved by Mary's story, Pringle enthusiastically took up her cause (as one of several slave cases he was working on during this period) and arranged for her to meet with a solicitor, George Stephen, to see what could be done. In the meeting, Mary 'expressed, in very strong terms, her anxiety to return [to Antigua] if she could go as a free person, and, at the same time, her extreme apprehensions of the fate that would probably await her if she returned as a slave'. Pringle quotes her as saying, overcome by emotion, 'I would rather go into my grave than go back a slave to Antigua, though I wish to go back to my husband very much – very much – very much!' Stephen's advice, however, was not heartening. The recent case of the slave Grace Jones had given them no reason to hope. Brought to England by her owner Mrs Allen in 1822, she had been returned to slavery in Antigua the following year, and although the customs officers had considered this illegal, a ruling in the High Court of Admiralty by Lord Stowell in 1827 had stated that her freedom had only applied during her residency in England. The moment she returned to Antigua and its colonial laws, it was invalidated, making Grace a slave once more. British law was therefore powerless to make Mary free in Antigua, so for now, her new friends could only boost her funds with a little cash and attempt an 'amicable negotiation' with Mr Wood to try to secure her freedom.

Unfortunately, Wood was in no mood to be amicable. Mary's advocates reasoned, they argued, they offered him generous remuneration in return for his slave, but he proved as stubborn and vengeful as ever. The solicitors found him 'so full of animosity against the woman' that the case seemed hopeless. Wood declared that he 'would not move a finger about her in this country, or grant her manumission on any terms whatever; and that if she went back to the West Indies, she must take the consequences'. The Anti-Slavery Society took the only course left to them: they decided to bring the case before Parliament, and set about drawing up a petition on Mary's behalf. Alarmed by this turn of events and keen to avoid having his dealings publicly picked over in the House of Commons, Wood was crafty: he entered into negotiations but delayed and prevaricated at every opportunity, even hinting that he might agree to free Mary 'in his own time and way' if he wasn't antagonised by the threat of exposure. Wood was confident in his manipulations – for a powerful white man, nothing could be easier than bringing down a black female slave. He fell upon the obvious recourse, which was to smear Mary's reputation and portray her as 'an abandoned and worthless woman, ungrateful towards him, and undeserving of sympathy from others', and procured letters from West Indian friends to support his view. In doing so, he 'neutralised' the Society's efforts until the session end of Parliament in 1829, at which point he and his wife quietly set sail for Antigua – leaving Mary behind in London – and slipped through their fingers entirely.

THE HISTORY OF MARY PRINCE

It was a frustrating outcome, but Mary's immediate concern was survival, for during that first winter in London, the cold weather aggravated her rheumatism, leaving her unable to work and reliant on charity. Never one for idleness, she took on jobs as a charwoman and domestic servant as soon as she was well enough – which seemed 'handsomely paid' compared to what she was used to – though after a year, when her latest employer Mrs Forsyth left London, she found herself out of work again and back at the Anti-Slavery Society, in dire need of help.

As it happened, reliable work and an extraordinary new chapter in her life were just around the corner. By now Thomas Pringle was well acquainted with Mary and convinced of her good character, so in December 1829 he decided to hire her as a servant in his own household. With stable, paid work, kind employers, a roof over her head and a team of well-connected new friends all working for the abolition of slavery, Mary was now experiencing the best life she had known as an adult, though of course it was bittersweet. She was no closer to returning home to Antigua as a free woman, and could only pray that God would 'find a way to give me my liberty, and give me back to my husband'.

After another 12 months of 'seeing the poor woman's spirits daily sinking under the sickening influence of hope deferred', Pringle tried again, via the Moravian Missionaries and the Governor of Antigua, to persuade Wood to free Mary, offering him ample compensation for his loss, but the man was immovable: Mary was a liar, he claimed, guilty of 'baseness' and 'depravity'; to grant her manumission 'would be to reward the worst species of ingratitude'.[22] Even her husband had abandoned her, he said, and 'taken another wife'. The intermediaries declared the case a lost cause, while Pringle began to realise that he 'had not yet fully appreciated the character of the man we had to deal with'.

Slandered by her obstinate master, and stranded in limbo between freedom and captivity, Mary now took the history-making decision to assert the truth and tell her story to the world. It was the only act within her power that might just create change. Perhaps she wasn't aware that she would be the first black woman in history to do this in Britain, or perhaps she was and was undaunted. All we know, as Pringle stresses in his preface, dated 25 January 1831, is that 'The idea of writing Mary Prince's history was first suggested by herself', and she was clear about her purpose. 'She wished it to be done, she said, that good people in England might hear from a slave what a slave had felt and suffered.' Mary was a woman with an important message, and she now had friends who could put it into print and broadcast it for her.

As editor and amanuensis respectively, Thomas Pringle's and Susanna Strickland's tasks were to head off the public's prejudices and establish Mary's veracity from the off. If this was to be a successful polemic that won over public opinion to the abolition cause, they would have to approach it almost as a court testimony, in which the evidence was corroborated and the witness irreproachable. In his preface, Pringle reveals that he cross-examined Mary on every point of her story to ensure its authenticity, helped by Joseph Phillips, an active abolitionist who had lived in Antigua and knew both Mary and the Woods. Pringle also stated for the record that the Anti-Slavery Society was not connected to the publication; their involvement was disinterested and all proceeds from the pamphlet, he insisted, would go directly to Mary.

In his supplement, Pringle published the details of his battle with John Wood for Mary's freedom, systematically dismantling Wood's list of accusations like a lawyer cross-examining him in a court of law. Mary's account, he argued, had all the finer details of the truth; if she were so morally reprehensible, why did the Woods keep her in their house tending to their children for 13 years? Why keep her when they had sold five other slaves? And why would Daniel James still send affectionate letters wishing for her return if he had taken another wife? Every statement Wood had made, Pringle refuted, before proceeding to offer glowing character references of Mary from himself, her previous employer Mrs Forsyth and Joseph Phillips. Phillips could only damn the Woods with faint praise (they were not 'more severe, probably, than the ordinary run of slave owners'), but he observed that, contrary to the story Wood had put forward, Mary was viewed by them 'as their most respectable and trustworthy female slave'. And after 27 years in the West Indies, Phillips recognised in her account 'the genuine stamp of truth'.[23] By the end of the supplement it was Wood who looked like the liar, and, certainly in Pringle's view, one whose chief motive was vengeance, 'to *punish* [Mary] for leaving his service' and daring to stand up to him.

Strickland's involvement was rather more covert, and consequently her fingerprints are a little harder to spot. Pringle explains in his preface that Mary's account 'was written out fully' by Strickland, 'with all the narrator's repetitions and prolixities, and afterwards pruned into its present shape; retaining, as far as was practicable, Mary's exact expressions and peculiar phraseology'. Immediately, this differentiates Mary's account from other, more 'authentic' slave memoirs, such as Olaudah Equiano's, whose life story, published in 1789, was 'Written by Himself'. As Mary was unable to write, there was no way of avoiding Strickland's act of transcription. Pringle insists, however, that her interference was minimal. The account is 'essentially [Mary's] own', he says, 'without any material alteration farther than was requisite to exclude redundancies and gross grammatical errors, so as to render it clearly intelligible'.

By this account, Pringle's and Strickland's interventions sound no more obtrusive than a light edit. Unfortunately, a comparison with other sources reveals that their tweaks could be overzealous, occasionally veering into spin-doctoring and even censorship. When Pringle claims, for example, that 'No fact of importance has been omitted', he isn't being strictly truthful. In reality, he and Strickland made the conscious decision to edit out any hint of Mary's pre-marital sex life, particularly her long-term relationship with Captain Abbot and the details of Darrell's sexual abuse, partly to pander to the delicacy of their readers, but also – at a time when women could only be virgin, wife or whore, and those with black skin were publicly regarded by some as more animal than human[24] – to present Mary as a pure and innocent victim and a fellow human being, rather than a mutinous, sexualised, morally ambiguous slave.

It was all done with the best of intentions, to present an image of a woman the British public couldn't fail to warm to and have faith in, but in their efforts to filter Mary's words and repackage her for public consumption, Pringle and Strickland ran the risk of compromising her voice instead and exposing it to charges of falsification.[25] Perhaps this was the only way in the prudish nineteenth century, but in retrospect it has one key detrimental effect on the abolition cause's legacy: that 'Black agency in undermining slavery is devalued, and under the auspices of the Anti-Slavery Society, freedom is gained as the gift of white philan-thropists'.[26] In other words, it becomes a white saviour narrative – a sticky point, which can only be countered by remembering that the abolition movement would have had little momentum without the vital resistance of the slaves themselves. Indeed, it was slaves who began the movement, with revolts and uprisings on the plantations (there had been significant slave rebellions in Jamaica in 1760 and Guyana in 1823, which had been violently crushed by the British), individual runaways and the searing first-hand testimonies of outspoken rebels such as Mary all contributing to the campaign. These acts of vocal and physical protest wrested back some agency for the black community in reclaiming their own freedom. Despite the difficulties it presents, Mary's *History* – the first instance of black female protest in Britain

– is an example of black and white activism working effectively together.

Certainly, Pringle and Strickland's involvement is indivisible from the narrative, but even though the text has been compromised and questioned, Mary's ownership of her story remains intact and should not be taken from her. In her powerful closing speech, which Pringle asserts was given 'as nearly as was possible in Mary's precise words', her protest activism reaches its crescendo. On hearing the extraordinary claims circulating in pro-slavery camps that slaves did not want to be free, that 'slaves are happy', she urgently felt it her duty to disabuse the English of this absurd fallacy:

> How can slaves be happy when they have the halter round their neck and the whip upon their back? and are disgraced and thought no more of than beasts? – and are separated from their mothers, and husbands, and children, and sisters, just as cattle are sold and separated?

She wondered, too, at how Englishmen and women who went out to the West Indies seemed to be transformed into monsters by their involvement in slavery:

> … they forget God and all feeling of shame, I think, since they can see and do such things. They tie up slaves like hogs – moor them up like cattle, and they lick them, so as hogs, or cattle, or horses never were flogged; – and yet they come home and say, and make some good people believe, that slaves don't want to get out of slavery. But they put a cloak about the truth. It is not so. All slaves want to be free.

Any man who said otherwise, she argued, was 'either ignorant or a lying person'. And in response to any slaver who insisted they couldn't do without slaves, she demanded to know why, since they did perfectly well without them in England. Like any employee, she said, slaves wanted the right to leave a bad employer behind and find another who treated them properly. In the end, it was a simple plea for fairness:

> *We don't mind hard work, if we had proper treatment, and proper wages like English servants, and proper time given in the week to keep us from breaking the Sabbath. But they won't give it: they will have work – work – work, night and day, sick or well, till we are quite done up; and we must not speak up nor look amiss, however much we be abused … This is slavery. I tell it, to let English people know the truth; and I hope they will never leave off to pray to God, and call loud to the great King of England, till all the poor blacks be given free, and slavery done up for evermore.*

Her final words are a passionate indictment of slavery from a place not just of righteous indignation, but of visceral experience. Her appeal to the King would have fallen on deaf ears – William IV, who had succeeded his brother George IV in 1830, was against abolition – but others were not so myopic. After decades of campaigns that had presented the British people with evermore stark evidence of the disturbing truth of slavery and the injustice of its existence, they were approaching a turning point, and Mary's story would help them reach it.

TRIAL BY ORDEAL

The publication of *The History of Mary Prince* in early 1831 was by no means the end of Mary's story. It had taken considerable courage for her to publish it, not just because it was an unprecedented act for a black woman in Britain, but because it exposed her to the suspicions of the public, as well as their praise and pity. Pringle and

How can slaves be happy when they have the halter round their neck and the whip upon their back?

Strickland had been right to predict it and had done their best to protect her, but for some, that wasn't enough. They wanted proof.

Pringle included in his Appendix to the third edition of the pamphlet that, on publication, members of the public began to write in 'respecting the existence of marks of severe punishment on Mary Prince's body'. Her descriptions of her floggings did not satisfy them; they wanted to see the scars. By way of evidence, Pringle printed a letter from his wife to a Mrs Townsend of the Birmingham Ladies' Society for the Relief of Negro Slaves, in which Mrs Pringle assures her 'that the whole of the back part of [Mary's] body is distinctly scarred, and, as it were, *chequered*, with the vestiges of severe floggings. Besides this, there are many large scars on other parts of her person, exhibiting an appearance as if the flesh had been deeply cut, or lacerated with *gashes*, by some instrument wielded by most unmerciful hands.' As if Mary had not suffered enough indignities, Mrs Pringle confirms that she, her sister, Susanna Strickland and another friend were all present 'in a second inspection of Mary's body', revealing that, to ascertain the truth of her testimony – which was automatically doubted – Mary had been subjected to not one but two humiliating physical examinations.

Mary's story had clearly hit a nerve, because not long after its publication came two libel cases in which she had to testify. The first, in February 1833, was instigated by Pringle himself, in response to an article in *Blackwood's Edinburgh Magazine* in November 1831 that attacked both 'the malicious falsehood of Mary Prince's narrative'[27] and 'the venomous Anti-Colonial Manifesto' that Pringle and Joseph Phillips represented.[28] Pringle took the publisher, Thomas Cadell, to the Court of Common Pleas, where Mary was called to give evidence, though on this occasion she was only required to confirm that she had given Pringle an account of her life. The case went in Pringle's favour, but Cadell was ordered to pay only nominal damages of £5.

Just a couple of weeks later a second trial followed, and this time Mary would not have such an easy ride – John Wood was suing Thomas Pringle for libel, and in retaliation for what she had said about him, Mary would undergo a nasty, targeted character assassination in full view of the public. First to the Court of the King's Bench, Guildhall, came several witnesses who attempted to undo all of Pringle's hard work in making Mary respectable by discrediting her testimony with accusations of laziness and lying. The Woods were 'always very mild and gentle' to their slaves, they testified, and Mary 'always appeared cheerful and satisfied'[29] while under their control.

Stung and humiliated, Mary herself then had to take the witness stand. A report in *The Times* on 1 March 1833 quoted her evidence at length and, in a mark of authenticity, it matched closely the story she told in her *History*, except for a few key details that Pringle and Strickland had been careful to remove. It was now that her seven-year affair with Captain Abbot came to light, and although Joseph Phillips was of the opinion that such liaisons were so common in the colonies between masters and slaves 'as scarcely to deserve the name of immorality',[30] the fact that Mary had 'told all this to Miss Strickland when that lady took down her narrative', along with the details of another relationship she'd had with a freeman named Oyskman, yet none of it had been mentioned in her *History*, suddenly looked like dishonesty.[31]

Almost as damaging was the revelation that one night Mary had found another woman in bed with Captain Abbot and, in her jealousy, had taken a whip to her. The incident had ended up before a magistrate, only for the judge to laugh at the women's squabble and dismiss the case. The courtroom laughed, too, when they heard the story, unsurprised perhaps that, contrary to what her *History* would have us believe, Mary Prince was no angel. Pringle mentions in his supplement that as well as finding Mary honest, loyal, discreet, industrious, grateful and 'anxious to do her duty', he also saw in her 'a somewhat violent and hasty temper'. To us it might not seem strange that a woman kept in human bondage her entire life might harbour a degree of unresolved rage, or that it would manifest itself in behaviour learned from her masters, but Pringle doesn't acknowledge this. He does note, however, with disapproving undertones, that she also had 'a considerable share of natural pride and self-importance'. Black women, it seems, were not allowed to possess such traits, and yet it's since been argued that it was these very qualities that enabled Mary to stand up to her owners and survive her ordeal without being utterly crushed by it. Her indomitable spirit was used as another stick to beat her with, but it was her determination to answer back, run away, save her money, actively pursue her freedom and campaign for abolition by publishing her story that made her the remarkable woman she was.[32]

In Mary's defence, Pringle brought his own supportive cast into court to vouch for her character, including Joseph Phillips and Pringle's sister-in-law, Susan Brown, who bore witness to the scars on her body and the fact that her constitution was now 'a good deal broken' by decades of hard labour. It left the jury torn. They 'returned a verdict for the plaintiff on some of the issues, and for the defendant on others',[33] but ultimately it was Pringle who lost out. Through gritted teeth he was forced to pay Wood £25 in damages, while Mary walked out of court that day made to look and feel like a liar. Still, she could hold her head high, defiant and proud in the knowledge that she had spoken truth to power, as no other black woman in England ever had before.

AM I NOT A WOMAN AND A SISTER?

Despite its defeat in the law courts and the controversies and slurs it provoked – or maybe because of them – *The History of Mary Prince* was ultimately a successful piece of propaganda for the abolition cause. In its first year of publication it ran to three editions, and bolstered the movement at a critical time. The sugar-loving, tobacco-smoking, salt-sprinkling British public devoured Mary's disturbing account of the shocking brutality of the supposedly genteel plantation owners, and their consciences were pricked. The time was ripe for change and a number of complex factors now converged to finally turn the tide. Alongside personal protests such as Mary's and the persistent campaigning of the abolitionists, there had been more recent slave uprisings in the colonies, parliamentary reform and a change in the economic climate that meant trading in slave goods was no longer so lucrative. This perfect storm was enough to convince Parliament at last, and on 28 August 1833, the crucial ruling was passed that slavery was to be abolished throughout the British colonies.

The fight was won, but such seismic atrocities cast long shadows. Britain's leading role in the slave trade is a bitter pill to swallow; that the base greed of our powerful elite led to such barbarism, that much of our country's wealth and prosperity was dearly bought with the lives of countless human beings, that many of our great cities were built on the proceeds, that Britain's slavers were awarded £20 million in 'compensation' for the loss of their 'property' and that this vast national debt was only fully paid off by British taxpayers in 2015 – these are grisly truths that even today we find hard to face and try to ignore.[34] The genteel folk of nineteenth-century Britain would have preferred to ignore them, too. Thinking of the many slaves who had wept and bled to provide them with their sweet tea and comfits greatly spoilt their enjoyment, and most weren't happy to forego such luxuries.[35] But Mary Prince, and the handful of others like her who managed to make their voices heard, forced them to think about it. Her *History* occupies an important place among the slave narratives and early black writings that were published on both sides of the Atlantic – from Ignatius Sancho, Olaudah Equiano, John Marrant, Ottobah Cugoano, James Albert Gronniosaw and Phyllis Wheatley in the eighteenth century to Harriet Jacobs and Solomon Northup in the nineteenth – to document the horrors of slavery and sing out a protest cry for freedom: a few powerful agents from the ranks of the powerless who helped to bring about a pivotal moment in both black and white history.

Britain took a huge step forward in 1833, but in the aftermath of this revolution, what became of Mary? Slavery had polluted her entire life. Even once she'd found the immense courage she needed to lay claim to her freedom and hold her persecutors to account, she was dragged through the courts, doubted and discredited. Justice ought to dictate that she triumphed in the end. The frustrating truth, however, is that we do not know how Mary's story ends. Just as the emancipation of slaves becomes enshrined in British law throughout its Empire, Mary Prince vanishes from the records. The last we see of her is in the courtroom in early 1833. Pringle observed at the time that her health was poor, her eyesight failing and her constitution broken; it's entirely possible, even likely, that she died soon afterwards, maybe even before the victorious ruling of August 1833, her body wracked and ruined from 40 years of exhaustive hard labour and physical torment.[36] Or maybe she didn't. John Wood was never going to budge and grant Mary her freedom, and it took several years for the Slavery Abolition

Act to gradually take effect throughout the Empire,[37] but once it did, perhaps Mary made it back to Antigua to live out her days, free and happy, with her husband. It may be hopeless optimism, but until new evidence comes to light, it remains a possibility.

Mary was by no means a woman destined to go down in the history books. On the contrary, every circumstance of her life seemed designed to prevent it. Her 'owners' did everything in their power to obliterate her life from the earth; they stole her agency, her humanity, her dignity, her nationality, her name – and they were legally entitled to do so. This was the kind of total erasure that a woman like Mary faced. No portrait of her survives – undoubtedly there never was one; she was a woman not just of low status, but of no status. Like countless other slaves, her only visual representation is in the generic image on the Society for the Abolition of the Slave Trade's seal, which in the 1780s was mass-produced on a medallion by Josiah Wedgwood to support the cause. It depicts a slave kneeling and shackled in supplication, and asking one simple question: 'Am I not a woman and a sister?'[38]

What has survived, however, despite the filters applied to it, is Mary's voice – distinctive, defiant, resilient, dignified and passionate, without vitriol or hate. She came close to being broken by her ordeal time and time again, but was never 'done up' by it; though her body began to fail from its decades of abuse, her spirit survived. After more than 40 years of slavery, her final known acts were of rebellion, courage and protest. To speak the unpalatable truth, she had to expose herself to insult, suspicion and humiliation, but it was a price worth paying – she had suffered much worse in the past, after all. A woman with no power, no image, no legal recognition and little education had nonetheless managed to draw her own portrait in words, and in that radical act of self-assertion, she spoke loudly and unashamedly not just for herself, but for every slave who couldn't speak for themselves, acknowledging experiences that would otherwise have been denied and memorialising human lives that would otherwise have been forgotten. Mary Prince didn't just publish her history, she *made* history.

Anne Lister

GENTLEMAN JACK

When Anne Lister was 15 years old, she began to write a diary. Not a gauche, incoherent, excruciating teen diary, but a four-million-word masterpiece, spanning 24 hardback volumes, two exercise books, various loose papers – and almost her entire life. The work started out as little more than lists on scraps of paper but bloomed into bitty entries in notebooks and, from 1816, when she was 25, into intensely detailed chronicles, in which she scratched out in black ink the dramas and banalities of her everyday life. It became a serious occupation, documenting her frank observations in surgical detail, even an obsession, until the diaries became so profusive that she had to create painstaking indices just to keep track of them.

For Anne, the purpose of all this labour was threefold. First, it was commemorative; Anne was aware that she was a remarkable creature, and 'resolved not to let my life pass without some private memorial that I may hereafter read, perhaps with a smile'.[1] She also had ambitions to be a published writer and earn herself 'a name in the world',[2] so what better way to train? Above all, though, her diary was her confidante: 'By unburdening my mind on paper', she wrote, 'I seemed to have opened my heart to an old friend. I can tell my journal what I can tell none else.'[3]

*'I love, and only love, the fairer sex and
thus beloved by them in turn, my heart
revolts from any love but theirs.'*

ANNE LISTER (1791–1840),
DIARIST, BUSINESSWOMAN, TRAVELLER AND THE 'FIRST MODERN
LESBIAN'

She certainly could, because what is most remarkable about Anne Lister's diaries is that one-sixth of them is written in a secret code of her own devising, an arcane combination of Greek, Latin, algebra and punctuation marks. Her 'crypt hand', as Anne called it, had to be undecipherable, for she would use it to safely express the most private, most intimate details of her life, to write what was unwritable and to be free and honest about her 'disguised & hidden nature that suits not with the world'.[4] If these coded passages had become public during her lifetime, they would have been considered some of the most shocking and scandalous documents ever set down in the English language.

'THE MOST BEAUTIFUL GIRL I EVER SAW'

Anne's first diary entry, written on a spare piece of paper on 11 August 1806, when she was 15, begins with the words, 'Eliza left us.' This was Eliza Raine, Anne's devoted schoolfriend, who had just spent the summer holidays with the Listers in Halifax. She was also Anne's first lover. The girls had met at the Manor House School in York, where both were boarders and both stood out as different; Anne because her ways were odd and her clothes noticeably shabby; Eliza because she was rich and her skin was dark.

Eliza was an heiress of British-Indian descent. Her father, William Raine, had been a British Army surgeon for the East India Company in Madras (now Chennai), where he'd married an Indian woman, whose name is lost to history. After his death in 1801, their two daughters, Jane and Eliza, were sent to school in England, aged 13 and 11, leaving their mother behind in India. They would never see her again, for she died the following year. By 1804, the girls had arrived at the Manor School, in the knowledge that on their twenty-first birthdays, or when they married if that came first, they stood to inherit £4,000 each from their father's will.

Decades later, Anne would still consider Eliza 'the most beautiful girl I ever saw'.[5] She ought to have been a good catch, but as her parents' marriage hadn't been registered in England, she carried the stigma of being both foreign and illegitimate. Neither she nor Anne were sent to sleep in the dormitories with the other girls; they were given an attic room to share, just the two of them, where they quickly developed an intense sexual relationship that, in the privacy of their room, was surprisingly easy to get away with. Women were so often each other's only company; closeness between them was common and sharing a bed standard. The cultural acceptance of 'romantic friendships' – believed to be loving but platonic – provided the perfect smokescreen for female lovers.

After six months the two 14-year-olds made a solemn vow of marriage, exchanging rings and hatching a plan to set up home together with Eliza's inheritance once they turned 21. Encouraged by Anne, Eliza started a diary, too, and the girls began to use code words between them to express the inexpressible. Again and again, Eliza jotted down the word *felix* – Latin for 'happy' or 'lucky' – in her diary, to denote that she and her 'husband' had had sex. So began Anne Lister's crypt-hand and her first marriage. It was an advantageous match on both sides, for Anne brought the lineage, and Eliza the fortune.

Indeed, fortune was all the Listers lacked. As one of Halifax's most important landowning gentry families, they peered down their noses at the nouveau-riche cloth manufacturers who were bringing profitable industry to their Yorkshire town, while at the same time envying them their ready cash. The Listers had to rely on their estate of Shibden

Hall, a fifteenth-century manor house situated in rolling fields on the outskirts of the town, to make their money the old-school way – from the land. Anne took great pride in being of the landed gentry, though it irked her that she was from the wrong branch of this illustrious clan. Her father, Jeremy, was a youngest son; it was his brother, Anne's bachelor uncle James, who owned Shibden, leaving Jeremy and the rest of his siblings with precious little. His four sisters had no dowries and so they remained spinsters at Shibden, while Jeremy had to make his own way in the world. He chose the military, though by the time Anne was born, on 3 April 1791, he'd been invalided out in the American War of Independence and become a recruitment officer. There was never much money to support his wife, Rebecca, or their four surviving children: John, Sam, Anne and Marian.

Indeed, Anne would always feel more than a little ashamed of her immediate family. Her mother was a drinker, 'tipsy 25 nights',[6] and her father a coarse soldier – 'so unlike a gentleman' – who had a knack for losing money.[7] To Anne, they were never quite smart enough, or rich enough, to match their Lister ancestry, of which, conversely, Anne was immensely proud, and from an early age, it was apparent that she would demand more out of life.

By her own description, Anne was 'a curious genius' even 'from my cradle', who before long grew into a 'very great pickle'.[8] As a child she would habitually escape from her maid at the family home in Market Weighton and spend her evenings exploring the town, seeing all manner of things she shouldn't – 'curious scenes, bad women, etc'.[9] By the age of seven, she was deemed such an 'unmanageable tomboy' that she was sent off early to a dame school in Ripon, 'because they could do nothing with me at home', where she was 'whipped every day except now & then in the holidays, for two years'.[10] It made no difference; she remained boisterous, boyish and unrepentant.

She got on much better with Uncle James and his sister Anne than she did with her parents, and consequently gravitated more and more towards Shibden. In 1803, she moved in for nearly a whole year. Although her brother John was the one set to inherit the estate, it was Anne who showed a burgeoning interest in the nuts and bolts of how it was run. But then, as the breadth of detail in her diary attests, Anne was interested in everything. By the time she arrived at the smart Manor School in 1805, courtesy of her Aunt Anne, she had developed a taste for serious scholarship, particularly Latin and Greek, and had every intention of learning everything a boy could learn.

At school, Anne and Eliza were rarely apart; even during the holidays, Eliza was welcomed like another daughter into the Lister household, just as Anne was at the York home of Eliza and Jane's guardian, William Duffin. Enforced separation would soon come, however, because after the summer holidays of 1806, Anne Lister did not return to the Manor School. If this was intended to divide the girls in the hope of weakening their bond, it didn't work – at least not immediately, for when 'Eliza left us' in August 1806 to go back to school, leaving Anne at home, the two teenagers corresponded avidly, with Anne recording every letter and every gift they sent each other in her diary. Later that year, when Eliza received a proposal of marriage from Rebecca Lister's adoptive son Mr Stubbs, she would not even entertain the idea – she couldn't explain it to Mr Stubbs or to Mrs Lister, but she considered herself as already married.

Indeed, in early nineteenth-century Britain, in the days before we humans had begun to categorise our sexuality, there were no words with which to describe the relationship that existed between Eliza and Anne. Cultural understanding of lesbianism was a mixture of blindness, bafflement and denial. While sodomy was vehemently condemned and punishable by death, there was no legal punishment for sex between women, for the simple reason that it was not believed to exist. A legal case in Edinburgh in 1811 involving two boarding-school mistresses made this official. Marianne Woods and Jane Pirie had been accused of 'improper and criminal conduct' after being discovered canoodling in bed by one of their pupils. After eight years of deliberation in the courts, however, they were acquitted by the House of Lords on the grounds that the 'crime here alleged has no existence'. Respectable women, it was thought, were too pure, too asexual, to even contemplate sex if it was not for the purposes of procreation or pleasing their husband, and even if they did, the question of what two women might actually *do* together in bed was met with general incomprehension and a distinct lack of imagination. They might form intense, loving friendships, they might express those friendships in physical affection – all this was laudable – but, as the Lord Justice Clerk confidently asserted, 'according to the known habits of women in this country, there is no indecency in one woman going to bed with another'.[11] Clearly, if it didn't involve a penis, it didn't count.

But incomprehension did not equate to acceptance. With 'no polite language in which to talk about lesbianism'[12] (the word itself didn't enter common usage until the twentieth century), the inability to discuss or even acknowledge the existence of gay women rendered them remarkably free to indulge their desires, yet at the same time wholly repressed by their negation. By necessity, their relationships had to be just as clandestine as those of gay men, not because they were in danger from the law but because their inexpressible otherness meant they were neither recognised, understood nor accepted.

In 1806 the Listers had moved from Market Weighton to a rented house in Halifax, where Anne continued her scholarly education of

Greek, Latin, algebra, geometry, rhetoric and her own voracious reading with the Reverend Samuel Knight and the Misses Mellin, of a local ladies' school. Her social circle was now widening and, as any teenager might, Anne began to push the boundaries of social acceptance to see just how 'different' the people of Halifax would allow her to be. What to wear was the most pressing issue. For a girl who felt no affinity with conventional female fashion and whose frayed cuffs and patched petticoats regularly attracted attention, this was no easy decision – Anne was so anxious about her clothes that she always referred to them in code in her diary. Almost since birth she had felt more boy than girl, and now she was ready to make a statement: she started to replace the dainty, colourful dresses of the Georgian era with a strikingly austere riding habit – a dark, high-necked, long-sleeved jacket and plain skirt. After attending a local concert in this outfit, she noted airily that she 'was much stared at and well quizzed as an original. Care despised on my part.'[13]

Far from being disconcerted by this reaction, Anne enjoyed the frisson she had created, and over the next couple of years consciously indulged the 'masculine' elements of her character with increasing swagger. In private, she bought herself men's braces and kept pistols under her pillow; in public, she walked out alone, openly flirted with young women, ignored her parents' curfews and socialised, unchaperoned, with men. She played cards with the gents, walked to church with them, even visited them alone in their rooms. When one such rumour reached her despairing parents, Anne was forced to offer an explanation. Yes, she had visited Captain Bourne alone in his rooms, but nothing improper had occurred – she had gone there to look at his guns.[14]

It was inescapable now that Anne looked and behaved more like a young man than a fine lady; her manners, dress and interests were all 'softly gentleman-like',[15] and inevitably this drew comment. 'What a pity that she does not pay more attention to her appearance,' declared one drawing-room gossip, 'for those who do not know her judge from this.' The same woman observed, however, that 'she is such a pleasant companion that I myself could have listened to her till I had forgot it'.[16] When Anne got wind of this chatter, she was gratified rather than hurt, for it proved what she already suspected: that her natural charisma was more than enough to outweigh her 'oddities'.[17]

By the age of 17, Anne was spreading her wings, and in consequence her marriage was beginning to flounder. While Eliza's letters only grew more impassioned – 'How my heart throbs for thee!'[18] – Anne was enjoying a dalliance with her flute pupil Maria Alexander and putting practical hindrances in their way. She now told Eliza she thought it unrealistic for them to live together at 21 – 27 seemed much more likely. By the spring of 1809 it was clear to both of them that Anne was backing away, but instead of confronting this painful truth, they attempted to paper over the cracks – a distraction technique that became increasingly difficult to maintain. The new year of 1810 brought with it a spate of influenza, which felled Anne's younger brother John. Anne nursed him at home alongside her other brother, Samuel, but John died on 24 January, aged just 14, leaving Sam the new heir to the Lister estate. Eliza, meanwhile, had her own crosses to bear. Having now finished school, she was obliged to go and live with her grumpy older cousin, Lady Crawfurd, in Doncaster, which would prove a miserable experience. Lady Crawfurd had a dreadful temper, she was 'a child' and 'a tyrant',[19] and conniving, too – by April she had taken to hiding Anne's letters and rejecting social invitations on Eliza's behalf.

Eliza's sister was also a desperate worry. In May 1808 Jane had married a cadet named Henry Boulton who was stationed in India, and the couple had spent the last two years in Calcutta. A letter from Jane in April 1810, however, revealed that the marriage had collapsed. Once in possession of Jane's £4,000, Boulton had abandoned her, leaving her with no option but to make the long journey back to England alone. When she arrived more than six months later she was traumatised, penniless – and pregnant. It's not known what happened to Jane during those months – she may have been seduced, raped or forced into prostitution to survive – but in nineteenth-century Britain the details were irrelevant. A 'fallen' woman, and particularly one with brown skin, was regarded as criminal and had only one fate: her guardian, Mr Duffin, found her a place to live, but beyond that either would not or could not help her, while Anne and Eliza were told to avoid her. Like many women before her, Jane Boulton was shoved out of sight and out of mind.

Amid the ongoing turmoil, Eliza's mental health was suffering. During that spring of 1810, Lady Crawfurd's behaviour became unmanageable; antagonised by Jane's misfortune and suspicious that Eliza and Anne were plotting against her, she resorted to regular tantrums and verbal abuse. Eliza began to feel 'orphan like & unprotected' in her cousin's house; her spirits, she wrote, were 'sometimes so broken I don't know whether life or death more desirable'.[20] And to complete her misery, it was becoming increasingly obvious that Anne Lister had met someone else.

NEW FRIENDS

Isabella Norcliffe was a horse-and-hounds kind of girl, whom Anne had met in York in 1809. Lively, fun and from a well-respected family, 'Tib', as she was nicknamed, was everything Eliza wasn't. The Norcliffes were wealthy, too, with a townhouse in York as well as the elegant, newly refurbished Langton Hall, near Malton, where Anne would make frequent and lengthy visits over the years. This was just the kind of refined society that Anne had always longed to associate with, so when Eliza inevitably left Lady Crawfurd's and returned to Halifax in the summer of 1810, Anne was far too preoccupied with her high-flying and far more entertaining new friends to see much of her. Eliza's low spirits were becoming a drag; oblivious to her own part in contributing to them, Anne was unsympathetic and impatient, believing an 'ill temper' to be a self-inflicted 'malady, which most can prevent, and all can cure'.[21] The relationship staggered on, but as the tiffs increased, so the contact dwindled.

By the spring of 1811, Anne and Tib were in the throes of a full-blown affair. Anne was 20 and Tib 26, but they had plenty in common: Tib was also boyish in her ways; she was a hunter, a horse rider and a creative swearer, and though she wasn't academic like Anne, she shared her love of guns and the theatre. Smitten with Anne's clever words and open sexuality, Tib dreamed of making Anne her life partner, and for a while at least Anne fantasised about this, too.

The lovers spent weeks at a time visiting one another's homes, and soon began to venture further afield. In February 1813 Anne took a trip to Bath with the Norcliffes, followed in May by a week in Wiltshire alone with Tib. The freedom and privacy this trip afforded them, with a shared bedroom at every guesthouse, suddenly opened up new possibilities. Anne had lately confessed to her brother Sam, before he had marched off to join the army in the autumn of 1812, that 'sometimes I could envy you, if it were not impious and unjust'; as a man he was free to explore the world, while she was condemned to inaction, and the constraints were beginning to chafe: 'Never till this moment did I feel a wish to be freed from that petticoat slavery that but ill subdues a mind superior to its tyranny,' she complained.[22] Anne was a natural thrill-seeker who yearned for the adventures that her brother or the well-travelled Norcliffes took for granted. For a woman to travel alone was risky and frowned upon, but Anne had now found the loophole she needed: travelling with a 'friend' could raise no objections, and it offered the added bonus of time alone with her lovers away from prying eyes.

For now, that friend was Tib, though during a stay in York in February 1813, Anne told her brother Sam that she had felt 'no small pleasure in seeing again Miss M. Belcombe. But who is *she*, perhaps you'll say?' *She* was Tib's closest friend, whom Anne had met on a previous visit to Langton Hall, making it a 'doubly interesting' trip.[23] Poor unsuspecting Tib had introduced Anne to the love of her life.

Mariana Belcombe was a year older than Anne, and quite the opposite of Tib, as Tib well knew: 'she is milder than any thing I ever saw, & you know what *I* am'.[24] She lived in York, in similarly modest circumstances to Anne, with her parents (her father was a doctor who specialised in psychological problems), her brother Stephen and four sisters: Anne (known as 'Nantz'), Harriet, Louise and Eliza. Though Tib offered Anne more social and financial advantage, it was Mariana who now became the focus of her emotional and sexual life. Once Tib had seen for herself the intensity of their relationship, any hopes she'd had of making Anne her life partner were dashed.

There is no record of how or when the affair with Mariana began – Anne's diaries between 1810 and 1816 are lost – but they first met in 1810, when Anne told Tib she thought her a 'sweet looking girl'.[25] It's known that, in December 1812, when Anne was 21 and Mariana 22, the two women spent a fortnight in York alone together, and by the following year they were writing to each other every few days, passionately in love and in the midst of a heady sexual relationship that would last for over two decades.

In the mid-1820s, years after they first got together, Anne was still writing candidly in her diaries of the ecstatic sex she had with Mariana. Freed by her crypt-hand code, she catalogued every 'kiss' they enjoyed (the word had multiple meanings for Anne, referring not just to kisses, but to sex and orgasms), recording both their quantity and quality. Mariana knew precisely how to please Anne in bed. She would excite her with words – 'She often murmurs, "Oh, how delicious," just at the very moment. All her kisses are good ones'[26] – and viewed Anne as she wished to be viewed: as a man. In a world where same-sex couples were invisible, the lovers had to improvise when it came to the dynamics of their own relationship. To make sense of feelings that were never talked about or legitimised, and to allow Anne to inhabit the gender identity that felt most natural to her, they emulated the familiar heterosexual couplings around them. Anne could now 'play the man' in every sense: Mariana called her 'Freddy'; she ignored Anne's periods and was acutely aware of 'my sensitiveness of anything that reminded me of my petticoats'.[27] Anne was in raptures – Mariana was sweet, kind and feminine; just the sort of woman she wanted to spend her life with.[28]

Anne's happiness was interrupted when in June 1813 she received the shattering news that her brother Sam, the only member of her family she actually liked, had drowned in a terrible accident.[29] Of the Lister siblings, there was now only Anne and her younger sister, Marian, left – two very different and wholly incompatible characters – and with the last male heir now gone, the question of who would inherit her bachelor uncle's estate, which included Shibden Hall, as well as land and businesses around Halifax, was suddenly open for debate. Uncle

James wasn't keen on leaving his complex concerns in the hands of his rather feckless brothers, Joseph and Jeremy, being more inclined to favour the Welsh branch of the family, the Listers of Swansea. Ever alert to new ways of improving her lot, Anne spied a chance; she set about convincing her uncle that, despite being a woman, *she* was the perfect candidate. She had already demonstrated her interest in estate management, she stressed; she had a deep veneration for the land as part of the Lister family heritage and had resolved never to marry, ensuring that the estate wouldn't fall into the wrong hands. She was nothing if not persuasive. Eventually Uncle James agreed that she could move in and learn how the estate was run, so in May 1815, when she was 24, Anne duly arrived at Shibden as heir apparent.

It wasn't quite the life she had dreamed of. Her aunt and uncle lived frugally, and Shibden was no spacious neo-classical Georgian pile like Langton Hall; it was a draughty, damp, medieval manor house with low ceilings, small leaded windows and dark oak-panelled walls. Anne was always short of the cash she needed for the life she thought she should have, but at least now she was free of her irksome parents and sister. Her aunt and uncle were accepting of her boyish ways and preference for women, even if they didn't quite understand the true nature of them. And most importantly, Anne now had a promising future ahead of her as an independent landowning woman.

Eliza Raine, meanwhile, had had to figure out for herself that her 'husband' had lost interest in her. She'd still harboured some hope in 1812 when she'd rejected a proposal of marriage from one Captain John Alexander (a decision she later came to regret), but her twenty-first birthday – a date she and Anne had both once longed for – passed by barely noticed by Anne. She had lost patience with Eliza's depression, and with fun, wealthy, respectable new friends like the Norcliffes, she no longer needed Eliza's money. Nor did she wish to be associated with Eliza's scandalous sister, Jane, who had now fallen as low as life could bring her: to drink, prostitution and consumption. Eliza was cut from social occasions, and when she left Halifax for York, Anne was glad, writing to Sam shortly before his death that 'Upon the whole, her leaving our neighbourhood, is rather a good thing for me … home is, by this means, made considerably more agreeable.'[30]

As her friends deserted her, Eliza's misery became abject. Even her guardians, the Duffins, and her governess Miss Marsh turned against her. In an effort to keep her crumbling sister safe, Eliza tried to have Jane committed to an asylum in London, and in response Miss Marsh began to spread gossip that 'of the two sisters', Eliza was 'the most deranged'. Seeing only a malicious and ungrateful foreigner in her former charge, Miss Marsh declared that she was 'done with her & all the black progeny forever'.[31]

Like her sister, Eliza was now ostracised, and in the autumn of 1814 her rage and despair at their treatment triggered an aggressive confrontation with Mr Duffin, after which she was declared insane and taken to Clifton Green, the new private asylum on the edge of York run by Mariana's father, Dr Belcombe.[32]

Far from being supportive of the girl she had once loved, Anne kept her distance, though she was eventually persuaded to visit Eliza at the asylum in December 1817. She found her placid enough at first, but on her second visit Eliza was tetchy and keen to confront her ex-husband with some stark home truths: 'I had never done her any good,' Anne was told plainly. 'I might have genius, I might have talent but … I had made bad use of them.'[33] Such was the damning judgement of Anne's first wife, the beautiful heiress whose skin colour, illegitimacy, unhappiness and anger would condemn her to the mad-house for the rest of her life. She died there in 1860, at the age of 68.[34]

BETRAYAL

By the time Anne's diaries resume in August 1816, when she was 25, her steamy relationship with Mariana Belcombe had been ongoing for four years, but she was reeling from a recent schism between them that had changed everything. On 9 March that year, Mariana had married a rich 44-year-old widower named Charles Lawton, having sneakily arranged the match behind Anne's back. Persuaded by parental pressure, the veneer of conventionality and the grand Lawton Hall in Cheshire that Charles offered, Mariana had chosen pragmatism and materialism over romance, and Anne was crushed by the betrayal. Over a year after the marriage she was still haunted by 'the trick' Mariana had 'once played'[35] and couldn't help but mourn the loss of their halcyon days: 'Surely no one ever doted on another as I did then on her. I fondly thought my love & happiness would last forever.'[36] Looking back years later, she truly believed that she 'never was so wretched in my life' as she was now.[37]

Mariana, however, had no intention of allowing her marriage to Charles Lawton to put a stop to her relationship with Anne. Far from it. She insisted that as a wealthy married woman she would have more freedom to see Anne, not less, and so the lovers continued their affair in the cynical hope that the middle-aged Charles would die soon enough, leaving them free to set up home together with his fortune. They sealed their secret pledge with a symbolic exchange of rings, and, in a grand test of their devotion, agreed to patiently wait out the next decade or so, stealing moments of intimacy whenever the opportunity arose.

It was a plan that would frequently depress Anne over the years, leaving her full of doubt over Mariana's love. To be a woman's mistress rather than her wife was never enough for Anne. As far as she was concerned, Mariana had sold out: 'She believed herself, or seemed to believe herself, over head & ears in love, yet she sold her person to another for a carriage & a jointure.'[38] To Anne, it was nothing more than 'legal prostitution'.[39]

So when the diaries begin on 14 August 1816, Anne is in the mood to take a little revenge on her faithless lover – by conducting an affair with her sister, Nantz.[40] As was common practice, Anne and Nantz had accompanied the bride on her honeymoon and stayed with her for the first six months of her marriage to help her adjust to her new life, and by the end of this trip, Anne's seduction was underway. Nantz was 31, unmarried and curious, but she was also cautious, so it took some time for Anne to persuade her into bed. Come November, however, when Nantz visited Anne at Shibden, she was finally able to share the news with her diary: 'Had a very good kiss last night. [Nantz] gave it me with pleasure, not thinking it necessary to refuse me any longer.'[41]

Anne's sexuality had never given her much angst – she had been active with girls since her teens and by her mid-twenties was in full control of her body and her desires. Her resolution never to marry a man for the sake of money and appearances, as Mariana had, was unshakeable: 'I love, & only love, the fairer sex & thus beloved by them in turn, my heart revolts from any other love than theirs.'[42] But Nantz was new to this experience and she had worries. As sex between men was forbidden in the Bible, she feared sex between women might be, too, and 'asked if I thought the thing wrong'. Anne barely turned a hair. She 'dextrously parried' Nantz's concerns, reassuring her with the conclusion she had long since come to in her own mind: 'I urged in my own defence the strength of natural feeling & instinct, for so I might call it, as I had always had the same turn

The girls
liked me &
had always
liked me

from infancy. That it had been known to me, as it were, by inclination. That I have never varied & no effort on my part had been able to counteract it. That the girls liked me & had always liked me.' To Anne, her sexuality was an integral, accepted part of her nature. The literary precedents she had found in classical poetry had convinced her she was not abnormal, and as sex between women 'was certainly not named' in the Bible, she didn't believe for one minute that it excluded her from God's love.

Indeed, at a time when love between women was 'not named' in the Bible, or anywhere else for that matter, it was this self-awareness, this ease and confidence in her feelings that made Anne so remarkable in her own day and so seemingly in step with ours. Few of the women she had relationships with felt so at peace with their sexuality, and none of them pursued gratification of it so aggressively. Anne's wider social circle certainly noticed her 'oddities', but as they had no way to articulate their suspicions, Anne could take liberties that few gentlemen could get away with. A little discretion was all it took to avoid becoming a social pariah – and Nantz was the not the first, or the last, to see the wisdom in Anne's sexual manifesto.

Alone again at Shibden, Anne threw herself into a strict regime of study in the spring of 1817, to distract herself from her loneliness and satisfy her curious mind. Her timetable was military: 'I mean to devote my mornings, before breakfast to Greek, & afterwards, till dinner, to divide the time equally between Euclid & arithmetic … I must read a page or 2 of French now & then, when I can. The afternoons & evenings are set apart for general reading, for walking, ½ an hour, or ¾, practice on the flute.'[43] Her days were stuffed with activity – if there were any spare moments, they were given over to helping Uncle James run the estate – but she still found time to fret over her clothes, and that summer she came to an important decision about how she would present herself to the world. She wanted to look different, unfeminine, but to maintain a respectability that befitted her family's status. Full cross-dressing was not an option, so on 2 September 1817, she 'entered upon my plan of always wearing black'[44] – a happy compromise to her mind. Black was rarely worn by women and had a simple, striking androgyny that pleased her. It would be her signature look for the remainder of her life – one that she would only deviate from on the rarest of occasions.

That summer, Anne was also beginning to despair that the plan she and Mariana had cooked up to one day live together would ever come off. Mariana's visits to Shibden were scarce, brief and clandestine, made all the more so because Charles was now 'terribly jealous'[45] of Anne and didn't trust her an inch. He had intercepted a letter from her in January that had hinted at their wish for him to be out of the way, which left Anne no longer welcome at Lawton Hall and both women 'in constant fear of him forbidding her writing to me at all'.[46] To enable them to communicate in confidence, Mariana learned Anne's secret code, but all the sneaking around left Anne deeply unsatisfied: 'I am often miserable & often wish to try to wean my heart from her & fix more propitiously.'[47] Her heart was set on finding a life partner, and in these moments of frustration, when she was left hankering after a woman who was forever out of reach, she tried to convince herself that Tib would do. She could never quite succeed.

Following the deaths of both her Uncle Joseph and her mother – whom she hadn't seen in two years – within a week of each other, Anne consoled herself with a trip to York in December, where Mariana was staying with her family. Even this meeting was fraught, however. The Belcombes had noticed the strangely romantic attentions Anne paid to their daughter, and although they couldn't accurately express their concerns, they had made their displeasure known. Anne turned on the charm and assured Mrs Belcombe that she had 'changed my manners to M— as soon as I was properly told of the folly of them'.[48] Within hours, she proceeded to flirt with three of the Belcombe sisters – Eliza, Harriet and Lou – while still enjoying secret quickies with Mariana behind locked doors. Poor Nantz, on this occasion, didn't get a look-in.

'DOES YOUR COCK STAND?'

The following year, 1818, Anne began to cut her losses with Mariana and look about for someone else. An infatuation with a pretty local girl called Miss Browne came to nothing, so when Tib returned from a three-year trip abroad, Anne tried again to persuade herself that she could love her. Tib was as keen as ever, but their reunion at Langton Hall in September was a disappointment – Tib had grown fatter and a good deal more worldly since her travels, and for Anne, this spoiled her. In bed, it was obvious to both of them that something was wrong: 'Tried for a kiss a considerable time last night but Isabella was as dry as a stick & I could not succeed.'[49]

The sex may not have been inspiring, but Tib's tales of her adventures abroad most certainly were. Anne was desperate to explore the continent, which had long been off-limits due to the French Revolution and the Napoleonic Wars, so in May 1819, she persuaded her aunt to go with her to Paris. She was confident they would make good travelling companions – Aunt Anne was 'fond & proud' of her and not in the least perturbed when she heard of her niece's preference for women: 'Talked of my fancy for Miss Browne … She said she knew very well & that I should like Miss Browne better than Tib or M——, if I durst.'[50] So at the respective ages of 28 and 54, the two Anne Listers embarked on their first ever trip abroad, spending a month in post-revolutionary France. Anne was so fascinated by this first glimpse of the wider world that she observed every detail, penning a 71-page account for the Duffins that could have acted as an official travel guide. The two women, usually so cooped up in their remote corner of Yorkshire, had never 'felt better in our lives'.[51]

The autumn after their return, however, Anne was at a low ebb. Mariana seemed further away than ever and Tib's habits, she'd decided, 'are very little suited to mine' – particularly her excessive drinking. 'I could not live happily with her. At all events the experiment shall not be tried.'[52] Her mood only darkened when, at home in Halifax, she became the subject of a hate campaign that targeted her visible difference to other women. Anne strode around Halifax in her great coat and gaiters, with her deep voice and mannish walk, looking every inch the dapper gent, yet through a judicious mix of restraint and charm, she had always got away with mostly being herself among her peers. They gossiped about her and eyed her a little warily but were 'accustomed to my oddities' [53] and usually greeted her flirty ways with nothing worse than a smirk. Certainly, she felt confident enough to state openly in company 'how very much I preferred ladies to gentlemen'.[54] Strangers, on the other hand, weren't quite so tolerant. 'The people generally remark, as I pass along, how much I am like a man', she noted in her diary. Prostitutes solicited her in the street; behind her back they called her 'Gentleman Jack', while to her face one man even asked, 'Does your cock stand?'[55]

Anne met every jeer with majestic indifference, but in the autumn of 1819, a series of more sinister incidents called for decisive action.

On 1 October, she received a threatening letter from 'William Townsend', followed by another a few weeks later, which began by claiming that she had 'advertised in the *Leeds Mercury* for a husband ...' Anne read no more – she resealed it and sent it back. More letters arrived towards the end of the year and by now she was rattled enough to expect some kind of physical assault. If it came to that, she was ready to fight. She suspected the culprit was a 'little-ish, mechanic-like, young man' who had hassled her in the street back in July and was confident that, if that were the case, she would be a match for him. 'I will never fear. Be firm. Learn to have nerve to protect myself & make the best of all things. He is but a little fellow & I think I could knock him down if he should touch me. I should try.'[56]

The harassment continued into the New Year. One man stopped her in the street to ask if she wanted a sweetheart and a kiss (Anne felt she 'could have knocked him down'[57]); another 'suddenly attempted to put his hands up my things behind. In the scuffle, I let the umbrella fall but instantly picked it up & was aiming a blow when the fellow ran off as fast as he could.' They had picked the wrong woman to try to intimidate. 'I did not feel in the least frightened, but indignant & enraged.'[58] When the next letter arrived, Anne immediately consulted a magistrate about taking legal action, though they proved hopelessly ineffectual. As usual, she felt able to talk frankly with her aunt about the matter and took heart from the fact that both she and Uncle James stood in solidarity with her, suggesting not that she pander to these bullies by changing her ways, but that she frighten them off with her pistols instead.

Over the following year, Anne sought refuge with the various women in her life. She and Mariana were reunited at York and Shibden from February to April 1820, where they pored over their past and renewed their vows of love and commitment. Mariana begged her to be as faithful as a husband, and Anne agreed, skilfully evading any binding promises so that she felt 'as much at liberty as ever'.[59] With all the indifference of a rake, she then went to Langton Hall in October and proceeded, over several months, to have sex with both Tib and Tib's new girlfriend, Mary Vallance, and to flirt with Mariana's sisters, Nantz and Harriet. This bedroom-hopping farce, in which Anne made all the ladies jealous of one another, culminated in a return to the Belcombes' in York in January 1821 where she slept with Nantz, too – though with little enthusiasm. She saw no significance in her infidelity to Mariana, even when it was with her sister. There was hardly a woman Anne did not try to seduce, and hardly a woman who resisted her. Her confidence, silver tongue and sexual assertiveness were evidently intoxicating.

Anne's sex life became even more complicated in the summer of 1821, when she was reunited with Mariana after nearly a year and half's separation and soon afterwards noticed 'a queer, hottish, itching sensation ... about the pudendum'.[60] She knew enough to guess that she had caught a venereal disease from Mariana, who must in turn have caught it from Charles, who made no great secret of his infidelities. Unfortunately, there was no easy, effective way to deal with it. Deploying the age-old trick of pretending to have a friend with similar symptoms, Anne consulted Mariana's brother Steph – a doctor like his father – and managed to get a prescription for 'cubeb powders & lotions' – a pepper solution to be applied with a sponge. The apothecary made up the medicine for her, as well as a concoction of calomel (noxious mercury chloride) ground up with oil, to be injected into her vagina,[61] though these remedies would offer little relief from her complaint. That didn't stop Anne from sleeping with both Tib and Mariana as usual over the following year.

THREE STEPS IN ONE

Anne's prospects began to look up a little in June 1822 when, after years of proving her worth and reliability as a future estate manager of Shibden, Uncle James officially wrote Anne, now 31, into his will as his heir and gave her a biannual allowance of £25. The first thing she did with it was to travel. In July, she and her aunt took a tour of North Wales – Anne driving them in the new one-horse gig she had recently bought for £65 – during which they indulged her love of walking and scrambling up mountains, taking in the beautiful scenery and climbing Mount Snowdon. The most enlightening stop of this trip, however, was the house of Lady Eleanor Butler and Miss Sarah Ponsonby, commonly known as the Ladies of Llangollen. These intriguing women had met in County Kilkenny in 1768 and, defying the disapproval of their well-to-do families, had eloped and set up home together in a small cottage in the Welsh village of Llangollen. The ladies wore gentlemen's jackets and top hats, and had transformed their house and gardens into a Gothic rural paradise, which they lovingly named Plâs Newydd, or 'New Hall'. They would live there together for 50 years.

The ladies' unconventional story soon won them wide-reaching fame. Far from inviting social exclusion, this eccentric couple fascinated both the press and the beau monde. Wordsworth, Southey, Shelley, Byron, Scott and the Duke of Wellington all flocked to meet them. Even Queen Charlotte showed an interest, persuading her husband, King George III, to grant them a pension. Acceptance came surprisingly easily, but only because Miss Butler and Miss Ponsonby were upper-class ladies, traditional in every other respect, who exemplified the euphemistic, non-threatening, ennobling ideal of platonic 'romantic friendship'.

Anne had read about the Ladies of Llangollen in the paper in 1810 and been instantly fascinated, recognising herself in their story. Mariana and her sister Lou had already visited and 'very much admired' their set-up ('M— wished we had such a one'[62]), so naturally Anne was keen to see it for herself. The ornate house and beautiful grounds were enough to trigger in her a wave of wistful fantasies of living such a life with her wife – 'I could have mused for hours, dreamt dreams of happiness, conjured up many a vision of … hope'[63] – while her meeting with the learned and genteel Miss Ponsonby left her full of wonder. Eager to know for certain if the ladies were, as she suspected, like her, Anne tried to subtly divine the information from their conversation. Miss Ponsonby would not be drawn to say anything explicit, but on parting, in what seemed like a gesture of tacit understanding, she gave Anne a rose from their garden, which Anne tenderly resolved to press and keep 'for the sake of the place where it grew'.[64] She came away from Plâs Newydd 'much pleased', convinced that the ladies' relationship could not possibly be platonic – 'Heaven forgive me, but I look within myself & doubt'[65] – and reassured that such a life was possible. She felt more hopeless than ever, though, that she would ever create that utopian future with Mariana.

As if to confirm her premonition, a scene between Anne and Mariana in August 1823 undermined their relationship almost to the point of collapse. Mariana was due to pass through Halifax on the 19th, so, early that morning, unable to stand the 'suspense and anxiety of waiting' for her love to arrive, Anne marched out of Shibden on no breakfast and walked ten and a half miles in the rain to meet her coach on the moors. By the time she found it she was wild-haired and drenched; she bounded into the carriage, taking the three steps in one, and flumped down in the seat next to Mariana and Lou.

Mariana was 'horror-struck. Why did I say I had walked from Shibden? Never saw John's eyes [Mariana's servant] so round with astonishment; the post-boys, too; & how fast I talked!' The way Anne had leapt up those three steps was so unladylike – she had abandoned all caution in showing such unbridled excitement to see her. Always the more conventional of the two, Mariana was mortified.

They patched things up, but this episode played on Anne's mind continually, especially when Mariana then showed a reluctance to go ahead with a planned trip to Scarborough. They went, in mid-September, though at the seaside Anne's heavy black outfits stood out even more. In this unfamiliar society, acquaintances snubbed her, 'all the people stared at me' and worse: 'M— owned afterwards she had observed it & felt uncomfortable.'[66] She admitted, too, that she would have preferred Anne to have 'a feminine figure', and that the dark hairs growing on her upper lip 'made her sick'.[67] Anne couldn't escape the conclusion that her lover was now ashamed of her and terrified that their relationship might be discovered. It confirmed what Anne had always suspected: that Mariana was 'a weak & wavering companion'[68] whose 'feelings were cooler' than hers and governed by the 'paltry selfishness of coward fear'.[69] With a growing cynicism, Anne blamed her lack of status. Wealth and prestige protected and excused eccentricity, but as it was, neither she nor Mariana had the 'éclat' to 'pass me off'.[70] The two women talked, sobbed, had sex, reaffirmed their devotion and carried on regardless, but something between them had irrevocably broken.

Meanwhile, Tib had fallen ill and Anne was convinced it was her doing. Her own infection was no better after three years of suffering – she had even given leeches a try by now, an antiquated quack remedy that had been abandoned by most. Desperate for a cure, she confided in her aunt and uncle, who thankfully were not so worldly in these matters. Aunt Anne was under the impression that such maladies could be passed on by drinking from the same glass or 'going to the necessary'.[71] They decided to send Anne to a doctor in Manchester, though his prescriptions were as hopeless as all the others.[72]

Anne's suggestion was that perhaps a restorative trip to Paris might succeed where all else had failed, and as usual she got her way. With £125 in hand from Uncle James, she set off with her maid on 24 August 1824, for what was supposed to be a three-month trip to learn French and regain her health. It turned out to be a seven-month trip, which only made her health worse. The best doctor in Paris, Guillaume Dupuytren, who was physician to Louis XVIII and Charles X, listened to Anne's cock-and-bull story of having contracted the infection from her unfaithful husband (using Mariana's story as her own), and prescribed a rationed diet, hour-long baths every other day at 35°C and a toxic mercury rub. After a week of this punishing treatment, Anne was a physical wreck: 'I begin to look pale and ill,'[73] she observed, as the mercury brought on 'profuse bleedings'.[74] Her health only improved when she stopped Dupuytren's treatment.

Aside from tending to her health concerns, the main reason for Anne's prolonged stay in Paris was her involvement in a rather messy affair with a 37-year-old widow who had taken up residence there. Mrs Maria Barlow presented just the kind of challenge that Anne found thrilling. They prowled around one another, flirting and insinuating, until Maria edged into Anne's bed, but she wanted a commitment first, so not without some guilt, Anne told her what she wanted to hear: that she loved her and they would be married – 'How she is deceived', she told her diary. 'Why have I done this?'[75] The two women took an apartment together, and within a week and a half

Anne was having doubts. Before long, their fling had ended, Maria was left weeping and heartbroken, while Anne walked away dry-eyed and unmoved. The relationship would sputter on and off over the next two years, but ultimately Maria had neither the money nor the social éclat that Anne required. Even more irreconcilable was the fact that Maria treated her 'too much as a woman' – both in bed and out of it.[76] They managed to remain on friendly terms, though Anne still considered this liaison 'the worst scrape I have ever been in'.[77]

LADY OF THE MANOR

Anne returned from Paris in April 1825, still a little distracted by Maria Barlow. When she saw Mariana for the first time in over a year on a trip to Buxton in August, she 'felt restrained' at first and it took a while for the couple to warm to one another again. But warm they did. Within a few days, the lovers had fallen into their usual pattern of raking over their problems, renewing their marriage vows and continuing as rampant as ever, only this time they exchanged unconventional gifts before parting – a lock of their pubic hair, which, in a sexualised riff on the classic courtship custom, they kissed and put into lockets 'for us always to wear under our clothes in mutual remembrance'.[78]

In practice, such gestures had little effect on Anne's constancy. With her 'wife' technically married to another, she always felt a licence to stray, to the extent that over Christmas at Langton Hall, she actively pursued Mariana's sister Harriet (with whom, Anne surmised, 'I might have taken any liberty I pleased'[79]) and slept once again with Tib. Days later she was in York chatting up Mr Duffin's niece, followed by Mariana's other sister Lou, who had also made it clear that Anne could have her if she wanted. 'Here I am flirting again,' Anne mused. 'How can I trust myself?'[80]

While her love life reigned chaotic, one of the most decisive moments in Anne's life occurred one January morning at Shibden Hall in 1826. On the 26th, while Anne was brushing her teeth, her Uncle James collapsed suddenly in his bedroom and died. Later that same day, the family gathered to read his will and, as expected, he had left his entire estate to Anne, with the income from the estate to be shared with his remaining siblings while they lived. Anne felt strangely calm; she had lost a dear, kind uncle who had taken her in, quietly supported her peculiar ways and now revolutionised her fortunes, and yet, 'There is not that sorrow there ought to be.' She felt the sin of it – it frightened her that her thoughts could turn to 'temporal gains' at such a moment[81] – but the truth was, at the age of 34, she had finally got what she wanted: she was an independent landowner, in control of her own money and her very own property.

The first task on Anne's agenda as lady of the manor was not, perhaps surprisingly, to dedicate herself to estate life, but to travel. As soon as she had sorted her business affairs and received the rents from her tenants, she and her aunt set off, on 16 June 1826, leaving Anne's hapless father Jeremy and crotchety sister Marian to look after Shibden. The plan was to be away for two years, though it would turn out to be almost five.

During those years, Aunt Anne remained happily settled in Paris, while Anne flitted like a hyperactive child from place to place and person to person in a permanent restless fever. One minute she was in Paris with Mariana, the next she had embarked on a four-month tour of Switzerland and northern Italy with Maria Barlow. Hastily, she moved on to Scotland to pursue a love affair with her aristocratic and consumptive friend Sibella MacLean – another doomed relationship, though one that would introduce Anne to several influential contacts, including the British ambassador to Paris and his wife, Lady Elizabeth Stuart de Rothesay, and Sibella's young niece, Vere Hobart, whom Anne fixed her eye on as her next romantic conquest. With these illustrious new friends, she socialised at embassy soirées and travelled through Belgium and northern France, before returning to Paris, where she attended palaeontology and anatomy lectures at the Collège de France, and undertook her own grisly dissections. These were grand, thrilling, mind-stretching adventures, but none of them would have quite as lasting an impact on Anne as her visit to the Pyrenees.

She was there as part of a three-month tour of the South of France with Lady Stuart de Rothesay and her two daughters, having set out with them on 21 July 1830, narrowly avoiding the July Revolution in Paris by a week. For all that she revelled in the social upgrade, however, Anne quickly found herself yearning for a much freer life than the one her lofty new companions allowed for. As the party neared the mountains that Anne so adored, their 'life of trammel' began to make her 'heartily sick'; she was itching to scramble up the peaks, but her friends were not so intrepid: 'I get no real walking, am getting fatter and all day tortured by dress too tight. Oh, that I was unknown and walking and riding about at my ease.'[82]

One day at the end of August the wanderlust became irresistible. Without telling anyone, Anne took herself off on a four-day hiking expedition; she hitched up her skirts and climbed first to the top of the Brèche de Roland (2,807 metres), negotiating treacherous glaciers on the way, and then Mont Perdu (3,355 metres), the third-highest mountain in the Pyrenees. At the summit of Mont Perdu, with breathtaking views towards Spain, the 'perfect solitude, the profound stillness' gave Anne 'a sensation I had never had before'.[83] The exertion of the climb and the three-hour descent along the gorge d'Ortessa was so extreme it made her throw up afterwards, but Anne later stated that 'no moment of my life has made a deeper impression on me, than the memory of my return from Mt Perdu'.[84]

Anne and her aunt reluctantly left Paris for Yorkshire on 23 May 1831; their funds were running low, and since the July Revolution the previous summer the political tensions in the country had remained high, which had led to their embassy friends falling out of favour in the diplomatic corps. No sooner had they arrived back at Shibden, however, than Anne was agitating to leave again. She could hardly bear to live with her father and sister any longer than necessary, so after issuing instructions for a few estate improvements, she was off in less than three weeks, first to York to see the Duffins and the Belcombes, then to Langton Hall to see Tib. Her old friends lacked the sheen of the society types she was now used to associating with, though. Bored and twitchy, Anne moved on to a three-week tour of the Netherlands at the beginning of August with Mariana – though this, for unknown reasons, Anne regarded as an 'ill-fated journey'. After 15 years of trying to defy their separation, it was now undeniable that she and Mariana had drifted apart. A visit to Lawton Hall the following year would confirm that the relationship had fizzled into little more than 'common friendship'.[85] So Anne returned from the Netherlands with a fresh resolve. It had been a restless, exhilarating, exhausting few years, spent searching for – or perhaps running away from – the one thing she lacked. It was now time to settle down and find herself a suitable new wife.

'THE NEXT TENANT OF MY HEART'

Anne's quest for a new life partner didn't run smoothly. Come the summer of 1832, she was 41 and back at Shibden, licking her wounds after six months in Hastings, where she had made a last-ditch attempt to court Vere Hobart, only for the trip to culminate in what Anne saw as another great betrayal: Vere's engagement to a Captain Cameron. In a bid to conquer this latest bout of heartbreak, Anne occupied herself by hatching grand plans for re-landscaping the grounds of Shibden, exploiting the estate's mining potential and improving the old house.

An appealing distraction soon arrived, however, in the form of Miss Ann Walker of Lidgate, a shy 29-year-old orphan and heiress from the neighbouring village of Lightcliffe. Anne had met and even flirted with the flaxen-haired Miss Walker a handful of times over the years, but socially she had kept her at arm's length. The Walkers were new money – cloth manufacturers – and until now Anne had always considered tradespeople beneath her. Following the sudden death of Ann Walker's brother, she and her sister Elizabeth had unexpectedly inherited the Walker estate; Elizabeth's husband, Captain Sutherland, had claimed his wife's share, and convinced Ann to bequeath hers to his son – though that could always be changed ... Financially this girl was a catch. Anne dismissed the past rumours of her 'mental derangement' – 'Her mind warped on religion'.[86] The wealthy, vulnerable, impressionable Miss Walker seemed like the ideal quarry.

After one or two neighbourly visits in July and August, Anne began to woo Miss Walker in earnest in September, obeying all the rules of heterosexual courtship. The scene was set. Among her extensive plans for the house and gardens – for which she commanded a small army of workmen, with whom she enjoyed rolling up her sleeves and mucking in – Anne had had a small thatched hut, or *chaumière*, built in the lower part of the grounds, which she called the moss-hut – the perfect secluded spot for private assignations. Meanwhile, the phrase 'Incurred a cross thinking of Miss Walker' (her code for masturbation) became a frequent refrain in her diary.[87]

Timid, nervous Miss Walker was surprisingly receptive to Anne's advances, and by the end of the month, they were 'bordering on love-making in the hut'. Anne was confident that 'our liaison is now established'.[88] They got on 'beautifully'; they even talked of travelling together, a significant commitment, which Ann remarked, tellingly, 'would be as good as a marriage'.[89] All the signs looked positive, so at the beginning of October Anne proposed that Miss Walker move in to Shibden.

There's more than a little of the libertine in Anne's record of the seduction. Although she was hoping to find the life partner she had long been looking for, it was Ann Walker's fortune that attracted her most – almost £3,000 a year. 'Thought I, "she little dreams what is in my mind – to make up to her – she has money and this might make up for rank."'[90] Another bonus was that Ann was indeed a malleable soul, who looked up to Anne: she 'seems to take all I say for gospel', Anne wrote happily, and 'consults me about her affairs'.[91] Unlike her previous partners, Anne felt sure she could 'gently mould Miss W— to my wishes'. She had every intention of making them both happy, but it was her own happiness and comfort that took precedence: 'We shall have money enough. She will look up to me & soon feel attached & I, after all my turmoils, shall be steady, &, if God so wills it, happy.'[92]

Anne knew she was not in love with Miss Walker, but she was on a mission to be so: 'I shall think myself into being in love with her,' she told herself firmly.[93] This was easier said than done, however, for as their courtship progressed, Ann's behaviour gradually began to infuriate and repel her. At first, Anne played the considerate gentleman when Ann refused to respond one way or the other to her proposal. Miss Walker was reluctant to live at Shibden after the comforts of her own homes: Lidgate, Cliff Hill (where Ann hoped to live after her aged aunt's death) and the (now empty) family seat of Crow Nest were all bigger and rather more elegant than Shibden. She worried, too, that she might change her mind, so Anne gallantly gave her six months to decide.

In the meantime, as they began fumbling towards sex, she noticed that Ann Walker seemed rather too 'man-keen' for her liking.[94] Such easy conquests were never a turn-on for Anne. Like every gentleman of her day, she expected her wife to be pure, and when she began to suspect that Ann might in fact be 'one of the initiated',[95] any love-like feeling towards her evaporated: 'her mumbling kisses have cured me of that'.[96] Still, she continued to 'grubble' her on the drawing-room sofa and make her way further up her petticoats towards her 'queer', and persisted with the relationship, only with less patience. She now wanted a decision by the end of the year.

But Ann Walker had secrets that were paralysing her into indecision. It emerged that she had been furtively engaged to a Mr Fraser, who had died suddenly just three months before, leaving her careering guiltily between grief for him and lust for Anne. She had also been receiving anonymous letters warning her of Anne Lister's predatory nature. The stress had brought on low spirits, back pains and sleepless nights. The very antithesis of Anne Lister's positive, kinetic dynamism, Ann spent most of her days cooped up, languishing on the sofa, her thoughts bleak, her energy zapped. Then, on 26 October, came a letter with black edging, informing her that her friend Mrs Ainsworth had been thrown from her carriage and killed. Coming so soon after the loss of her parents, her brother and her fiancée, this was too much grief. The final straw came when, within a week of his wife's death, Mr Ainsworth started paying his addresses. Hamstrung by a misplaced sense of obligation because Ainsworth had once 'taught her to kiss' and (she eventually admitted) put pressure on her to have sex, she felt unable to refuse his indecently hasty proposals outright.[97] Ann Walker was grappling with feelings and concepts she had no knowledge or understanding of, and the result was mental, spiritual and physical turmoil.

For her part, Anne did not take kindly to having a rival – she had been hurt too many times before to countenance losing out to a man yet again. Her response was to issue an ultimatum: on the Thursday she told Ann Walker she must choose between her and Mr Ainsworth before the following Monday – which only panicked Ann all the more, making her vacillate wildly from complete indecision one minute to offering Anne a lock of her pubic hair the next.

While Anne Lister told herself that she would be 'easily reconciled either way' to the outcome of this affair,[98] Ann Walker spent days in turmoil, and on the Monday, 5 November, she sent an agitated note. She had lived the last 12 months, she explained, 'under circumstances of no common moment' and 'with my health impaired & with vivid regrets of the past, I feel that I have not the power fairly to exercise my own judgement'. Instead, she would let God decide. She had placed two pieces of paper in a purse, one saying yes, the other no, and whichever Anne should draw out first would decide their fate. But to evade the question in this way and leave such important life choices to chance was as alien a notion to Anne Lister's decisive nature as it was inherent to Ann Walker's. She returned the purse to Ann and promised to give her until New Year's Day to decide.

Ann's prevarication continued right up until the eleventh hour. Several times during those weeks Anne believed the matter settled in her favour; in mid-December they were talking of solemnising their commitment before God, by 'declaring it on the Bible & taking the sacrament' together in church.[99] But by Christmas, Anne was despairing of ever getting an answer, and wasn't even sure she wanted one: 'I never saw such a hopeless person in my life ... thank God my own mind's not like hers – what could I do with her?'[100]

As the deadline approached, the couple parted in tears, their affair seemingly over, leaving Anne sanguine rather than heartbroken, and already looking ahead. 'I never stood so alone – & yet I am far happier than I have been of long ... what adventure will come next? Who will be the next tenant of my heart?'[101]

A week later, however, she received a letter that shed new light on the real source of her lover's anguish: in having sex with and marrying Anne, Ann Walker feared she was consigning herself to 'everlasting torment in hell-fire' – her punishment for provoking God's ire. 'This explains all,' Anne told her diary. 'The poor girl is beside herself.'[102] Between Anne and Ann Walker's brother-in-law, Captain Sutherland, it was agreed that, as the rumours had foretold, her mental health was not what it ought to be, and that she should join the Sutherlands up in Inverness where she could receive care. Anne divined that the Sutherlands had another motive beyond their regard for Ann's welfare – to marry her off to a Scottish relative who was knee-deep in debt – but this realisation sparked little jealousy. Ann Walker left Yorkshire on 16 February 1833, and Anne Lister rejoiced: '"Heaven be praised," said I to myself as I walked homewards, "that they are off & that I have got rid of her & am once more free."'[103]

I feel a wish
to be freed from
that petticoat slavery

Anne now got down to estate business. Ploughing on with her ambitious plans, she redrew the landscape around Shibden and proved herself a formidable businesswoman and hardnosed negotiator, earning the begrudging respect of the men she dealt with. With steam power set to dominate the future, Anne read up on geology and set about developing the coal seams underneath her land. Months were spent haggling over coal leases with her business rivals Christopher and Jeremiah Rawson – Anne drove a hard bargain, for she suspected they were already trespassing on her land and stealing her coal, so she set her price high and would not budge. When the negotiations finally broke down in February 1833, Mr Jeremiah Rawson admitted that 'he was never beaten by ladies & I had beaten him. [I] said gravely, "It is the intellectual part of us that makes a bargain, & that has no sex or ought [to] have none".'[104] It was a view still not shared by many.

She proved herself an indomitable force when it came to politics, too. As an old-school Tory, Anne was opposed to the radical reforms of Earl Grey's Whig government that sought to redistribute the privileges of her class, which might have seemed beyond her control – as a woman she had no vote, after all. As a landowner, however, she now wielded more political influence than most men. In the first election following the Reform Act of 1832, in December, Anne had 'talks' with her enfranchised tenants, such as John Bottomley, and persuaded – or perhaps intimidated – them to vote for her favoured Tory candidate.[105] If this seems like a corrupt practice, it was, but a common enough one across the country that wasn't technically illegal and often worked. With the ballot cast publicly, Bottomley knew he'd better oblige his landlady, so he promised to vote her way and he kept his word.[106] In this instance it made no odds; Anne's Tory candidate still lost, but she had found a new form of agency in the world, however underhand, and would use it again in future.

A year after her return to Shibden, in mid-June 1833, still restless and hungry for new experiences, Anne set off on another adventure. She spent the next six months visiting several of her old aristocratic friends in London, Paris and Copenhagen, and was thrilled to be mixing with the elite once more. To her mind, she had reached the pinnacle of her social ambitions when she was received at the Danish court. Despite one cringe-making gaffe in which she mistook one of the ladies in waiting for the Queen, Anne styled it out and was invited to attend the Queen's birthday ball – an occasion so grand and gratifying to Anne that 'for the first time these 17 years, I was in white satin'.[107]

Anne had tried to convince herself that she didn't much care about Ann Walker, that she was glad to be rid of her, but she acknowledged that Ann had a knack of 'unhinging' her, and during their ten-month separation she thought of her often – still occasionally incurring a cross as she did so. There was some excitement, therefore, when Ann Walker returned from Scotland at the close of 1833. There was hope in the news that she had finally refused Mr Ainsworth, yet still, on their reunion, the two women fell into much the same pattern as before. It seemed to Anne that Ann Walker's health hadn't much improved, so in the New Year of 1834, she organised for her to stay in lodgings just outside York, where she could receive regular treatment from Dr Steph Belcombe – whose reassuring diagnosis of Ann's complaint the year before had been that there was 'nothing the matter with her but nervousness'.[108] Anne hoped to God he was right. She had invested precious time, energy and emotion in Ann Walker, and despite what she told herself, she cared for her. It doubtless crossed her mind, too, that they had already discussed changing their wills in one another's favour, and for that, she would need her wife to be sane.

By the time they met again in Halifax in mid-February, Ann Walker seemed to have finally put all her doubts aside. She was ready to commit, and her union with Anne would have all the hallmarks of a traditional dynastic marriage. 'She agreed it was understood that she was to consider herself as having nobody to please, & being under no authority, but mine.'[109] To make it official (Anne in particular was keen for a solemn, binding promise from her wavering lover), on 27 February, Ann Walker placed a ring 'on my left third finger in token of our union – which is now understood to be confirmed for ever'.[110] A month later, the two Annes took the sacrament together at Goodramgate church in York, before a congregation who had no understanding of the cultural significance of what they were witnessing. For Ann Walker to demonstrate her love before a God she unequivocally believed in, whose wrath she genuinely feared, showed a courage that most today do not have to find, and suggests that she finally had faith in His acceptance of their union. Anne Lister, meanwhile, felt free now the marriage had been solemnised to set about merging their two estates and appropriating her wife's money, as any husband would. In possession, finally, of the advantageous marriage she had hoped for her entire adult life, she tried to be positive about their future: 'I soon shall be satisfied with her and I really hope we shall get on very well together.'[111]

NEWLYWEDS

In the first weeks and months of their marriage, the two Annes visited one another regularly and, as they relaxed into their relationship,

Ann Walker's health – and their sex life – improved. Jeremy, Marian and Aunt Anne were all unfazed at the prospect of Ann Walker moving into their home – on the contrary: they liked Miss Walker and thought she would suit Anne very well. Ann Walker herself, however, remained anxious about relocating to Shibden – not just because it was less comfortable than what she was used to, but because of what people might say. 'Will it be wise to irritate or brave public opinion further just now?' she asked Anne. Perhaps, after all, it would be better if she stayed at Lidgate. This further indecision only irritated Anne, and the unwillingness to show off their union to the world offended her. 'Affront! Does this seem as if she really thought us united in heart and purse?'[112] Unable to empathise with her wife's nervousness at her new lesbian lifestyle, or to abide the idea of settling anywhere other than her own estate of Shibden, she wasn't willing to compromise.

Perhaps Anne hoped that her improvements to Shibden would make all the difference, for she was now consulting an architect about adding Gothic castellations to the exterior, and a carriage drive and lodge to the entrance, as well as using her wife's money to buy new land to expand her coal-mining schemes. She began to act as Ann's informal business advisor and employed her steward Samuel Washington to manage both of their estates jointly.

Avoiding the question of when and how they would live together for the time being, the two Annes spent June, July and August on a honeymoon of sorts in France and Switzerland, and mostly got on well. Anne was the more adventurous of the two, but Ann Walker found that she also loved travel, and proved herself capable of roughing it with good humour; she wrote to Aunt Anne of the 'magnificent hotels' they met with – one of them a barn, where they slept between the cows and the hay loft, another a cramped shoe-box apartment where they bunked in with their host's sickly children.[113] At Chamonix they toured Mont Blanc on muleback; at St Etienne they descended into a mine and emerged covered in coal dust. Ann grew stronger every day and both women felt revived, so that, notwithstanding the occasional irritation ('Never in my life saw such a fidget in a carriage'[114]), Anne wrote to her aunt of what a splendid time they were having and what a 'blithe, and happy' traveller Ann Walker was.[115]

They returned to Halifax on 28 August 1834, and now, finally, Ann Walker moved in to Shibden. She was welcomed by the Listers, while Anne rented a pew for the two of them in the front row of Lightcliffe church in a defiant signal to the community that they were a respectable, godly couple. A visit alone to Mariana over Christmas 1834 tested Anne's loyalty, but although she observed with some satisfaction that Mariana 'cannot get over her love for me', Anne 'behaved with perfect propriety'.[116] For the first time in her life, she felt officially married and therefore obliged to be faithful. When she was greeted with delight by her loving wife on her return to Shibden, she found herself astonished at 'how little I had thought of M—' and felt 'very glad to be back again'.[117]

Despite their inauspicious start, the newlyweds were doing well, but as Ann Walker had feared, not everyone took kindly to the news of her move. Her relatives, particularly the Sutherlands, were baffled and deeply suspicious of this intense closeness between her and Miss Lister and her sudden change of address, and barely a month after Ann had moved in to Shibden, the gossips got to work. 'All the town talking of A—'s coming here,'[118] Anne reported, though with no words to explain their real objections, they could only accuse Ann Walker of abandoning her old aunt and imposing on Jeremy Lister. Then came the local by-election in the new year of 1835. Anne again supported the Tory candidate, and when he won by only one vote, the working people of Halifax rose up in widespread protests against the bribery and intimidation used by landowners such as her to drum up votes. Some local Tories found their property damaged, but for the Annes, public humiliation was the weapon of choice. On 10 January, a mysterious notice in the *Leeds Mercury* announced the marriage of 'Captain Tom Lister of Shibden Hall to Miss Ann Walker', which was followed a couple of days later by an anonymous letter of congratulation.[119] This was political revenge, but also a highly personal attack that mocked both Anne's masculinity and her relationship with Ann Walker. The girls tried to laugh it off; even in her diary Anne was all dignified stoicism – 'Probably meant to annoy, but, if so, a failure'[120] – though when the announcement appeared in the *York Chronicle* and the *Halifax Guardian*, too, they were swift to demand an apology from the editor.

The bad feeling in the town persisted towards them. Anne's acquaintances, who had always been so tolerant of her 'oddities', were now becoming openly hostile at her blatant show of unconventionality. Some, like Anne's good friend Mrs Priestley, who had once walked in on the Annes mid-grubble and had been frosty ever since, simply cut them; others tried to articulate their displeasure. Mrs Waterhouse 'hoped A— would not learn to walk and be like me – one Miss Lister quite enough';[121] an anonymous letter in March contained 'extreme abuse of me – pity for A—' and a promise to 'aid her getting away from me & Shibden';[122] and a month later reports dogged them of 'my tricking or getting out of [Ann] all she had'.[123]

Anne's critics were perhaps justified in their concerns over her control of Ann Walker's fortune, for she was now using it to fund her multiplying business interests, which included coal mines (Anne had been extracting coal from her first mine, which she named the Walker Pit, since 1834 and had plans to set up another, powered by a water-wheel), selling off land for the encroaching railway and converting one of her properties, Northgate House, into a hotel and casino. In defiance of public disapproval, Anne made an open state-ment of her marriage by having Ann Walker lay the hotel's foundation stone alongside her before a crowd of 100 people on 26 September 1835.

As Ann Walker saw her cash drain away on extravagant ventures that were yet to pay off, however, she began to fear ruin. Arguments between the couple became frequent and Ann's depression resurfaced. She began to say that they might be better off apart, and more and more often Anne's diary entries open with the words: 'No kiss.' It was becoming obvious 'that we shall not stick together for ever';[124] she was certain Ann 'would be glad to be at liberty again',[125] and indeed, she felt the same, professing a weary acceptance of their inexorable break-up. The truth was, though, that Anne Lister could not afford to give up on her marriage. Her projects would all collapse if she did. Their second anniversary on 10 February 1836 was as flat as Ann's mood ('she can hardly perhaps own to herself that she repents'[126]) and any attempts to cheer her up were futile. Anne feared that she was 'getting all wrong again in her spirits',[127] and a stressful legal dispute in March with the residents of a nearby slum, during which they 'burnt A— & me in effigy', did nothing to help her lover's mental state.[128]

Financial independence came to Anne Lister in 1836 when her two dependants, her father and Aunt Anne, both died within six months of each other. She had always been slightly ashamed of her shabby family, but Jeremy and Aunt Anne had been reliably loving and supportive of her and her unusual lifestyle, and Anne was perhaps more grateful for it than she knew. She saw to their funeral arrangements, watched her sister, Marian, move out to the family home at Market Weighton and then started to make changes. Even before Jeremy's death on Anne's 45th birthday, the two Annes had been preparing to arrange their wills. Now each left the other a life interest in her estate. If Anne Lister should die first, Ann Walker would have the right to live at Shibden and claim its income until her death, and vice versa. When they were both dead, Shibden would go to John Lister of the Welsh Listers, while Ann Walker's assets would go to the Sutherland heirs. Both women included a clause that would disinherit the other should they ever marry a man. The enormity of this legally binding agreement, however, seemed to revive all Ann Walker's old doubts. She was reluctant to sign on the dotted line; began to say that 'she could not make me happy'[129] and talked of 'her duty to leave me'. Anne was typically brusque in her response: 'said I could not stand this – she must make up her mind and stick to it'.[130] So she did. Ann Walker signed her will along with Anne on 9 May 1836 – though she refused to publish it until a year later.

Anne was now free to remodel Shibden as she wished, and her wish was to emulate the grand houses she had visited over the years. With her architect, John Harper, she planned to open up the house-body (hall) by ripping out the low ceiling, and to add a grand staircase, modern fireplaces and a Norman tower that would house her own personal library. With her garden designer, Samuel Gray, she discussed a romantic parkland, with a great lake, cascade, rockpool and wilderness garden. But with her business ventures not yet making a profit, it was still Ann Walker's money that had to pay for it all. As Anne piled on the pressure for Ann to publish her will and grant her more powers over her estate, the arguments continued and so did their misery. There was no fixing a marriage with such a weak core: Anne Lister did not love Ann Walker, and all the money in the world couldn't change that. While Anne hoped they could stick it out another year or two until she had righted her finances, Ann talked again and again of leaving, but, insecure, indecisive and in love as she was, she could never bring herself to do it.

LADY TRAVELLERS

By the spring of 1838, the conversion of Anne's Northgate House hotel was complete, her new Listerwick Colliery was up and running and the building work at Shibden was well underway. With their affairs in good order and the couple's unhappiness now of long-standing, Anne suggested what had always worked for her in the past: travel. She could conduct much of her business from abroad by letter, while the adventure would provide a welcome distraction from their problems and remove them from local hostility. Russia was her preferred destination, but Ann Walker recoiled from the idea of a long trip, so for now their plans were a little more modest. They set off for Paris on 2 May 1838, travelling via Antwerp, Brussels and Liège, then onwards to Anne's favourite place, the Pyrenees.

For six weeks in July and August they holidayed at Saint-Sauveur, bathing in the waters and exploring the surrounding mountains. Anne would often spend all day striding up the peaks of the Pyrenees, pushing herself sometimes beyond her limits. Ann was less ambitious, and perhaps more sensible: she preferred either to negotiate the mountains on horseback or to sketch them. It was alone, then, that Anne pulled off her most historic feat during this trip: becoming the first tourist, and the first woman, to reach the summit of the highest peak of the French Pyrenees: Vignemale. This 3,298-metre mountain had been thought inaccessible, but the year before two men had found a route to the top and were now selling the first official tourist ascent as guides. Experienced climber that she was, Anne was determined to do it.

The excursion was set for Saturday, 4 August 1838, but bad weather delayed it until the Monday. Having slept the night before on a bare rock floor in a shepherd's hut below the peak, Anne woke at 2 a.m., donned her riding gear and nailed leather boots, hitched up her skirts,[131] picked up her crampons and, on hardly any food, set off at 2.45. Nearly 10 hours later, at 1 p.m., the group reached the summit. Anne vomited from the exertion, but proudly wrote her name and those of her companions on a piece of paper, which she tucked inside a bottle and placed under some stones. After taking a few moments to inhale the view, they began the long descent and arrived back at the hut at just gone 8 p.m. Not relishing the prospect of another night spent on the floor with rocks jabbing her in the back, however, Anne insisted on pushing on until they reached the hostel. They finally made it back at 1.15 a.m., after nearly 22 hours of walking.

This was an extraordinary and hard-won achievement, so Anne was dismayed when just days later she found her crown challenged. Napoléon Joseph Ney, Prince de la Moskowa, had climbed the mountain the Thursday after her and, having been told by the guide that the English lady hadn't made it to the top, he assumed the title as his own. Anne's response was decisive: she had a lawyer draw up a certificate that laid out the truth for the guide to sign and send to the Prince. Even so, an article appeared in the 21 August edition of *Galignani's Messenger* (an English newspaper published in France), stating that the Prince and his brother had reached the summit first. This time Anne had the editors publish a correction, but as she was only ever referred to as the 'English lady', it was the Prince's name that stuck as the victor of Vignemale. Not for the first time or the last, a woman's achievement had been claimed by a man. Even today the route bears his name, not hers.[132] Anne feigned indifference in her diary – 'What matters it to me? I have made each ascent for my pleasure, not for éclat'[133] – though her determination to put the matter right betrays that, on the contrary, it mattered to her a great deal.

The Annes arrived back at Shibden on 27 November 1838 to a barrage of problems. The building work was not finished and snow-storms had ravaged Cliff Hill, leaving it in dire need of repairs. With funds running low, debts mounting and Anne's vast investments yet to pay off, it again fell to Ann Walker to stump up the cash, straining the couple's relationship further. Meanwhile, much to Anne's irritation, the Chartists had arrived in Halifax. To make their call for electoral reform heard, the working classes were marching through the streets, brushing the boundaries of Shibden, and Anne, whose instinct was always to jealously guard her privilege by aligning with the old feudal establishment rather than the working man, made her stance quite clear. When the town council requested troops against the protesters in May 1839, she happily housed them in her hotel, only heightening the 'deep-rooted feeling of hostility against the dignities of the olden time'[134] that simmered in industrial towns like hers.

With the atmosphere at home proving so unpleasant, within six months of their return from the Pyrenees Anne was desperate to get away again. She was determined to get to Russia this time, and hopefully Persia, too, so once Ann was persuaded and their prepara-tions were made, they set off in a laden carriage on 20 June 1839. From Calais, they travelled overland, via Denmark, Sweden, Norway and Finland, before arriving in St Petersburg on 17 September.

Russia lived up to Anne's every expectation. After three happy weeks admiring the art, royal palaces and gardens of St Petersburg, they headed to Moscow – 'the most picturesquely beautiful town I have ever seen'[135] – where they took in the Bolshoi and Red Square, and found St Basil's Cathedral 'gorgeously grotesque'.[136] Anne's letters of recommendation from her embassy friends meant that in almost every port of call they were welcomed by high-ranking officials and their wives and looked after well. They mixed with the Russian aristocracy, saw 'handsome houses, balls in the best Parisian style, and a great many pretty girls'.[137] They explored private palaces, experienced Russian Orthodox Church ceremonies and took part in Friday Muslim prayers. They hungrily consumed this new culture, from high to low, but after several months, and with winter approaching, Ann Walker was sated and ready to go home. Anne Lister, unsurprisingly, was not.

Her heart was still set on Persia and her plan was to make her way there along the Volga River, via the Caucasus Mountains on the border with Georgia. Most people thought her mad – to attempt such a thing during the winter months was foolhardy enough, but there had also been reports of kidnappings in the region by the Cherkess, the Circassian people from the remote North Caucasus. Ann tried to dissuade her – for financial reasons if nothing else – but Anne was intractable, and so her wife deferred to her authority. It was now a real possibility, acknowledged between them, that once they returned home they might decide to separate.

For now, though, they made the preparations for their next adventure. The first task was to equip themselves with Russian *kibitkas* (wooden wagons that doubled as both carriage and sleigh), wolfskins and fur-lined leather boots, coats and hats. They then found local servants who knew the region and were willing to escort them, and after a trial run that took them 45 miles out of Moscow in January, after which Anne was raring to go and Ann Walker was not, they set off on 5 February 1840. Four days later they arrived at Nizhny Novgorod, and from there travelled along the frozen Volga, towards the Caspian Sea, to Astrakhan and beyond, to Tbilisi. During this epic journey, in temperatures as low as -40°C, Anne's fingers ached so much that she was barely able to write, yet still she managed to record every detail. As well as the daily minutiae she observed of the new cultures around her, she wrote of how their horses broke through the ice on the Volga and plunged into the river, and of her visit to a harem: 'Except an asylum for insanes I have never seen any sight so melancholy and so humiliating.'[138] They slept in palaces one night and in beds infested with bedbugs the next. And as they neared the Greater Caucasus, they were ambushed, as predicted, by about 20 Cherkess bandits. Anne made a quick calculation – with their servants, drivers, the Russian officer accompanying them and the four Cossacks escorting them, she hazarded a guess they were a large enough party to 'make a tolerable fight'. She was ready: 'I got out and reprimed my one loaded pistol' and the Cossacks, too, prepared to fight. This show of defiance was enough: after a brief stand-off, their assailants retreated, leaving Anne's party victorious. 'I felt not the least afraid,' she wrote proudly, 'nor did Ann.'[139]

After a vertiginous but breathtaking journey through the mountains, they arrived at Tbilisi, the capital of Georgia, on 12 April, after more than two months of travelling. There they paused for breath, but ever restless, Anne wanted to move on almost immediately to Tehran and Baghdad. She was told this was impossible, and Ann Walker, concerned now about their dwindling budget and sick of feeling bulldozed by Anne's itinerary, was firmly against the idea. Anne relented but insisted they at least go to Baku, on the Caspian

Sea, the smallest and most remote outpost of the Russian Empire. She got her way, so a month after arriving in Tbilisi, the two women – now travelling in oppressive heat and fighting off fleas – made the five-day journey through Azerbaijan to Baku, before returning to Tbilisi on 1 June.

Surely now Anne would stop and agree to go home? No, she wanted to see more of the Caucasus and the Black Sea. It may have been pure wanderlust, or perhaps she was reluctant to return home, knowing she would have to deal with mounting debts and the potential break-up of her marriage when she got there. There were no regrets, however, for their June journey along the Mtkvari River and the Surami Pass to the city of Kutaisi in West Georgia was 'one of the most beautiful drives I have ever taken in my life'.[140] And the several weeks they spent exploring the Greater Caucasus mountains in July, where they saw forests, gorges, waterfalls and glaciers, enjoyed local hospitality, slept out under the stars and had a tame bear-cub eat out of their hands, was the high point of the trip for both of them.

The two Annes were seeing sights that few nineteenth-century Europeans had ever seen, let alone women. Difficult, dangerous and expensive, off-piste exploration such as this was an option only for the brave and the independently wealthy. Alongside Celia Fiennes, who had ridden the length and breadth of England side-saddle in the late seventeenth century, and Lady Hester Stanhope and Lady Mary Wortley Montagu, who had blazed their way across Europe, the Middle East and the Ottoman Empire in the eighteenth century, Anne Lister and Ann Walker must take their place among the great lady travellers of British history.

THE MADWOMAN IN THE ATTIC

Anne Lister seemed unstoppable – she thought so, too – but even she had physical limitations. After 26 days in the mountains, the intrepid explorers returned to Kutaisi, then ventured almost to the Black Sea, to Zugdidi, but there in the hot, muggy swamplands they found sickness everywhere they went. On their hurried journey back to Kutaisi in pursuit of healthier air, they stopped overnight at a farm in Lia where they had to share a room with men, women and children who all appeared 'pale and yellow and unhealthy'.[141] They quickly moved on, but on 11 August 1840, as they were passing through Jgali, Anne Lister's diary comes to an abrupt halt. Six weeks later, on 22 September 1840, she was pronounced dead at Kutaisi.

In her obituary on 31 October, the *Halifax Guardian* put Anne's death down to '*la fièvre chaude*', a vague diagnosis of fever that could apply to any number of illnesses – she may have contracted typhus, malaria or a plague-like disease carried by ticks; whatever it was, it was decimating the population around her, and claimed her, too. Given the six-week lapse in Anne's usually obsessive diary writing, it's possible that, after a life crammed full to bursting, she lay hot, sick and helpless for much of that time. She was 49.[142]

What Ann Walker endured in the months following Anne's death can only be imagined. Already brittle, she was now alone, thousands of miles from home, weighed down by grief and facing the dreadful ordeal of having to escort her partner's embalmed remains on the long journey back to Yorkshire. It took her seven months, but she managed it, arriving in Halifax on 24 April 1841. Anne was buried five days later in the parish church. The hostility of former days forgotten, the local newspapers glowed with respect for this 'lamented' and 'distinguished' lady, whose 'public spirit in the improvement of our town and neighbourhood is attested by lasting memorials'. They honoured her ancestry, her 'mental energy and courage' and her charitable contributions – barely scratching the surface of the real Anne Lister.[143]

Anne had not lived to see it, but her renovations at Shibden were now nearly complete, and there Ann Walker returned alone, as was her right. Anne's will stipulated that until the day Ann Walker died, or married, Shibden and its income were hers. As it turned out, her tenure would end before either could come to pass. She struggled to manage both Anne's estate and her own, and perhaps her grief, too, and retreated into melancholic reclusion. So much so that, after two years, her Sutherland relatives judged her to be of 'unsound mind', and on 9 September 1843 they staged an intervention to forcibly remove her from Shibden Hall and commit her to an asylum. A party including Ann's sister Elizabeth Sutherland, her lawyer Robert Parker, Dr Belcombe (who was now 'convinced of Miss W's insanity'[144]) and a local constable arrived at Shibden to do the deed but met with a strange scene when they got there. Fearful of the outside world, Ann had barricaded herself in, locking all the rooms in the house and shutting herself in the master bedroom, known as the Red Room. The constable forced open the door, and Parker later recorded what they found:

> ... *the room was in a most filthy condition, and on the side of the bed were a brace of loaded pistols ... The shutters were closed – an old dirty candle stick near the bed was covered with tallow, as if the candle had melted away on it ... Papers were strewn about in complete confusion. In the Red Room were a [great] many handkerchiefs [spattered] all over with blood ...*[145]

To her contemporaries, this was a certified vision of lunacy. Ann was taken away to Dr Belcombe's private asylum near York (the very one where Eliza Raine was still living) – another tragic example of a grieving, traumatised, depressed woman being mistaken for a mad one. Shibden Hall, meanwhile, fell into a legal limbo, becoming the subject of years of legal disputes between the Swansea Listers and Captain Sutherland.

After Ann had spent two years in the asylum, her aged aunt brought her back to live at Cliff Hill, where she died in 1854, aged 51, stripped of most of her wealth. With the Sutherlands and their eldest son also now dead, the Walker estate fell to Ann's sole surviving nephew, while John Lister Sr of the Welsh cousins inherited Shibden. Order had been restored. It was as if the Lister–Walker marriage had never happened.

It's a tragic end to the story, and one that prompts some uncomfortable questions. Anne Lister and Ann Walker's relationship was complex; on both sides there was desire, affection and courage as well as loneliness and unhappiness. But it's hard not to question Anne Lister's motives. Was it mere coincidence that her first and last wives both ended up in the madhouse? Could it be that the domineering Anne Lister was drawn to rich, fragile, vulnerable women she could manipulate with her brute strength? Or was it simply easier for society to brand such discomfiting, unhappy, 'unnatural' women as sick?

If Captain Sutherland was guilty of the latter he couldn't say so, but he certainly believed the former. A letter to John Lister reveals that he saw Anne as a 'designing and unprincipled person' who found it all too easy 'to deceive and dupe' Ann Walker, first instilling in her 'a mistrust and hatred of her closest relatives', then convincing her to hand over the Walker estate and its profits. There are flecks of truth in Sutherland's words, though when he accuses Anne of being some kind of would-be murderess ('Whether Miss Lister intended that Miss Walker should ever return [from their travels], God only knows!!'[146]) he rather damages his case, revealing only his ignorance of the couple's complex relationship and his determination to demonise a woman who he felt had done *him*, more than Ann Walker, a great 'injury'.

Money, manipulation, murder, madness: this was the stuff of nineteenth-century Gothic novels, particularly those by Anne's near neighbours and contemporaries, the Brontës. The case for Anne's life providing some inspiration for *Jane Eyre*, *Shirley* and *Wuthering Heights* has been made – not least that the mixed-race Eliza Raine, given to bouts of aggression, or Ann Walker, locked up in the Red Room, could have been models for Mr Rochester's secret wife, Bertha.[147] Whether their stories seeped into literature or not, it's hard now not to view Eliza and Ann as the archetypal madwomen in the attic – problematic, inconvenient, distressed women whom society could not comprehend and had no idea what to do with. Like so many others, they were shut away out of sight, their fortunes dissolved, their voices muffled, their lives erased.

'WHAT OLD HALIFAX SCANDAL KNOWS ABOUT MISS LISTER'

Anne Lister was dead, but her diaries survived her and have since lived an extraordinary and perilous life of their own. Anne's descendant, John Lister Jr, would be the first to bring them to public attention when he took possession of Shibden and its mish-mash of family papers in 1867. Finding in her notebooks an extraordinary wealth of historical local interest, he began to publish extracts from the uncoded sections in the *Halifax Guardian* in May 1887. To an antiquarian like John Lister, however, the coded passages presented an irresistible puzzle. With his friend Arthur Burrell he set about cracking Anne's code – and when they managed it, they got the shock of their lives. These sections were 'entirely unpublishable' and the friendships they described 'criminal'. Burrell's advice was to 'burn all 26 volumes', but thankfully, Lister's antiquarian instincts were too strong.[148] Legend has it, he hid them away in a secret hatch in a quiet corner of Shibden, and there they stayed for the next 40 years.

In 1933, when John Lister died and Shibden became the property of the local council, the diaries and letters were unearthed again, and it fell to trainee librarian Muriel Green to begin the daunting task of archiving them. To help her, Green's father tracked down the now-elderly Arthur Burrell, who eventually handed over the key to Anne's code, though with the portentous warning of 'what old Halifax scandal knows about Miss Lister'.[149] It's no great surprise that Burrell remained cautious. With Radclyffe Hall's novel *The Well of Loneliness* banned in 1928, and E. M. Forster still unwilling to even attempt to publish his 1932 draft of *Maurice*, homosexuality was clearly still an unpublishable subject, so when Green produced her collection of Anne's letters in 1938, there was no mention of it whatsoever. 'It would have cast a slur on the good name of the Lister family if it were known then,' she later said.[150]

And so the silence continued. Homosexual acts were decriminalised in the UK in 1967, but even the Swinging Sixties were too prudish for Anne Lister's racy sex life. Dr Phyllis Ramsden, one of two academics who decoded, read and summarised the diaries in their entirety in 1966, dismissed whole crypt-hand sections as 'sentimental exchanges with her friends' that contained 'nothing of historical importance'.[151]

.It wasn't until the 1980s that the full significance of the diaries' contents was revealed, thanks to the heroic efforts of Helena Whitbread, who decoded and published extensive excerpts dating from 1816 to 1826. When this work was added to in the 1990s by Jill Liddington, and more recently by Anne Choma, who have both focused on Anne's relationship with Ann Walker, for the first time the true, unspoken history of lesbianism, romantic friendship and female desire was blasted out of the closet. Anne Lister's diaries are now considered some of the most important documents in British LGBTQ+ history. There is nothing else like them in pre-twenti-eth-century British women's writing.

Today, Anne Lister can command her own Sunday-night TV drama and be publicly celebrated as the force of nature she was and the emblem of gay pride that she is. But this interest in her comes only after 150 years of persistent squeamishness, suppression and silence. The honest, uncensored portrait of Anne we now have access to reveals a woman who is by no means an easy feminist icon. For all her magnetism, there's plenty not to like. She could be calculating and cruel, mercenary and manipulative. She was a snob, a social climber, a flirt and a seducer. And despite her own radical lifestyle, she wasn't always so progressive – she clung doggedly to the outmoded and unfair political systems that benefited her class, and made no attempt to break down boundaries for other women besides herself.

From this angle, Anne can seem almost villainous – a cad in a Victorian novel. But she was other things, too: fiercely intelligent and insatiably curious, a courageous eccentric, an intrepid adventurer, an indomitable businesswoman and a complicated romantic – one who longed for a life partner but could never find one who met her exacting standards. Those who negotiated with her were trounced, those who tried to humiliate her failed, those who suspected her found themselves tongue-tied and those who loved her were utterly enthralled.

When judged by the standards of her own day, Anne behaved no worse, and in many cases much better, than any number of nineteenth-century gentleman. At a time when marriage more often resembled a business transaction than a sweeping romance, Anne saw hers to Ann Walker as just another dynastic alliance, no different to any heterosexual one, and she laid claim to her wife's money and property accordingly. Captain Sutherland – indeed, all husbands – did the same, but the blatant outrage that this partnership provoked in him and the Halifax locals suggests it was the legal merger of the two hereditary estates belonging to these propertied women that really disturbed people. Anne Lister may not have outwardly challenged the patriarchy, but by playing the marriage game as if she were a man, to ensure her own financial advantage, she had inwardly subverted it instead. In his denunciation of her as a grasping predator, Sutherland unwittingly delivered a damning indictment of the patriarchal system that he and every other man benefited from – and that Anne Lister, to everyone's dismay, had dared to appropriate for herself.

By tweaking the patriarchal template to her own ends, Anne retained control of her own assets, and enhanced her status and wealth into the bargain. To her, laying claim to masculine freedoms didn't just mean wearing eccentric clothes and enjoying a penchant for guns; it meant economic power and political influence; it meant physical autonomy and hereditary control; it meant knowledge and exploration, owning her sexuality and pursuing the gratification of it. This was perhaps the most progressive part of her character, and in her belief that she could marry a woman and have the commitment solemnised like any heterosexual couple – with all the legal ramifications that entailed – she was centuries ahead of her time.

This is why Anne Lister has been called 'the first modern lesbian': not because there's anything modern about homosexuality, but because she embraced it with an easy acceptance and confident self-awareness that has only recently become mainstream. Unlike several of her lovers, she had no doubt, no shame and no guilt about her feelings for women. She was free and open about her 'oddities' and keen to display her marriages to the world. Forever striving to balance her clandestine private desires and her determination to maintain a respectable public life, she was a woman on a mission to understand and define her own sexuality, and to find a way to live happily, without compromise or apology.

Whole books could be written on each of the sprawling elements of Anne Lister's life – with four million words to explore, her life is documented more fully than possibly any other figure in history. As a landowner, entrepreneur, political influencer, traveller, mountaineer and industrialist, she was as active in the male world as it was possible for a woman to be in early nineteenth-century Britain. Just as remarkable is that she found the time to document it all in forensic detail in her diaries – less than 10 per cent of which have been explored to date.

These diaries were Anne's therapy, but they were also an ambitious attempt at autobiography, to capture and remember every moment of her life, and define herself, mind and body, on paper. And she recorded the world around her with the same obsessive, fierce scrutiny that she applied to herself. Life was a continual adventure, a source of endless fascination. Nothing was too small or mundane to be beneath her notice, from conversations to business transactions to sexual encounters to bowel movements to the scaling of her teeth.[152]

In writing so frankly about sex from a female perspective, she was also putting into words (albeit encrypted ones) what British culture found unspeakable, and reclaiming women's bodies and desires – feared, objectified, ignored and taboo as they had been for millennia – from obscurity in the process.

Anne Lister's story, her legacy, her life's work, came within a whisker of going up in smoke; if it had, we would have lost an intricate socio-historical document of pre-Victorian gentry life, certainly, but we would have missed out on much more than that. Anne's diaries offer us an intimate insight into the mind of a brilliant, complex woman and a privileged peek into the secret history of forbidden love between women. Shibden Hall stands to this day, a museum to Anne's life and achievements, and there, from high on the wall in the main hall, she watches from her portrait, mistress of all she surveys, a look of supreme confidence on her face. It's as if she knows that, against your better judgement, she will seduce you, too.

Caroline Norton

A PAINTED WANTON

22 June 1836. A young reporter for the *Morning Chronicle* settles in his seat in Westminster's Court of Common Pleas, ready to take down every particular of the day's trial. It's early morning, and the room is filled to capacity, mostly by curious barristers who've paid five or even ten guineas to secure themselves a spot. All the same, the public are pressing at the doors, eager to squeeze themselves into the smallest available space, and as the doors give way to the pressure, there is 'a simultaneous rush', followed by 'the greatest excitement, confusion, and uproar'.[1] Every corner of the small, stuffy courtroom is 'instantly crammed'.[2] The judge, irritated by the disturbance, calls for the doors to be closed and threatens to adjourn the court if order is not restored.

The reporter's name is Charles Dickens; smooth-chinned at 24, curls to his collar, he sits to attention and flexes his fingers. The trial of the century is about to begin: the Honourable George Norton, barrister and magistrate, suing the Prime Minister, Lord Melbourne, for 'criminal conversation'[3] – adultery by another name – with his delectable wife, Caroline. With such a high-profile defendant and so captivating a woman at its centre, the papers have rarely witnessed 'so great an anxiety to hear proceedings in a court of law'.[4] This is a trial of national significance: not just husband versus lover, or even husband versus wife, but Whig versus Tory.

'A woman is made a helpless wretch
by these laws of men.'

Caroline Norton (1808–1877),
WRITER AND WOMEN'S RIGHTS CAMPAIGNER

The plaintiff, George Norton, is not present; he's at home in Mayfair – but his lawyers stand to make a great deal of money for him if they win. As with all criminal conversation cases, the charge is not simply the grievance of a cuckolded husband; it is a claim for compensation for breach of his conjugal rights and the theoretical theft of his property – and she is an expensive item. The proposed damages to be awarded to Norton for the loss of his enjoyment of his wife have been set at £10,000. Fletcher Norton, 3rd Lord Grantley of Wonersh, sits glowering over proceedings on the Lords' bench in his younger brother's stead – a well-known Ultra-Tory[5] and a conspicuous presence, whom many believe to be the mastermind behind the whole sordid scandal.

The defendant, William Lamb, 2nd Viscount Melbourne and Britain's Whig Prime Minister, is also not present, though everyone in the room knows him of old. Witty, debonair, charming; even now, in his late fifties, this man can draw women of all ages – Norton's wife is young enough to be his daughter.[6] And he is certainly no stranger to scandal. Everyone knows of his late wife's notorious affair with Lord Byron in 1812,[7] and that he has been sued for criminal conversation before, by Lady Branden's husband in 1828. On that occasion he settled out of court, but this time he is fighting it out and pleading not guilty. As the country's Premier, he can't be called to testify as a witness, but if he is found guilty, he will lose more than just the £10,000 in damages. His government will fall and so will his political career.

Mrs Caroline Norton will not be called, either, nor will she have a team of lawyers to defend her honour. As the wife of the plaintiff, her testimony has no legal value. The trial will rake over the most intimate details of her life, paint her as the very picture of sin and determine the course of her future, yet she has no right to call on a single witness or speak a word in her defence. As she is a society beauty, a writer and a Sheridan, too, the public wants to believe her guilty, and if the verdict goes that way, it will mean the loss of her reputation, her career and her children. As her former servants line up to testify against her and a jury of 12 men prepare to pronounce on where her life will now lead, Caroline Norton sits at her mother's house at Hampton Court, fidgety and powerless, waiting to hear her fate.

THE HANDSOMEST FAMILY IN THE WORLD

Everyone agreed that the Sheridan sisters were entrancing. The 'Three Graces' – Helen, Caroline and Georgiana – came from a long line of beautiful women and dazzling men, and had inherited all their glamour and allure. Their grandfather was Richard Brinsley Sheridan – 'Old Sherry' – the Irish playwright, poet, satirist and Whig politician famed for his love of wine, witticisms and high living. The story of how he had eloped with their grandmother, the soprano singer Elizabeth Linley, and fought two duels in her honour was common knowledge, as was the fact that their only son, Thomas, was a chip off the old block. A promising comic actor, writer and singer, Tom Sheridan nonetheless found it difficult to apply himself to anything in particular. After a failed attempt at politics and a brief stint as a soldier, he took on the management of Old Sherry's theatre at Drury Lane, though he strug-gled to keep that afloat, too. His greatest talent was joviality. When his father remarked it was high time he took a wife, Tom's reply was, 'Yes, Sir, but whose?'[8] He soon lived up to the quip by having an affair with a married woman, whose husband sued him in 1807 for criminal conversation. By then Tom had taken his own wife – the handsome, sweet-natured Caroline Callander, fledgling novelist and poet – though he had done so in true Sheridan style, by eloping with her to Gretna Green in June 1805.

It was a romantic family history, with a raffish streak that Tom and Caroline's children – Brinsley, Helen, Caroline, Georgiana, Thomas, Frank and Charles – could never quite shake off. All possessed of the fierce dark beauty that was characteristic of a Sheridan, they were 'the handsomest family in the world', according to Benjamin Disraeli, and a close and affectionate one, too, with dramatic flair and a tendency to show off. In keeping with tradition, people *talked* about the Sheridan children – especially the girls. Lady Cowper, sister of Lord Melbourne, noted that Helen, Caroline and Georgie were 'much admired but are strange girls. They swear and say all sorts of things to make men laugh. I am surprised so sensible a woman as Mrs Sheridan should let them go on so. I suppose she cannot stop the old blood coming out. They are remarkably good looking … and certainly clever.'[9]

Perhaps Lady Cowper was thinking of Caroline in particular, for more than all her other siblings she had inherited the famous Sheridan wit, as well as the charm, intelligence and confidence to wield it. Rather too much confidence, some thought. On her birth in London on 22 March 1808, her mother declared Caroline 'stout and strong and the prettiest infant I ever saw',[10] but when faced with her intense gaze, Old Sherry wasn't so sure: 'That is not a child I would care to meet in a dark wood,' he declared.[11] Although blessed with the same fiery dark eyes, raven hair and creamy complexion as her sisters, a slight masculine quality coupled with an outspoken, flirtatious character and a gift for mimicry meant Caroline was considered the least conventionally attractive of the three. At 15, she was sent to a boarding school at Shalford, in Surrey, to iron out her coarse language and stroppy temper. There she would perfect her sketching, dancing and etiquette, and, most importantly, 'learn not to argue with men but to please them'.[12]

Marriage was imperative for the Sheridan girls, because despite their celebrity, they had no money. His fortune long lost, Old Sherry had died impoverished in 1816 and a year later Tom succumbed to another family trait – consumption[13] – leaving his wife and seven young children (Caroline was just nine) with virtually nothing. Mrs Sheridan was only saved from penury by the patronage of Tom's old friend the Duke of York, who in 1820 arranged for her to receive a pension and a grace-and-favour apartment at Hampton Court Palace. For now, the family were comfortable, but the girls would have no dowries – nothing to lure a husband besides their good looks and charm.

Caroline Sheridan had more to her than that, however. She and her sister Helen had displayed a precocious talent for drawing and poetry as children, and an entrepreneurial zeal to go with it – they were just 11 and 12 when they had their first book published: *The Dandies' Rout*, which satirised foppish young Regency beaux in comic rhymes and caricatures. Its success motivated the sisters to begin writing and selling their own sentimental songs and ballads, so that by the time she had reached her teens Caroline was earning her own money and working as a professional writer. But while this was one of the few acceptable ways for a genteel lady to make a little extra cash, it could hardly be relied upon for lifelong financial security. Writing could be her hobby, but marriage must be her career.

The business of finding a husband began unexpectedly for Caroline, in a strange episode that occurred while she was still at boarding school. In 1824, she and her classmates were sometimes taken to visit the nearby Grantley estate at Wonersh, home of the Nortons. These outings were pleasant enough; Caroline remembered later how one of the Norton daughters had taken quite a shine to her. She hadn't remembered, or even noticed, the girl's 24-year-old brother, George, lurking in the shadows, so she was surprised, shocked even, when her governess told her she was not to visit Wonersh Park again unless her mother permitted it, because Mr George Norton had expressed a desire to marry her. This was all very odd. 'I had not exchanged six sentences with him on any subject whatever', Caroline later wrote.[14] Silently George had watched her, transfixed by her beauty, and resolved to write to her mother and ask for her hand. A little taken aback, Mrs Sheridan did the sensible thing, responding that, at 16, her daughter was too young to be married; if he was serious, George would have to wait three years. It was flattering, Caroline supposed, to have inspired such a reaction in a man she had barely spoken to, but mostly she was relieved that this bizarre proposal had been put off, hopefully to be forgotten – he wasn't exactly the Byronic hero she imagined herself with. She returned to her studies and her songwriting, and thought nothing more about Mr George Norton.

Once Caroline had left school the following year, she and her sisters prepared for their first seasons, when husband-hunting would begin in earnest. Helen went first and soon attracted the attentions of Captain Price Blackwood, heir to the Irish peer Lord Dufferin. Caroline's turn came in 1826, but although she was admired, no declarations were made. Men might be entertained by her sharp wit and forthright opinions, but they didn't, it seems, want such pert cleverness in their wives.

It came as a great relief to Mrs Sheridan when Helen secured the first eligible match and married Captain Blackwood on 4 July 1826. And when Georgie made her debut the following season and attracted plenty of attention, Caroline began to worry. There was now a risk of being pipped to the post by her younger sister – or worse, ending up an old maid. So when George Norton renewed his offer after the agreed three-year hiatus, she was obliged to give it some serious thought. On paper, at least, Norton seemed like a good prospect – he came from a grand, wealthy family, and although he wasn't the current heir to the Grantley estate, his older brother was married but childless, so the title could one day be his. And he had certainly proved his constancy. Perhaps in time she would learn to like him, maybe even love him. It was with an air of resignation, then, perhaps even desperation, that Mrs Sheridan finally accepted George Norton's proposal on behalf of her daughter.

If the Sheridans noticed any warning signs before the marriage, they ignored them. For in reality, the couple were a spectacular mismatch and George Norton a deeply unpromising character. At 27, his career and his manner were decidedly less impressive than Caroline's at 19. She was all vivid energy, radiant beauty, magnetism and cheek; he was dull, slow-witted and humourless. She was a precocious, ambitious literary talent who earned her own money; he was an indifferent MP and lacklustre barrister who excelled at nothing, was late for everything and relied on his family expectations to one day release him from work altogether. She, like her ancestors, was liberal and Whiggish, passionately drawn to progressive, reforming politics; he came from a long line of bullish political dinosaurs – unpleasant, extreme right-wing Ultra-Tories, who were determined to preserve all the feudal systems, social injustices and religious intolerances of the past.

Still, the wedding went ahead on 30 July 1827 in Mayfair's Hanover Square. It didn't begin well. George arrived late (as usual), making Caroline understandably snippy: 'Well, Mr Norton, you are come at last, and look handsomer, I declare, than I expected.' Even their guests were struck by what an unlikely couple they made; one of them remarked that Caroline was 'too splendidly, magnificently, furiously beautiful. Cleopatra sailing on the Nile ... Mr Norton rather fidgeting around her'.[15] She may have been the blushing bride, but Caroline was far more in command of the situation than her groom.

LOVE, HONOUR AND OBEY

The dynamic between the Nortons changed almost as soon as the ceremony was over. Just a few weeks into the marriage, George showed his new wife exactly what sort of man he really was: one quick to irrational anger and brutal violence. On their return from honeymoon they moved into his pokey rooms in his Temple chambers, where their first row culminated in George flinging an inkstand and most of his law books at Caroline's head. Their second, when the couple were in Scotland to introduce Caroline to her in-laws, was worse. As they retired to their rooms one evening, continuing an earlier discussion, Caroline stated plainly that she had 'never heard so silly or ridiculous a conclusion' as the one George had come to. This remark 'was punished by a sudden and violent kick' to her side,[16] and the blow left Caroline in pain for days.

This was a whole new disturbing world for the teenage bride. To one who'd been blanketed by warmth and affection in the Sheridan household, where pert, lively talk was welcomed and enjoyed, this cold tyranny, when any frank opinion that contradicted her husband's resulted in unjustifiable rage, was both bewildering and terrifying. To make matters worse, Caroline had received a frosty welcome from most of her in-laws, particularly George's eldest brother, Lord Grantley, to whom she took an instant dislike. The family's objections were manifold: she was too poor to help them, too Whiggish to agree with them, too clever to be moulded by them, too beautiful to be trusted by them. But it was not in Caroline's nature to be battered into submission: the war of the Nortons had begun.

The miserable newlyweds took a house in Storey's Gate, Westminster, overlooking Birdcage Walk and St James's Park, where Caroline threw herself into her work. She had no intention of giving up her writing; it was her ambition, her solace and her income – and, unexpectedly perhaps, George had no objections; after all, now they were married, every penny she earned went straight into his pocket. This was particularly handy for George, because contrary to what Caroline had been led to believe before the wedding, he was constantly hard up. An unsuccessful barrister who received few briefs, his own income was less than he'd pretended, so Caroline's earnings were the couple's main source of income. This suited lazy, lethargic George perfectly, as he considered it his wife's duty to further his career for him. 'He never ceased impressing upon me', she later wrote, 'that as I brought him no present fortune ... I was bound to use every effort with the political friends of my grandfather, to get him lucrative promotion in his profession.'[17] In the end, it was Mrs Sheridan who secured him a decent, though undemanding, position as the commissioner of bankrupts in the Court of Chancery.

While her husband got away with doing as little as he could, Caroline worked hard in that first year, branching out from song-writing to (anonymously) publishing her first book, *The Sorrows of Rosalie*, a collection of Byronic poems that reflected her bleak state of mind. *The Times* found in it 'some passages which are beautiful and full of true poetical feeling' but complained of a 'sickliness in the sentiment which is probably the result of inexperience'.[18] It sold well nonetheless, running to several editions, though with her profits and copyrights now belonging to her husband, the success was bittersweet.

There was never any let-up in George's attacks; they kept coming and only grew more menacing. His cruelty was unhinged, unpredictable and unprovoked; he would pick fights over nothing and exact petty revenge for imagined offences. Having not bothered to get to know Caroline before asking for her hand, he had perhaps hoped for a wife he could easily master, yet she continued to answer back, disagree and ignore his absurd demands. His beatings, he told her, would teach her 'not to brave him', but it was a lesson she refused to learn.[19] His inability to crush her into utter, degraded submission only made him increasingly enraged. She would later write that, even when she was a child, she could not recall 'a single instance in which I was subdued by harshness', and George's kicks and blows were no exception.

Caroline's family were aware of the abuse, and they attempted to protect her, but beyond extracting a feeble promise of better behaviour, they had no real power to do so. There were no women's refuges and the law was so wilfully murky on the matter of marital abuse as to effectively condone it, allowing husbands to 'correct' their wives in the belief of their impunity and wives to endure it in the belief of their helplessness.[20] Marital rape, meanwhile, was not legally recognised at all, though given that sex was considered a wifely duty no matter how unwelcome, it seems inevitable Caroline was subjected to this, too.[21]

Into this toxic environment, the Nortons' first child, Fletcher, was born on 10 July 1829 – a delicate creature, whose health would always be fragile – making Caroline now a working mother. She leapt straight back into writing and published *The Undying One, and Other Poems* in 1830, for which she asked for, and was paid, the respectable sum of £500, and received glowing reviews. In her growing confidence, she proudly displayed both her name and her portrait on the book this time.

That same year, the country's political course swerved dramatically. On 26 June, the preening, pampered, bloated King George IV died and was not much mourned. He was cheerfully replaced by William IV, and a new king meant a new general election. Out went the Tories, undone by their own infighting, and in came the Whigs; George Norton was ousted from his family seat as Tory MP for Guildford, never to regain it.

Of this new Whig government, one member in particular caught Caroline's eye: the phlegmatic, indecisive (some said indolent) Home Secretary, Lord Melbourne. The man's scandalous romantic history was enticing enough, but he had also been a great friend and admirer of Caroline's father and grandfather – a connection that inevitably drew the pair together. By early 1831, despite a 30-year age gap, they had developed an intimate friendship; he captivated by her wit, energy and beauty, she by his rakish charm and vivid tales of Sheridan high-jinks.

There were no complaints from George about his wife's new acquaintance; he saw only an opportunity to exploit it. He badgered Caroline to use her influence with Melbourne to find him a better-paid job, and Melbourne obliged, securing him a position as magistrate for Whitechapel at the Lambeth Street court in April 1831. The role offered a good salary of £1,000 a year for relatively little work – just three short days a week – so it suited George well.

Although his wife's ministrations had improved George's prospects, in a rare reversal of the norm she was still the main breadwinner – in one year she made £1,400, significantly more than George, and she 'rejoiced' in her achievement. It was with 'romantic pride' that she later remembered how, 'woman though I was', the 'first expenses of my son's life were defrayed from the price of that first creation of my brain'[22] – even if it sometimes meant sitting up all night working while nursing a baby to meet her deadlines. Buoyed by the confidence and sense of purpose that supporting her family gave her, she 'rose undiscouraged' after every quarrel with her feckless, abusive husband.

'IS SHE NOT DAZZLING?'

On 14 November 1831, six months after Caroline's first play – a weepy melodrama called *The Gypsy Father* – was performed at the Covent Garden Theatre to mixed reviews, her second son, Brinsley (or Brin), was born. And as before, his birth had no effect on the sudden bouts of abuse that continued to punctuate her marriage. But still, Caroline would not be brought to heel. Instead, she waged a blatant campaign of defiance against her husband. When the Whigs presented their social and electoral reforms to Parliament, including the Roman Catholic Relief Act in 1829 and the Great Reform Act of 1832 – both strongly opposed by the Ultra-Tory Nortons – she was vocal in her support of them. When in London, she hosted glamorous society soirées where every guest oozed talent, cleverness and charm. Armed with her scintillating conversation, Caroline moved through these gatherings like a goddess, radiating beauty, flirting outrageously and batting away admirers, while her dull, bovine husband flailed in her wake, hopelessly out of his depth.

Both men and women fell head over heels for Mrs Norton. The artist Benjamin Haydon developed a troubling obsession with her that became a nuisance for Caroline and a torture for his wife, though the attentions of adventurer Edward Trelawny – Byron and Shelley's wild, battle-scarred friend – were rather more enjoyable. 'Is she not a glorious being? ... Is she not dazzling?' he rhapsodised to Mary Shelley.[23] Mary could only agree, confessing her own attraction to Caroline, which bordered on sexual – 'I never saw a woman I thought so fascinating. Had I been a man I should certainly have fallen in love with her.'[24] The admiration was mutual and the two women became great friends.

Indeed, Caroline was adored by almost everyone except her husband. As she once observed: 'No man ever admired me more, or loved me less.'[25] George hadn't bargained on a wife so much cleverer than him, who mocked and mimicked him and openly flirted with other men. But as long as it was with powerful men like Lord Melbourne, he would encourage it. He could punish her in private, after all.

Melbourne certainly was Caroline's favourite. As well as a regular visitor at Storey's Gate, he was her preferred companion at plays and salons, while the frequent letters she exchanged with her dear 'Fatty' – which were often carefully constructed to make this famously insouciant man jealous – grew evermore playful, personal and intense. They would both always deny an affair, but Caroline's passionate declarations when they were apart – 'your name is always on my lips'; 'I cannot be with you always, and therefore I amuse myself as I can'[26] – certainly read like one.

Few could imagine how dark this sparkling woman's life was behind closed doors. At the start of 1833 Caroline was pregnant for the third time, and if anything, George's attacks only became more deranged. One morning, when he quibbled about wanting her seat at the breakfast table and Caroline refused to move, 'Mr Norton then deliberately took the tea-kettle, and set it down upon my hand.'[27] Skin seared, she ran out of the room in search of medical help, while George calmly took her seat and ate his breakfast. This disturbing scene had taken place in front of three-year-old Fletcher, who was playing in the room at the time.

Several months later, when Caroline was heavily pregnant, George launched his most dangerous attack yet. Now the editor of glamorous periodical *The English Annual*, Caroline was working flat out to get the edition finished before the baby arrived, so one evening she excused herself after dinner, asking George to remain where he was so that she could work undisturbed. 'He answered that the house was his, not mine; that he should sit in what room he pleased; and that I should find I could not carry things with such a high hand as I desired to do.' Weary of such petty arguments, and wary of where they could lead, Caroline called her maid to work with her in the drawing room – and locked the door against her husband. He soon demanded to be let in, and when she refused, he broke down the door and 'gave way to the most frantic rage, blew out the candles, flung the furniture about, and seized my maid to turn her out of the room by force'.

Caroline clung to her maid, near-fainting with panic. The outburst only ended when several servants came rushing in, at which point, faced with an audience, George abruptly left the room. Caroline gasped out her relief, but too soon: 'Mr Norton returned almost immediately, and seizing me, forced me out of the room and down on the stairs.' Fearing for her life now, Caroline screamed for help, shrieking that 'Mr Norton was "gone mad"'.[28] George was on the point of throwing her down the stairs when a manservant grabbed him and held him back.

This episode could not go unchallenged. Caroline wrote to her brother, explaining that if her husband's behaviour did not become more 'gentleman-like', she would be forced to leave him. Brinsley relayed her statement to George, adding that unless the family received a written apology for the assault and a solemn promise that it would never happen again within 24 hours, his conduct would be exposed to the public.

The mere possibility of losing his reputation as a gentleman was enough to elicit a begrudging apology from George, though in the same breath he attempted to justify his actions; he had broken the door down 'on principle', he said, 'thinking it necessary, as a husband, to resist such extravagant and disrespectful proceedings' as locking him out of the drawing room. He wrote confidently, too, that he and Caroline were 'all right again' and hoped the family would 'forget and forgive'.[29] It was paltry reparation, but at the very least, he had provided Caroline with a written admission of his guilt.

Uneasily, the Nortons continued their life together. When Caroline gave birth on 26 August 1833 it took her several weeks to recover, but miraculously the boy was healthy. They named him William, after their friend and benefactor Lord Melbourne, and the 'little tadpole', Caroline wrote, was 'destined to be the beauty of the family'.[30]

THE QUARREL

George Norton had long been earning the hatred of his in-laws, but on a disastrous family tour of Ghent, Antwerp and Cologne in the summer of 1834, matters came to a head. George hated foreign travel, and had already made a nuisance of himself by getting ill at Aix-la-Chapelle and demanding that his wife perform 'the functions of sick-nurse, valet, and chambermaid' around the clock. Once he had recovered, they journeyed on slowly in a cramped, stuffy carriage, where George sat blithely puffing away on a hookah. Suffocating from the smoke, Caroline begged him several times to stop, and when he refused to even answer, she snatched his precious pipe and flung it out of the window. George's immediate reaction was to leap out of the carriage to retrieve it, but when he returned he dealt out his punishment: 'He then seized me by the throat, and pinned me back with a fierce oath against the hood of the carriage.' Caroline managed to struggle free, slip out of the open carriage door and run to the others for protection, though 'the marks of his fingers were in bruises on my throat'. She was fully convinced that she 'should have been strangled in a minute or two more'.[31]

There could be no more pretence from the Sheridans that George was anything other than a brute, and from that day on there was 'an alienation from my husband on the part of my family'. They were done with him, but Caroline was shackled to him, and like many a battered wife before and since, she forgave him for this latest attack, persuaded that she was at fault for provoking him.

Then, in 1835, the family would learn that George was a liar as well as a thug. Despite their comparatively princely income, money was always a source of embarrassment for the Nortons, with appeals to family and friends a common occurrence. In the spring of 1834 Caroline had had to ask Lord Melbourne to secure her husband another, better-paid job as chief magistrate at Bow Street Court, but Melbourne, wiser now to George's character, had refused. When George cut to the chase and asked him for a £1,500 loan, Melbourne again demurred. George's recourse was to suck up to his rich relation Margaret Vaughan instead (yet another who despised Caroline) in the hope of financial reward.

It was only a matter of time before Caroline began to question exactly *why* they were so pressed for cash. When she voiced her 'astonishment that his own patrimonial resources never seemed to yield us anything', George finally disclosed the truth: there were 'no proceeds forthcoming from the hereditary estates'.[32] Caroline was stunned, and Mrs Sheridan horrified: it had been distinctly stated in the marriage negotiations that land worth £30,000 would go to Lord Grantley's younger siblings. Now it turned out to be a 'monstrous untruth'. One word from her daughter and Mrs Sheridan was ready to take it up with the lawyers 'to show how you have been cheated; which it is evident you have been'.[33]

Relations could hardly curdle much more, but the year had plenty of drama in store yet. While Caroline was busy reworking her experiences of domestic tyranny into fiction in *The Wife and Woman's Reward*, published in May 1835,[34] her brother Brinsley was living up to the Sheridan name by eloping to Gretna Green with rich heiress Marcia Grant, whose father, Sir Colquhoun Grant, took the news rather badly. He issued a court writ to Brinsley and accused the Sheridan sisters, George Norton and even Georgie's grand husband Lord Seymour of being accomplices.[35] A fellow of the old school, Grant was all for settling it with a duel (which were now illegal), though in the end a reconciliation was achieved without bloodshed. George Norton proved harder to appease. He had taken umbrage at being publicly implicated in this scandal, and it may well have been his implacable resentment over this that formed the basis of the unspecified 'quarrel which divided him from [her family] for ever' that same summer. Whatever ugly scene unfolded afterwards, it was serious enough this time to prompt Caroline, now pregnant for the fourth time in six years, to take the momentous step of leaving her husband.

She sought refuge with the Seymours, while Brinsley undertook the negotiations with George. He wanted her back, of course, but that wouldn't happen, Brinsley stated, unless certain conditions of good behaviour were met. There followed from George a great show of being both reasonable and contrite: to the intermediary he made his pledge that he would treat his wife well; to his in-laws he wrote in the 'extremest and most exaggerated terms of submission'; to Caroline he declared that 'no words could prove his remorse'. He would 'make any sacrifice' if she would return, and if he could not make her happy, they could 'quietly and rationally separate' – he would tell the world 'that the cause of it was not any imputation on you.'[36]

Piteous promises were easy to dole out, but George had other, stealthier ways of inducing his wife to return. He would 'be very unwilling', he told the intermediary, 'that any question of pecuniary affairs should prevent Mrs Norton seeing the children'[37] – a targeted remark, given that a married woman was invisible before the law. When a wife was separated or divorced from her husband, she had no automatic right to see her children again until they were 21. If her husband chose to withhold them from her, the law agreed that, as the only recognised parent, he had every right to do so. To prove that this was no idle threat, George was careful to keep the children from Caroline throughout this separation, knowing it was the most powerful injury he could inflict on her.

Lord Grantley, meanwhile – never far from the fray – was doing his damnedest to dig up dirt on his insubordinate sister-in-law, and Caroline was well aware of it: 'No one can help me,' she despaired in her letters. 'I am not in the hands of my weak and violent husband. I am in those of Lord Grantley.' Her alarm was justified, for although she maintained that, 'miraculous' though it might seem, she had been 'eight years the "faithful wife" of Mr Norton',[38] the mere imputation of harlotry could be enough to ruin her reputation. Lose that, and she would undoubtedly lose her children.

At the mercy of manipulative men and a law that didn't acknowledge her, Caroline was as good as trapped. And George's letters to her were those of a changed man:

> He implored me by all that was dear and holy to grant a 'complete' forgiveness – a 'real' pardon – to write it the moment I had read his letter – to seal and send it by post, and not to let any one see it ... He adjured me not to 'crush' him, and he ended his letter with the words, 'I go on my knees to you! Have pity!'[39]

Every friend advised her not to do it, but the letters were 'impossible to read without being touched'; she pitied him, believed him, forgave him, exactly as requested. It was only later that she would realise what a grave mistake this was and just how much calculation – by a lawyer who knew exactly what he needed in writing – had been behind every word.

It took only two days for George to break his pretty promises. Caroline was pregnant, but the violence reignited as if nothing had happened. The 'agitation and misery' he caused led to severe illness and, in turn, to a miscarriage – an event that left George unperturbed; he continued to treat his wife with the 'utmost harshness and neglect', refusing to pay the doctor's bill and leaving her brother Brinsley to nurse her through her grief. The magistrate was doling out his punishment to the wife who had tried to leave.

The situation was untenable. Caroline's family would now scarcely acknowledge George's existence, and the couple lived increasingly separate lives. So when Brinsley invited Caroline and the boys to spend Easter 1836 with him at his palatial new pad, Frampton Court, he pointedly left George off the list. The snub enraged George and, goaded on by Margaret Vaughan, he resorted to stamping his foot, declaring that if he wasn't invited, Caroline couldn't go either. Their bickering continued throughout the party they attended that evening, and peaked on the carriage journey home, when George, drunk and belligerent, jealously accused her and his brother-in-law Fitzroy Campbell of flirting. By the time they arrived home, he had decreed that the children, at any rate, would not be going to Frampton the next day. For now Caroline let it drop, but the next morning, she went straight to Lord Seymour's house to ask her sister Georgie for advice. While she was there, however, her manservant arrived with an urgent message: 'Something was going wrong at home,' he said. Miss Vaughan had whisked the children away in a hackney coach, no one knew where. There was only one explanation: Caroline's children had been kidnapped.

The whole thing reeked of pre-meditation. The children were traced to Margaret Vaughan's house and Caroline stormed to her front door, breathing fire. When Margaret denied all knowledge of the incident and threatened to hand Caroline over to the police, she was ready to throttle the woman, and might have done so had not Fitzroy Campbell arrived with news of the children's whereabouts. They were with Margaret Vaughan's house agent, Martin Knapp, who greeted them with George's callous instruction that the children were to be kept from their mother 'by any means they chose to employ'.

Caroline was frantic. She shouted and screamed and pleaded with Knapp to let her see them. Instead, he called the police. All the while the children were being held in the room just above her – she could hear 'their little feet running merrily over my head while I sat sobbing below – only the ceiling between us and I not able to get to them!'[40] In the end, she had to admit defeat and dragged herself away without so much as a glimpse of her boys.

Weeping and broken, she went straight to Frampton, and there the decision was made – she had to leave George now, once and for all. She scrawled out a desperate letter to Lord Melbourne, now the country's Whig Prime Minister, shrieking, 'He has taken my children from me!' – 'if they keep me away from my boys I shall go mad'.[41] She hadn't prepared for this. She had lost her children, and all her possessions – everything she owned was in George Norton's house and legally belonged to him. If she had tried to return home then, she later learned, she would have been denied entry, for George had left orders with his manservant that if either she or Brinsley should come to the house, he was 'to refuse admittance, and to open the house-door only with the chain across'.[42] Open war had been declared.

THE UNBLUSHING ONE

George Norton had no intention of letting his wife go 'quietly'. On the contrary, he would 'endeavour publicly to disgrace'her.[43] He meant to make no provision for her, and under no circumstances to allow her to have the children. He was humiliated, and he had the power to make her suffer for it. Caroline, meanwhile, like many women, was ignorant of just how legally powerless she was regarding her marriage and children, so she dug in, ready to fight.

George's initial plan was to try for a divorce, which, in 1836, could still only be attained via an Act of Parliament, by proving Caroline an adulteress. Caroline was confident he would find no evidence and, perhaps surprisingly, didn't actually want a divorce. It would mean public humiliation, shame and, very likely, her children being handed over to a new stepmother. What she wanted was a separation by mutual agreement with custody of the children, though she knew she would have to play her cards carefully: 'The proceedings in a Court of Justice must ruin a woman's reputation and my great object is to avert that.'[44]

George played dirty from the off. He interrogated his children – who were just seven, five and two – about their mother's conduct with other men, probed his servants on what she got up to when he was out and broke into her desk to go through her papers. He even bribed a cab-boy to try to steal Fitzroy Campbell's letters from his club, which, 'if attempted at the Post-office … would have been felony'.[45]

The gossips only aided him in his quest to ruin his wife. Stories were swapped in parlours all over town that Caroline Norton had run away with Edward Trelawny, or maybe Lord Seymour, and Margaret Vaughan had long been whispering tales of her adultery in George's ear – 'it is no wonder if I feel a little fatigued with all I am supposed to have done', Caroline sighed in a letter to Trelawny.[46] In the meantime, she had learned that George kept a mistress, though she decided not to make a public accusation. What would be the point? It was only in women that adultery was unforgivable.

All the while she was missing her children desperately. So desperately that she considered going back to George, or even abducting them. As far as she knew, they had been sent to stay with Lord Grantley at Wonersh and she fretted over the harsh treatment they would likely receive there. Lord Melbourne's pragmatic, though unhelpful, advice was to keep a stiff upper lip 'and not to give way to feelings of passion'.[47] It obviously worked for him. In an effort to avoid any implication in the Nortons' break-up, he was now backing away from Caroline, which only made her cling on the tighter. His tactical retreat came too late, though. It emerged in April that George had been persuaded by Grantley to sue the Prime Minister for criminal conversation with his wife. By the end of May the trial had been set for the following month.

The papers rejoiced at such a juicy scandal and with prurient glee the satirical cartoons lampooned everyone involved. Some sketches drew George as a horned cuckold and Melbourne as Caroline's adoring little 'Lamb', while others cast doubt over the paternity of her youngest child, and pointedly featured the ominous figure of Lord Grantley lurking in the background. The primary motive behind the trial was understood to be political – it was common knowledge that the Ultra-Tories wanted to bring down the Whig government and thwart their pesky reforms, and that Grantley was unscrupulous enough to manipulate his craven younger brother for the purpose.

That didn't stop the press from subjecting Caroline to a vitriolic smear campaign. Having already decided whose side they were on, the papers cast their protagonists accordingly: 'Mr Norton was represented as an amiable, injured, deceived husband; Lord Melbourne as a profligate impostor; and I myself as a painted wanton.'[48] The Satirist magazine particularly had it in for her; according to its pages she'd had every man in town – politicians, Edward Trelawny, the Duke of Devonshire – while other publications reckoned her conquests were global in scale, including 'a Crowned Head, the spawn of one of the Continental Revolutions, a Noble Duke ... and no less than three Titled Persons, at this moment high in the councils of their Sovereign'.[49] More than one paper dragged up her brother's elopement, ranting that the 'whole race of Sheridans have, from all time, been celebrated for anything but morality', while Caroline was 'Norty Mrs Norton', 'the unblushing one', possibly even in cahoots with George to extort damages from Melbourne. In one particularly bitchy swipe, The Satirist even suggested that those damages should be insultingly low: 'we have heard that one farthing would be about a reasonable sum'.[50]

Caroline was naturally stung by this barrage of scurrilous abuse, so when Melbourne's solicitor then came knocking with awkward questions for the defence, she fired off an indignant letter to the recoiling Prime Minister, causing his usual nonchalant façade to slip. 'I dare say you think me unfeeling,' he conceded, 'but I declare that since I first heard I was to be proceeded against, I have suffered more intensely than I ever did in my life.' He was not sleeping, not eating, he said, not because he was worried for himself, 'because, as you justly say, the imputation upon me is as nothing ... The real and principal object of my anxiety and solicitude is you, and the situation in which you have been so unjustly placed.'[51]

It was a scrap of comfort, but it didn't lessen Caroline's trauma. She had been slandered, her life was on the brink of ruin and she was powerless to prevent it. The outcome of this trial would determine her fate, yet she would be barred from the courtroom and denied a defence. As the day of reckoning approached and her spirits sank, her letters to Melbourne drifted from angry to melancholy to self-pitying. One minute she wrote of her love – 'my life has been divided ... into the days I saw you and the days I did not'[52] – the next of her sadness that he had 'ceased to feel the affection for me which you did'; she blamed herself for not 'quietly taking my place in the past with your wife Mrs Lamb – & Lady Branden'.[53] That she counted herself among these women seems the most conclusive proof yet that, despite their denials, Caroline and Melbourne were indeed lovers. It was now up to his lawyers to convince a jury that they weren't.

CRIMINAL CONVERSATION

At 9.30 a.m. on 22 June 1836, the trial began as it would go on: with none of the main parties present, and with speculation as its foundation. The jury was asked to dismiss all the 'idle rumour' surrounding the case and to judge 'upon the evidence alone'. They were reminded, too, that in criminal conversation cases, direct evidence of wrongdoing wasn't strictly necessary due to its rarity; circumstantial evidence would do. No one, of course, understood the true nature of the relationship they were being asked to evaluate – the room was told it was a 'marriage of affection, gentlemen – at least on the part of Mr Norton'.[54]

The prosecution, led by Sir William Follett, began proceedings, launching into a summary of the 'incriminating' evidence against Lord Melbourne – a man who had insinuated himself into George Norton's life as a benefactor, patron and friend, only to 'inflict upon him the deepest injury … one man can inflict upon another'. The damages for this injury were set at £10,000, and there followed a long list of suspicious observations: Melbourne was a frequent visitor to the house, for hours at a time; he would furtively use the back door rather than the front entrance, and when he was with Mrs Norton doors were bolted and blinds pulled down. Mrs Norton would take care over her appearance before his visits and look dishevelled after them. And more than once, a kiss on the cheek or a hand on the knee had been witnessed between the two. Follett had evidence of a more material nature, too, almost too excruciating for a nineteenth-century gentleman to articulate in public: 'I allude to the marks which are the consequence of intercourse between the sexes. I shall prove these marks to have been observed on the day linen of Mrs Norton.'

It looked bad. If these accusations were shown to come from reliable witnesses, Melbourne and Caroline were done for. It was up to Follett to keep the momentum going, though he began with an air of desperation. The notes Melbourne had sent to Caroline that were portentously read out to the courtroom were so innocuous in content – 'How are you?'; 'I will call about half past four' – that they provoked only sniggers.[55] Caroline's letters to George, on the other hand, filled with standard marital chitchat and occasional suggestions of affection, were denounced as showing nothing more than a 'pretended attachment'. The prosecution then called forward their informants – a string of 12 servants, all of whom had been dismissed from the Nortons' employ some time before. Servants were notoriously 'a race most dangerous in all cases, but particularly in cases of this sort' – they formed an army of spies in every upper-class household, and for any who became disgruntled, a crim con trial was the perfect opportunity to vent their displeasure.

One by one, Caroline's former lady's maids, housemaids and laundrywomen came forward with their incriminating tales of kisses on the cheek, 'tumbled' hair and tell-tale stains on her sheets. And one by one they damned themselves. Some, it transpired, had lied about why they left the Nortons' employ – usually because they had been unmarried and 'in the family way'. These women were instantly dismissed by the jury as immoral and untrustworthy.[56] Others made the mistake of admitting that they had been questioned by George Norton at his chambers, or entertained by Lord Grantley at Wonersh, leading to the reasonable supposition that they had been coached or even bribed as witnesses.

In none, however, was this fall from grace more dramatic than in the prosecution's star witness, John Fluke, the Nortons' former coachman. This Dickensian character endeared himself to the crowd immediately; his cheeky responses made them chuckle, while his tale of woe as an injured, impoverished Waterloo veteran invoked their pity. It was he who delivered the most damaging testimony of the day – a revealing glimpse of Caroline and her lover in the drawing room: he in a chair near the fire; she reclining on the hearth rug.

'Did you observe how her dress was?' asked Sir William Follett.

'Yes,' replied Fluke, 'when I got to the middle of the room, she shifted herself up on her right arm … the clothes were up on Mrs Norton's left leg, and I saw the thick at the knee part of her thigh.'

A flash of leg was enough to get any nineteenth-century jury a little flustered, but Fluke's testimony, like all the others, soon began to unravel under questioning. How did he come to leave the Nortons' employ? It emerged that on his last day he had driven George to work, Caroline accompanying him, when he'd had 'a drop too much' to drink. Inevitably, there was an accident – 'Mr and Mrs Norton fell out and of course they put the spite on me and I was discharged.' Fluke, it turned out, was regularly drunk on the job, but still it was 'that d—d b—h, Mrs Norton', as he'd been overheard to call her, whom he blamed for losing his job. The defence pressed on. Had he not also boasted that he was the 'principal witness against the Premier of England'? And that he stood to gain five or six hundred pounds for his trouble, which would come in very handy for paying off his debts …? Fluke was rattled. He couldn't remember saying such things, but he didn't sound sure. What he did remember was that he, too, had been a guest of Lord Grantley's at Wonersh.

It was now Sir John Campbell's turn to conduct Melbourne's defence, but after eight and a half gruelling hours, he was exhausted and the courtroom restless. He called for an adjournment, which was denied, so instead they took a short break. When Campbell returned to the courtroom he had a radical new strategy – he would call no witnesses. What was the point? No case had been made against his client. The prosecution's witnesses had all proved themselves liars, wantons and drunks, a bunch of 'discarded servants' with a grudge. What's more, they had all been coached and bribed by Norton and Grantley, whose presence in court seemed designed to intimidate them. Their testi-monies were worthless. The courtroom held its breath and looked to the Lord's bench. Grantley didn't flinch; he just scowled in silence.

Every argument from the prosecution was then easily picked apart. If George Norton had truly believed his wife guilty of adultery, why did he not bring his accusation forward years before, when these offences were alleged to have taken place? Instead, he had encouraged Caroline's close friendship with Melbourne, and happily taken a well-paid job as a magistrate from him. The true cause of the couple's falling out, Campbell argued, was their quarrel about spending Easter with Brinsley Sheridan at Frampton, and in the fallout, he claimed (doubtless with another glance in Grantley's direction), 'some person has made Mr Norton a dupe ... has persuaded him to allow his name to be used merely for party and political purposes'.

To close, Campbell read out a complete refutation of the charges from the Prime Minister himself – a gentleman of honour, in stark contrast to Grantley and Norton's blatant corruption. And although Caroline had no voice in this trial, Campbell also reminded the jury of their responsibility towards her: '[It] is impossible to forget that upon your verdict depends whether this lady, of beauty, of virtue ... of talent as we all admit ... shall from henceforth at this early age [28] ... be declared a disgrace to her sex.'

His work was done. The jury took just 'a few seconds' to confer before returning their verdict: Lord Melbourne was not guilty. The decision was met with 'a loud burst of applause, mingled with a few hisses',[57] while 'Cheers and cries of "Bravo!" rang through the court', soon to be taken up by the 'multitude outside'.[58] It was 20 minutes to midnight. The trial had lasted for 14 hours.

Charles Dickens's report of the trial that had seized the nation took up 27 columns of the *Morning Chronicle* the next day. The young reporter was so done in by the case that he could barely get out of bed, declaring to a friend that 'Norton v. Melbourne has played the devil with me.'[59] In the wake of the verdict, much of the press was forced to eat their words: Lord Melbourne stood 'as free of all suspicion of guilt in this matter as if his Lordship had never been accused'.[60] The prosecution's tactics had been shabby and ungentlemanly; the Honourable George Norton was now 'the simple noodle, Norton',[61] and Lord Grantley the arch villain. Some even attempted to rehabilitate Caroline's reputation, accusing the Tories of sacrificing 'one of the most lovely and distinguished of her sex' for political gain.[62]

Caroline ought to have been delighted. Melbourne had been exonerated and, by extension, so had she. Yet her position was now more difficult than ever. The taint of suspicion was not easily shed; many of her former acquaintances cut her and there now seemed even less chance, after George's public humiliation, that she would be reunited with her children. Her only option was to try for a 'Scotch divorce'. In Scotland, both husband and wife could apply for divorce on the grounds of adultery or desertion alone – but to Caroline's dismay she found that her triumph in the trial had now made that impossible. To be found innocent of adultery in a court of law meant that George could not now sue her for adultery as grounds for divorce. And to procure the evidence she needed to sue him for adultery and cruelty as a basis for her desertion would be nigh-on impossible. Not least because she had damned herself without even knowing it. When George had begged her to return in 1835, and persuaded her to offer her forgiveness in writing, he had tricked her into making the greatest error of all. By the law's reckoning, 'I could not plead cruelty which I had forgiven ... by returning to Mr Norton I had "condoned" all I complained of.'[63] It amounted to one unassailable fact: she would never be able to divorce George Norton. The words 'Till death us do part' had never sounded so chilling.

A HELPLESS WRETCH

In the aftermath of the trial, Caroline wrote to Mary Shelley in a state of furious agitation: 'it is impossible not to feel bitterly the disgusting details of the unhappy trial ... a woman is made a helpless wretch by these laws of men, or she would be allowed a defence, a counsel, in such an hour'. To count for nothing 'in a trial which decided one's fate for life, is hard'.[64] Her own plight had made plain to her the fundamental injustice of a woman's lot, and now her righteous anger was bubbling to the surface. Not least when confronted with her husband's ruthless stance regarding their children.

At first, Caroline had blithely assumed that, as their mother, she had the right to both see and care for her boys if she and George separated, when in fact, she had the right to do neither. She wrote to George on 26 June 1836 suggesting that, while his wishes would always be respected, the children needed 'a mother's care and instruc-tion'; she proposed that the two youngest live with her while the eldest went off to school and that they share 'such portion of the holidays as suits you'. When this was flatly refused, she learned with horror that 'the right was with the father; that neither my innocence nor his guilt could alter it; that not even his giving them into the hands of a mistress, would give me any claim to their custody'.[65] And, as the boys' only legally acknowledged parent, George intended to wield his rights as despotically as he could in revenge for his defeat in court. On 15 July he informed her that whether she was granted 'access or not, and the quantum of it, shall be entirely within my own breast in all future time to determine'.[66] A brief meeting with the two eldest at his solicitor's chambers was possible, but that was all. Caroline bitterly rejected this offer. To see them under such circumstances would associate her in their minds with 'secrecy and shame' – she was being treated as if she had been proved guilty, not innocent, of adultery.[67]

What followed was an increasingly distressing back and forth, in which George used the children, as well as Caroline's personal possessions and manuscripts, as bargaining chips to negotiate the most advantageous terms for himself. While he bartered over money (he would only agree to a separation if he was absolved of all liability for her debts and if she agreed to an annual allowance of his stipulation), Caroline would only discuss the boys: 'while I have control of my reason, and strength to guide a pen, I will sign nothing, do nothing, listen to nothing, which has reference to any other subject till it is decided what intercourse is to be allowed me with my children'.[68] More worrying still were the tales from her former servants at Storey's Gate that George had been asking if they saw any resemblance between Master Brin and Lord Melbourne, and was now insisting his youngest son be known as Charles, rather than William, to sever any connection with his namesake. If George were to disown his children for fear of illegitimacy, their futures would be ruined as well as hers.

With money tight, Caroline's brother Brinsley stepped in to help and by the end of July she had found a home in Green Street with her uncle, Charles Sheridan. That same month, however, she was also struggling to come to terms with the fact that her relationship with Lord Melbourne was gasping its last under the strain of the scandal. The new rules were that they couldn't see each other, and shouldn't write, but Caroline couldn't help it. Feeling victimised and spurned, she lashed out at the one she loved: he had brought this 'blight' upon her life, he was the cause of all the 'filth and insult' thrown at her, and now he was neglecting her. The suffering and punishment were all hers – he had lost nothing – and Caroline was livid: 'Can you give me back my children?' she stormed. 'Can you make all that shame pass away which has been the penalty for the amusement of *your* idle hours?'[69]

Melbourne could only acknowledge her pain and reassure her of just how deep his feelings ran: 'I miss you. I miss your society and conversation … You know well enough there is nobody who can fill your place.'[70] This love affair, if that's what it was, had by necessity to end, but to sever all ties between them was impossible; by the end of the month they were on better terms, and would always remain close.

Come August, Caroline had still not seen her children and, in desperation, she began to keep watch on Storey's Gate and follow them whenever they went out with their nurse. She managed to steal a few words with Fletcher one day and tried her best to explain how matters stood. In return, the boy handed her a dog-eared letter he'd been carrying around in his pocket that the servants had dared not post for him. It was the only real comfort she'd had in months – she was certain that Fletcher, at least, would not forget her – but these stealth tactics could not succeed for long. George's interfering cousin Margaret Vaughan soon began to take the children out in her carriage, to keep them out of Caroline's reach.

In mid-August the children were spirited away altogether, with no goodbyes, to George's relatives in Scotland, where Caroline was certain they would be mistreated. She was right. Under the care of his sister Grace, Lady Menzies – a 'haughty and intemperate' woman – seven-year-old Fletcher was flogged to '"impress on his memory" that he was not to receive letters from me', while Brin, not yet five, was stripped, tied to a bed-post and flogged with a riding whip – who knows why?[71]

As the year wore on, the fruitless haggling over the separation continued, with no resolution concerning the children. Caroline tried to write, tried to socialise – she 'laughed restlessly … to prove mortification and sorrow could not reach me' – though often it was just too hard.[72] Out of the blue, she was granted one strange meeting with her children, for just half an hour, in the presence of chaperones, but they were hurried away before she had a chance to compose herself, leaving her even more distraught than she was before.

The only welcome news she received that year, on 21 November, was that the odious Margaret Vaughan had died. George's constant fawning over her had got him what he wanted – she had left him her Yorkshire estates, including the grand Kettlethorpe Hall, and an annual income of £2,000 – but the extra money made him no more generous to Caroline. In a letter to Edward Ellice, who was attempting to act as intermediary between them, he dressed up his miserly, bullying behaviour as some kind of heroic of act: 'My endeavours to save the mother of my children from further exposure are fruitless', he opined. 'She is determined to drag herself yet more before the public.'[73] In her response to Ellice, however, Caroline was unbowed, powered by a new determination not to be shamed and muted: 'A woman has apparently no individual destiny. She is the property of those on whom she may reflect discredit or otherwise. If I succeed I hope my success will be a satisfaction and triumph to "my people" for nothing will ever be a matter of triumph or satisfaction to me again.'[74] Her struggle, she had realised, was the struggle of all women, and she would do more than drag it before the public. She was preparing to take her fight for her children to the highest level possible.

THE HARLOT'S PROGRESS

Nothing would change until the law changed, and as a writer, Caroline could channel her anger and influence public opinion in a way that most injured women couldn't. The absence of a mother's rights in existing custody law was something she now fully understood and felt passionately about, so between 1837 and 1839 she made manifest her fury in three powerful political pamphlets on the subject. The first, *Observations on the Natural Claims of a Mother to the Custody of her Children as Affected by the Common Law Rights of the Father*, appeared in early 1837, and included arguments based on her own experiences as well as case studies of other women.[75]

Caroline had big plans for this pamphlet. In a letter to Mary Shelley, who was helping her to edit it, she voiced their shared frustrations that there was still 'too much fear of publishing about women', resulting in women's lives, and the issues that affected them, being passed over in silence. 'I think it is high time,' she wrote, 'that the law was known at least, among the "weaker" sex, which gives us no right to one's own flesh and blood.'[76] Her plan, however, was not just to make the law known, but to change it once and for all – and she had the contacts to help her do it. Abraham Howard and Serjeant Talfourd were powerful lawyers whom Caroline enlisted to canvass Parliament on her behalf, and soon the Infant Custody Bill was introduced to the House of Commons. If passed, it would allow a judge to grant custody of a child under 12 to either parent.

The bill's first reading in Parliament was scheduled for April 1837, but it would face numerous delays, primarily because of George's suspiciously timed campaign of vacillation. To coincide with each scheduled reading, he would raise Caroline's hopes of seeing the children, and in the same breath impose new conditions he knew she wouldn't accept – that they could live with her but only with a chaperone, that she could see them but only at his convenience, that they be brought up 'with the strictness I require', that her allowance would be contingent on her irreproachable conduct. As George forever shifted the goalposts, so they went forever round in circles and Caroline's attention was drawn away from her campaign.

Then, on 19 May, a few days before the bill's second reading was due, George suddenly attempted to initiate a reconciliation. At his insistence, they met in an empty house in Berkeley Street, where they had a 'long wretched interview' and George begged her to '"forget the past" and return home. He laid the blame of all that had happened on his brother, friends and advisers; said the trial was against his will and judgement, and that he longed to "take me to his heart again".'[77]

Caroline was so desperate to have her children back that she seriously considered it, though naturally she was wary – every minute, the rules of the game changed. One day George claimed to believe in her innocence, the next he was threatening to withhold the children and 'bring forward revolting tales' about her if she didn't agree to his demands. Whenever she expressed her distrust of him, he would feign hurt and pretend to be reasonable, before issuing a whole new set of entirely unreasonable terms. Most disturbing of all was how he began to sign his letters using the moniker 'your affectionate intended, Greenacre' – a reference to one James Greenacre, who had recently been hanged for murdering and dismembering his fiancée. He used it playfully, she said, 'in allusion to my fear of meeting him', but it was a creepy touch she would never forget.[78]

If George and Grantley's motive *was* to distract Caroline from the serious business of pushing the custody bill through Parliament, it worked, for Talfourd was forced to postpone the second reading by two weeks, and again after that, because of Caroline's ongoing negotiations with Norton. Her involvement was crucial to the bill's success and he needed her to be focused – hardly possible when George continually dangled her heart's desire before her, only to snatch it away again. It looked worryingly like one elaborate, vicious trick, but she had to keep negotiations open.

By mid-June the situation had deteriorated even further. Caroline had heard that the children had been sent to Wonersh, where they had all caught measles, so naturally she rushed there to comfort them. An ugly scene followed. When Grantley arrived home and found her cradling Brin in her lap, he ordered her to leave. When that didn't work, 'He pulled and shook me fiercely by the arm.' In that moment Caroline was a lioness protecting her cubs. Sick of being manhandled by Nortons, her courage flared: she threatened to indict him for assault if he touched her again, at which Grantley released his grip and summoned his servants, who wrenched Brin from her 'by his arms and legs' and carried him away.[79] As the other boys ran away screaming, Grantley bellowed for them to be locked up and for Caroline to be thrown out of his house.

The mood was now as hostile as it had ever been. All talk of reconciliation had ceased, the children were sent back to Scotland, and correspondence between Caroline and George was banned – from now on, they would communicate only through lawyers. The next she heard from him was an advert he placed in *The Times* on 5 September 1837, which stated that he would not 'be liable for any debt … which the said Mrs Norton may hereafter contract or incur'. It was a low blow, publicly warning tradesmen away from her and attempting to cut off her credit, so a fuming Caroline appealed to her lawyers – 'Have I no remedy?' she demanded bluntly. 'The law can do nothing for you', was their limp response.[80] For now, Brinsley Sheridan could only publish a formal response in *The Times*, stating of George's ad that 'the whole of it is false' and the 'case will shortly appear before a court of justice'.[81]

Not even the arbitrator George himself appointed in November 1837 to settle their affairs out of court could fathom the chicanery of this man. John Bayley was hired because he was biased *against* Caroline – he believed her vain, extravagant and guilty of adultery – but once he learned of George's interminable lies, he soon switched sides, seeing 'no earthly reason' why the children should be withheld from Mrs Norton.[82] His decree was that the boys be summoned immediately, and George pretended to obey, writing the instruction to his sister in Bayley's presence. What Bayley didn't see was the second letter George sent after it, which immediately revoked the command. By the end of the process, poor Bayley was so confounded by George's ungentlemanly behaviour that he had resigned as arbitrator twice. 'If the devil is not with him,' he wrote to Caroline in distress, then 'there is no such spirit'.[83]

These months of endless shuffling only made Caroline all the more determined to push through the Infant Custody Bill, which now looked like the only way to regain access to her children, so over the next 18 months she dedicated herself to the campaign. The bill was due to be reintroduced in May 1838, and bang on time, George published another advertisement in *The Times*, absolving himself of his legal liability for his wife debts. Caroline would not be derailed. Instead, she wrote another new pamphlet to support the bill, *The Separation of Mother and Child by the Law of Custody of Infants Considered*, which again drew on her own personal nightmare to demolish a law that was made by men but destroyed women's lives.

It was published anonymously, but people soon cottoned on to who had written it. Caroline listed five women of impeccable reputation who had all been denied access to their children in the Court of Chancery, to demonstrate the law's bias towards fathers, regardless of their moral character. A wife had no access rights to her children whatsoever, she reminded her readers, even if 'she could prove that she was driven by violence from her husband's house, and that he had deserted her for a mistress. The father's right is absolute and paramount, and can no more be affected by the mother's claim, than if she had no existence.'

When the bill went for its second reading in Parliament on 28 May it became clear just how deeply entrenched in misogyny and hypocrisy the existing custody law really was. The speeches against it reflected a society so obsessed with the sexual purity of its women that, while adulterous husbands were patted on the back and handed their children no questions asked, wives – adulterous or not – had their maternal rights erased just in case. Many MPs panicked that the new custody bill posed an existential threat to both their society and their marriages: devoted wives would turn adulteress and become a 'most dangerous menace to society'; fathers would be unable to prevent 'unchaste women from getting access to their children' and polluting them with their sin.[84]

The fact that men in Caroline's own family (her uncle, for one, who knew all too well of her troubles) believed the law should stay as it was made her wonder 'how even kind and good men narrow their minds on this subject'. Apparently there were precious few men who were willing to accept a diminution of their own power in exchange for a modicum of justice. Many were not even interested. The turnout for the reading was dispiritingly low, yet the bill managed to pass through to the House of Lords for debate on 30 July.

Caroline now lobbied every liberal peer she could find, particularly

Lord Brougham, a former lord chancellor who was known to have had several affairs (one of them with Lord Melbourne's wife) and a very unhappy marriage, appealing for help in 'what I will not call my cause but the cause of all women'. Like so many others, however, Brougham's instinct was to protect the patriarchy that served him so well. He ignored Caroline's petitions and argued fervently against the bill in the debate, claiming, 'It would open the door to such frightful changes in the whole of this country, and in the whole of the principles on which the law of husband and wife was founded.'[85] That a woman stood to lose her children if she committed adultery was a prime deterrent, and if this law was passed, who knew how many women – weak, susceptible and insatiable as they were feared to be – would fall? Nowhere and by no one was it acknowledged that these were the words of a serial adulterer, who had suffered no consequences for it whatsoever, simply because he was a man.

The bill was rejected, nine votes to eleven, and it was obvious why: there was one rule for men, and another for women. It was self-preservation of the most heinous kind: frightened men building unassailably high walls of moral righteousness and legal protection around themselves, to conceal their own shortcomings and to punish them in women. They jealously kept all the freedoms and rights for themselves, and allowed women none, and the blatant hypocrisy of it made Caroline's blood burn like acid in her veins.

Hand in hand with Caroline's involvement in the bill came the inevitable attacks in the press, but, undeterred, as 1839 dawned she penned another polemic to support the bill's next reading, which was due in the spring. *A Plain Letter to the Lord Chancellor on the Infant Custody Bill* was written under the pseudonym Pearce Stevenson, as she feared that her name – now tarred as that of a 'she-devil', a 'she-beast' and 'something between a barn actress and Mary Wollstonecraft'[86] – would prevent the pamphlet from receiving a fair hearing. Despite the familiar diversions from George, it was third time lucky for Talfourd's bill. Read in April and July 1839, debated all over again and pelted with the same old objections, on 17 August it was finally passed as the Custody of Infants Act. After two years of bruising campaigning, during which her husband and the press had done their level best to distract, defame and derail her, Caroline had been instrumental in bringing the first act of feminist legislation into the British statute books. For the first time, women who were separated or divorced but had not been found guilty of adultery in court were now entitled to custody of their children until they were seven years old, and to access thereafter. And although it was only wealthy women who could afford to do battle in court for their children, it signified the stirrings of a dramatic sea change for women's legal rights.

'MY LITTLE LOST ONE'

Caroline's youngest son, William, was not yet seven, so naturally she hoped to use the new law to gain custody of him and access to Fletcher and Brin. But George, conniving as ever, found a way to evade this legal obligation. The law applied in England, but not in Scotland. Scotland was where the boys were, so of course he was adamant that was where they would stay. Caroline's lawyers investigated but found that, as long as George refused to move the children to England, they were powerless to force him.

By 1840, the estranged couple were in their fifth year of squabbling over the children and getting nowhere, so that in those years, Caroline had seen her sons only a handful of times. She was at least edging back into the warm glow of social and literary acceptance, though. In May, after months of badgering Lord Melbourne to use his influence with the new young queen, Caroline was finally presented at Buckingham Palace to Victoria – a vital step in her social rehabilitation – while her new book of poems, *The Dream*, a passionate encomium to motherhood by a woman who had been wrenched from her children, went down well with Victorian readers. Hartley Coleridge was so impressed that he called her 'the Byron of our modern poetesses'.[87] There could be no higher praise as far as Caroline was concerned.

But even these fine honours seemed to pall in the light of what she had lost. The 'petty successes' of admiration and inclusion that she had so valued and enjoyed in her youth seemed strangely hollow now. 'What is anything worth in this life,' she asked Mary Shelley, 'if the strongest of all ties is made the one means of poisonous discomfort?'[88] George's bartering was driving her to the edge. She raged at him in her letters, challenging his self-image as a 'gentleman', a good husband and a 'man of honour'. She was 'weary, utterly weary' of 'month after month passing away in useless and shuffling letters, which, while still affirming that you do not refuse access, leave things in fact exactly as they were.'[89] But George's responses were always calculated to exacerbate rather than ease her suffering. In one instance, in lieu of her actual children, he sent her some portraits he'd commissioned, triggering in her a fresh wave of grief. A few weeks later, he promised to send the boys to join her for a holiday on the Isle of Wight. To the Isle of Wight she went, and for ten days she waited, but the children never arrived. George had 'contrived that at least one of those boys would not know his mother if he met her by chance in the street',[90] and now he was laughing at her, too.

Then, in the spring of 1841, came a chink of opportunity. She discovered that George had secretly sent the boys to Laleham prep school in Surrey – a draconian establishment, though one that was at least in England, where she ought, by law, to be allowed to see them. Her hopes rising, she visited the school that June and requested access, but the housemaster deferred immediately to George. His reply was as unyielding as ever – 'No one is to see or have any communication with my children except under my express written authority.' When Caroline involved her lawyers, he predictably played the morality card: her 'conduct', he insisted, 'has not been such as to enable her to have intercourse with her children, nor to justify me in permitting it'.[91] Now, however, Caroline had the law on her side. She lost no time in making her application to the Lord Chancellor to demand her rights in accordance with the Custody of Infants Act, and though the Court of Chancery was notoriously sluggish, it was, at last, an affirmative step towards reclaiming her sons.

Sadly, the law moved too slowly for Caroline, and, in the end, it would take a tragedy to make George Norton relent. In September 1842, Caroline was taking the spa waters at Tunbridge Wells when she received an urgent message that her youngest son, nine-year-old William, whom she had hardly seen since he was a toddler, had fallen from his pony while at Kettlethorpe Hall and was now lying danger-ously ill. Stricken, she took the train over 200 miles to Yorkshire the following day and was met at the station by a grim-faced woman she had never seen before – Lady Kelly, the wife of George's lawyer. Desperate for information, Caroline blurted out, 'I am here. Is my boy better?' Lady Kelly's reply was brief, blunt and savage: 'No, he is not better, he is dead.'[92]

William had died some hours before and was already lying in his coffin – 'the senseless clay of my little lost one' – when Caroline reached the house. She now learned the full story of what had happened. The boys had been staying at Kettlethorpe virtually alone – George had not been with them, as usual, and there had been no one to look after them 'but an old woman who opens the gate'. This meant that William was unsupervised when he went out on his pony and was thrown two miles from home. His injuries were minor, only a scratched arm, so he made his way to the nearest house, where he was cleaned up by the servants. Not well enough, though. The scratch became infected and William developed tetanus, or lockjaw, named after the muscular spasms that quickly make the body seize up. The doctor told the already-broken Caroline that William had been conscious when he died, had prayed and asked for her twice, and 'bore the dreadful spasms of pain with a degree of courage which [he] has rarely seen in so young a child'.

This was a new kind of agony, more dreadful than any Caroline had ever experienced. And as much as she 'choked' back her anger at George, a constant refrain played in her head: 'This might not have happened had I watched over them!'[93] George seemed full of grief and remorse. He begged Caroline's forgiveness and made the kinds of promises he had trotted out many times before. He would let her see the boys, he would be reasonable about her allowance and not hinder their separation. By now, of course, Caroline knew not to believe these contrite displays, and sure enough, once Lord Grantley arrived, she observed with a shudder how quickly he returned to his old self: 'he humbled himself, and grieved for an hour … and then he buried our child, and forgot both his sorrow and his penitence'.[94] Bitterly she noted that with half the money George was lavishing on William's decorative coffin he could have paid for 'some steady man-servant to be in constant attendance in their hours of recreation'.[95] The more she dwelt on it, the more she blamed George utterly. He had stolen William's childhood from her, and William's mother from him; and now the boy was dead because of his neglect. To add to her pain, he had 'allowed the child to lie ill for a week – indeed to be at death's door – before he sent to inform me', so that she hadn't even been able to see him and say goodbye before he died.[96] There could be no forgiveness this time.

Caroline's new life was odd to her. She had lost one son, but regained the other two, for George had honoured at least one of his promises and allowed Fletcher and Brin to visit her in London before they returned to school. Able, finally, to be a mother again, though to only two children instead of three, her life was now an uneasy mix of grief and joy. As mother and sons got reacquainted, she found the boys 'so happy at being reknit to me that I can scarcely think of it without weeping'. She marvelled at the little strangers before her: Brin, not yet 11, was 'brimful of gratitude and love to all who ever loved or were kind to me', and Fletcher, now 13, was 'quieter, more thoughtful, less spirited, but seems like an angel to me'.[97] Both had taken their brother's death hard, while Brin, seeing his parents united in sorrow at the funeral, had naively hoped it might signal a reconciliation.

This was emphatically not the case, but William's death did bring about some important changes in the Nortons' relationship. The bad-tempered negotiations certainly continued, but eventually, softened by grief, George made two vital concessions: Caroline would have equal visiting rights to see the boys at school, and custody of them for half the year. It was the breakthrough for which she'd been striving for over six years, and here it was; the bittersweet compensation for her 'little tadpole's' death.

NORTON VERSUS NORTON

George was unnervingly quiet for six years after William's death, during which time Caroline attempted to make up for years of lost mothering, to re-establish herself as a society hostess and to set herself up as an independent woman. Now in her late thirties and as beautiful as ever, she could still attract glamorous types to her salon, including the rising star Charles Dickens, who by now had solicited Mrs Norton's company as a friend rather than a reporter.[98] And when Caroline's uncle died in 1843, resulting in the loss of her home, she resolved, rather radically, to live alone in Chesterfield Street. True independence, however, was hard for a woman to come by. Even Caroline, who earned a good living (she had recently been paid £500 for a new novel and was due another £500 for her poem of social injustice, *The Child of the Islands*),[99] had no legal right as a married woman to sign her own lease; her brother Brinsley had to act as surety for her. And occupying this strange limbo between reliance and independence made her peevish: 'It is a hard thing', she wrote to Brinsley in December 1844, 'to feel legally so helpless and dependent, while in fact I am as able to support myself as an intelligent man working in a moderate profession.'[100]

All the while her boys were growing up into very different but equally problematic young men. Sweet-natured Fletcher was adored by all but was a constant worry due to his health – he had developed a weak chest, a heart condition and the Sheridan predisposition for consumption, so once he had completed his schooling at Eton it was decided he should move to a hot climate – thought curative for consumptives. In 1847 he boarded a boat to Lisbon to take up a junior post with the British Legation there, though the sunshine didn't prevent him falling into a long-term pattern of relapses and recoveries. Caroline would spend much of the next decade toing and froing between England and Portugal, devotedly nursing him and occasionally taking him on tours of Europe. By now she had lost two brothers to the 'white plague' – Frank in 1843 and Charlie in 1847 – as well as her father, and was determined to stave off its effects from her son. Brin, meanwhile, had gone up to Oxford and suffered an 'hysteric attack' in his first term, leaving the dons, who 'could not understand his ways', utterly baffled.[101]

It was the summer of 1848 when George broke his silence and returned to his favourite pastime of pestering Caroline about money. He wanted to raise some cash on her trust fund and needed her written consent, so Caroline seized the opportunity to get the deed of separation she wanted in exchange, along with an allowance of £600 a year. George haggled, of course, knocking off £100, but before the deal could be finalised Caroline's brother Brinsley raised an objection: while the proposed agreement demanded that she pay all her own future debts *and* those from the previous ten years, George would issue no backpay of her allowance at all. The financial advantage was so overwhelmingly George's that Brinsley refused to act as guarantor, meaning that only an informal document could be drawn up. Caroline signed in good faith regardless, but what George well knew, and Caroline didn't, was that this agreement – signed by a legal non-entity with no guarantors – was worthless. She would learn it soon enough.

In the meantime, there was Lord Melbourne to worry about. Having lost power to the Tories in August 1841 after a vote of no confidence, he had retired, sore and despondent, to his estate at Brocket Hall and, in October the following year, had suffered a stroke that left him partially paralysed. As depression and loneliness closed in around him, Caroline wrote regularly, gossiping, teasing and flirting as always, determined to cheer up her dear 'Fatty', but then in October 1848 came another stroke and, a month later, his death. Caroline could hardly take it in. She had to resist picking up her pen to share her news with him, and instead wrote to his nephew William Cowper, 'I cannot believe I am never to have a letter from him again.'[102] The love of her life was gone.

According to Melbourne's wishes, his family made Caroline an allowance of £200 a year – Lady Branden, the other woman accused of criminal conversation with him, received the same. It was intended as a gentlemanly act of compensation for the slander they had suffered and was kept as discreet as possible, but when George Norton heard of it, he swiftly reduced Caroline's allowance by a corresponding £200, and stored up this suspicious-looking gesture for future use.

Distraction came in the form of work. Despite being passed over for the role of Poet Laureate in 1850,[103] Caroline's literary successes continued the following year, with a book of ballads inspired by her travels with Fletcher, *Music on the Waves*, and a novel, *Stuart of Dunleath: A Story of Modern Times*, which drew heavily on her own experiences of domestic violence and legal injustice. This provocative, tragic melodrama, in which the heroine Eleanor Raymond is trapped with a husband so violent he breaks her arm, and is left with nothing when she escapes him, was described at the time as 'one of the most brilliant productions in modern literature'.[104]

It was the death of her mother from stomach cancer on 9 June 1851 that sparked Caroline's next clash with George. Wise by then to just how avaricious and untrustworthy her son-in-law was, Mrs Sheridan had done her utmost to protect her daughter from his grasping fingers by leaving her a bequest of £480 under the laws of Equity, to be in no way 'subject or liable to the power or control, debts, interference or engagements of her said present or any future husband'.[105] George's response was to coolly reduce Caroline's allowance by £480, leaving him just £20 a year to pay. With mounting medical bills for Fletcher and debts to pay off for the increasingly wayward Brin (which George, despite now earning over £3,000 a year plus rents, refused to contribute to), Caroline was left financially crippled. When she reminded George that he was bound by their 1848 agreement to pay her a £500 allowance in return for the mortgage on the trust fund, he informed her that, as man and wife were one in law, there could be no contract between them, and therefore (as he had known all along) the deed they had signed was 'good for nothing'. It was little more than a gentleman's agreement – and George had long since proved he was not a gentleman.

Such a dirty trick could no longer be a shock, yet Caroline had been genuinely taken in by the phony agreement, faithfully paying all her own debts to fulfil her side of the bargain. But now that George had broken his word and drastically reduced her allowance a full six months before her mother's bequest would materialise, she could no longer afford to. An unpaid bill from a Mr Thrupps of £49 4s 6d for carriage repairs was duly referred to her husband, and inevitably he refused to pay it. Thrupps took George to court, and Caroline was subpoenaed as the primary witness. Husband and wife were about to meet face to face in court for the first time, Norton versus Norton.

The trial took place on 18 August 1853 in another Westminster courtroom packed to capacity with 300 avid spectators. The public and the press were thrilled at the prospect of a new instalment of the engrossing Norton saga, and they were treated to a riveting show.

Caroline later recalled that at her first sight of her husband in the courtroom her 'courage sank', and when she tried to speak, her words 'choked' in her throat. Seeing her wobble, George pounced; gathering his papers ostentatiously, he sneered, 'What does the witness say? Let her speak up; I cannot hear her!'[106] and came to sit so uncomfortably close to her that several officials complained (though their objections were ignored).

These attempts to intimidate her had the opposite effect to the one George intended, however. As Caroline was interrogated on her spending and made to look extravagant, and George issued his justification for breaking their agreement of 1848, the gall of injustice rose in her throat. He had learned of the payments from Lord Melbourne's family, and was now claiming that she had vowed in their agreement never to receive any money from the former Prime Minister. Surely, George declared, the payments were an admission that she had been guilty of adultery all those years ago after all.

At that moment, it dawned on Caroline what George was up to: he intended to rake up the old scandal (which he had since stated he had never believed) to distract the court from the real question of whether he had defrauded his wife; he was going to discredit her word by savaging her reputation all over again. This was a fight not just for an income but another 'struggle against infamy'. She would not stand for it – 'Scorn and desperation took the place of fear.'[107] Summoning every scrap of Sheridan skill she had, Caroline found her voice and gave a magnificent performance: 'I am here for justice,' she roared, clarion and confident, 'and as this is a court of justice, I insist upon stating what I have to say. Those tradesmen would have been paid if Mr Norton had not performed the greatest breach of faith that was ever accomplished by man.'[108] The judge objected immediately to this speech, but Caroline was adamant: 'I will speak.' When she was then cross-examined by Mr Joseph Needham, she coolly deflected his questions with lightning speed. To his accusations of evasion, she shot back with added steel: 'You are afraid of my answers when I give them.' The little woman was proving much harder to break than they'd anticipated.

When the questioning turned to Lord Melbourne, however, by her own admission, she 'lost all self-possession'. She had never been his mistress, she snapped; she had received nothing from him, only 'his solemn declaration, as a dying man' that she had been falsely accused of adultery – a slander that dogged her still. 'I stand here a blasted woman from that day,' she cried,[109] and the court erupted into applause. Sensing her advantage, she grew bolder: 'My husband can cheat me because I am his wife,' she said, stressing her legal vulnerability. Yes, she occasionally received money from Melbourne's family, but she saw no shame in accepting it as compensation for 'the wreck of her whole life' that had resulted from the trial. When George's own solicitor confirmed that his client had been lying when he'd said their agreement was conditional upon her not accepting such a bequest, and as Needham stooped lower and lower, attempting to turn proceedings into a retrial of her relationship with Melbourne, her victory seemed near at hand. By the time Needham accused her of running away from George, sniping, 'It is not *his* fault you stand in the degraded position you do,' the court's sympathy was all with her.[110]

Spurred on, Caroline revealed more and more of George's erratic, disturbing behaviour. If he believed she had committed adultery, why had he attempted a reconciliation with her after the trial? Why had he signed his letters 'Greenacre', 'after the man who had murdered the woman and cut her body into pieces'? Why ask her to meet him in an empty house? After years of oppressive silence, this was her chance to expose the man her husband truly was, 'the man who calls himself a magistrate, a barrister and a gentleman', and her pent-up fury spooled out of her:

I have no rights I have only wrongs

For seventeen years I have concealed these things, but they come out today
because you bully me; and I am ashamed for your client if he does not feel
ashamed of himself. My own means will perfectly suffice now that I know
Mr Norton can cheat me ... I do not ask for my rights. I have no rights
– I have only wrongs.[111]

The crowd bellowed their approval – she had won them over as
expertly as Old Sherry himself. No longer a wanton seductress, she
was now a slandered wife and a woman to be reckoned with.

Even so, in an infuriating twist, George Norton won the case on
a technicality: because the debt was incurred before he had reduced
Caroline's allowance. He was far from happy, though. His wife had
laid bare his baseness in a public court, and he couldn't let it go
unchallenged. He requested a hearing to refute her accusations, which
the judge refused, and at this he inadvertently revealed a little more
of his true character – he 'vehemently addressed' his wife, the judge
and the press, and loomed over Caroline, his fist clenched, spitting
threats in her face. The crowd 'hissed as he walked out of the court',
for in this grubby little drama, George Norton had proved himself
the indisputable villain.[112]

ENGLISH LAWS FOR WOMEN

Both riled, neither Norton felt able to let it rest there. As soon as
the case was over, their indignation spilled out onto the pages of the
newspapers. Caroline went first, restating her case in full in a letter
to *The Times* on 20 August 1853, railing against her husband's
treachery and deploring the English laws that allowed it. To air her
dirty laundry in public was risky, but necessary: 'This case, though it

is life and death to me, may not interest the public. But what does interest the public is the law.' This was a mission not just to rescue her own reputation, but to make everyone aware of the iniquity of the laws regarding women.

Five days later George sent his lengthy response to *The Times*, offering a largely fictional retelling of their marriage and its break-down, dismissing his wife's testimony as 'the most splendid piece of acting ever exhibited' and accusing the court and even his own solic-itor of being 'suspended in breathless, helpless inaction' by her wily charms. In an effort to claw back his 'public character', his interminable piece refuted her every word. He accused her of flagrant extravagan-cies aimed at getting him into debt and rejected the verdict of the 1836 criminal conversation trial.

This provoked numerous responses from numerous quarters. Against advice, Caroline wrote another letter, addressing his most inflammatory charges, picking holes in his story and exposing his contradictions. Many a disgraced woman must have inwardly cheered when they read her assertion that there were some 'in whose eyes the accusation of a woman is her condemnation, and who care little whether her story be true or false'. Her defence was righteous and emphatic: 'I did not deserve the scandal of 1836 and I do not deserve the scandal of 1853.'[113]

George's solicitor, Mr Leman, then weighed in by assuring readers that there had been no clause in the separation agreement relating to Lord Melbourne as George claimed, while Messrs Currie and Woodgate confirmed on behalf of Sir William Follett, who was now dead, that he had not advised George to prosecute Lord Melbourne in 1836. Finally, and decisively, the couple's arbitrator John Bayley stated in no uncertain terms why his allegiance had switched from George Norton to his wife, on his discovery that 'Nearly every statement he had made to me, turned out to be untrue. I found Mrs Norton anxious only on one point, and nearly broken-hearted about it; namely, the restoration of her children … I found her husband, on the contrary, anxious only about the pecuniary part of the arrangement.' There was never a more deeply injured woman, he wrote, and Norton's conduct towards her was 'marked by the grossest cruelty, injustice, and inconsistency, that ever any man displayed'.[114]

The retrial played out in the papers through September and by the end of the month, the press had reached its verdict: Mrs Norton was a wronged woman and Mr Norton a scoundrel. That she could find no legal redress and that he remained a magistrate, able to pass judgement on similar cases, was a 'wrong' that stood 'flagrant before the public'.[115]

Buoyed by this support, Caroline now threw herself into writing an epic pamphlet that laid out her experiences with George in detail – every horrific abuse, every shifty lie, every belligerent trick – from the start of their marriage to the present. Her aims were twofold: to set down her story definitively for public judgement; and to use herself as a case study to prove the fundamental injustice of a married woman's legal invisibility 'in the hope that the law may be amended'.

The timing was apposite; divorce and separation laws were in the process of being reviewed following a report in 1853 produced by the Royal Commission on Divorce, chaired by Lord Campbell (another veteran of the 1836 trial), which, though it recommended no actual changes to the laws, proposed replacing local ecclesiastical courts with secular divorce courts to simplify the process and make it more affordable. To ensure that a vital female voice was heard amid this all-male debate, Caroline published *English Laws for Women in the Nineteenth Century* in 1854, confronting politicians and lawmakers with a powerful account of how their decisions affected women's lives.

'Except for the purpose of suffering,' she explained, 'as far as the law was concerned, it could oppress but never help me.' It had rendered her signature on a lease or deed of separation worthless; it had left her unable to reclaim or dispose of any of her possessions from the husband she had been separated from for 17 years; it had left her unable to make a will, defend herself in a trial that dragged her name through the mud, prosecute for the many libels against her, claim the copyrights for her literary work or prevent her husband from claiming her money; and it had left her unable to divorce or straightforwardly separate from him, even though his cruelty and manipulation could be proved – 'that is the negative and neutralising law, for married women in England'.

In answer to those who accused her of campaigning merely for personal gain, she emphasised that it was 'of more importance that the law should be altered, than that I should be approved. Many a woman may live to thank Heaven that I had the courage and energy left to attempt the task.' Even men might thank her one day, she hazarded, if only for the sake of their sisters, daughters or friends. And besides, the hope of saving other women from wasting their youth as she had in 'struggle and vexation' had 'a certain degree of happiness attached to it; even if the law be remedied too late for me personally to profit much by the change'.

These were rousing, feminist-like words, though her reaction to those who branded her one of those irritating women shouting about equality (who in the 1850s were only just beginning to formulate into a cohesive and proactive group) was, to the modern eye, peculiar. Rather than proclaim her solidarity with the women's rights campaigners, she was quick to dissociate herself from them.

'Petitioning', she wrote, 'does not imply assertion of equality. The wild and stupid theories advanced by a few women, of "equal rights" and "equal intelligence" are not the opinions of their sex.'[116] It was an incongruous and problematic statement from a woman who fought so determinedly for married women's rights and was so confident of her own intelligence, but she, along with 'millions more', accepted 'the natural superiority of man' as readily as she accepted 'the existence of God' – without question, rationale or proof – simply because that was how it had always been. Patriarchal indoctrination remained as deep-rooted as ever, yet even women like Caroline – who were wary of being labelled some kind of radical termagant, who were unable to acknowledge or even recognise their own feminist instincts, and who softened their stance to make their arguments more palatable – were being compelled *in extremis* by their own sense of injustice to start hacking away at the root system.

The same woman goes on to decry the shredding of her reputation with all the moral outrage of a feminist agitator and the skill of a political rhetorician, demanding, 'Why should I bear it only because I am a woman?' She cites several other case studies from Britain, France and America in which women were the victims of legal injustice purely because of their gender and ends with a plea for justice: 'Think,' she says, 'if the smallest right be infringed for men … how instantly the whole machinery of the law is set in motion to crush out compensation.' And if her own tarnished reputation should damage her argument, she asks her readers to 'forget that it was advocated by me', for the matter 'concerns you all … Let my part in this, be only as a voice borne by the wind – a cry coming over the waves from a shipwreck, to where you stand safe on the shore – and which you turn and listen to, not for the sake of those who call – you do not know them – but because it is a cry for help.'[117]

Why should
I bear it only
because I am
a woman?

UNTYING THE KNOT

In 1855 the Whigs returned to power under the auspices of Lord Palmerston. The time was ripe for legal reform, and Caroline was determined to make it happen, so the latter half of the 1850s was taken up with campaigning. The Lord Chancellor Lord Cranworth had introduced a new bill to transfer the power to grant separations and divorces from the ecclesiastical courts (which viewed marriage as sacrosanct and saw husband and wife as one) to a new civil court, which would end the need for a private Act of Parliament. But Cranworth was a ditherer, and under his auspices the bill was withdrawn for amendments and delayed several times between 1854 and 1856. So in stepped Caroline – passionate and proactive – to push forward a meaningful version of the bill, writing two pamphlets that again drew on her own dire experiences to convince lawmakers of the need for drastic legislative change.

First came *A Letter to Queen Victoria on Lord Chancellor Cranworth's Marriage and Divorce Bill* in June 1855 – a fierce polemic that denounced a married woman's invisibility before the law. Mindful of her addressee, she began by pointing out what a 'grotesque anomaly' it was that 'a married woman in England shall be "non-existent" in a country governed by a female sovereign', before explaining the myriad ways this negation left women vulnerable, exploited and injured. Her expertise, authenticity and conviction rang out as clear as a church bell: a wife could be entirely blameless – she 'may have withdrawn from [her husband's] roof knowing that he lives with "his faithful housekeeper", having suffered personal violence at his hands; having "condoned" much, and being able to prove it by unimpeachable testimony: or he may have shut the doors of her house against her:

all this is quite immaterial ... As her husband, he has a right to all that is hers: as his wife, she has no right to anything that is his.' She would still be considered one with him. He could march her back to his house and forcibly demand his 'conjugal rights'; he could live off her money with no obligation to pay her a penny in support. The inequality of the divorce law reflected just what a gross injustice the marriage pact was: 'a civil bond for him, and an indissoluble sacrament for her', in which the same old sexual double standard ordained that a woman must tolerate her husband's adultery, while hers was condemned as a threat to social order. Even officially innocent women like Caroline were left in limbo with no redress: 'My reputation, my property, my happiness, are irrevocably in the power of this slanderer. I cannot release myself. I exist and I suffer but the law denies my existence.'[118]

Knowing the Queen was no feminist, she followed this with another uncomfortable disavowal of 'the wild and ridiculous doctrine of equality'; she argued only for justice, she said: her husband's other 'inferiors' to whom he was contractually obliged – his maid or apprentice – had legal protections that his wife did not. Nonetheless, when Caroline asserts that women are capable of great things, and that she will bear any abuse or ridicule to use her gift for words to change the law, she sounds an awful lot like a feminist issuing her battle cry:

I deny that this is my personal cause – it is the cause of all the women of England. If I could be justified and happy tomorrow, I would still strive and labour in it; and if I were to die tomorrow, it would still be a satisfaction to me that I had so striven. Meanwhile, my husband has ... the copyright of my works. Let him claim the copyright of this![119]

The pamphlet was a great success. Even Lord Brougham called it 'as clever a thing as ever was written' that had 'produced great good'.[120]

Caroline's words were making a difference; alongside that of her ally in Parliament, Lord Lyndhurst, hers was now one of the most prominent voices in the debate. So, as further delays hampered the bill's progress, in 1857 she published another new pamphlet, *A Review of the Divorce Bill of 1856*, to help chivvy the MPs along. It set down 20 propositions that she felt ought to be part of the new act, including the payment of alimony, the abolition of criminal conversation trials, for desertion to be allowed as a ground for divorce and for a divorced or separated wife to regain all rights over her property and wealth.

There was no shortage of opposition to the bill, not least from the High Anglicans in Parliament who despaired of any measure that might encourage divorce for fear of the disintegration of society that would surely follow. But further complications arose from an unlikely source: competition from another female activist. Barbara Leigh Smith (later Bodichon) was of radical middle-class stock and a natural political organiser. Inspired by Caroline's writings, she began to publish her own pamphlets and with her progressive outfit the Langham Place group, whose mission was to fight for women's education, employment and legal rights, she worked with Lord Brougham's Law Amendment Society to bring forward a Married Women's Property Bill, aimed at granting women the right to retain their own property after marriage.

The natural solution was surely to join forces, but the two women never even met, and moral queasiness seems to have been to blame. The Langham Place group disapproved of Caroline's scandalous taint and the use of her personal life in her polemics, and, despite her denials, saw a self-interestedness in her motives. Little wonder then, perhaps, that Caroline so demonstrably dissociated herself from the feminist movement of which Barbara Leigh Smith was a prominent part; they had rejected her, so she would reject them. Women's rights might have taken quicker strides if they hadn't, but as it was, the two bills jostled for attention at the same time, and it was the more radical Married Women's Property Bill that fell by the wayside.

So after three years of ferocious pamphleteering, antagonistic debate, and umming and aahing over the intricacies of the divorce and separation bill, it was the Matrimonial Causes Act that was passed by Parliament on 28 August 1857 – though only by a tiny margin. Lord Lyndhurst had spoken passionately and persuasively in the House, reading out passages from Caroline's pamphlets to illustrate his points. And although the new law had won out by dint of being progressive but not *too* progressive, and would only benefit those who could afford the legal fees, it was a vital step forward nonetheless. In the country's new dedicated secular courts, an Act of Parliament would no longer be needed for divorce, making it far more accessible, while the act itself contained four feminist clauses that derived directly from Caroline's pamphlets: a separated wife could now protect her earnings and property from her husband; in accordance with the Custody of Infants Act, she could be granted custody and visiting rights of her children as well as alimony payments; she could inherit or bequeath property as though she were a single woman ('*feme sole*'); and she now had the power to sue or be sued, and to sign contracts in her own right. If she were accused of adultery in a criminal conversation trial, she could now defend herself, and cite cruelty as a factor in a divorce.[121] Thanks in large part to Caroline's tenacious lobbying, separated wives now had a visibility and level of protection in law that they had never had before.

It was a painful irony, then, that this new act still didn't enable Caroline to divorce George – she had written proof of his cruelty, yet the law continued to view her return to him decades before as a conclusive pardon. It did, however, legally entitle her to sign a proper deed of separation, and so she triggered negotiations the moment the Matrimonial Causes Act became law in January 1858. George and his lawyers twisted and turned as always, for over 18 months, and then something peculiar happened. A chance meeting between the Nortons at the steam packet ticket office turned into a miraculously civil and productive encounter; they 'talked matters over without lawyers and agreed to sign and seal and settle and have done with grievous battling and uncertainties'.[122] The deed was duly drawn up without aggravation, and the conditions clearly laid out: Caroline would receive an allowance of £400 a year and a one-off payment of £1,000 to cover arrears, and could now live 'separate and apart from [her husband] as if she was sole and unmarried', with a right to her own money and property, 'free from the powers and command, restraint, control, authority and government of him'. On 2 September 1859, after 25 years of bluster and fury, both husband and wife calmly signed the deed and legally untied the knot that bound them.

Suddenly, it was done. Caroline had managed to extricate herself from the biggest mistake of her life, and the decades of exhaustive quarrelling and bitter mud-slinging were at an end. She may not have been free to marry again, but at the age of 51, she was at last free of George Norton.

LOST AND SAVED

The great struggle of Caroline's life was over, but less than three weeks after signing the deed of separation came a worrying letter from Fletcher, now based at the British embassy in Paris. He played it down, but he was spitting blood, and by the time Caroline reached him on 19 September 1859, he was in a pitiful state – thin and feeble, coughing incessantly and unable to sleep for the aching in his bones. He wept when he saw his mother, and over the following weeks, as he wasted away in front of her, she nursed and tried to comfort him. On 13 October, when he was 30 years old, her sweet, fragile boy died in her arms.

Caroline was 'stunned'. To lose a second child left her utterly bewildered; she wrote to friends of 'what a blank all is with me', that 'all the pleasant part of life' had gone.[123] But there was more pain to come. In April 1863, her enduring friend Sir William Stirling Maxwell, a Scottish art historian and Tory MP whom she had long wished to marry, married another woman. Caroline had met Sir William in the late 1840s and found him kind and dependable – everything George Norton wasn't – and although his wife, Lady Anna, became a close friend, their union still hurt. Then, in June 1867, Caroline lost her sister Helen, too – a failed mastectomy led to an extremely painful death from cancer, which Caroline could hardly bear to witness.

Her most attritional ordeal during the 1860s and '70s, however, was with her son Brin. In 1853, when he was 21, he had scandalised the family by marrying an illiterate 'peasant girl' in Capri, Maria Federigo. Caroline was easily reconciled to this – she found Maria, or Mariuccia as they called her, sweet and intelligent. Harder to accept was that, over the years, as if to quash any lingering doubts about his parentage, Brin was growing more and more like George. Nervous, ill, indolent and disturbed, he flitted from Brittany to England to Capri, perennially unable to settle, and showed little interest in his two children. Then came the habitual drinking, which led to 'cause-less rages' and violent outbursts aimed at both Mariuccia and his mother. It was all so horribly familiar: 'I can scarcely give you a better idea of the life I led with my husband than by describing my life with my son', Caroline told Lady Anna Stirling Maxwell.[124] But there could be no turning her back on her only surviving child; instead, she pitied Brin's 'strange confused hypochondriacal state of mind' and tried to manage the paranoia that made him distrust his family and fear he was being poisoned.[125] Since George had mostly washed his hands of his son, it fell to Caroline to cover Brin's medical bills, support his family and help look after his children.

She continued to write poems and novels throughout the 1860s, often with her own scarred life buried in the subtext, though the Victorian public were proving harder and harder to please. Her 1863 novel *Lost and Saved* divided readers with its story of an innocent teenage girl who is tricked into an elopement and then abandoned, pregnant and ruined, but who manages to claw back her independence and her reputation. To some, this was gritty realism – Caroline's best work; others balked at the notion that a woman, once 'lost', could ever be 'saved'. Caroline had lived this story of ruin and recovery – she knew women could not be so easily categorised into virgin or whore – but Victorian culture, which canonised the wife as the 'angel in the house', couldn't countenance the redemption of the fallen woman as anything other than immorality rewarded. The public took fright and sales began to wane, so much so that Caroline felt compelled to write a defence of the work in the press – a move that only made sales drop further.

By the time her final novel, *Old Sir Douglas*, appeared in 1867, Caroline was weary of justifying herself and beginning to feel the effects of ill health, so she decided the time had come to stop writing. This included pamphleteering, so when the Married Women's Property Act reappeared for debate in 1870, Caroline didn't enter the fray. Perhaps, though, as it passed into law on 9 August that year, allowing married women to keep possession of their earnings, and to inherit property that wasn't held in trust, as well as up to £200 in cash, she felt some satisfaction that they had at last been granted some of the rights she had argued for back in the 1850s. The battle for women's legal equality was finally underway, but Caroline, who had worked so hard to win those vital first victories, was now in her sixties, tired and ill, so she passed the baton to younger, fitter warriors to continue the fight.[126]

On 24 February 1875, while Caroline was in Capri visiting Brin, George Norton died of liver disease at Wonersh, swiftly followed by Lord Grantley on 27 August, at the ages of 74 and 79 respectively. Their obituaries were terse and unenthusiastic, and, gratifyingly, remembered them chiefly as 'the husband of the well-known authoress'[127] and brother-in-law of the 'brilliant' Mrs Norton. They noted, too, that in their unhappy dealings with her, 'public opinion generally was on the side of the lady'.[128] Perhaps it's poetic justice that these 'gentlemen', whose only achievements in life amounted to using their wealth, power and brutality to torment an unprotected lady, should go down in history as the triggers for dramatic legal improvements to the lot of all women. No doubt they would have been livid.[129]

Caroline was in her late sixties before a little joy finally came her way – and it would be brief. By now she was virtually housebound, creaky and stiff with rheumatism, yet rumours of her love life were still circling. As she was now a free woman, the talk was that she planned to marry Sir William Stirling Maxwell, who, following the tragic early death of Lady Anna in February 1874, was also now a widower. The gossips were right, and on 1 March 1877, after 30 years of unfaltering friendship, these two world-weary veterans made the most optimistic of commitments. At the age of 69, Caroline acknowledged that it was 'very, very late in life' to 'welcome happiness and peace', and after all she had endured, it was a revelation. 'If you knew the years and years of alienation,' she wrote to a friend, 'of being ashamed of one's name and persecuted to the last ... to live in dread, and then suddenly to change to real "home" and real love and be proud and grateful, after so much suffering – you would not wonder I have accepted my good lot and cling to the giver.'[130]

Just months after the marriage, however, on 15 June 1877, Caroline died of jaundice and peritonitis. And once she was gone, they fell like dominoes: Brin, who had been too ill to attend her funeral, died six weeks later on 24 July, followed by Sir William, who died from typhus seven months after his new wife.

Caroline's obituaries were several degrees warmer than George's had been, though they also insisted on dredging up the Melbourne scandal. Her notoriety ensured that she was quickly immortalised in the novels of the day,[131] while the *Athenaeum* magazine assured its readers that she was 'one of the women of our time who have left a name not soon to be forgotten'. It was wrong about that. Today, Caroline is not ranked alongside Mary Shelley and Charles Dickens as one of the great nineteenth-century writers. Like much Victorian melodrama, her books – so highly praised and popular in their day – had fallen out of fashion and out of print by the end of the century. But then Caroline's greatest achievement was not as a poet or a novelist. It was as a survivor, a fighter and a political campaigner that she made a lasting impact on the world – though even that has been largely forgotten.

If she's remembered at all it's for the sordid scandal that marred her youth and the interminable struggles with her husband that consumed almost her entire life. Indeed, had she married a different man she might have been just another successful writer and society wit – and, for her, that would have been enough. A fighter by necessity rather than nature, she had no aspirations to be a legal crusader or a pioneer of women's rights, but her blighted existence with George Norton pushed her to it. Once she understood the grave injustices of a married woman's life, her outrage demanded that she stand up and shout about them. Many women before her had suffered the same and stayed silent, too frightened, too disenfranchised, too overwhelmed to speak out. Caroline's only advantage was that she was a rebel spirit, blooood with courage, means, cleverness and contacts. And she would use them wisely. Facing down disapproval and defying every insult, she would roar out her message loud and clear to force lawmakers to acknowledge, for the first time in British history, that she and every other married woman existed – and that they deserved to be both seen and heard.

A reluctant, inadvertent feminist, Caroline Norton nonetheless changed women's lives. Every wife, every mother, every divorced or separated woman who faces her own George Norton in Britain today owes her a great debt of gratitude. Branded a harlot in her own time, she is a true heroine in ours.

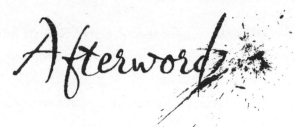

UNFINISHED BUSINESS

'The growing good of the world is partly dependent on unhistoric acts; and that things are not so ill with you and me as they might have been, is half owing to the number who lived faithfully a hidden life, and rest in unvisited tombs.'

MARY ANN EVANS ('GEORGE ELIOT'), *MIDDLEMARCH*, 1871

The stories in this book are just eight out of millions – eight precious women who snuck into the records through the back door of history, most of whom now lie in unmarked graves or unvisited tombs, their lives forgotten, their achievements ignored. Their 'unhistoric acts' may not have made it into the textbooks, but instead they did something even more valuable: helping to demolish, bit by bit, the towering walls that have hemmed in women for millennia, nudging us ever closer to where we now stand.

And in the wake of a frenetic century of particularly dramatic progress, it's all too easy to feel complacent. Today, we enjoy rights and freedoms that these women could scarcely dream of. We are less trammelled by the confines of our gender than we have ever been. At long last, both men and women are realising that the arbitrary rules we've imposed upon ourselves only hinder rather than help us, and that when we discard them, society doesn't disintegrate; in fact, it flourishes. In an age when intelligence, talent, ambition, grit, desire and courage are not just seen as masculine traits, but as human traits, surely we can pat ourselves on the back and say our work here is done?

It's a nice idea, but if recent times have shown us anything it's that progress can stumble backwards as well as forwards, attitudes can be rewound, hard-won rights can be rescinded – and true parity suddenly looks a long way off when confronted with the cold, hard stats. In the UK in 2019, for example, the gender pay gap still stands stubbornly at an average of 17.9 per cent.[1] Only 208 out of our 650 MPs are female (a record high, at just 32 per cent),[2] as are only six CEOs in the FTSE 100.[3] Having been held back for so long at the start, women, it seems, are forever having to play catch-up. The picture looks even more grim when we consider the reality of modern-day sexual dynamics. When two women on average are murdered every week by their partner,[4] when opinionated women receive a barrage of rape and death threats from online trolls, when a proud pussy-grabber gets voted into the White House and millions of women around the world say #MeToo about being sexually harassed, we really should take the hint that misogyny is alive and well in Western society and that the work is by no means done. As the struggle to gain respect and equality for women continues the world over, is it any wonder that we find ourselves looking to the past for a little inspiration to help us keep going?

That's one reason why the current enthusiasm for reclaiming women's rightful place in history mustn't be a passing fad. The stories we tell about our collective past matter – they seep into our conscious-ness, shape our cultural understanding, and influence how we define ourselves and our experiences. And if those stories are only ever about men, then the tale will only ever be half told, and the cycle of excluding women continues. It may not seem like much, but by retrieving women's lives from the dustbin, brushing them off and sending them out into the world, we can at least rebalance the history books and, quite literally, change the narrative.

These lost stories deserve to be unearthed, talked about, remembered and learned from, not least because if we're ever to fully combat the inequalities and misogyny of today, and understand why we're still having to deal with them, we have to understand where it all comes from. To fathom just how deeply entrenched gender inequality is in our culture, and to acknowledge the ignorant and misguided principles upon which it was originally based, is half the battle won.

Perhaps we haven't made quite as much progress as we thought we had, and in such moments, the prospect of trying to unpick thousands of years' worth of damage may seem overwhelming, but if the life stories of these women show us anything, it's that we should never be daunted by the task ahead. Our individual efforts may seem small, insignificant, unhistoric. We may be ridiculed, abused and told to shut up. But we already know that if we persist – if we take heed and take heart from the past; if we notice, challenge, disrupt and question; if we call out the injustices, smash up the rules and redraw the templates – then before we know it, we'll have an army of Roaring Girls demanding to be heard, who can no longer be ignored.

When quoting from the same source extensively, the edition has been credited once, at the first instance, to avoid obtrusive page references.

INTRODUCTION

1   More common were Roaring Boys or 'Roarers' – roisterers, thieves and trouble-makers who became a recurrent feature of sixteenth- and seventeenth-century litera-ture, particularly Jacobean city drama. These stock characters suggested either boisterous young gallants who drunkenly brawled, rioted and swore in the streets or lower-class tricksters and thieves, upsetting the veneer of civility and social order as they went. They make notable appearances in Nathaniel Field's *Amends for Ladies* (1611), Ben Jonson's *Bartholomew Fair* (1614), the 1622 edition of Middleton and Rowley's tragicomedy *A Fair Quarrel* and Philip Massinger's *The City Madam* (1632). The 1626 broadside ballad *The Cheating Age* describes one Roaring Boy as a 'grim rascal' fresh from Newgate who swindles the balladeer out of his money, while *Overbury's Characters* (1615) describes another who 'cheats young gulls that are newly come to town', is a 'supervisor to brothels' and 'sleeps with a tobacco-pipe in's mouth'. Mary Frith appears to be their first and only female counterpart in the drama of the period, and

given their prevailingly negative connota-tions, the playwrights' depiction of her in *The Roaring Girl* as a paragon of virtue seems all the more radical.

2   This legal obliteration of wives remained in place long into the nineteenth century. As William Blackstone put it in his *Commentaries on the Laws of England* (1765–9), 'By marriage the husband and wife are one person in law, that is, the very being or legal existence of the wife is suspended during the marriage, or at least is incorporated and consolidated into that of the husband.'

3   The 1632 document *The Law's Resolutions of Women's Rights* explains this particular law succinctly enough in the titles to Section VIII – 'That which a husband hath is his own' – and Section IX – 'That which the wife hath is the husband's'.

4   Ephesians 5:22–24.

5   Although the statistics suggest that women ran only a 6–7 per cent risk of dying in childbirth in the eighteenth century, it was in practice 'probably the single most common cause of death in women aged twenty-five to thirty-four, accounting for one in five of all deaths in

this age group', and because every woman would likely know of at least one woman who had died either in childbirth itself or from infection contracted soon after it, their fear of it was real and tangible, albeit magnified. See Amanda Vickery, *The Gentleman's Daughter: Women's Lives in Georgian England* (Yale, 1999), pp.97–98.

6   Anne Laurence, *Women in England 1500–1760: A Social History* (Phoenix, 1996), p.34.

7   In his 1728 pamphlet *Augusta Triumphans*, Daniel Defoe wrote of his despair at the prevalence of this practice, condemning the rise in private madhouses, where treacherous husbands dumped their discarded wives. 'If they are not mad when they go into these cursed houses', he wrote, 'they are soon made so by the barbarous usage they there suffer.' Catharine Arnold, *Bedlam: London and Its Mad* (Simon & Schuster, 2008), p.125.

8   Wife sales were not common or legal, but they went on – there were at least 300 recorded cases in the eighteenth and nineteenth centuries, and the prices involved were often meagre – shillings rather than pounds. They hardly ever took place before the eighteenth century, but one was recorded as late as 1928. See Vickery, *Suffragettes Forever! The Story of Women and Power* (BBC) and Laurence, 1996, p.54.

9   Laurence, 1996, p.55.

10   All of these punishments were particularly common practice during the seventeenth century. The use of the scold's bridle, also known as the branks, was first recorded in Scotland in 1567 and was most prevalent during the seventeenth century, but its usage continued into the late eighteenth century.

11   Witchcraft first became a felony in England in 1542 under Henry VIII, and the first woman known to be hanged for it was Agnes Waterhouse at Chelmsford in 1566. Witchcraft trials were at their peak, particularly in Scotland, at the turn of the seventeenth century under the influence of witch-obsessive James VI, later James I of England, with panics also occurring in Lancashire in 1612 and Essex in the 1645. Collectively, this led to thousands of women – usually lower-class widows and spinsters – being hanged or burned in the UK for this non-existent crime. In 1712, Jane Wenham became the last woman in England to be condemned for witchcraft, though she received a reprieve, while the last woman to be burned for it in Scotland was Janet Horne in 1727, before it officially ceased to be a capital crime in 1736. Burning women for other capital crimes, however, continued until 1790. See capitalpunishmentuk.org; Catharine Arnold, *Underworld London: Crime and Punishment in the Capital City* (Simon & Schuster, 2013), p.176.

12   As Mary Beard explains in her pocket-rocket volume *Women and Power* (Profile Books, 2017), the ancient world has bequeathed us a problematic legacy in this respect. In life, women were barred from political discourse and, like slaves, denied formal political rights, while in literature they were often metaphorically or physically silenced: from the moment Telemachus tells his mother Penelope to shut up in Homer's *Odyssey* to the many rape victims of Classical mythology who are mutilated or transformed into mute beasts to prevent them from accusing their attackers.

13   See the work of psychologists, neuroscientists and journalists such as Cordelia Fine, Gina Rippon, Lise Eliot and Angela Saini for the evidence that is debunking many of the powerful myths that have long misinformed our gender politics, telling us that men and women's brains have evolved differently.

14   1 Corinthians 11:3–9.

15   Today, women who display an absence of solidarity towards other women might be termed 'footsoldiers of the patriarchy', to borrow a phrase from feminist writer Mona Eltahawy, who is particularly coura-

geous at calling out this kind of anti-feminism in the modern world.

16   See cartoonist Jacky Fleming's 2016 book *The Trouble with Women*.

17   Virginia Woolf, *A Room of One's Own*, 1929 (Penguin, 2004), p.88.

18· Oxford English Dictionary.

19   The term 'feminism' derives from the French *féminisme*, coined in 1837 by French socialist Charles Fourier. It didn't enter common parlance in Britain until the mid-1890s.

MARY FRITH

1   St Paul's Cross was the open-air pulpit in the churchyard of old St Paul's Cathedral. It was London's most important public pulpit where state and religious news were broadcast, preachers and dissidents sermonised and sinners did penance.

2   In the absence of pockets in Jacobean clothing, money was usually kept in a small leather pouch or purse that hung from the waist by a string. All a thief had to do was cut the string and they had the purse, hence the nickname 'cutpurses'.

3   Laurence, 1996, p.166.

4   In the seventeenth century, before the novel had fully developed, the biographies or supposed autobiographies of notorious criminals and adventurers such as Mary Frith, the highwayman James Hind or the 'counterfeit' princess, thief and bigamist Mary Carleton emerged as the true-crime bestsellers of their day – lurid tales that offered plenty of thrills and embellishments, and a bit of moral instruction, too. The trend reached its peak in the eighteenth century, as sham autobiography morphed into the earliest novels, the first being Daniel Defoe's *Robinson Crusoe* (1719) and *Moll Flanders* in 1722.

5   All quotes from Randall S. Nakayama (ed.), *The Life and Death of Mrs Mary Frith: commonly called Moll Cutpurse*, 1662 (Garland, 1993), unless otherwise stated.

6   The fact that, in her will, Mary Frith made her niece Frances Edmonds her executrix suggests that she had at least one sibling, whose family she was close to, though they get no mention in any sources.

7   The number of capital offences in England had risen from three (theft, murder and treason) to 11 in around 1540, during Henry VIII's reign, and with the introduction of the brutal legal system known as 'the Bloody Code' in the late seventeenth century, that number rose even higher. By 1688, there were 50 crimes that would earn you execution; by 1699 the Shoplifting Act decreed that the theft of property over the value of five shillings was punishable by death and by 1765, 160 crimes carried the death sentence, including the theft of any item worth over one shilling. See Arnold, 2013, pp.48 and 121.

8   Gustav Ungerer, 'Mary Frith, Alias Moll Cutpurse, in Life and Literature', *Shakespeare Studies*, Vol.28 (2000), pp.62–4.

9   The name Moll as a pet form of Mary held seedy connotations, equating Mary's thievery, and undoubtedly her cross-dressing, with whoredom.

10   England and the Netherlands appear to have had the highest number of cases of female transvestism in Europe during this period, with at least 50 authentic cases recorded in the former and 119 in the latter, most during the seventeenth and eighteenth centuries. As seafaring nations that were frequently at war, both countries offered ample opportunity for women to run away to become soldiers and sailors (see 'Hannah Snell', Chapter 5). More often than not, the women who did it were poor and unmarried, just like Mary Frith, and usually young – their high voices, smooth faces and slight figures passing easily for those of pubescent boys. Many of these women were also aware that they were part of a trend, citing in their defence the fact that other women had done the same. See Rudolf M. Dekker and Lotte C. van de Pol, *The Tradition of Female*

Transvestism in Early Modern Europe (Macmillan Press, 1989).

11 Beard, 2017, p.54.

12 These strict gendered distinctions of dress didn't apply straight away. Babies of both sexes were dressed in gowns for the first few years of their lives. The differentiation only began, with some ceremony, when, anytime between the ages of two and eight, boys would be 'breeched' – put in breeches for the first time. The practice of 'breeching' went on until the late nineteenth/early twentieth century, when the concept of keeping boys in dresses beyond babyhood faded out.

13 Deuteronomy 22:5.

14 Men were at it, too, during this period, though not in the same numbers as women. One in particular is mentioned in Mary Frith's 'diary': Aniseed-Water Robin, a so-called hermaphrodite 'as remarkable' as Mary, whom she apparently took against as a threat to her crown – he was 'a kind of mockery ... of me', she says, who had been sent 'into the world to mate and match me, that nothing might be without a peer'. The disdain reserved for this character is unsurprising. Today, cross-dressing is more often associated with men, but consistent from that day to this has been the extra scorn men have received for adopting the practice, for the supposed crime of emasculating themselves and imitating that which is beneath them.

15 Letter from John Chamberlain to Sir Dudley Carleton, 25 January 1620, Norman Egbert McClure (ed.), *The Letters of John Chamberlain* (The American Philosophical Society, 1939), Vol.2, pp.286–7.

16 *Hic Mulier* was the first of these pamphlets, which condemned cross-dressing women as monsters and whores who had flouted the rules of custom. It provoked a response a week later, in *Haec Vir*, in which a cross-dressing woman passionately proclaims her freedom to dress how she wants, arguing against the arbitrary and irrational diktats of gender convention, because 'Custom is an Idiot'. (She also, however, takes aim at effeminate men, somewhat damaging her impressively right-on credentials.) See Linda Woodbridge, *Women and the English Renaissance: Literature and the Nature of Womankind*, 1540–1620 (University of Illinois Press, 1984), pp.139–51.

17 Chamberlain to Sir Dudley Carleton, 25 January 1620 (1939), pp.286–7.

18 See Jean E. Howard, 'Cross-dressing, the Theatre and Gender Struggle in Early Modern England', *Shakespeare Quarterly*, Vol.39, No.4 (Winter 1988), pp.418–40; Ungerer, 2000, p.66.

19 In the Netherlands, in the eighteenth century, there were parallel cases of female thieves using cross-dressing to aid their nefarious deeds. Female members of the Bokkenrijders Band, for example, thieved and even tortured victims during raids alongside men. Such stories only reinforced the connection between transvestism and criminality. See Dekker and van de Pol, 1989, p.35.

20 Frank Kermode, *The Age of Shakespeare* (Phoenix, 2005), p.28.

21 *The Roaring Girl*, Prologue, 1–30, James Knowles and Eugene Giddens (eds), *The Roaring Girl and Other City Comedies* (Oxford University Press, 2001).

22 Ibid., Scene 1, 95–7.

23 Ibid., Scene 2, 125–8, 134, 213–14.

24 Ibid., Scene 4, 129.

25 Ibid., Scene 11, 216–17.

26 Ibid., Scene 4, 192.

27 In the drama that has come down to us, Dekker and Middleton's portrayal of a notorious contemporary figure is unique, as are her characteristics. The closest we can get to a stage antecedent for Moll Cutpurse is in the lost play *Long Meg*, dating from around 1594/5, which was based on another sword-fighting, cross-dressing folk heroine, known only through tales and a 'jest-biography' entitled *Long Meg of Westminster*, and who may or may not have been real. In the legend of Long

Meg, however, there are some crucial differences between her and Moll. Meg's cross-dressing is occasional and for a specific purpose, and at the end of her story she conforms to a conventional submissive marriage. It's always possible that with Long Meg featuring in the popular ballads and plays of her childhood, Mary Frith grew up hearing tales of this fabled woman and drew some inspiration from her. See Dekker and Middleton, *The Roaring Girl*, Paul A. Mulholland (ed.), (Manchester University Press, 1990), Introduction, pp.15–17.

28 See Howard, 1988, pp.418–40.

29 'Gaskins' was another name for a gentleman's voluminous hose or breeches. A 'gaskin-bride' therefore refers to a bride in wide breeches.

30 The concept of Moll Cutpurse as a defender of women was taken up by the 1662 chapbook (pamphlet) version of *The Life and Death and Mrs Mary Frith*, which was entitled *The Woman's Champion; or The Strange Wonder*.

31 *The Roaring Girl*, Scene 5, 67–107.

32 Ibid., Scene 10, 322–3.

33 Middleton and Dekker revel in these saucy gender games in *The Roaring Girl*, for instance when Moll happens upon Sebastian and Mary canoodling. For this secret assignation, Mary has disguised herself as a page, and contrary to the refrain in the play that a woman dressed as a man is repellent, Sebastian is positively turned on by kissing Mary in drag: 'Methinks a woman's lip tastes well in a doublet,' he croons. The scene becomes even more provocative when the playwrights consciously break the illusion and remind their audience that in fact they are witnessing – undoubtedly with a frisson of the forbidden – two male players kissing, a point teasingly made by Moll: 'How strange this shows, one man to kiss another.' (Scene 8, lines 46–8.) Strange to the characters in the play, maybe, but not to the audience. When the character

Goshawk later says that 'it was never known, / Two men were married and conjoined in one', he and the audience can share a chuckle, knowing that, in fact, it happened at the end of every stage comedy. (Scene 11, lines 107–8.)

34 Ibid., Epilogue, 35–8.

35 Perhaps the most tantalising element of this appearance is that it implies Mary became personally acquainted with Jacobean London's players and playwrights and worked closely with them. With contacts such as Middleton, Dekker, Henslowe and Alleyn, it's possible, even likely, that she knew, or at least brushed shoulders with, Shakespeare, too.

36 Aristocratic women performed at private court masques in the early seventeenth century (and before), but Mary Frith appears to be the first woman known to have performed on the public stage in Britain, some 50 years before the first professional female actresses were officially allowed to do so at the Restoration of Charles II.

37 *A Counterblast to Tobacco* was King James I's tirade against the newly fashionable and expensive habit of smoking. A clay pipeful cost three pence – three times more than a theatre ticket – and Mary Frith was an early female adopter (though not, as claimed in her diary, the first). Kermode, 2004, p.27.

38 *Consistory of London Correction Book*, 27 January 1612, *Counterfeit Ladies: The Life and Death of Mal Cutpurse; The Case of Mary Carleton*, Janet Todd and Elizabeth Spearing (eds), (William Pickering, 1994), Introduction, pp.xiv–xv.

39 Ungerer, 2000, p.58.

40 *Consistory of London Correction Book*, 27 January 1612, Todd and Spearing (eds), 1994, Introduction, pp.xiv–xv.

41 In the early seventeenth century, old St Paul's was a place where all manner of folk gathered to barter, buy, gossip and steal. A stew pot of society, the nave and central aisle of the cathedral, known as St

Paul's Walk, would roil with prosperous merchants, businessmen, booksellers, tobacconists, beggars, prostitutes, hawkers, pamphleteers – and thieves like Mary.

42   *Consistory of London Correction Book*, 27 January 1612, Todd and Spearing (eds), 1994, Introduction, pp.xiv–xv.

43   Ibid., p.xv.

44   The anecdote in question tells of a woman who had made a respectable marriage but had a wandering eye. With Mary working as her madam, she was prostituted out to various men – merchants, doctors, knights, noblemen – and on her deathbed felt compelled to confess to her husband that all but one of their 12 children were not fathered by him. When faced with the cuckold's wrath, Mary 'bid him be quiet' and told him that 'if he would follow my advice I would make him a gainer by his hard fortunes, which I effected by procuring him round sums of money from his respective rivals to the maintenance of their illegitimate issue, which they honestly paid; and all was hushed up in a contented secrecy.' It's an entertaining tale, though one that bears the faint hallmarks of absurdity and invention.

45   *Consistory of London Correction Book*, 27 January 1612, Todd and Spearing (eds), 1994, Introduction, p.xv.

46   Penance in a white sheet usually took place in a church or some other public space such as St Paul's Cross, and required the penitent to stand or kneel, bare-headed and barefooted, swathed in a white sheet and holding either a candle or the 'white rod of discipline', while listening to a sermon denouncing their sin. They were then expected to confess, apologise and ask God's forgiveness. The practice can be traced back to the Middle Ages and continued even into the nineteenth century. Today, although the medium may have changed to trial by media, the spirit of public shaming continues.

47   The drunkard's cloak was a barrel with holes cut into it for the offender's head

and arms to pass through, so that they could 'wear' it as a punishment for drunkenness. 'Carting', or being paraded through the town on a cart (or sometimes backwards on a horse) wearing a placard that named your crime, was reserved for fornication and incest, while the stocks and the pillory were meted out for a variety of offences.

48   Letter from John Chamberlain to Sir Dudley Carleton, 12 February 1612, McClure (ed.), 1939, Vol.1, p.334. It's worth noting that Chamberlain refers to Mary as 'Mall Cut-purse', not Mary Frith. By now, the real woman had been eclipsed by her alter-ego.

49   Ungerer 2000, pp.54 and 69.

50   *The Roaring Girl*, Scene 11, 158–64.

51   It is possible, however, that Mary was one of the first women to visit tobacco shops. These establishments were reserved for men, and yet frequenting them was listed among her misdemeanours in the Bishop of London's court as yet another example of her insubordination and debauchery. See Ungerer 2000, p.61.

52   William Banks was a Scottish entertainer who had been famed during the 1590s for having a dancing horse named Marocco. He settled in London as a wine merchant during the 1630s, which would date this anecdote to sometime during Mary's mid-forties.

53   Nothing is known of Mary's husband, Lewknor Markham, although it has been speculated that he may have been the son of the poet, writer and playwright Gervase Markham. If that were the case, Mary may well have met him through the theatre.

54   In the diary, Mary lies on her deathbed at the age of 74. Her death was recorded in 1659, yet the introduction states that she was born in 1589, which would have made her 70 at her death. Scholars have settled on 1585 as the more likely birth date. See Ungerer (2000), p.48.

55   The diary has Mary as a resolutely single woman, though it presents a

muddied and misogynistic picture of why. The introduction first suggests that Mary was 'not made for the pleasure or delight of man' – in other words, she was too ugly to attract one – but then changes tack, arguing that it was because she had no sexual interest in men. Mary is now single and celibate by choice, until another contradiction links her to a shoemaker who 'squandered away' her money. It was this bad experience, the writer now insists, along with 'such other like chouses [cheats] and tricks', that put her off the idea of marriage. As these wayward motives show, a single woman was a bewildering concept to the seventeenth-century mind.

56 *The Roaring Girl*, Scene 4, lines 35–8.

57 Ungerer, 2000, p.59.

58 When questioned in court, Mary hazarded a guess that she and Markham had been married 'about some seven years sithence', while the plaintiff's attorney brought to light that the couple had not lived together 'this ten years or thereabouts', which in 1624 would equate to the full length of their marriage. The deliberate opacity that Mary encouraged regarding her married state might also account for its omission from her biography. See Ungerer, 2000, p.70.

59 Bridewell Court Books, Vol.9/129; Ungerer, 2000, p.71

60 Robert Burton, *The Anatomy of Melancholy*, 1621, Vol. I, p.87.

61 See Ungerer 2000, p.71. We know Mary wasn't averse to a bit of sham acting, but if she was faking insanity to escape the unrest, it couldn't have been a great success. Bedlam was hardly much of a refuge, and she was released long before the hostilities were over.

62 Westover treated 44 women and 14 men for mental disorders. Thirty of those women were diagnosed as 'melancholic', compared with 11 men; six female patients were considered to be suffering from 'hysteria'. Eight women were judged 'mad' or 'distracted', compared with three men.

The Casebook of John Westover of Wedmore, Surgeon, 1686–1700, transcribed by William G. Hill; Laurence, 1996, p.98.

63 See Arnold, 2008, pp.217–18.

64 Donald Lupton, quoted in Jonathan Andrews, Asa Briggs, Roy Porter, Penny Tucker and Keir Waddington, *The History of Bethlem* (Routledge, 1997), p.51.

65 The sense of social responsibility associated with Puritanism did lead to some improvements at Bethlem hospital around the time of Mary's confinement. A year before she was discharged, in June 1643, the court of governors ordered the hospital to be enlarged, and over the following year extra accommodation for 20 more patients was built. The governors also began to implement a system of random inspections to try to maintain decent standards. After one such inspection, it was decreed on 18 July 1646, two years after Mary had left, 'that no officer or servant shall give any blows or ill-language to any of the mad folks on pain of losing his place'– suggesting that, until then, these were common occurrences. See Arnold, 2008, p.77.

66 Other literature of the period suggests Mary may have joined hundreds of women who petitioned and blockaded Parliament in August 1643, demonstrating for peace. The politician and writer Henry Neville, who sided with the Parliamentarians during the Civil War, places Moll Cutpurse at a similar scene in his 1647 satirical pamphlet *The Parliament of Ladies*, in which he jokes that the 'forces of the city' were 'under the command of Mall Cutpurse and Mall Sebran', who, 'being there placed with pipes in both their mouths, with fire and smoke in a very short time, had almost choked both the passage and the passengers'. He appears to have been taking aim both at Royalist supporters and women's involvement in politics. Ungerer, 2000, p.72.

67 The publishers of *The Life and Death of Mrs Mary Frith* and its chapbook, William Gilbertson and George Horton,

had already made a career of rebranding famous criminals in the wake of their king's execution, such as the highwayman James Hind, morphing them into Royalist folk heroes and champions of the poor, exploited and oppressed. Now, it seems, they and their team of hack writers would do the same for Mary Frith. See Ungerer, 2000, pp.44–6 and 49–52.

68 In 1664, a two-room house in Fetter Lane with a shop, cellar, kitchen, two chambers and a garret could be let for £14 a year with a £10 premium. See also Gregory King's 'Scheme of income and expenses of the several families of England' of 1688 – a tabulation of various incomes by profession, which though unreliable in its figures gives a rough idea of the hierarchy of wealth in late-seventeenth-century London. Liza Picard, *Restoration London: Everyday Life in London 1660–1670* (Phoenix, 2003), p.19; pp.248–9.

69 *The Roaring Girl* vanished from theatres for centuries after the early 1600s, before finally resurfacing for performance in the 1950s, and again in 1983 for a Royal Shakespeare Company production in which Helen Mirren starred as Moll. As it stands, the last woman to play her in the UK was Lisa Dillon in the RSC's 2014 production.

70 Daniel Defoe, *Moll Flanders*, 1722, G.A. Starr (ed.), (Oxford University Press, 1998), p.201.

71 Alexander Smith has it in his 1719 work *A Complete History of the Lives and Robberies of the Most Notorious Highwaymen, Footpads, Shoplifts and Cheats of Both Sexes* that Mary Frith held up Thomas Fairfax, commander-in-chief of the New Model Army, on Hounslow Heath, shooting him through the arm and lifting 200 Jacobuses (a gold coin worth 25 shillings, minted during the reign of James I) from his purse, landing her in Newgate Prison. It appears to be pure fiction, another opportunity to paint Mary as a heroic scourge of the Parliamentarians.

MARGARET CAVENDISH

1 Queen Christina of Sweden was famed for her brilliant mind, her strong will and her habit of wearing men's clothes. In 1654 she shocked the whole of Europe when she abdicated the throne, only to make later attempts to reclaim it and become queen of Naples and Poland, too. Pepys's reference to such a queen would have pleased Margaret, but it carried barbed suggestions of notoriety and extravagance.

2 *The Diary of Samuel Pepys, Vol.VIII, 1667*, Robert Latham and William Matthews (eds), (HarperCollins, 2000), pp.163–4, 186–7, 196, 209 and 243.

3 *The Diary of John Evelyn, Vol.II*, William Bray (ed.), (J. M. Dent & Sons Ltd, 1907), p.25.

4 Margaret Cavendish, 'A True Relation of My Birth, Breeding, and Life' in *Nature's Pictures Drawn by Fancies Pencil to the Life*, 1656, pp.374 and 385.

5 Cavendish, 'A True Relation of My Birth', 1656, pp.376–7 and 369–70.

6 Cavendish, *Sociable Letters*, 1664, CLXXV.

7 Cavendish, 'A True Relation of My Birth', 1656, p.371.

8 Cavendish, 'To His Excellency the Lord Marquess of Newcastle', *Sociable Letters*, 1664.

9 Cavendish, 'A True Relation of My Birth', 1656, p.387.

10 Margaret loathed violence, not just against humans but animals, too (a rare thing at a time when blood sports were the hobby of almost every fashionable gentleman), so much so that she might even be called an early proponent of animal rights. She would write poems from the perspective of hunted birds and stags, and professed that 'it troubles my conscience to kill a fly'. (Cavendish, 'A True Relation of My Birth', 1656, p.388 and 390.)

11 Margaret's brother, John Lucas, now

head of the family as the legitimate heir, was a particularly unpopular character. As a major local landowner and High Sheriff of Essex since 1636, he had caused growing resentment among the Colchester locals during the 1620s and '30s by enforcing some of the King's most resented levies – collecting the county's ship money, for example (a tax imposed on coastal counties to boost the country's naval defence), which many refused to pay. He would also ruthlessly pursue every last groat he could make out of his tenants, often by litigious means.

12   Cavendish, 'A True Relation of My Birth', 1656, p.372.

13   Ibid., p.374.

14   Ibid., p.374.

15   Ibid., p.375.

16   Cavendish, *Sociable Letters*, 1664, XCIII.

17   Cavendish, *The Life of William, Duke of Newcastle*, 1667, in C. H. Firth (ed.), (John C. Nimmo, 1886), p.88.

18   This assumption is debatable. Given William's age and his past as a womaniser, it's likely that he had contracted venereal disease at some point during his exploits (he offered Sir Kenelm Digby his 'secret recipe' against syphilis) and passed it on to his wife, which could have caused her to become infertile. He was also taking 'powder of vipers' as a 'miracle cure' for impotence, recommended to him by Digby. See Katie Whitaker, *Mad Madge: Margaret Cavendish, Duchess of Newcastle, Royalist, Writer and Romantic* (Chatto & Windus, 2003), pp.104–5 and 113.

19   Cavendish, *Sociable Letters*, 1664, XCIII.

20   During the siege at Colchester in June 1648 that preceded Sir Charles's death, the Lucas family home of St John's Abbey was ransacked again, though this time, as there was nothing left to plunder, the soldiers vented their ire on the only things they could find: first the 'bare walls' and then the family vault, where they smashed up

the tombs of Margaret's recently buried mother and sister. An ugly scene of desecration followed – the soldiers 'scattered the bones about with profane jests' and, in a grotesque act of disdain, even cut off the women's hair, not yet decomposed, and 'wore it in their hats'. (Historical Manuscripts Commission, 12th Report, Appendix, Part IX, pp.27–28.)

21   Cavendish, *Life of William*, 1886, p.49.

22   Cavendish, *Sociable Letters*, 1664, XC.

23   Margaret's physician, Sir Theodore Mayerne, despaired at her wilfulness, though his prescriptions were no better than hers. His prize treatment for melancholy involved more laxative purges, more bleedings, then a course of his 'steel liquor' – a toxic solution made from steel shavings, wine, oil of brimstone, apples, fern roots, flowers, 'nephritic wood', ivory and spices – to be taken daily, for months at a time and for years on end. (Whitaker, 2003, p.114.)

24   Letter from William Cavendish to the Duke of Buckingham, 8 February 1651, 'Letters of the Duke of Newcastle and Colonel Hutchinson', *Notes and Queries*, 7th Series, 8, C. H. Firth (ed.), 1889, pp.422–3.

25   Cavendish, 'A True Relation of My Birth', 1653, pp.379–80.

26   Patricia   Crawford,   'Women's Published Writings 1600–1700', in *Women in English Society 1500–1800*, Mary Prior (ed.), (Methuen, 1985), pp.212–13.

27   The seats of royal authority were gradually being dismantled by Parliament in the early 1640s, and in 1641 the Star Chamber lawcourt was abolished, and with it the country's censorship laws. Parliament intended to replace the laws with its own, but for a short while, a licence was no longer needed to publish a book and a slew of religious and political works ensued. The number of pamphlets and tracts produced increased from 900 in 1640 to 2,000 in 1641 and 4,000 in 1642. Parliament established its own censorship laws with An Ordinance for the Regulating of Printing

in 1643. See Peter Ackroyd, *Civil War: The History of England, Vol.III* (Macmillan, 2014), p.216.

28   Crawford, 1985, p.217.

29   Such was the fate of the first prose fiction by a woman in England. Lady Mary Wroth hit back at Denny, however, with her own satirical verse closely paralleling his own in 'Railing Rimes Returned Upon the Author': 'Your spiteful words against a harmless book / Shows that an ass much like the sire doth look'.

30   Anne Bradstreet seems to be the only other woman writer of the period to attempt to tackle such 'masculine' subjects as politics, history and natural philosophy, including verses on the elements and the four humours of the body, and may have served as inspiration for Margaret. Much of her work was only published after her death in 1672, except her book of poems, *The Tenth Muse Lately Sprung Up in America*, which appeared in England and America in 1650 – supposedly without her knowledge.

31   Cavendish, 'The Poetresses Hasty Resolution', *Poems and Fancies*, 1653.

32   Ibid., 'To the Reader', 1653.

33   Ibid., 'To All Noble and Worthy Ladies', 1653.

34   Ibid., 'To the Reader', 1653.

35   While the sixteenth century had boasted educational nunneries, a brief flurry of learned court ladies (thanks to the sophisticated influence of Catherine of Aragon) and reformers who advocated education for aristocratic women, by Margaret's day women's learning was falling out of favour, particularly for those in the upper classes, who were thought to have no use for it.

36   Ruth Perry, *The Celebrated Mary Astell: An Early English Feminist* (University of Chicago Press, 1986), pp.104–5.

37   Cavendish, 'A True Relation of My Birth', 1656, p.384.

38   Cavendish, 'The Epistle', *The World's Olio*, Book I, Part III, 1655.

39   Cavendish, 'The Clasp', *Poems and Fancies*, 1653.

40   See Whitaker, 2003, pp.167–70, for her argument for Margaret's dyslexia.

41   Cavendish, 'Epistle Dedicatory to Sir Charles Cavendish My Noble Brother-in-Law', *Poems and Fancies*, 1653.

42   Cavendish, 'To All Writing Ladies', *Poems and Fancies*, 1653.

43   Cavendish, 'An Epistle to Mistris Toppe', *Poems and Fancies*, 1653. Toppe was the married name of Margaret's maid and dearest friend Elizabeth Chaplain.

44   Cavendish, 'To All Noble and Worthy Ladies', *Poems and Fancies*, 1653. Margaret was paraphrasing Denny's verse here. His original couplet read: 'Work o th' works leave idle books alone / For wise and worthier women have writ none.'

45   Whitaker, 2003, p.26; Crawford, 1985, p.212. Of those 42, only seven were literary works and none were written with the intention of earning a living. Until Margaret came along, no woman had ever written more than one literary work.

46   Aphra Behn is the one other woman writer of the century who can rival Margaret in this regard – in 1670 she published and staged her first play (of many) and would frequently touch on risqué subjects, including sex, gender and politics.

47   *Philosophical Fancies* put forward Margaret's new theory that the world was composed, not of different-shaped atoms (an idea she now rejected) but of a single kind of living matter that was capable of innate motion.

48   Dorothy Osborne, Letter 18, *Letters from Dorothy Osborne to Sir William Temple*, Edward Abbott Parry (ed.), (London, 1903), pp.81–2.

49   Ibid., Letter 21, p.100.

50   Cavendish, 'The Clasp', *Poems and Fancies*, 1653.

51   Letter from Sir Edward Hyde to William Cavendish, quoted in Whitaker, 2003, p.166.

52   Margaret is here referring to the

traditional belief, dating back to Aristotle and Galen, that women were composed of cold and wet elements, which supposedly rendered them softer and weaker than men, who were believed to be hot and dry.

53   Cavendish, 'Preface to the Reader', *The World's Olio*, 1654.

54   Cavendish, 'A True Relation of My Birth', 1656, p.378.

55   William Cavendish, 'An Epistle to Justify the Lady Newcastle and truth against falsehood, laying those false, and malicious aspersions of her, that she was not author of her books', *Philosophical and Physical Opinions*, 1655.

56   Cavendish, 'To the Two Universities', *Philosophical and Physical Opinions*, 1655.

57   Margaret plays a fascinating game with her heroine's gender identity in 'Assaulted and Pursued Chastity'. She starts out as a nameless female, but when she falls prey to the married Prince, nearly kills him in self-defence, becomes his prisoner and begins to fall in love with him, she becomes Miseria. When she escapes in disguise as a boy, however, freed from the dangers and restraints of being female, and with her life, gender and identity in flux, Miseria commits a symbolic act of self-determination and changes her name to Travellia, allegorically reflecting her changing state. By the end of the tale, the girl's changeable name is finally fixed as she becomes the Princess, just as her strategically shifting personal pronouns settle on the feminine.

58   See 'Evading Rape and Embracing Empire in Margaret Cavendish's *Assaulted and Pursued Chastity*', Marina Leslie, in *Menacing Virgins: Representing Virginity in the Middle Ages and Renaissance*, Kathleen Coyne Kelly and Marina Leslie (eds), (University of Delaware Press, 1999), pp.179–97.

59   Cavendish, 'A True Relation of My Birth', 1656, pp.389–91.

60   Cavendish, *Playes*, 1662.

61   1 November 1660, *The Diary of Samuel Pepys, Vol.I, 1660*, Robert Latham and William Matthews (eds), (HarperCollins, 1995), p.280.

62   2 May 1660, ibid., p.122.

63   Cavendish, *Life of William*, 1886, p.127.

64   A jointure was a marriage settlement in which certain property or money was bequeathed to a wife for the period after she survived her husband. She gained legal control over those assets, which as a married woman she was denied; consequently, widows of rich men could enjoy relative independence and power.

65   Though they were chalk and cheese in character and philosophy, Margaret's fantasies of all-female secular communities were important antecedents for the women's college that Mary Astell would argue for in reality 30 years later (see Chapter 3). It's interesting to note that Mary, as a single woman, was considered to be motivated by bitterness and disappointment, while Margaret found the idea of an all-female retreat just as enticing despite being happily married.

66   Margaret felt she'd found a kindred spirit in Shakespeare – a man whose wit had also overcome his relatively meagre education. She particularly admired his ability to draw characters from all walks of life, especially women. 'And so well he hath expressed in his plays all sorts of persons, as one would think he had transformed into every one of those persons he hath described … nay, one would think that he had been metamorphosed from a man to a woman, for who could describe Cleopatra better than he hath done, and many other females of his own creating?' (Cavendish, *Sociable Letters*, CXXIII, 1664.)

67   Cavendish, 'To the Reader', 1666, *The Blazing World and Other Writings*, Kate Lilley (ed.), (Penguin, 2004), p.124. The Frenchman Margaret refers to is the novelist Savinien Cyrano de Bergerac (1619–1655), whose *Comical History of the States and*

Empires of the Moon (1657) involved a trip to a fantastical world on the moon.

68　Cavendish, 'Epilogue to the Reader', *The Blazing World*, 2004, p.225.

69　*The Blazing World* indicates how at home Margaret would have been in the age of the novel. With its freewheeling structure, capacity for invention and reliance on storytelling, this was the genre Margaret was made for but never quite found. Her short 'romancical' fictions – almost fantasy novellas – are important and oft-ignored stepping stones in the English novel's journey to conception.

70　This was Anne Maxwell, who had taken over her husband's publishing business after his death – one of the few ways in which women could acquire their own businesses in the seventeenth century.

71　18 March 1668, *The Diary of Samuel Pepys, Vol.IX, 1668–9*, Robert Latham and William Matthews (eds), (HarperCollins, 1995), p.123.

72　This observation came from fellow Royalist Sir Charles Lyttelton, writing of a visit made by the Duke and Duchess to Nottinghamshire in August 1665. He noted that Margaret 'was very pleasant, but rather to be seen than told. She was dressed in a vest [a masculine riding coat], and, instead of [curtsies], made legs and bows to the ground with her hand and head'. Her boosted confidence as an author and duchess had evidently encouraged her to play even more overtly with gender conventions. Quoted in Douglas Grant, *Margaret the First* (Rupert Hart-Davis, 1957), p.184.

73　John Evelyn, quoted in Whitaker, 2003, p.303.

74　18 April 1667, *Diary of Evelyn Vol.II*, 1907, p.24.

75　Letter from Mary Evelyn to Mr Bohun, undated (1667), *Diary and Correspondence of John Evelyn Vol.IV*, William Bray (ed.), (George Bell & Sons, 1887), pp.8–9.

76　Cavendish, 'A True Relation of My Birth', 1656, p.364.

77　Letter from Mary Evelyn to Mr Bohun, 4 January 1672, *Diary and Correspondence IV*, 1887, pp.31–2.

78　Ibid., undated, 1667, pp.8–9.

79　30 March 1667, *Diary of Pepys, 1667, Vol.VIII*, p.137.

80　Whitaker, 2003, p.298.

81　26 April 1667, *Diary of Pepys, 1667, Vol.VIII*, p.186.

82　Letter from Mary Evelyn to Mr Bohun, undated (1667), *Diary and Correspondence IV*, 1887, pp.8–9.

83　Welbeck's chaplain Clement Ellis, *Letters and Poems in Honour of the Incomparable Princess, Margaret, Duchess of Newcastle*, 1676, p.176.

84　From an anonymous mock-epitaph about Margaret, recorded by antiquarian John Stainsby (quoted in Whitaker, 2003, p.355). This was one of the most vitriolic jibes ever aimed at Margaret, in which the Devil describes her as the 'Shame of her sex, Welbeck's illustrious whore'. Given Margaret's unblemished reputation as a loyal wife, the accusation seems entirely defamatory.

85　Cambridge University, *Letters and Poems*, 1676, pp.32–34; Walter Charleton, quoted in Whitaker, 2003, p.315; Charles Cheyne, *Letters and Poems*, 1676, p.79.

86　George Ballard, *Memoirs of Several Ladies of Great Britain who have been Celebrated for Their Writings or Skill in the Learned Languages, Arts and Sciences*, 1752, p.305.

87　Horace Walpole, *A Catalogue of the Royal and Noble Authors of England, Scotland, and Ireland*, 1758, Vol.II.

88　Despite antiquarian Mark Anthony Lower's assertion in his *Life of William* (1872) that her contemporaries named Margaret 'Mad Madge of Newcastle', there is no evidence to suggest that the nickname had its genesis during her lifetime. The comments made by Dorothy Osborne, Samuel Pepys and Mary Evelyn must have been influential, as perhaps was writer Charles Lamb's affectionate name for her of 'Madge Newcastle'. Sir Walter Scott referred to her as 'that old madwoman the Duchess of Newcastle' in his 1822 novel *Peveril of the Peak*, suggesting that by the early nineteenth century the image of Margaret as mad had firmly embedded itself into popular consciousness. (See Whitaker, 2003, pp.362–3.)

89   Virginia Woolf, *The Common Reader Vol.I*, 1925 (Vintage Classics, 2003), p.72.

90   Woolf, *A Room of One's Own*, 1929 (Penguin, 2004), pp.71–2. While there was some truth to this view, it ignored Margaret's lack of access to education, her active role in intellectual life, and her own acute awareness of the criticisms she received and the dangers of flattery. Indeed, in *The Blazing World*, the Empress challenges Margaret on this very thing: 'If you were not a great lady,' she says, 'you would never pass in the world for a wise lady; for the world would say your singularities are vanities.' Margaret is unconcerned: 'she did not at all regard the censure of this or any other age concerning vanities'. (p.218)

91   Woolf, 1925, p.77.

92   Cavendish, *Sociable Letters*, 1664, LXXXII and 'To the Two Universities', *Philosophical and Physical Opinions*, 1655.

MARY ASTELL

1   Mary Astell, *The Christian Religion As Profess'd by a Daughter of the Church*, 1705, p.293.

2   Ruth Perry, *The Celebrated Mary Astell: An Early English Feminist* (University of Chicago Press, 1986), p.53.

3   George Ballard, *Memoirs of Several Ladies of Great Britain who Have been Celebrated for their Writings or Skill in the Learned Languages, Arts and Sciences* (Oxford, 1752), p.445.

4   Mary Astell, 'Solitude', 1684.

5   Ballard, 1752, p.458.

6   Astell, 'In Emulation of Mr Cowleys Poem call'd the Motto', 7 January 1687–8.

7   In dissolving the nunneries, which took place between 1536 and 1542, the Reformation had taken away one of the key recourses open to respectable single women who either wished to take orders, gain an education or simply live outside of society.

8   Virginia Woolf, still analysing the conditions required for women to be able to write in 1928, dramatised perfectly the quandary Mary now faced: 'For now Aphra Behn had done it, girls could go to their parents and say, You need not give me an allowance; I can make money by my pen. Of course, the answer for many years to come was, Yes, by living the life of Aphra Behn! Death would be better! And the door was slammed faster than ever.' Virginia Woolf, *A Room of One's Own*, 1928 (Penguin, 2004), p.74.

9   Perry, 1986, p.242.

10   Mary Astell and John Norris, *Letters Concerning the Love of God*, 1695, pp.1–2.

11   Ibid., p.6.

12   Ibid., Preface, 1695.

13   So said the writer Sarah Chapone in 1742 when interviewed by George Ballard for his research for *Memoirs of Several Ladies of Great Britain*.

14   Astell and Norris, 1695, p.53.

15   Taking his cue from Aristotle and Galen and the ancient theory that women's bodies were made up of cold and moist elements while men's were hot and dry, Malebranche expounded the view that their brains were made of softer, more delicate fibres, which couldn't bear the strain of rigorous or abstract thought. Mary greatly admired Malebranche's works in general, so we can only wonder how she squared this particular circle.

16   Women, it seems, didn't need education so much as moral reform. Popular works like *The Education of a Christian Woman*, by Spanish Humanist Juan Luis Vives, in 1524, meant well, arguing in favour of women's education, but they were too short-sighted to see any intellectual

need in a woman beyond the moral and spiritual instruction thought necessary to make her a fitting companion for a man. The question would be broached more fully by Dutch writer Anna Maria van Schurman, whose *The Learned Maid: Or, Whether a Maid May Be a Scholar?* was translated into English in 1659. Although not a great leap forward from Vives's scheme of a century earlier, van Schurman at least considered all the variables that might affect a woman's ability to be a scholar, such as her family's wealth, and any children and housewifely duties she might have.

17 Ballard, 1752, p.447.

18 Christine de Pizan, *The Book of the City of Ladies*, 1405, translated by Rosalind Brown-Grant (Penguin, 1999), Part I, p.57.

19 Europe was far ahead of England in this respect; France, Italy and Spain – where no Reformation had taken place – were still equipped with educational nunneries and women's scholarship was becoming a recognised and accepted part of their culture. By the eighteenth century women could be both students and professors at the great universities, as demonstrated by the Italian physicist Laura Bassi, who was given a PhD from the University of Bologna in May 1732.

20 In England, women's voices in the debate were conspicuous by their absence until, in 1589, Jane Anger (undoubtedly a pseudonym) published *Her Protection for Women*, the first defence of women written by an Englishwoman. The debate gained pace at the beginning of the seventeenth century and there was a noticeable pattern to it – men like Swetnam, who were panicking at the threat to their supremacy, would issue vicious attacks on women's sexual inconstancy and intellectual inferiority, prompting women (under such aliases as 'Mary Tattle-Well' and 'Joan Hit-Him-Home') to respond with indignant defences of their moral character and learning ability, usually relying on biblical

references and historical examples to argue their case. With logic and intellectual reasoning rarely applied, this reactionary debate went round in circles.

21 It particularly annoyed Mary Astell, with her firm belief in the class system, that gender was more of a barrier to education than class, with men of lower status than her granted access that she was denied. As Ruth Perry puts it, 'The universities were open to the male offspring of brewers and haberdashers, but closed to the daughters of the oldest noble families in England.' (Perry, 1986, p.104.)

22 Figures reported by David Cressy for the Norwich and London dioceses based on court depositions. He reported that by the 1690s women's illiteracy had reduced to around 52 per cent in London but remained around 80 per cent in the provinces. (Perry, 1986, p.489.)

23 Margaret Cavendish, 'The Epistle', *The World's Olio*, Book I, Part III, 1655.

24 One of the few men to suggest seriously an educational college for women was Clement Barksdale, schoolmaster and translator of Anna Maria van Schurman's work, who in his 1675 pamphlet *A Letter Touching a College of Maids or a Virgin Society* proposed a women's academy based on the Oxford model, where the teachings would extend beyond religious and moral instruction to prepare women for 'decent employments and exercises, both divine and humane'. See Introduction, Sharon L. Jansen (ed.), *Mary Astell: A Serious Proposal to the Ladies* (Saltar's Point Press, 2014), p.24.

25 The 'Mrs' was a courtesy title afforded many single women to lend them an air of respectability – a strange custom that merely added weight to the idea that being single was in some way shameful.

26 Ballard, 1752, p.452.

27 Perry, 1986, pp.99–100.

28 Jansen, 2014, p.37.

29 Lady Mary Chudleigh's best-known feminist poem 'The Ladies Defence' was

written in 1701 in direct response to Sprint's blatant attack on women. She was incited to write it, she said, by the appalling realisation that many men agreed with his sentiments. She was eloquent in her anger and proved a true disciple of Mary Astell's teachings: 'Tis hard we should be by the men despis'd, / Yet kept from knowing what wou'd make us priz'd: / Debarr'd from Knowledge, banish'd from the schools, / And with the utmost industry bred fools … But spite of you, we'll to our selves be kind: / Your censures slight, your little tricks despise, / And make it our whole business to be wise.'

30 Ballard, 1752, p.446.

31 Astell, 1705, pp.402–3.

32 Women would not be admitted to Britain's universities until the late nineteenth century – to the universities of London, Edinburgh and Cambridge in 1869, and to Oxford in 1879 – but even then they were prohibited from graduating with a degree. The University of London awarded its first degrees to women in 1878, Edinburgh in 1894, Oxford in 1920 and Cambridge not until 1948.

33 See Amanda Vickery's *The Gentleman's Daughter: Women's Lives in Georgian England* (Yale, 1999) for a detailed study of the lives of conventional genteel women in the North of England; their letters and diaries afford us a glimpse of their everyday experiences of marriage. The examples range from the happy to the miserable, though the majority lie somewhere in between. As Vickery puts it, 'As far as can be gathered from letters, none of these husbands expected blind obedience in every detail of domestic life … Unequal partnership was workable if a wife observed the general proprieties and a husband tempered his authority.' (p.72.)

34 The dangers of being a woman trapped in a bad or unwanted marriage would become a preoccupation of eighteenth- and nineteenth-century novels, notably those by Henry Fielding, Samuel

Richardson and Jane Austen. Richardson, for one, was known to have read Mary Astell, so perhaps we shouldn't be surprised at his heroine Pamela's dismay for brides when their 'fond lovers, prostrate at their feet' morph into 'surly husbands trampling on their necks' after the marriage ceremony.

35 This is a stumbling block for twenty-first-century readers of Astell. In any sexual encounter between men and women, Mary implies that male seduction is always to blame: 'Sometimes a woman is cajol'd, and sometimes hector'd, she is seduc'd to love a man, or aw'd into a fear of him.' Female desire is not even considered. See Perry, 1986, pp.144–47.

36 Elizabeth I had understood that as a woman of rare power, she would only make herself vulnerable by marrying. As a queen regnant, rather than a consort, she forced the husband-as-sovereign-over-his-wife issue to its paradoxical apex – how could a queen be subject to one of her own subjects? It would mean diluting her power and relinquishing much of it to her husband. And then of course there were the dangers of childbirth. Sex, marriage, motherhood – she had seen them destroy her own mother, three stepmothers and her cousin, and she would not risk it for herself. In the face of constant pressure to conform and continue her dynastic line, she chose instead bodily safety and absolute, unadulterated power as the Virgin Queen.

37 Ballard, 1752, p.450.

38 Ibid., p.449.

39 Astell and Norris, 1695, pp.34–5.

40 'Romantic friendships' between women were common, and society accepted them with little concern. For some, these relationships simply provided the source of companionship and support they couldn't get from men. For others, it allowed them to engage in under-the-radar sexual relationships, as revealed by Anne Lister's diaries (see Chapter 7). Given Mary Astell's abstemious religious

beliefs, however, it seems almost certain that her friendships, however intense, did not cross over into sexual activity.

41 Mary had always carefully employed the language of state and religion to frame her arguments in an effort to demonstrate that her ideas were not dissent, but rational, pragmatic, Christian sense. Evidently, this wasn't quite clear enough to some of her readers. (Preface to the third edition of *Some Reflections Upon Marriage; To which is added a preface, in answer to some objections*, 1706.)

42 The first of these pamphlets, *Moderation Truly Stated*, picked apart the Nonconformist minister James Owen's defence of 'occasional conformity', *Moderation a Vertue*. Her second, *A Fair Way with Dissenters and Their Patrons*, took on Daniel Defoe, whose *The Shortest Way with the Dissenters* had satirised the views of High Church Tory zealots who argued hysterically of the dangers of toleration. And her third, *An Impartial Enquiry into the Causes of Rebellion and Civil War in this Kingdom*, contested a sermon by the Whiggish Dr White Kennett, exalting Charles I and citing dissent as the root cause of the Civil War.

43 In his pamphlet, Shaftesbury had made a bid for a moderate response to religious fanaticism, arguing that it was an unreasonable superstition, a 'pannick' that could not be legislated against and should therefore be dismissed with 'good humour', as a puppet show at Bartholomew Fair had recently done when it gently ridiculed some troublesome French Protestant zealots. As a Whig politician and pupil of John Locke, Shaftesbury represented all the ideas that Mary vehemently disputed, and, of course, she was outraged at the notion of her profound beliefs being belittled as a 'pannick'; to her, religion was both sacred and founded entirely on reason.

44 Elinor James is the most notable example, who a generation before had written politically agitating pamphlets of a similarly conservative Tory nature. (See Perry, 1986, pp.183–85.)

45 Frances Atterbury, the Bishop of Rochester, was so staggered by Mary's critique of an essay he had written after she had dined at his house one night that he could scarce believe the comments had come from a lady: 'There is not an expression that carries the least air of her sex from the beginning to the end of it,' he wrote. Indeed, her mode of address was altogether too unladylike for him: she 'would be perfect', he insisted, if she had as much 'good breeding as good sense', but instead she had 'not the most decent manner of insinuating what she means'. Ballard was quick to refute these charges and, if anything, Atterbury's response reads like nothing more than a man affronted by a clever, forthright, opinionated woman. It's joyous to think of Mary so inflamed by her ideas that she was considered an 'offensive and shocking' guest at dinner parties. (Letter from Francis Atterbury to Dr Smalridge, quoted in Ballard, 1752, p.453.)

46 Following the death of Queen Anne in 1714, the Whigs would hold power for the majority of the eighteenth century, and their anti-Jacobite stance, toleration of religious dissenters and commitment to constitutional monarchy and free trade would shape the country throughout the Georgian era.

47 By 1733, 20,000 children in England had been educated at charity schools, 15,761 of whom had been placed in respectable positions. For the boys, this mostly meant apprenticeships to watermen and fishermen, labourers or craftsmen; for girls, it usually meant apprenticeships with dressmakers or a place in domestic service. (Perry, 1986, p.236.)

48 Perry, 1986, p.265.

49 Perry, 1986, pp.284–86.

50 This is the only area of London that bears any trace of Mary Astell's existence, as intersecting with Cale Street now sits Astell Street.

51 In July 1720 Mary wrote to Sir Hans Sloane, physician, naturalist and, upon his death, founder of the British Museum, to discuss some land he was offering as a site for her school, suggesting that plans were afoot to move it from the Royal Hospital to its own premises – maybe even to expand. There was no more talk of these plans after the South Sea Company crash.
52 Letter to Lady Anne Coventry, 7 March 1723, quoted in Perry, 1986, p.396.
53 Although she abhorred dissent, as a fervent Stuart supporter it's plausible that after Queen Anne's death in 1714 and the inauguration of George I, the highly politicised Mary Astell did become embroiled in Jacobite plots to restore James II's son to the throne. She certainly followed the rebellion's progress closely and had friends who were active Jacobites, such as the Duke and Duchess of Ormonde, and Francis Atterbury, who was imprisoned in the Tower and then exiled for his affiliation with the Pretender. As far as we know, however, Walpole did not question her in court. (See Perry, 1986, pp.172–9.)
54 The two treatments recommended by Mary's friends don't inspire much confidence in their efficacy: one was a concoction made of warts sliced from a horse's foreleg and boiled in white wine; the other, a plaster made of mutton suet, beeswax and flaxseed. (Perry, 1986, p.319.)
55 Ballard, 1752, p.459.
56 Mary's stoicism is all the more remarkable when considered alongside the novelist Fanny Burney's jaw-clenching first-hand account of the same operation in 1811. Burney was a courageous woman and she, too, refused to be held, but even so, 'When the dreadful steel was plunged into the breast, cutting through veins – arteries – flesh – nerves ... I began a scream that lasted unintermittently during the whole time of the incision.' Burney endured 20 minutes of 'utterly speechless torture' as the doctors scraped the resistant flesh from her breast bone. (Letter from Frances Burney to her sister Esther Burney, 22 March–June 1812, Frances Burney, *Journals and Letters* (Penguin, 2001), p.442.
57 Ballard, 1752, p.459.
58 Ibid., pp.459–60.
59 Letter from Lady Elizabeth Hastings to Bishop Wilson of the Isle of Man, quoted in Perry, 1986, p.323.
60 As Mary saw it, her successor ought to have been the captivating, unconventional Lady Mary Wortley Montagu, in whom she recognised a great literary talent who had the brains, wit and insight to challenge the world around her. When Mary read Lady Mary's travelogue-style Embassy Letters of life in Turkey written in 1717–18, she urged her to publish them, writing a preface for her in readiness, but Lady Mary was dissuaded by her high-ranking family against making such an immodest show.
61 Ballard echoed Mary's sentiments on this subject in his preface, making the point we are still repeating today, that 'many ingenious women of this nation who were really possess'd of a great share of learning and have, no doubt, in their time been famous for it, are not only unknown to the public in general, but have been passed by in silence by our greatest biographers'. In righting this wrong, Ballard was performing a great historical service, for if he hadn't sought out the last remaining few who knew her, much of what we know of Mary Astell would have been lost.
62 The Blue Stockings Society was an informal literary group established in the early 1750s by like-minded well-to-do women to allow them a place to congregate for intellectual and high-minded discussion. It became an important social and educational movement for women who craved mental stimulation beyond the tea table and card room, and was of course satirised and ridiculed by many – Horace Walpole referred to their gatherings as 'petticoteries' – and the term 'bluestocking' has since acquired a pejorative slant, suggesting prim, lofty women with pretensions to learning.

63 Defoe's Roxana likens a married woman to an 'upper-servant', just as Mary did, while Richardson's devout, eloquent Clarissa Harlowe tries to live the Astell ideal of independence. It's surely no coincidence that Clarissa also shuns company and summons her coffin to her bedside in anticipation of her death, just as Mary did. It's telling, however, that neither novelist could envisage a successful, respectable life for an independent woman – she must either live scandalously or die. (See Perry, 1986, pp.100 and 536.)

64 Letter from Elizabeth Elstob to George Ballard, 24 December 1736, cited by Perry, 1986, p.296.

65 This Chinese whisper came from Lady Mary Wortley Montagu's granddaughter, Lady Louisa Stuart. Quoted in Florence Smith, *Mary Astell* (Columbia University Press, 1916), p.16.

66 Astell, *A Serious Proposal to the Ladies*, 1694, p.111.

CHARLOTTE CHARKE

1 All quotations from Charlotte Charke, *A Narrative of the Life of Mrs Charlotte Charke*, 1755 (Scholars' Facsimiles & Reprints, Leonard R. N. Ashley (ed.), 1969), unless otherwise stated.

2 Charlotte's performance history has been verified by theatrical playbills and accounts, but for her personal anecdotes we have only her word. Her reputation with her contemporaries and her father's surviving letters, however, confirm that she was following a path both on and off stage that was deemed outrageous and unacceptable, suggesting that, self-dramatisation aside, the foundations of her story are true.

3 The playwright John Dennis was one of those who claimed that Colley had 'neither tenderness for his wife, or natural affection for his children', accusing him of squandering thousands of pounds at their expense. Charlotte's biographer Kathryn

Shevelow points out that Colley's biographer Helene Koon challenges the biases behind this irredeemable image of Colley, and adds that 'there is no credible evidence' that Colley's gambling prevented him from caring for his family. Colley himself reputedly made no bones about his selective attitude to morality. 'I am for the Church, though I don't go to church,' was apparently a motto of his. See Kathryn Shevelow, *Charlotte* (Henry Holt, 2005), pp.43 and 61.

4 Charlotte makes a habit throughout her narrative of likening herself to characters in plays – a device that displays not only her complete immersion in the theatre, but also her tendency to view herself as the chief protagonist in the continuous drama that is her own life.

5 It's been argued that, due to Colley's conspicuous absence from Charlotte's teenage life, she developed an obsession not just with imitating him, but actually taking his place as man of the house, though this Freudian take on her masculine tendencies undermines what Charlotte herself suggests: that they derived primarily from natural inclination. See Shevelow, 2005, pp.75–6.

6 Contrary to what might be supposed, it was not common for girls to be married as teenagers in the early modern period. It was legal for girls as young as 12 and boys of 14 to marry, but on average they waited until their mid-twenties. Teenage unions were usually confined to the aristocracy, where dynastic betrothals from childhood were often arranged. See Laurence, 1996, p.45, and Lawrence Stone, *The Family, Sex and Marriage in England, 1500–1800* (Penguin, 1990), pp.40–44.

7 As we know, these foundations still underpin the acting profession today, with female actors often having to play catch-up to achieve parity while battling sexual objectification, underrepresentation, a narrow choice of roles, unequal pay and harassment by powerful men.

8   Actors employed by a theatre company were usually granted one or two benefit performances a year, when they could take home the profits of that night's show. In effect, it was a bonus to supplement their usually meagre income. If ticket sales were good, they could almost double their annual wage.

9   George Farquhar, *The Beaux' Stratagem*, Act V, Scene iv.

10   Charlotte doesn't disclose the date of when the couple chose to separate, but Shevelow argues for the spring of 1733 as a likely time based on their performance history together and apart. (See Shevelow, 2005, p.135.)

11   The fuss generated today by the suggestion of a woman playing a male role – a female James Bond, Doctor Who or Hamlet, for example – seems particularly unwarranted in light of the fact that this practice has a centuries-long tradition, from Charlotte's Roderigo in the eighteenth century to Sarah Bernhardt's Hamlet in the nineteenth.

12   There might be several reasons for employing a woman to play a male part in the eighteenth century: to add an extra erotic charge, an element of sexual ambiguity or layers of complexity to gendered roles and jokes, or perhaps to portray young, effeminate dandies or soppy, weak or foolish men like Roderigo. More to the women's credit, it might also be to skewer and satirise masculine pride, chauvinism and affectation in rakish or bullying characters.

13   Bartholomew Fair took place annually in Smithfield, where entertainments abounded for the masses, including dancers, singers, jugglers, contortionists, acrobats, freak shows and theatre troupes.

14   Several of Charlotte's contemporaries also made their name playing breeches and travesty parts, most notably the Irish actress Peg Woffington, who began her career playing Macheath in John Gay's *The Beggar's Opera* in 1732, two years before Charlotte would do the same and make it

her own, establishing it as a traditionally gender-bending role.

15   By March 1733 Colley Cibber was done with theatre management and retiring from acting, preferring his less demanding roles as Poet Laureate and professional bon vivant, so he sold his share of the Drury Lane patent – not, as expected, to his son Theophilus, who had been renting it from him in the hope of purchasing (or better yet inheriting) it, but to John Highmore, a man who already held a third of the patent but had no practical skills in running a theatre or managing a team of players. This poor decision set off the disastrous chain of events that followed.

16   See Shevelow, 2005, pp.156–66, for a full account of the actors' mutiny.

17   Shevelow, 2005, p.186.

18   Always an innovator, Henry Fielding is best known for his part in creating the modern novel with *The History of Tom Jones, a Foundling* (1749) and his reforming roles as a justice of the peace and founder of the Bow Street Runners – the antecedents of the police force. Early in his career, however, he was an avant-garde playwright and a key player in Charlotte's life.

19   Although no year is given, Colley's letter is dated 27 March, and it seems likely that this and his final meeting with Charlotte occurred soon after the 1737 performance of *The Historical Register* on 21 March. The 'worthless scoundrel' Colley feels no need to name must surely be Fielding, and the reference to never being 'any good' a personal dig at her career. For the offence of wounding his pride, he would hit her where it hurt. (Letter printed in Fidelis Morgan, *The Well-Known Troublemaker: A Life of Charlotte Charke* (Faber, 1988), p.87; Shevelow, 2005, p.237.)

20   This censorship had long-standing ramifications for British theatre. In the short term, it meant actors and playwrights were out of work. New plays were often neglected in favour of safer, older plays, especially Shakespeare, while theatre managers had to

think up inventive new ways to sidestep the Licensing Act, often incorporating musical pieces into their productions. In the longer term, it rid the government of pesky political dissent, practically eradicated competition between theatres and 'effectively stifled the development of theatre in London for centuries', with a variant of its censorship law remaining in place until 1968. (See Shevelow, 2005, pp.246–7.)

21 Indoor tennis courts were often converted into theatres when the fashion for real tennis faded during the seventeenth century. These were usually a far cry from the glamorous venues Charlotte was used to working in.

22 See Morgan, 1988, p.64.

23 It's only from the marriage register and newspaper adverts listing Mrs Sacheverell as appearing at the New Wells Theatre in Clerkenwell in the summer of 1746 that we know of this second marriage at all (Charlotte later reverted back to the name Charke). She clearly didn't want to draw attention to it, even wishing to erase it from her history.

24 Richard Charke had been among the mutineers to return to Drury Lane, so had remained an unwelcome fixture in Charlotte's life for several years after their split. As he was heavily in debt, his plan was to start a new life in Jamaica, living there with his mistress as unofficial husband and wife, but it appears he died before she could join him. Charlotte was dispassionate at the news, but magnanimous enough to wish him peace and forgiveness in death.

25 Theophilus and his second wife, the celebrated actress Susannah Cibber, were involved in a notorious scandal in 1737–8. In need of money, Theo turned pimp and encouraged an intimacy between Susannah and her wealthy admirer William Sloper. He is even said to have forced her at gunpoint into Sloper's bed. His villainous plan backfired, however. Susannah and Sloper fell in love, and eventually she left

Theo, who then took the matter to court in a lurid criminal conversation trial in December 1738, in an attempt to regain his wife and £5,000 damages. He won the case but was awarded paltry damages of £10. Typically, it was Susannah's reputation that was destroyed. She disappeared from the stage for two years before rebuilding her career to become one of the most successful actresses of the eighteenth century.

26 See Stark, 1998, pp.116–17; *Annual Register*, 1760, pp.84–5; *Annual Register*, 1777, pp.191–2.

27 Catharina Lincken served in the Prussian armed forces for several years, before being dismissed when her sex was discovered. In 1717, still in the guise of a man, she married Catharina Mühlhahn, who later claimed to have no knowledge of her husband's subterfuge. The case ended up in court and the legal transcript, dated 13 October 1721, gives graphic details of their sexual activities, including how Lincken used a makeshift dildo of stuffed leather to have sex with her wife. She was executed for sodomy – a capital crime – while Mühlhahn was imprisoned. Lincken's story is particularly distressing, and she was unlucky – due to the confusion over lesbian sex and the reluctance to class it as sodomy, it was more usual in such cases for women to have their death sentence commuted to exile, imprisonment or whipping. In the Netherlands, for example, Maria van Antwerpen feared being put to death for having married another woman in 1747 and again in 1762, and having 'seduced and debauched' a young girl while living as a man, but in her case the authorities didn't pry into how this might have been achieved. In the end, she became a celebrity and was sentenced to nothing worse than banishment from her home city. See Rudolf M. Dekker and Lotte C. van de Pol, *The Tradition of Female Transvestism in Early Modern Europe* (Macmillan, 1989), pp.75–80.

28   Like all theatre managers, Charlotte had to innovate to evade the strictures of the Licensing Act. During one of her returns to the stage, she rented a building for a short season and advertised the venue as a 'tavern', where a ticket would buy punters a pint of ale, with theatre entertainment thrown in for free. It was a neat trick to avoid the ire of the authorities.

29   This letter is dated 21 September. Again, no year is given, but Shevelow argues that the tone suggests it comes later than his other letter, and even that it may have been written by Catherine at Colley's dictation. (Letter printed in Morgan, 1988, p.124; Shevelow, 2005, p.297.)

30   Whyte notes that during the financial negotiations, Mrs Brown was an 'attentive listener', leaning forward with 'an eye of anxious expectation', suggesting that she had a shared interest in Charlotte's earnings, as any wife would.

31   Samuel Whyte's visit took place in December 1754, but his article describing the event appeared in the *Monthly Review* in June 1794.

32   'The Lover's Treat; or, Unnatural Hatred'; 'The Mercer: or, the Fatal Extravagance' and 'The History of Charley and Patty'. These pieces are undated but are likely to have been written between 1757 and 1759 as they come after *Henry Dumont*, which is mentioned on the title pages. (See Shevelow, 2005, pp.366–7.)

33   Letter to the Duke of Devonshire, 7 August 1759 (printed in Morgan, 1988, pp.186–7; Shevelow, 2005, pp.369–70).

34   *Public Advertiser*, 26 September 1759.

35   *London Evening Post* and other newspapers, 17–19 April 1760.

36   William Shakespeare, *As You Like It*, Act II, Scene vii, 142.

37   Dr Burney, *Memoirs of Dr Charles Burney, 1726–1769*, p.185, cited by Shevelow, 2005, p.353.

38   Playwright and theatre manager Charles Dibden, 1820s, quoted in W. Clark Russell, *Representative Actors*; David Erskine Baker, Isaac Reed, Stephen Jones, *Biographia Dramatica*, 1812, p.103; George Speaight, *The History of the English Puppet Theatre*, 1955, pp.107–8, cited by Morgan, 1988, pp.192–4.

HANNAH SNELL

1   Letter from Admiral Collingwood to Rear Admiral Purvis, 9 August 1808, Edward Hughes (ed.), *The Private Correspondence of Admiral Lord Collingwood* (Navy Records Society, 1957), pp.251–2.

2   The sea has long been identified as an unpredictable female force – life-giving one minute, deadly the next – while its predatory mythical monsters are usually women gone wrong: seductive sirens who lure men to their deaths or transformed nymphs such as Scylla and Charybdis, who devour ships whole. Even ships themselves can be both motherly protectors and dangerous leaky vessels. Traditionally, all must be mastered and tamed by men to ensure safe passage and prosperity.

3   Most of the women who were unofficially allowed on board were prostitutes. Others might be hired to work as nurses on hospital ships. Wives, on the other hand, who accompanied their husbands at the Captain's discretion, would often work as cooks or washerwomen, and even participated in battle, helping to tend the wounded or acting as powder monkeys, sometimes dying in the process. Despite these contributions and sacrifices, officially these women did not exist on board. Their names weren't recorded in the muster lists; they were afforded no pay and no food rations – they and their children (some of which were born at sea) had to share what meagre handouts their husbands received. See Suzanne J. Stark, *Female Tars: Women Aboard Ship in the Age of Sail* (Pimlico, 1998), pp.47–81.

4   All quotes, unless otherwise stated, from Robert Walker, *The Female Soldier; or*

The Surprising Life and Adventures of Hannah Snell, 1750, reprinted in *The Lady Tars: The Autobiographies of Hannah Snell, Mary Lacy and Mary Anne Talbot* (Fireship Press, 2008).

5   Sailors' wives left behind on shore, especially by those who had been pressed into the navy, often lived a wretched existence, with no money and no means of supporting themselves (or any children) for years on end. A sailor's pay took a long time coming, and methods of sending money home were unreliable at best. The streets and workhouses of port towns such as Plymouth and Portsmouth were filled with the starving and distressed families of men gone to sea. See Stark, 1998, pp.23–7.

6   The surge in women sailors in the eighteenth century coincided with the general trend for cross-dressing that swept Britain at the same time, and was no doubt encouraged by the continual military conflicts that characterised the era. The decline came in the early 1800s, when the wars with France and America ended. The navy duly reduced in size and began to implement identity checks and physical examinations on recruits, as well as more stringent rules on cleanliness, making it almost impossible for a woman to hide her gender on board. See Stark, 1998, p.122; Dekker and van de Pol, 1989, pp.102–3.

7   Christian Davies was granted a pension of one shilling a day for her lifetime by Queen Anne for her services and was admitted as the first female pensioner at the Royal Hospital Chelsea in November 1717. She was buried there with full military honours in 1739. Her story, *The Life and Adventures of Mrs Christian Davies*, published in 1741, has in the past been attributed to Daniel Defoe, though it seems unlikely, as he died 10 years before its publication.

8   'Tar', probably short for 'tarpaulin', was a common nickname for a sailor dating from the mid-seventeenth century.

9   This phenomenon of women running off to war to become soldiers and marines was so striking that by 1762, men were beginning to joke that there were so many ladies in the army it would be better to create separate regiments for them. See Dekker and van de Pol, 1989, p.100.

10   Stark, 1998, p.100.

11   Mary Lacy, *The History of the Female Shipwright*, 1773, reprinted in *The Lady Tars*, pp.60 and 63.

12   For Christian Davies, the outward accoutrements of masculinity were the most important elements to get right in her transformation: 'I cut off my hair, and dressed me in a suit of my husband's, having had the precaution to quilt the waistcoat, to preserve my breasts from hurt, which were not large enough to betray my sex, and putting on the wig and hat I had prepared, I went out and bought me a silver hilted sword, and some Holland shirts.' With the window dressing mastered, the rest would naturally follow. *The Life and Adventures of Mrs Christian Davies* (London, 1740), p.20.

13   It's a common feature in the accounts of female cross-dressers that their disguise succeeded because they could pass for youthful, fresh-faced men. Maria van Antwerpen, for example, enlisted as a soldier in the Dutch army in 1746 as a boy of 16 when she was 28, and again as a young man of 23 when she was 42. See Dekker and van de Pol, 1989, p.15.

14   See Matthew Stephens, *Hannah Snell: The Secret Life of a Female Marine, 1723–1792* (Ship Street Press, 1997), pp.18–21, for his unpicking of the discrepancies in Hannah's narrative.

15   The records also disagree with Walker on the location of General Guise's regiment when Hannah is supposed to have been there. Ibid., p.21.

16   *Boswell's Life of Johnson* in six volumes, George Birkbeck Hill (ed.), (Clarendon Press, 1887), Vol.1, p.348.

17   Admiral Charles Vinicombe Penrose, *Observations on Corporal Punishment*

(Bodmin, 1824), pp.51–65, quoted in Stark, 1998, p.18.

18   When a ship was in port, hundreds of prostitutes would pile on board to service the needs of sailors who had been at sea for months, even years, and the open space of the lower deck, already jam-packed with reeking, unwashed bodies, would become one grubby, frantic scene of mass debauchery. Most of these prostitutes were half-starved, ill and extremely young – in 1758, the magistrate John Fielding stated that most women in London's brothels were under 18, and many scarcely older than 12 (then the legal age of consent for girls; it would not be raised to 16 until 1885). Besides the inevitable emotional and physical abuse, venereal disease and pregnancy were the usual consequences. Only the most desperate of women would resort to it. See Stark, 1998, pp.32–7.

19   *Annual Register* 1771, p.71.

20   Newspaper report quoted in Stark, 1998, pp.111–12.

21   The British troops launched their attack on Devicotta on 11 June and were back on board the *Eltham* on 13 June. The ship then stayed at Porto Novo for another six weeks before returning to Fort St David on 1 August.

22   For a full analysis of the inconsistencies between Walker's account and the muster lists, see Stephens, 1997, pp.29–33.

23   Ibid. p.33.

24   Quoted in Dekker and van de Pol, 1989, p.16.

25   See Stark, 1998, pp.89–90.

26   See Stephens, 1997, p.35.

27   Conduct money was paid to sailors to cover the costs of getting them home after they were discharged from their ship.

28   *Newcastle Courant; Whitehall Evening Post,* 23 June 1750.

29   *The Female Soldier* wasn't just a hit in Britain. Like other such biographical accounts from across Europe, particularly France and Italy, it was also translated into Dutch and published in the Netherlands, where there was a particular appetite for such tales, it being the only country in Europe to have an even higher incidence of female cross-dressers than the UK. See Dekker and van de Pol, 1989, p.93.

30   *Whitehall and General Evening Post,* 30 June 1750; *Derby Mercury,* 29 June–6 July 1750.

31   This tradition stretched back to Mary Frith (see Chapter 1) in the early seventeenth century and would culminate in the music-hall performers of the late nineteenth and early twentieth centuries. But the female soldier had a particularly fond place in Restoration and eighteenth-century drama. Thomas Shadwell's *The Woman-Captain* (1680) and George Farquhar's *The Recruiting Officer* (1706) both involve female characters donning regimentals. And martial displays make early appearances, too: in 1701 an 11-year-old girl was recorded as performing at the New Tunbridge Wells 'musick-house' (now the Sadler's Wells site), 'Arm'd *Amazon* like, with abundance of Rapiers'. And in Charles Shadwell's *The Humours of the Army* (1713), the female officer Belvedera delivers the epilogue while performing manual exercises with a musket. See Georgina Lock and David Worrall, 'Cross-dressed performance at the theatrical margins: Hannah Snell, the Manual Exercise, and the New Wells Spa Theater, 1750', JSTOR, *Huntington Library Quarterly,* Vol.77, No. 1 (Spring 2014), pp.17–36.

32   Ibid.

33   *Derby Mercury,* 29 June–6 July 1750; *Whitehall and General Evening Post,* 30 June 1750.

34   *Penny London Post,* 27 June 1750; *Newcastle Courant,* 30 June 1750.

35   Note the implication here that it's the woman's responsibility not to invite such evils, rather than a man's not to perpetrate them – a pernicious idea that continues to linger in the public consciousness.

36 The Chelsea Hospital's admission book for 1746–1754 logs Hannah's acceptance as an out pensioner but only adds to her mystery, as it records her time of service as four and a half years, rather than three, and her wounds as being received 'at Pondicherry in the thigh and both legs' rather than at Devicotta. With the hospital board following Walker's version of events rather than the official records, as Stephens notes, this must surely be a case of either 'bureaucratic incompetence or collusion'. See Stephens, 1997, pp.44–6.

37 *Derby Mercury*, 15 November 1751.

38 Hannah's second marriage to Richard Eyles may also have been by necessity, as her son George was born the same year as their wedding.

39 *Leeds Intelligencer*, 8 January 1771. The anecdote was repeated in the *Chester Chronicle* on 6 December 1776, with the added detail that at the time of the incident Hannah 'kept the Three Tuns, a public house at Kennington-Butts'. If so, then her ambition to become a publican seems to have been realised, though clearly not by trading as the 'Woman in Masquerade' as planned, since the story pointedly has her back in petticoats.

40 21 May 1778, John Beresford (ed.), *The Diary of a Country Parson: The Reverend James Woodforde 1758–1781* (Oxford University Press, 1924), pp.224–5. Woodforde's account shows just how easily Hannah's story could be mythologised. Either by error or Hannah's own embellishments, he extends her length of army service to 21 years, changes her pseudonym to John Gray and reports that one of her fingers was cut off at Pondicherry.

41 *Derby Mercury*, 15 September 1791; *Northampton Mercury*, 17 September 1791.

42 Chelsea Hospital journal, 9 June 1785, quoted in Stephens, 1997, p.51.

43 *Derby Mercury*, 15 September 1791; *Northampton Mercury*, 17 September 1791.

44 Stephens, 1997, p.51; Arnold, 2008, pp.134–6 and 167–8.

45 See Stephens, 1997, pp.56–7; Lock and Worrall, 2014, p.17.

46 Women officially became part of the Royal Navy during the First World War, in 1917, with the creation of the Women's Royal Naval Service; the WRENs was still an auxiliary force, however, so despite the vital work of its women then and in the Second World War, they were, as ever, relegated to support roles – indeed, their wry motto was 'Never at Sea'. In 1993 the WRENs was fully integrated into the Royal Navy and its women finally allowed to go to sea.

MARY PRINCE

1 Britain would overtake both Spain and Portugal as the most successful slave-trading nation. It's estimated that between 1640 and the abolition of the slave trade in 1807, Britain transported a total of 3.1 million slaves across the Atlantic from Africa to the Americas and the British colonies in the Caribbean. Approximately 2.7 million of them survived the journey. (nationalarchives.gov.uk/help-with-your-research/research-guides/british-transatlantic-slave-trade-records/)

2 James Somerset's defence lawyer cited the ruling from 1569 that confirmed the absence of slavery in England, and Lord Mansfield agreed: Somerset should be set free, he decreed, on the grounds that 'No master ever was allowed here to take a slave by force.' The case was instrumental in setting a legal precedent for the oft-cited belief that all men and women were free in England, even if it wasn't always respected in practice. See Sara Salih (ed.), *The History of Mary Prince: A West Indian Slave* (Penguin, 2004), Introduction, p.xviii; Miranda Kaufmann, *Black Tudors: The Untold Story* (Oneworld, 2017), pp.6 and 15–16.

3 Due to the patchy records, it's difficult to ascertain precisely how many black or

brown people there were living in Britain in Mary's time. Estimates vary but a general figure agreed between scholars is between 10,000 and 15,000 in the mid- to late eighteenth century. (Salih, 2004, Introduction, p.xvii; Laurence, 2002, p.20.)

4   In 1773 the American slave Phillis Wheatley, for example, had been rigorously examined by a group of Boston nobles before her poems could be published in England (she'd been unable to publish them in America at all), to attest that she was 'qualified to write them' despite being 'brought an uncultivated Barbarian from Africa'. She succeeded in the end, becoming the first black woman to publish her writing in Britain. See Salih, 2004, Introduction, p.xiv.

5   All quotes from Mary Prince, *The History of Mary Prince: A West Indian Slave*, Sara Salih (ed.), (Penguin, 2004), unless otherwise stated.

6   Olaudah Equiano, *The Interesting Narrative of Olaudah Equiano, or Gustavus Vassa, the African, Written by Himself*, 1789 (Isaac Knap, 1837), p.52.

7   This is not simply an emotive metaphor. Reports of masters flogging their slaves and then rubbing salt and pepper in the wounds as further torture were common.

8   Maryprince.org.

9   It's not stated, or even hinted at, in the narrative, but it's possible, even likely, that the father of Hetty's child was Captain Ingham – sexual liaisons between masters and slaves, both consensual and non-consensual, were common.

10   Mary seems to be describing the symptoms of a dropsy, or build-up of fluid in the body.

11   It's thought Mary is referring to Grand Turk, of the Turks and Caicos Islands, still a British territory.

12   Maryprince.org. Robert Darrel appears to be unconnected to Mary's second owner, Mrs Williams's father Richard Darrell.

13   Taking ownership over their slaves'

names as well as their bodies was one way in which slave owners effaced their individuality and undermined their confidence, agency and sense of self. Even Mary's paternal surname Prince was likely attributed to her father as a mocking nickname by his owners, while the Woods changed her name entirely to Molly Wood, to accentuate both her lowly status (the name Molly had dubious connotations as a slang term for prostitute) and their possession of her. See A. M. Rauwerda, 'Naming, Agency, and "A Tissue of Falsehoods" in *The History of Mary Prince*' in *Victorian Literature and Culture*, Vol.29, No.2 (2001), pp.397–411.

14   Pringle adds in a footnote that by the time she arrived in England, Mary knew little of what had become of her family. She had seen her mother just once during her time on Turk's Island and that had been upsetting, 'for she had gone from her senses' and didn't recognise her. This seems to have been temporary (Mary believed it was brought on by the trauma of a violent storm at sea), for she worked on Turk's Island for several years before returning to Bermuda. Her father died while she and her mother were on Turk's Island, and it was a long time before they knew of it; her mother died after Mary went to Antigua. Mary knew virtually nothing of what had happened to her siblings (now seven brothers and three sisters), except that the eldest sister, 'who had several children to her master', was taken by him to Trinidad, while the youngest, Rebecca, was enslaved in Bermuda.

15   Harriet Jacobs, *Incidents in the Life of a Slave Girl*, 1861 (Dover Publications, 2001), Chapter XIV, p.66. Jacobs wrote this after finding out her baby was a girl. Her heart sank, because, 'Superadded to the burden common to all, they have wrongs, and sufferings, and mortifications peculiarly their own.'

16   The real nature of Mary's relationship with Captain Abbot would come out in

court in 1833, during the libel trial brought against Thomas Pringle.

17   The Moravian Church is a denomination of the Protestant Church, with founding links in fifteenth-century Bohemia and Moravia, in what is now the Czech Republic. The first Moravian congregations were established in England in 1642, but from the 1730s onwards they also had missionaries established all over the world, with a strong footing in the colonies. The Moravians still have over a thousand congregations worldwide.

18   Daniel and Mary could not be married in the Church of England, she tells us, because an 'English marriage is not allowed to slaves; and no free man can marry a slave woman'.

19   See Miranda Kaufmann's *Black Tudors* (Oneworld, 2017), a fascinating study of the lives of black Africans in sixteenth-century England, from John Blanke, who played trumpet at Henry VIII's coronation, to deep-sea diver Jacques Francis, who helped salvage from the *Mary Rose*, and Diego, who circumnavigated the globe with Sir Francis Drake.

20   In 1781, 133 slaves (regarded as cargo) were deliberately thrown overboard on the *Zong* slave ship in order to cash in on their insurance value and save on diminishing water reserves. When the ship owners made an insurance claim for the loss of their slaves, the insurers refused to pay up, and the dispute led to two trials in 1783. In the first, the jury found in favour of the ship owners; in the second, however, when evidence came to light that the water shortage was due to the crew's own errors, the ruling went against them.

21   The Anti-Slavery Society was formed in 1823, a revised organisation to come out of the Committee for the Abolition of the Slave Trade, a largely Quaker group formed in 1787 by William Wilberforce, to better tackle the different challenges faced in the wake of the end of the slave trade in 1807. The society began by campaigning for gradual abolition but would eventually change its stance to demand immediate abolition instead.

22   Letter from John Wood to Mr Taylor, Secretary to Sir Patrick Ross, 20 October 1830, Prince, 2002, pp.43–44.

23   Letter from Joseph Phillips to Thomas Pringle, 18 January 1831, Prince, 2002, pp.50–2.

24   In the nineteenth century there were still those who were all too ready to doubt, ignore or discredit anyone with black skin, arguing that they were an inferior race, or not even human – a sub-species who were savage, dishonest and incapable of learning beyond mere imitation. Such repugnant views were a hangover from the previous century, derived from the likes of philosopher David Hume, who wrote in his essay 'Of National Characters' in 1753 that he was 'apt to suspect the negroes ... to be naturally inferior to the whites', and Edward Long, who in his 1774 *History of Jamaica* made the spurious claims that white and black were 'two distinct species' and that a black person 'fills up the space between mankind and the ape'. See Salih, 2002, Introduction, p.xv.

25   Susanna Strickland, later Susanna Moodie, makes reference to her transcription of Mary's narrative in one of her short stories, 'Rachel Wilde, or Trifles from the Burthen of a Life', in which she defends the work as 'strictly true' against the accusation that it is a 'tissue of falsehoods from beginning to end'. She would later write a biography of the alleged murderess Grace Marks, which has also been charged with inaccuracy and embellishment. (Rauwerda, 2001, pp.404–5.)

26   See Clare Midgley, *Women Against Slavery: The British Campaigns, 1780–1870* (Routledge, 1992), pp.86–92.

27   *Morning Post*, 7 November 1831.

28   James McQueen, 'The Colonial Empire of Great Britain', in *Blackwood's Edinburgh Magazine*, Vol.30, No.187 (November 1831), pp.744–64.

29 *Evening Mail*; *The Times*, 1 March 1833.
30 Letter from Joseph Phillips to Thomas Pringle, 18 January 1831, Prince, 2002, p.51.
31 *The Times*, 1 March 1833.
32 Midgley, 1992, p.90.
33 *Evening Mail*; *The Times*, 1 March 1833.
34 As well as the moral stain, the slave trade left a deep financial scar on the British people, while lining the pockets of its slavers. The grand total of £20 million that the government paid out to its 46,000 slave owners equates to over £16 billion today. This debt was only paid off in full by British taxpayers in 2015. (independent.co.uk/news/uk/home-news/britains-colonial-shame-slave-owners-given-huge-payouts-after-abolition-8508358.html; theguardian.com/commentisfree/2018/feb/11/lets-end-delusion-britain-abolished-slavery).
35 There were notable exceptions among the abolitionist community. A particularly interesting form of protest came from women. Many of the early anti-slavery factions had been set up by women, particularly Quakers, and although they had little or no power politically and were still generally excluded from activism on the grounds of impropriety (William Wilberforce was against their involvement), the abolition cause saw a surge in organised female campaigning. Ladies' anti-slavery associations sprang up around the country, notably in Birmingham, Liverpool and Sheffield; some campaigners, like Elizabeth Heyrick, took to pamphleteering, while others found a way to make clear their disgust in a domestic form, by exercising their powers as consumers and organising a sugar boycott – which, by the late 1790s, up to half a million people had joined. For the most part this middle-class activism was overwhelmingly white – until, that is, Mary Prince stepped forward to become the first black female slave to join their ranks. Even then, however, she would be treated as a victim rather than a comrade by these well-meaning philanthropists. See Midgley, *Women Against Slavery* (Routledge, 1992); Paula Byrne, *Belle: The True Story of Dido Belle* (William Collins, 2014), pp.215–18.
36 Within 18 months, Pringle himself – Mary's employer, her chronicler and her champion – would be dead, succumbing to tuberculosis in December 1834 at the age of 45. His death may partly account for Mary's coinciding disappearance from the records.
37 When the Act first became law, only slaves under the age of six were immediately freed. Over the next six years there followed a transition period in which slaves over that age were gradually freed, being first 'apprenticed' and paid a wage for a small portion of the week when they were considered free.
38 The more common version of Wedgwood's medallion depicted a male slave and the words 'Am I not a man and a brother?'

ANNE LISTER

1 19 February 1819, Helena Whitbread (ed.), *The Secret Diaries of Miss Anne Lister* (Virago, 2010), p.94.
2 3 March 1819, Whitbread, 2010, p.96.
3 22 June 1821/16 September 1823, Whitbread, 2010, pp.171 and 319.
4 31 May 1824, Whitbread, 2010, Introduction, p.xx.
5 Letter to Anne Lister Sr, 13 June 1834, Muriel Green (ed.), 'A Spirited Yorkshirewoman: The Letters of Anne Lister of Shibden Hall', 2nd edition, Library Associations Honours Diploma (British Library typescript, 1939), p.471.
6 27 [December 1816], quoted in Angela Steidele, *Gentleman Jack: A Biography of Anne Lister* (Serpent's Tail, 2018), translated by Katy Derbyshire, p.27.

7   3 September 1819, Jill Liddington, *Presenting the Past: Anne Lister of Halifax 1791–1840* (Pennine Pens, 1994), p.31.

8   10 November 1819, Whitbread, 2010, p.402.

9   13 November 1824, Whitbread (ed.), *No Priest but Love: The Journals of Anne Lister, 1824–1826* (Smith Settle Ltd, 1992), p.49.

10   10 November 1819, Whitbread, 2010, p.402.

11   Liddington, 1994, p.30; Lillian Faderman, *Surpassing the Love of Men: Romantic Friendship and Love Between Women from the Renaissance to the Present* (The Women's Press, 1985), pp.147–53.

12   Jill Liddington, *Nature's Domain: Anne Lister and the Landscape of Desire* (Pennine Pens, 2003), p.11.

13   27 November 1806, Patricia L. Hughes, *The Early Life of Miss Anne Lister & the Curious Tale of Miss Eliza Raine* (Hues Books Ltd, 2015), p.19.

14   Within the Lister family, it was Anne who wielded the weapons, not the men. One night in May 1809, she proved herself more than capable of stepping up as chief protector of the household, when her mother rushed into her room to tell her there was a man in the house in bed with one of the servants. 'With nothing on but my night jacket over my shift, my stockings & night cap on,' Anne 'took the pistols loadened with ball which were ready under my pillow & a sword', and went upstairs with her mother and brother Sam – who brandished only a candle – to confront them. No shots were fired, but she threw the rascal out on his ear. (8 May 1809, Liddington, 1994, p.27)

15   4 October 1820, Whitbread, 2010, p.152.

16   21 March 1809, Liddington, 1994, pp.26–7.

17   16 December 1832, Liddington, 2003, p.100.

18   Letter from Eliza Raine, 5 December 1909, Hughes, 2015, p.37.

19   Letter from Eliza Raine, 25 April 1810, Hughes, 2015, p.67.

20   Letters from Eliza Raine, 25 April 1810/23 May 1810, Hughes, 2015, pp.67 and 78–9.

21   Letter to Eliza Raine, 19 November 1809, Green, 1939, p.85.

22   Letter to Samuel Lister, 13 April 1811, Green, 1939, p.50.

23   Letter to Samuel Lister, February 1813, Muriel Green (ed.), *Miss Lister of Shibden Hall: Selected Letters 1800–1840* (The Book Guild Ltd, 1992), p.36.

24   Letter from Isabella Norcliffe, 1 September 1810, Green, 1939, p.33.

25   Letter to Isabella Norcliffe, 30 August 1810, Green, 1939, p.31.

26   22 July 1824, Whitbread, 2010, p.378.

27   25 May 1826, Whitbread, 1992, 173.

28   Like many men of her day, Anne liked her women to be sweet, innocent and not too well educated. Her friend Miss Francis Pickford, for example, whom she met in February 1823 and found strikingly similar to herself, didn't attract her at all. Known as Frank, Miss Pickford was clever and also dressed in a dark, mannish riding habit, but Anne 'would rather have a pretty girl to flirt with'. Nonetheless, she was still fascinated to have found another so like her: 'Are there more Miss Pickfords in the world than I have ever before thought of?' It seems there were. (12 March/5 August 1823, Whitbread, 2010, pp.262 and 296.)

29   On the last letter Anne ever received from Sam, dated 15 May 1813, she wrote on the bottom, 'Poor fellow! He was drowned abt 3 o'clock in the afternoon … while bathing in the river Blackwater.'

30   Letter to Samuel Lister, 24 April 1813, Green, 1939, p.72.

31   Letters from Miss Marsh, 16/20 October 1814, Hughes, 2015, pp.203 and 212.

32   Whether Eliza was indeed mad is by no means certain. Anne was clearly ready to believe it and, nervous, perhaps, of what

Eliza might blurt out about their relationship, she encouraged others to think so, too. The year after she was committed, Anne was of the opinion that Eliza should be made a ward in Chancery, which would strip her of her legal rights as an adult. Mr Duffin, however, wasn't so sure; according to Dr Belcombe, Eliza had 'intervals of perfect sanity, and has a correct recollection of what has occurred since her derangement began'. She was 'very wayward and obstinate', but 'perfectly aware of what she is saying and doing, so much so that it may be difficult to prove her insanity to persons appointed by Chancery to examine her'. (Letter from Mr Duffin to Anne Lister, 6 May/23 August 1815 Green, 1939, p.89.)

33 18 December 1817, Hughes, 2015, p.217.

34 Jane and Eliza both met a sad end. In 1817 Jane's illegitimate son died, aged six. Two years later her husband, Henry Boulton, was killed in action, at which point she inherited his money – or rather regained her own – but it came too late to help her. She died of consumption at the age of 30. Eliza inherited her money, but as a permanent resident of Clifton Green who was still prone to occasional bouts of violence and had to be restrained by a straitjacket, she could make no use of it either. When she died in 1860 she was a rich woman, possessed of nearly £8,000, but with no relations left and her will (once made out in favour of Anne but now leaving everything to Captain Alexander) invalidated, her money was claimed by the Crown.

35 30 June 1817, Steidele, 2018, p.35.

36 13 September 1817, Whitbread, 2010, p.24.

37 5 March 1823, ibid., p.261.

38 31 August 1818, ibid., p.69.

39 18 November 1819, ibid., p.120.

40 Anne later gives a clue as to what might have happened to her missing diaries, and indeed many of her letters from Mariana. She writes in 1824 of reading out to Mariana some of the entries from these years concerning her treatment of Anne when she married. Mariana was so distraught by their contents that she entreated Anne, half-fainting, to burn them, 'saying she should never feel secure till I did'. (12 December 1824, Whitbread, 1992, p.63.) Anne confirms that she burnt some letters on 20 November 1823 (Whitbread, 2010, p.338). Other papers may have been burned years later, perhaps by a jealous Ann Walker after Anne's death.

41 11 November 1816, Whitbread, 2010, p.4.

42 29 January 1821, ibid., p.161.

43 13 May 1817, Whitbread, 2010, p.14.

44 2 September 1817, ibid., p.24.

45 19 May 1817, ibid., p.16.

46 22 May 1817, ibid., p.17.

47 13 September 1817, ibid., p.24.

48 9 December 1817, ibid., p.35.

49 21 September 1818, ibid., p.79.

50 3 March 1819, ibid., p.96.

51 Steidele, 2018, p.67; Letter to Mr Duffin, 22 December 1819, Green, 1992, pp.40–54.

52 27 August 1819, Liddington, 1994, p.36.

53 Letter to Mariana Lawton, 16 December 1832, Liddington, 1994, p.40.

54 2 February 1819, Whitbread, 2010, p.91.

55 26 June 1818, ibid., pp.60–1.

56 1 October 1819, ibid., p.116.

57 5 January 1820, ibid., p.128.

58 11 January 1820, ibid., p.129.

59 30 August 1820, ibid., p.148.

60 3 August 1821, Whitbread, 2010, p.177.

61 10–11 August 1821, ibid., pp.179–80.

62 30 June 1817, ibid., p.19.

63 14 July 1822, ibid., p.214.

64 23 July 1822, ibid., p.222. Plâs Newydd in Llangollen, Denbighshire, still stands, a museum to the ladies' lives and a visitor attraction for those wishing to pay homage to these pioneers of same-sex partnerships.

65   3 August 1822, ibid., p.229.

66   15 September 1823, ibid., p.317.

67   16 September 1823, ibid., p.319.

68   31 August 1818, ibid., p.69.

69   23 August 1823, ibid., p.308.

70   17 September 1823, ibid., pp.320–1.

71   27 August 1823, ibid., p.310.

72   It's been deduced that Anne probably had trichomoniasis, a parasitic STI, which often doesn't carry symptoms, particularly in men, but in women can cause itching, discharge, burning with urination and pain during sex. It is more easily transmitted between women than, for example, syphilis or gonorrhoea. Today, it can be easily treated with antibiotics, but Anne, Mariana and Tib had no such luxury. See Steidele, 2018, p.127.

73   15 December 1824, Whitbread, 1992, p.64.

74   8 May 1826, ibid., p.172. Anne's revulsion at this was evident in her description in her diary that she 'used to sit on the pot & bleed like a stuck pig.'

75   23 November 1824, ibid., p.55.

76   Unlike Mariana, Maria didn't ignore Anne's periods, and wanted to reciprocate in bed, taking her turn to 'play the man', but Anne recoiled at the thought of being penetrated: 'This is womanising me too much.' (19 March 1825, Whitbread, 1992, p.85.) Her fantasies reveal quite the opposite inclination. Following a conversation with her friend Miss Pickford, who told her about once 'putting on regimentals & flirting with a lady under the assumed name of Captain Cowper', Anne was intrigued and imagined 'her using a phallus to her friend' (30 August 1823/14 September 1823, Whitbread, 2010, pp.314–15). On another occasion she imagined herself taking her friend Caroline Greenwood to a secluded shed on the moors and 'being connected with her. Supposing myself in men's clothes & having a penis, tho' nothing more.' (23 March 1821, Whitbread, 2010, pp.167–8.) See also Steidele, 2018, pp.129–130.

77   31 March 1825, Whitbread, 1992, pp.88–9.

78   21 September 1825, ibid., p.131.

79   26 December 1825, ibid., p.149.

80   Ibid, p.150.

81   26 January 1825, ibid., p.156.

82   Early August 1830, Steidele, 2018, p.173.

83   Letter to Anne Lister Sr, 13 September 1830, Green, 1992, p.134.

84   (Draft letter to Lady Stuart de Rothesay, 21 February 1839, Green, 1939, p.509.) It was so unusual for a woman to undertake an expedition such as this alone that it attracted controversy – a local policeman questioned Anne and examined her notebook, suspecting her of drawing up military plans. On another hike that took her over the border into Spain, she was stopped by soldiers who, following the revolution, were on the look-out for suspicious foreigners. Anne later implies that she was in fact arrested and put in prison – though if so, she managed to successfully talk or buy her way out, for she returned to her friends soon enough, only to be told off by Lady Stuart for continually absconding in search of adventure: 'I think she does not much like my character of enterprise,' Anne remarked. (Late September 1830, Steidele, 2018, p.176.)

85   2 May 1832, Liddington, 2003, p.17.

86   30 August 1828, Jill Liddington, *Female Fortune: Land, Gender and Authority* (Rivers Oram Press, 1998), p.35.

87   5 September 1832, Liddington, 2003, p.56.

88   28 September 1832, ibid., p.65.

89   27 September 1832, ibid., p.64.

90   17 August 1832, ibid., p.49.

91   27 September 1832, ibid., p.64.

92   27 September 1832, ibid., p.64.

93   28 September 1832, ibid., p.65.

94   5 October 1832, ibid., p.73.

95   11 October 1832, ibid., p.78.

96   5 October 1832, ibid., p.73.

97   7 November 1832, ibid., p88; Anne Choma, *Gentleman Jack: The Real Anne*

Lister (BBC Books, 2019), p.197.

98   2 November 1832, ibid., p.85.

99   14 December 1832, ibid., p.99.

100   25 December 1832, ibid., p.102.

101   31 December 1832, ibid., p.104.

102   8/10 January 1833, Liddington, 1998, p.70.

103   18 February 1833, ibid., p.72.

104   24 December 1832, Liddington, 2003, p.102.

105   It had become increasingly clear to the government that electoral reform was necessary – as public anger rose, the call for secret ballots, broader enfranchisement, the abolition of rotten boroughs and a redrawing of constituency lines were growing louder. The Reform Act of 7 June 1832 opened voter enfranchisement to men who had rented land for at least £10 a year for at least 60 years (either themselves or jointly with their father), or had held land of their own, worth £50, for at least 20 years. In Halifax, this still only accounted for about 7.5 per cent of its 20,000 residents (none of them, of course, women). Anne had few tenants who met this criteria, but John Bottomley was one of them.

106   Seemingly oblivious to the unenviable position she put him in, Anne was scathing about men like Bottomley: 'It is quite useless to leave such men as he uninfluenced – he knows nothing & cares nothing about it, & is likely best satisfied with the idea of pleasing somebody he knows.' (11 December 1832, Liddington, 2003, pp.97–8.)

107   Letter to Anne Lister Sr, 9 November 1833, Green, 1939, p.459.

108   23 October 1832, Liddington, 2003, p.80.

109   10 February 1834, Liddington, 1998, pp.92–3.

110   27 February 1834, ibid., p.95.

111   28 February 1834, ibid., p.95.

112   8 March 1834, ibid., p.98.

113   Letter from Ann Walker to Anne Lister Sr, 22 July 1834, Green, 1992, pp.183–4.

114   21 July 1834, Liddington, 1998, p.109.

115   Letter to Anne Lister Sr, 13 June 1834, Green, 1939, pp.471; Liddington, 1998, p.109.

116   25 December 1834, Liddington, 1998, p.136.

117   26 December 1834, ibid., p.137.

118   2 October 1834, ibid., pp.115–16.

119   10 January 1835, ibid., p.143.

120   12 January 1835, ibid., p.144.

121   11 February 1835, ibid., p.148.

122   15 March 1835, ibid., p.156.

123   8 April 1835, ibid., p.161.

124   23 August 1835, ibid., p.187.

125   23 November 1835, ibid., p.198.

126   10 February 1836, ibid., p.206.

127   13 March 1836, ibid., p.212.

128   27 March 1836, ibid., p.221. This dispute arose due to a poisoned well that had its source on Ann Walker's land. The residents of the Caddy Fields slum had always taken their drinking water from this well, but believing it to be hers, Ann Walker had attempted to stop them. Acting on the suggestion of her lawyer Robert Parker, she had ordered that a barrel of tar be added at the source to make the water unusable for a year. The dispute then hinged on whether the well belonged to Ann Walker or to the public, and when the case went to court, the public won. Ann's four employees who dumped the tar barrel (though not Ann herself) were made to pay damages, but the locals still felt the need to make visible their displeasure.

129   4 May 1836, ibid., p.233.

130   8 May 1836, ibid., p.233.

131   Anne would not be hindered by her detested skirts. She had customised her petticoats with 'tape loops put round the bottom' and 'strings at the top' so that she could tie them up around her waist, making them knee-length rather than full-length. (7 August 1838, Steidele, 2018, p.248.)

132   See Steidele, 2018, p.251.

133   August 1838, Steidele, 2018, p.251.

134   Letter to Lady Stuart, 26 May 1835, Green, 1939, p.481.

135 23 January 1840, Steidele, 2018, p.264.

136 12 October 1839, Steidele, 2018, p.262.

137 Letter to Vere Cameron, 13 January 1840, Green, 1992, p.197.

138 21 February 1840, Steidele, 2018, p.272.

139 4/5 April 1840, Steidele, 2018, p.278.

140 27 June 1840, Steidele, 2018, p.287.

141 11 August 1840, Green, 1992, p.205.

142 Anne's closest friends would all outlive her. Tib died five years later, in 1846, aged 61, and Mariana in 1868. Her husband Charles, whose death they had once so looked forward to, outlived them both. Anne's sister Marian lived a life of obscure poverty until 1882, when she died aged 84.

143 Local Intelligence: The Late Miss Lister of Shibden Hall, Whitbread, 2010, p.393.

144 Dr Belcombe to Parker, 8 September 1843, Liddington, 1994, p.11.

145 Parker memorandum, 9 September 1843, ibid.

146 Letter from Captain Sutherland to John Lister, 27 September 1844, Liddington, 1998, p.238.

147 The Brontës breathed the same air as Anne Lister. She was a good 25 years older, but they lived not far from Halifax, in Haworth. It's a tantalising prospect that such remarkable, unusual and uncompromising women might have passed one another on the moors and even exchanged a few words. Charlotte's biographer, Claire Harman, certainly believes that 'it would have been strange if Emily Brontë had not met Anne Lister', as she spent seven months working as a teacher at Law Hill, next door to Shibden, from September 1838, while Anne was industriously developing her estate. With local gossip about Miss Lister so prevalent, it seems likely that, at the very least, the Brontës had heard the stories of her and her 'friends', who were both locked away in Dr Belcombe's nearby asylum when Charlotte

was writing *Jane Eyre* (1847). See Claire Harman, *Charlotte Brontë: A Life* (Viking, 2015), pp.110–11 and p.196; Steidele, 2018, p.254; Liddington, 'Anne Lister and Emily Bronte 1838–39: Landscape with Figures', *Brontë Society Transactions*, Vol. 26, No. 1, April 2001, pp.46–67 for the potential crossovers between Anne Lister and the Brontës.

148 Liddington, 1994, p.15, quoting Arthur Burrell, 12/20 December 1936.

149 Ibid., p.17, quoting Burrell, 20 December 1936/1 January 1937.

150 Liddington, 1994, p.17, quoting Muriel Green in interview, 18 September 1991.

151 Ibid., pp.20–1, quoting Phyllis Ramsden. Ramsden embarked on the work with Vivien Ingham, who died in 1969 and of the two appears to have been the less coy about Anne's lesbianism.

152 Anne's diaries become particularly hard-going during the 1830s as she became more reliant on them, perhaps unhealthily so. She records 'every weather measurement, every tree planted or walk taken in her grounds, every boulder moved or pit-sinking negotiated, every conversation conducted (however transient), and even every letter written or received' in obsessive, repetitious and often tedious detail. Her days, always rammed, are delineated right down to every quarter-hour. As a result, about half the entire volume of her total diaries was written during the 1830s. See Liddington, 1998, pp.77–80.

CAROLINE NORTON

1 *Evening Mail*, 22–24 June 1836.

2 *Dublin Evening Packet and Correspondent*, 25 June 1836.

3 'Criminal conversation' – the euphemistic legal term for adultery – addressed the civil injury to a cuckolded husband, entitling him to claim damages from his

wife's lover. It was often abbreviated to crim con. There was no equivalent civil injury for a wronged wife.

4 *Waterford Mail*, 29 June 1836.

5 Ultra-Tories were a political faction that formed in the 1820s from a group who felt the Tories were too liberal. They were doggedly opposed to the reforms being ushered in by the Enlightenment and Industrial Revolution, including wider electoral enfranchisement and Catholic emancipation.

6 Queen Victoria, who would come to throne aged just 18 the following year, was even younger than Caroline and would also adore Lord Melbourne; he became a close friend, advisor and possible crush.

7 It was Lord Melbourne's wife, Lady Caroline Lamb, who famously branded Byron 'mad, bad and dangerous to know'.

8 Ian Kelly, *Beau Brummell: the Ultimate Dandy* (Hodder, 2005), p.60.

9 Clarke Olney, 'Caroline Norton to Lord Melbourne', *Victorian Studies*, 8: 3, March 1965, p.258.

10 Letter from Mrs Caroline Sheridan to George Callander, 30 March 1808, quoted in Diane Atkinson, *The Criminal Conversation of Mrs Norton* (Arrow, 2012), p.30.

11 Jane Gray Perkins, *The Life of Mrs Norton* (John Murray, 1909), p.2.

12 Alan Chedzoy, *A Scandalous Woman: The Story of Caroline Norton* (Allison & Busby, 1992), p.31.

13 Consumption, or pulmonary tuberculosis, was a bacterial lung infection and the single biggest killer in the nineteenth century. It led to a gradual wasting away of the sufferer and ran like a plague through the Sheridan family – it had done for Tom's mother, Elizabeth Linley, and would kill off numerous other family members, too.

14 Caroline Norton, *English Laws for Women in the Nineteenth Century*, 1854, p.24.

15 Mrs Sullivan to Mr Sullivan, quoted in Atkinson, 2012, p.53.

16 Norton, 1854, p.32.

17 Ibid., p.25.

18 *The Times*, 26 December 1828.

19 Norton, 1854, p.33.

20 For centuries it was commonly believed (though never officially enshrined in law) that a man had the right to beat his wife as long as he used a stick no thicker than his thumb. A major culprit for perpetuating this myth was a judge named Francis Buller, who is said to have cited the phony law in a case in 1782. There's no direct evidence for this, though he was caricatured by James Gillray in a contemporary cartoon as 'Judge Thumb'. An ancient law whose origin no one could quite remember, which allowed a husband to administer 'moderate correction' and 'domestic chastisement' to his wife, was often cited in court and only gave credence to this belief. Indeed, men who had murdered their wives argued it as their defence. Judges were inconsistent on whether they would allow it, though. In 1828, the year after the Nortons were married, a man named Nicholas Barker beat his wife to death in what he considered 'proper punishment' for her suspected adultery. The judge in this case stated that a man had no right to administer such punishment and sentenced Barker to be executed. In the 1852 case of Wyatt versus Birchell, however, the judge decreed that 'a married man had, by law, a right to chastise his wife'. (*Commentaries on the Laws of England*, William Blackstone, 1765; historyofwomen.org.)

21 Marital rape was only recognised as a criminal act by UK law in 1991. Caroline would later tell her lawyers that George commanded her to become familiar with high-ranking gentlemen for his own pecuniary gain and forced her 'to perform unnecessary and disgusting acts' for him, suggesting that sexual coercion was indeed a feature of his abuse. (Atkinson, 2012, p.273.)

22 Norton, 1854, pp.25–6.

23 Letter from Edward Trelawny to Mary Shelley, 25 September 1836, H. Buxton Forman (ed.), *Letters of Edward John Trelawny* (Oxford University Press, 1910), p.203. Trelawny, who had travelled the world, fought wars, seduced women and sparked endless trouble and endless talk wherever he went, captivated Caroline. In 1835 the two became close friends and, so the rumour goes, lovers as well. However, 'Wolf', as she called him, grew too intense even for Caroline and eventually she was forced to keep her distance.

24 Letter from Mary Shelley to Edward Trelawny, October 1835, Florence A. Marshall (ed.), *The Life and Letters of Mary Wollstonecraft Shelley, Vol.2*, 1889, pp.273.

25 Letter to Lord Melbourne, 21 June 1836, James O. Hoge and Clarke Olney (eds), *The Letters of Caroline Norton to Lord Melbourne* (Ohio State University Press, 1974), p.89.

26 Letter to Lord Melbourne, 29 September 1832, quoted in Atkinson, 2012, p.102.

27 Norton, 1854, p.33.

28 Ibid., pp.34–6.

29 Ibid., pp.35–6.

30 Letter to Georgie, Lady Seymour, 1833, quoted in Atkinson, 2012, p.108.

31 Norton, 1854, pp.37–8.

32 Norton, 1854, p.28.

33 Letter from Mrs Sheridan to Caroline Norton, Norton, 1854, pp.28–30.

34 This book featured two stories in one. In 'The Wife', the beautiful Susan Dalrymple is trapped in a loveless marriage to the jealous Lord Glenalton. While in 'Woman's Reward', the heroine Mary is charged by her dying father to look after her listless, boorish, penny-pinching brother Lionel. Both men bear a noticeable resemblance to George Norton.

35 Caroline's younger sister Georgie had made a splendid marriage in June 1830 to Lord Seymour, heir of the 11th Duke of Somerset.

36 Norton, 1854, pp.38-9.

37 Letter from George Norton to the intermediary George Bentinck, 25 June 1835.

38 Letter from Caroline Norton to William Cowper, 1835, quoted in Atkinson, 2012, p.130.

39 Norton, 1854, pp.38-9.

40 Letter to Lord Melbourne, 2 April 1836, Hoge and Olney, 1974, p.64.

41 Ibid., p.64

42 Norton, 1854, p.42.

43 Norton, 1854, p.42.

44 Atkinson, 2012, p.168.

45 Norton, 1854, p.43.

46 Letter to Edward Trelawny, 6 April 1836, quoted in Atkinson, 2012, p.162.

47 Atkinson, 2012, p.161.

48 Norton, 1854, pp.46-7.

49 *Newcastle Journal* (and other publications), 21 May 1836.

50 *The Satirist*, 29 May 1836, quoted in Atkinson, 2012, pp.172–73.

51 Letter from Lord Melbourne, 9 June 1836, Norton, 1854, pp.62–3.

52 Letter to Lord Melbourne, 21 June 1836, Hoge and Olney, 1974, p.89.

53 Letter to Lord Melbourne, 20 June 1836, Hoge and Olney, 1974, p.83.

54 Court transcript printed in the *Morning Chronicle*, 23 June 1836, written by Charles Dickens.

55 Charles Dickens enjoyed this absurd detail so much that he decided to add it to his first novel, which he was currently writing. *The Pickwick Papers* was already being published in monthly instalments at the time of the trial, spanning from March 1836 to November 1837. Innocent notes with insinuated sinister intent would play a pivotal role in his comic trial of Bardell versus Pickwick.

56 The double standard that required female sexual morality to be absolute was on full display during this trial. The female servants were routinely discredited on the basis that they had had extra-marital sex, even if they had gone on to marry the man in question. The assumption that they were

mendacious, wanton characters naturally followed in the minds of the jury.

57 *Morning Chronicle*, 23 June 1836.

58 *Perthshire Advertiser*, 30 June 1836.

59 Letter from Charles Dickens to John Macrone, 23 June 1836, quoted in Atkinson, 2012, p.182.

60 *Worcester Herald*, 25 June 1836.

61 *The Satirist*, 26 June 1836, quoted in Atkinson, 2012, p.184.

62 Political Review, *Huntingdon, Bedford and Peterborough Gazette*, 25 June 1836.

63 Norton, 1854, p.49.

64 Atkinson, 2012, p.182.

65 Norton, 1854, p.49.

66 Letter from George Norton, 15 July 1836, quoted in Atkinson, 2012, p.191.

67 Norton, 1854, p.50.

68 Letter to George Norton, 20 July 1836, quoted in Atkinson, 2012, p.193.

69 Letter to Lord Melbourne, 8 July 1836, Hoge and Olney, 1974, p.97.

70 Letter from Lord Melbourne, 24 July 1836, Norton, 1854, p.71.

71 Norton, 1854, p.51.

72 Atkinson, 2012, p.200.

73 Letter from George Norton to Edward Ellice, 4 December 1836, quoted in Atkinson, 2012, p.203.

74 Letter to Edward Ellice, 3 November 1836, quoted in Atkinson, 2012, p.201.

75 This pamphlet made everyone around Caroline nervous. Her publishers bolted for fear of being sued for libel by George (she ended up printing it privately with borrowed money), her brother Brinsley worried about the 'indelicacy' of going public and any retaliation it might provoke, and her sister Georgie persuaded her to cut out the more 'callow wrestling bits' in an effort to give the appearance of 'calmness and fairness'. Caroline, on the other hand, worried she had not gone far enough. See Atkinson, 2012, p.207.

76 Letter to Mary Shelley, 5 December 1836, quoted in Atkinson, 2012, p.204.

77 Norton, 1854, p.54.

78 Ibid., p.54.

79 Letter from Caroline Norton to Miss A (possibly Augusta Cowell), August 1837, quoted in Atkinson, 2012, p.233.

80 Norton, 1854, p.55. A husband was legally responsible for his wife's debts; it was the one element of marital law that didn't favour him, and he could frequently wriggle out of it. Over the next few years George was taken to court several times by tradesmen for non-payment of his wife's debts. Every time, his lawyers painted Caroline as a profligate, mischievously trying to get her husband into debt, and every time the all-male jury stuck with their own and found in favour of George.

81 *The Times*, 12 September 1837.

82 Letter from John Bayley to George Norton, 30 November 1837, quoted in Atkinson, 2012, p.241.

83 Letter from John Bayley, 30 December 1837, quoted in Atkinson, 2012, p.245.

84 Perkins, 1909, pp.145–6

85 House of Lords Debates, 30 July 1838, Vol.44, cc772–291. Brougham's objections were seconded by Lord Wynford, George's godfather, who had been closely involved with the 1836 action against Melbourne and had written a pamphlet against the bill, accusing Caroline of using it for revenge.

86 John Mitchell Kemble in the *British and Foreign Review*, quoted in Atkinson, 2012, pp.265–6.

87 *Quarterly Review*, 1840, quoted in Atkinson, 2012, p.288.

88 Atkinson, 2012, p.286.

89 Letter to George Norton, May 1840, quoted in Atkinson, 2012, p.288.

90 Letter to George Norton, August 1840, ibid., p.290.

91 Letter from George Norton to Caroline's lawyers, 21 June 1841, ibid., p.297.

92 Norton, 1854, p.53.

93 Letter to Samuel Rogers, 13 September 1842, quoted in Perkins, 1909, pp.166–7.

94 Norton, 1854, p.53.

95 Letter to Samuel Rogers, 13 September 1842, quoted in Perkins, 1909, p.167.
96 Norton, 1854, p.53.
97 Letter to Samuel Rogers, 8 October 1842, quoted in Perkins, 1909, p.171.
98 Dickens was smitten with Caroline like all the rest. The artist Daniel Maclise, who had produced a portrait of her for the frontispiece of *The Undying One*, teased him before he was due to dine with her at a literary soirée in 1840 that he hoped he would not have to sit between 'the Heavenly Norton and the Blessed Seymour [Georgie] for this is too much to bear'. (Atkinson, 2012, p.285.)
99 *The Child of the Islands* tackled some of the big social problems of the day, including poverty, hunger and class division, calling for a 'more intimate union between all classes'.
100 Letter to Brinsley Sheridan, December 1844, quoted in Atkinson, 2012, p.318.
101 Letter to Mrs Sheridan, 1848; letter to Georgie, Lady Seymour, September 1848, ibid., pp.334–5.
102 Letter to William Cowper, November 1848, ibid., p.336.
103 In 1850, when the Poet Laureate William Wordsworth died, it was mooted in the newspapers that in a nation now ruled by a great queen, it was surely high time a woman was given the accolade. Both Caroline Norton and Elizabeth Barrett Browning were named as worthy contenders possessed of 'poetic genius', though in fact Caroline had the idea first. Back in 1843 when the previous Laureate, Robert Southey, had died, she had quietly applied for the post, seeing no reason why a woman – especially one who had been compared with Byron – shouldn't take it. She had lost out then to Wordsworth, and she lost out again now – to Alfred Tennyson. There would not be a female Poet Laureate in its 300-plus-year history until Carol Ann Duffy was appointed in 2009.

104 *Weekly Chronicle*, quoted in Atkinson, 2012, p.353.
105 Atkinson, 2012, p.357.
106 Norton, 1854, p.82.
107 Ibid., pp.86 and 82.
108 *Dublin Evening Mail*, 22 August 1853 and other newspapers.
109 Ibid.
110 Norton, 1854, p.89.
111 *Dublin Evening Mail*, 22 August 1853 and other newspapers.
112 *Dundee Courier*, August 1853, quoted in Atkinson, 2012, p.367.
113 *The Times*, 2 September 1853.
114 Letter from Sir John Bayley to *The Times*, 13 September 1853.
115 *Morning Chronicle*, 26 September 1853.
116 Norton, 1854, p.166.
117 Norton, 1854, p.170.
118 Caroline Norton, *A Letter to the Queen on Lord Chancellor Cranworth's Marriage & Divorce Bill* (Longman, Brown, Green and Longmans, 1855), pp.12–13 and 96.
119 Ibid., p.153.
120 Letter by Lord Brougham, December 1855, quoted in Perkins, 1909, p.248.
121 Women would not be allowed to petition for divorce on the grounds of adultery alone, as men had always been able to do, until the Matrimonial Causes Act of 1923. Further divorce reforms in 1937 extended the grounds to include cruelty, desertion and insanity.
122 Atkinson, 2012, p.401.
123 Letter to Henry Newcastle, 1859; letter to Edward Ellice, 8 December 1859, quoted in Atkinson, 2012, pp.404–5.
124 Letter to Lady Anna Stirling Maxwell, November 1873, quoted in Atkinson, 2012, p.418.
125 Letter to William Le Fanu, 1873, quoted in Atkinson, 2012, p.417.
126 Under the Married Women's Property Act 1870 many women saw no benefit at all, as any property or money a woman possessed before she was married still became her husband's on the big day, and

the Act was not retroactive – so any woman who had married before it came into force could not reclaim from her husband any property she had formerly owned. It was therefore only a stepping stone until the second Married Women's Property Act of 1882, which finally decreed that a wife had equal legal status to her husband, as a separate entity, and had the right to retain and acquire all her own property and money as if she were a *feme sole*.

127 *The Times*, 26 February 1875.

128 *York Herald*, 27 February 1875.

129 Characteristically, both men issued a final swipe from beyond the grave. George's will forbad Brin from taking up residence at Kettlethorpe Hall, while Lord Grantley's revealed that he had broken the entail on his estate and, in his loathing for Caroline, disinherited Brin altogether. Incensed at this posthumous spite, Caroline launched herself into yet another legal battle to contest Grantley's will and reinstate her ungrateful, abusive son as his heir, though on this occasion the law bested her. The will was upheld, and when Lady Grantley died, it was Brin's son Richard who inherited the Grantley title and estate.

130 Letter to Mrs Le Fanu, 4 March 1877, quoted in Atkinson, 2012, p.422.

131 Caroline's old friend Benjamin

Disraeli treated her with a light satirical edge when he drew on her younger self for the character of Berengaria Montfort in his 1880 novel *Endymion*. But George Meredith's more scandalous depiction of her in his 1885 novel *Diana of the Crossways* got him into trouble with her relatives. See Chedzoy, 1992, pp.291–3.

AFTERWORD

1   UK gender pay gap figures for median gross hourly earnings for all employees, from April 2018: Office for National Statistics: ons.gov.uk/employmentandlabourmarket/peopleinwork/earningsandworkinghours/bulletins/genderpaygapintheuk/2018

2   Figures following the General Election 2017: https://researchbriefings.parliament.uk/ResearchBriefing/Summary/SN01250

3   Figures from July 2018: theguardian.com/business/2018/jul/17/number-of-women-in-top-boardroom-positions-falls report

4   Average figure for England and Wales from the Office for National Statistics, 2018, womensaid.org.uk.

ACKNOWLEDGEMENTS

A team of stellar Roaring Girls helped bring this book into being, and some pretty great Roaring Boys, too.

First off, thank you to my HQ commissioning editor, the fabulous Rachel Kenny, for making it happen in the first place – you've made a geek's lifelong dream come true. It was harder than I could ever have imagined, but thank you for having faith that I was up to the task.

And a huge thank you goes to the whole team at HQ: Kate Fox, Celia Lomas and Nira Begum – sorry for being the author/editor hybrid from hell! Thank you for your patience, your understanding, your insights and all your hard work. Thank you to Louise McGrory and Kate Oakley for the scrumptious cover design; to Lily Capewell and the publicity team and all those in sales and marketing and production for getting it out there and championing it; to Lisa Milton for publishing it; to the audio team for making it sound great, and to Helena Caldon and Sue Lascelles for your keen eyes.

Becky Glass, your illustrations are exquisite and your talent enviable. You had difficult (and sometimes non-existent) material to work with, yet you've made every image a thing of living, breathing beauty. Thank you so much.

Inevitably a book such as this relies heavily on the work of others, so I'm also indebted to all the scholars, historians and biographers whose labour-intensive and important research I've drawn on as sources. Thank you also to the merry staff at Shibden Hall for going above and beyond to show me round Anne Lister's home when I visited.

Grateful thanks must also go to Lucy, Ben, James, Simon and Sarah, Julia, Ally, Paul and Dan, for ideas, advice, photography and emergency courier services. I owe you all some cake at the very least.

And, of course, to Mum and Dad – in every sense, I could not have written this without you. Thank you for everything. A special shout-out goes to Mum, Dr Jackie Kyte, for being my first reader and for giving me constructive criticism with your teacher's hat on, as well as the praise and encouragement that only a mum can.

Last but definitely not least, thank you to all my wonderful family and friends for their enthusiasm, support and words of wisdom, and for the teabags, wine and hugs when I was flagging. What a great bunch you are.